Mary McAuley is a member of the International Advisory Committee for the website Rights in Russia. Between 1995 and 2002 she headed the Ford Foundation's Moscow Office, with particular responsibility for the human rights and legal reform programme. Previously she pursued an academic career, teaching Politics at the universities of Oxford and Essex, with visiting appointments at Madison, Wisconsin and Berkeley, California. Her books include *Soviet Politics 1917–1991; Russia's Politics of Uncertainty* and, more recently, *Children in Custody: Anglo-Russian Perspectives*.

'[McAuley] has met everyone who matters in the Russian human rights movement. She brings them all to life, and this is surely one of the best accounts of what it has really been like in Russia's opposition.'
— **Bill Bowring, SCRSS Digest**

'She brings to an English-speaking audience voices that have not often been heard [and] she sets down a unique record of concern about rights.'
— **Masha Gessen, New York Review of Books**

'This is a highly informative account of an important and interesting topic. It charts the development of human rights in Russia, from the disintegration of the USSR to recent times. Written by an internationally renowned specialist of Russia who has extensive first-hand experience of Russian domestic politics and the development of civil society after communism, it uses that experience and a large number of interviews with Russians engaged in the field to chronicle the rocky development of human rights organizations in Russia.'
— **Margot Light, Professor Emeritus of International Relations, London School of Economics and Political Science**

HUMAN RIGHTS IN RUSSIA

Citizens and the State from Perestroika to Putin

Mary McAuley

I.B. TAURIS
LONDON · NEW YORK

This book is dedicated to the memory of Valery Abramkin, penal reformer, to Liudmila Alekseeva, with affection, and in admiration for her indomitable spirit, and to the activists of an undaunted and resourceful younger generation.

New paperback edition published in 2016 by
I.B.Tauris & Co. Ltd
London • New York
www.ibtauris.com

First published in hardback in 2015 by I.B.Tauris & Co. Ltd

ISBN: 978 1 78453 679 4
eISBN: 978 0 85773 931 5
ePDF: 978 0 85772 585 1

A full CIP record for this book is available from the British Library
A full CIP record is available from the Library of Congress

Library of Congress Catalog Card Number: available

Typeset in Garamond Three by OKS Prepress Services, Chennai, India

CONTENTS

LIST OF ILLUSTRATIONS

PREFACE AND ACKNOWLEDGEMENTS

Writing a book about activists, many of whom are defending unpopular causes, is a hazardous undertaking. And when the author is an outsider, albeit a sympathetic outsider, and the topic is defending rights in Russia today, the hazards increase. Some of the activists will feel I lack an understanding of 'their Russia', that my criticisms are misplaced; others, observers from the wider community, that I am too sympathetic towards them. Some Western scholars will argue that I overestimate the significance of the human rights community; others, including activists, will take issue with my view of human rights. Perhaps too I should have written one book for my Russian colleagues, another for the Western reader. All I can do here is to acknowledge my debt to all who have contributed, one way or another, to this book, a book that crosses disciplines, has elements of a personal memoir, is written not only for students and scholars but also for a wider readership of those with an interest in Russia or human rights.

A further acknowledgement is in order, and that is to the legacy left by a lifetime engagement with Russia. Whether that is for good or bad, is another matter. In generation terms I fall into the category known in Russia as 'the people of the sixties', those who were young adults when Khrushchev advanced his destalinization campaign in 1956, and that inescapably has a bearing on the way I viewed and view the changes since 1991. I first visited Russia in 1959, as a student, then spent 1961–3 as a visiting graduate student at the labour law department, in the law faculty at Leningrad (now St Petersburg) University. Neither politics nor sociology existed as a discipline then (nor, one might add, did sociology exist at Oxford University). This was the time of the New Left. I chose the settlement of labour disputes as my thesis topic. I spent time in the factories and in the district courts. Thereafter I studied and taught Soviet politics and history in the UK and in the USA, returning for research periods to Leningrad.

In 1990 Russia opened up, unbelievably, and for the first time I could travel where I pleased, stay where I pleased, talk to anyone and everyone. With British Academy support, and academic leave, I spent most of 1991–4 researching the changing political scene, travelling from Siberia to Tatarstan, from the Urals to Krasnodar in the south, Arkhangelsk in the north, and back to St Petersburg. I kept a diary. Sometimes my path crossed with individuals who would subsequently set up a human rights organization, but I do not remember participating in any discussions on human rights in Russia before 1995. But, then, I had never been particularly interested in the topic. I had never read the Universal Declaration, nor the conventions. Membership of Amnesty International did not include discussions of human rights, only those of political prisoners. As for so many in Russia at the beginning of the nineties, it was the democratic movement and its opponents, the new political parties, and the economic collapse that occupied all my attention.

This was the baggage I took with me when in 1995 I resigned my post at Oxford University and abandoned both academe and St Petersburg for Moscow – to head the Ford Foundation's new Russian office, and with responsibility for a programme which included supporting Russian organizations in the field of human rights and legal reform. I had a steep learning curve to climb. My greatest debt is to the activists themselves, to those I came to know from 1995 onwards. For the next seven years I learnt all I could by listening, attending meetings, events, observing NGOs, judges, prison officers in action, making grants and seeing what happened to them, and travelling the country. To list all to whom I owe a debt is impossible. Some, sadly, who made significant contributions to the new human rights community, and who taught me much, have died: Valery Abramkin, Olga Alekseeva, Leonid Gordon, Alexander Gorelik, Veniamin Ioffe, Boris Pustintsev, Yury Shmidt, Mikhail Timenchik. A deep bow to them all.

The Ford Foundation, one of America's richest charitable foundations, believed in learning from other countries, and this took me to Chile, Brazil, South Africa and China. I am grateful to all those in the Foundation offices, whether in those countries or in New York, who offered support, or advice, and in particular to Joseph Schull and Shep Forman who, working out of New York, had begun to support activities in Russia from the early nineties. In Moscow itself, once we had set up the office, Elena Ivanova and Dmitry Shabelnikov are owed a special word of thanks – and so too are Miriam Aukerman, Maria Chertok, Catherine Fitzpatrick, Borislav Petranov, and Mizanur Rahman for their different contributions.

In 2002 I returned to London, but maintained contacts with organizations and individuals, attending events, and undertaking the occasional consultancy. I was fortunate to be given the status of an Associate by the International Centre for Prison Studies, then at King's College, London, and wrote on juvenile justice reform in Russia. In 2010 I decided to trace the path followed by the human rights community through the two decades since Communist party rule collapsed and the USSR disintegrated. A wealth of old and new materials, published by the Russian activists themselves, initially on paper, now increasingly on their websites, exists. Russians love writing, at length, and publishing. Then there were my notes, my memories of events and people. I had an overabundance of sources. But I needed to take my questions back to the activists themselves, including young individuals with whom I had never worked.

In 2010–11, with support from the British Academy, I interviewed perhaps 50 activists, from the elderly to the young, from Moscow and regional cities, attended their events, watched them at work. Ten Foundation grant makers, journalists, and commentators gave me their time. I sent the relevant passages I wished to quote to their authors, to gain permission; some requested slight changes, others gave approval, some simply replied that they trusted me. All quotations that are *not* referenced are taken from these interviews. The tapes and transcripts are held by the Center for Independent Social Research, St Petersburg. I am grateful to Natalya Gorinova for her painstaking transcription of the tapes. ('You still use tapes! How classy!' said one of the younger respondents when I took my tape recorder out of my bag.)

But there are many others from whom I have learnt much. A longer list would include Jan Rachinsky, Elena Zhemkova, Tanya Kasatkina, Vladimir Shnitke, Vyacheslav Bituitsky, Yury Vdovin, Irina Flige, Karina Moskalenko, Sergei Pashin, Mara Polyakova, Alexei Simonov, Sergei Belyaev, Boris Altshuler, Alexander Podrabinek. And Marek Nowicki, from Warsaw, who died in 2003, was an outstanding teacher.

A different word of thanks to Todd Landsman of the University of Essex, to Margot Light of the London School of Economics, and to colleagues at the European University at St Petersburg, who gave me opportunities to try out my arguments on different audiences. By 2012 I had a manuscript ready for comments. I am truly grateful to those who took the time to read it and respond: Vyacheslav Bakhmin, Catriona Bass, Rose Glickman, Eleanor Keen, Margot Light, Margo Picken, Boris Putsintsev, and two unknown reviewers. But by the summer of 2013 it was clear that Putin's onslaught on the human rights organizations, which had started in the spring, meant further revision was in order. I was fortunate to be asked by the Open Society Foundation to undertake a review of its grant-making programme in Russia, which includes human rights. This brought both known activists, and new, into the picture of 2013. While I may refer to their views, I do not attribute them without permission. I am grateful to the Open Society staff for their assistance, and for permission to draw from the review.

I have kept endnotes to a minimum, and included only a short Further Reading. But I hope I have included, in one or the other, references to all those authors from whom I have drawn directly. A Dramatis Persone is designed to help the reader recognize those who reappear at intervals throughout the text, and their organizations. To include all those who feature would make it unnavigable and defeat the purpose. The plate section features only a small sample of the activists and events. I try to illustrate the generational change within the community and a variety of events or activities that demonstrate the change over the period. Many individuals, equally worthy of inclusion, make no appearance (but the Dramatis Personae includes references to other easily accessible photo materials). I am especially grateful for help with the photographs to Irina Flige, Dmitry Borko, Andrei Blinushov, Alexander Baroshin and Maria Razumovskaya. Permission to use photographs has been received from the owners.

INTRODUCTION

Today 'human rights' is part of political, activist, and academic language. There are several international conventions, a UN Commissioner, there is a European Court for Human Rights, even the UK has a Human Rights Act (perhaps under threat), in the USA and UK courses on human rights appear on university curricula, there are human rights law departments and degrees, even a European University for Human Rights, supported by the European Commission. Human rights advocacy groups exist at national and international levels. The academic literature, with its debates – philosophical and historical – on what constitutes or what should constitute human rights is extensive.[1]

In Russia too there is an active human rights community which includes internationally known, national, and small local organizations. There is a Presidential Council for the Advancement of Civil Society and Human Rights, set up originally by President Putin in 2004, on which many respected rights activists have had or have a place. Issues are openly discussed, even if few gains are made, and the protocols published on the Kremlin website. The federal and regional ombudsmen are active. Young lawyers successfully take cases of police brutality through the courts. Dozens of small organizations, at local level, are occupied with infringements of social rights (housing for orphans, non-payment of wages, pensions). Human rights organizations submit alternative reports to the UN committees. The European Court of Human Rights is inundated with cases from Russia, presented by young lawyers, and in large part its verdicts against the Russian government are implemented. Textbooks on human rights law stand on the shelves in book shops, and leading law faculties are proposing its inclusion, under international law, in their curricula.

In this book I describe and attempt to account for the human rights community that came into being, and has evolved, in post-Soviet Russia since 1991. The attack on the organizations in 2013 provides the cut-off point. The achievements, and failures, of those who gathered under the banner of human rights deserve to be chronicled, not only because this is a fascinating story, set in a period of turbulent social and political change, when state and society struggled to find a new modus vivendi, but also for the light it sheds upon the way past and present can influence attempts to create a new order. Russian traditions, the Soviet past, the impact of moving to a market economy, attempts to introduce democracy, Western aid and ideas, the international environment, the appearance of a younger generation [. . .] all have played a part. I try to assess the contributions they have made to the community's successes and failures.

During the period Russia moves from being an imperial Communist-party state to a federal democracy and, thence, gradually, to one of 'electoral authoritarianism'. To explain how this happened would require much more than a study of a new civic entity, the human rights community, but a case study can illuminate parts of a process, and contribute to an understanding of the factors that play a part in post-Soviet politics. On the one hand, then, this is a book for all interested in Russian politics.

The legacy of the Soviet or Communist past is a topic that is increasingly attracting the attention of scholars. It has a place here. By way of introduction, I simply say: the effect of developments during the Yeltsin years upon a quite conservative, inward-looking society, with little knowledge or experience of other countries was, in many ways, traumatic. Soviet practices and traditions were still part of everyday life. And, one might ask, how could they not be? Engrained patterns of behaviour or attitudes do not vanish overnight, especially if they provide some defence in a strange and sometimes frightening environment. My concern is whether there were perhaps *particular* legacies that made the task of defending rights unusually difficult in Russia, or encouraged a belief that human rights should be the focus. Another topic that has attracted attention is the influence and consequences of Western assistance, and here too this study makes a contribution to a wider debate. Finally, this is a chronicle not only for those interested in Russia or post-Communist developments. The experience of the Russian human rights activists also speaks to a wider audience – to those pursuing a human rights agenda in other societies, and under different political regimes. While not a manual for those who emerge out from under an authoritarian or military regime (as, for example, happened in the Arab Spring of 2011) – indeed I shall argue that the specific country context is of paramount importance – there are lessons here for others to heed.

✳✳✳✳✳✳✳✳✳✳✳

'How fortunate,' said Irina Flige, chair of the St Petersburg Memorial Society's Research Centre, in May 2012, 'that you decided to write about the period from 1991 to 2011. Now it's clear that a period is ending, a new epoch is beginning.' By 2013, the sense of a period ending was even stronger. It was not just that a younger generation had stepped out, waving new banners, on to the streets of the major cities, and that they had occupied the internet, while the opposition politicians of the previous decade seemed to have lost their footing. Socially and economically, and in its technological infrastructure (communications), in the conducting of politics either at home or on the international stage, Russia was a very different country from that even of 2001.

By 2013, Russia had re-established itself as a player on the world scene. Its leverage over former countries of the Soviet Union varies from case to case but it remains a key player, wielding economic, political and security weapons, one whose interests none in the region can ignore. By 2015, as the book went to press, developments in Ukraine had thrown an uneasy 20 years dialogue between the USA, Europe and Russia into disarray, with worrying implications for all in the region. Anti-Americanism, anti-Western sentiments ride well at home, but the Russian elite takes its access to Europe and its goods for granted (a money haven, quality education for their children, property, and residence) and has no intention of losing them. In turn Western governments, business, and financial interests welcome the Russian elite and its money, regardless of the owners' credentials, or the government's treatment of political opponents. Concerns over armed conflict in Eurasia or the Arab world relegate talk of human rights to a back burner. While Russia increasingly looks to China, a densely populated competitor on its eastern border, and is aware of the dynamism of the other BRICs, it remains a huge, energy-rich, middle-income country, and the dominant player in the region.

Does this suggest back to the Soviet Union? Emphatically not. This is not a Soviet regime, a regime with control over a closed society, albeit with its imperial wings trimmed. Society is open to the outside world, with a wealthy sector that moves in and out, and an intellectual community with international connections. It is a consumer society, with porous borders, across which labour migrants, narcotics, and arms move in and out, and communications link its citizens to each other and to the outside world. It is post-Soviet, and post-imperialist, with a heady combination of grievances. By 2011, after a decade of minimal interest in civil, political, and human rights, people were coming together, to take up local social and political issues, and to pursue their grievances, and in 2012 the falsification of election results brought large numbers out in protest demonstrations. The human rights community in Russia was changing too. Its most important founding elements – democratic activists of perestroika and dissidents – were giving way to younger generations. The authorities too were struggling to find new ways of relating to the non-governmental sector. In 2013, legislative amendments required NGOs that engage in 'political activity' (undefined) and receive foreign funding to register as 'foreign agents', and a campaign of inspection and harassment began. For those who wish to pursue a human rights agenda (and what kind of an agenda will it be?), the terrain has changed. But let's start with the origins of the community.

Introducing human rights

During the 20 years following the UN Assembly's passing of the Universal Declaration of Human Rights in 1948, human rights barely featured in the political debates and policy decisions in the advanced Western world. The Universal Declaration was taken up as a weapon by some challenging colonialism and seeking national independence, in some cases demands for social and economic rights were advanced with reference to the UN conventions. But those participating in the uprisings in the Soviet bloc (in East Germany in 1953, Hungary in 1956) did not base their demands for an end to Soviet hegemony and the existing type of Communist-party rule on 'human rights'. The Prague spring of 1965 saw no calls for human rights, but rather for 'socialism with a human face'. The American civil rights movement of the 1960s did not make its claims with reference to human rights, or the Universal Declaration. The students in Paris in 1968 did not fight the police because of their or others' human rights. The Solidarity movement in Poland spoke of rights, of labour rights, of freedom for Poland and democracy, and only after its suppression did an underground 'Helsinki' group form.

But, by the mid-1970s, agreements between the major powers – the USA and the USSR – were to have indirect but far-reaching consequences for the future human rights community in Russia. In 1972 the two powers had set up a new institution, the Conference on Security and Cooperation in Europe (CSCE, renamed OSCE in 1998) to resolve outstanding issues relating to boundaries and security. In 1975, the Final Act was signed in Helsinki. Article III referred to the inviolability of existing frontiers (strongly advocated by the Soviet leadership); Article VII referred to respect for human rights and fundamental freedoms, as listed in the Universal Declaration on Human Rights. The publication of the Final Act in the Soviet press, accompanied by statements on its binding nature, prompted a small group of individuals in 1976 to set up the Moscow Helsinki Group. In Czechoslovakia a group, Charter 77, based itself on reference to the Helsinki agreements and the Universal Declaration.

In the late sixties and early seventies small groups of dissident intellectuals, Moscow based, had set up informal human rights groups. An Initiative Group on Human Rights appeared following the imprisonment of writers for the publication of critical materials. Its appeal to the UN was on the grounds that Article 19 of the Universal Declaration (on the right to disseminate information) was not observed by the Soviet courts. Members of an informal Committee on Human Rights cited violations of the law and human rights, emphasizing that their concerns were with 'illegality', the non-observance of clauses in the Soviet constitution or Soviet laws.[2] 'Observe the constitution!' not 'overthrow the system', was their rallying cry. This concern with legality earned them the name *pravozashchitnik* or 'rights-defender', a term that subsequently would acquire a much wider connotation.

During its short life from 1976–82 the Moscow Helsinki Group's members championed the cause of human rights, basing their case both

on the Soviet government's signing of Article VII, on the observance
of international agreements, and on specific articles in the Soviet
constitution. Their appeal was to law as the instrument for ensuring such
rights were observed. They and others were harassed, exiled, and
imprisoned by the authorities for continually raising issues and
publishing information abroad on the infringement of human rights in
the Soviet Union. Few of the original members were still active at the
end of the 1980s. Some had died in prison, others were abroad.[3]

By this time, human rights was part of the international lexicon
used by governments and human rights groups. The USA made use of
human rights to exert pressure on the Soviet government during the
closing years of the Cold War. (Under Gorbachev, the politburo
recognized, at least to itself, that the arms race, Afghanistan, and human
rights were three issues on which they needed to respond in order to
improve relations with the West.[4]) Human Rights Watch appeared in
America in 1976. Amnesty International, which since the early sixties
had taken up the rights of political prisoners with reference to the
Universal Declaration, began to diversify its activities and take up a
variety of human rights issues. However, while by the 1980s human
rights as a subject was beginning to appear on university curricula,
sometimes under philosophy, it was not a topic in the study or teaching
of politics, or in everyday politics, in Europe or in the USA. We talked in
terms of political rights, civil rights, campaigns for equality and social
justice, and defending interests, but not in terms of human rights. For
those who studied Soviet politics, their interest in the dissidents covered
a wide spectrum that included, among others, the nationalists, the
Baptists, writers such as Solzhenitsyn, as well as those arguing for the
observance of international conventions. However, as the ideological
commitments to communism or capitalism that had divided the world
for nearly a century evaporated, it seemed to some that a global
community, sharing a commitment to the Universal Declaration, could
emerge into the daylight. All of this would have consequences for
developments in Russia post-1991.

State and society as Gorbachev comes to power

In 1985 Russia, itself a country with more than 100 different nationalities,
dominated a multi-national empire, the USSR, whose control extended

over eastern Europe. The urban population, and even the shrinking rural peasantry, was highly literate; there was a well-educated professional and intellectual elite. There were recognizable social groups – the party *nomenklatura* or officials, the artistic and scientific elite, the military elite, and national minorities – and there were others, in the shadows – the victims of Stalin's and subsequent repressions, the security services, prisoners. It was a closed society where very few indeed had any knowledge of the world outside, or access to their own country's history of the twentieth century. The media was tightly controlled; censorship was tight, and it was only small groups of individuals, in the major cities, who had access to *samizdat* or underground unofficial publications

An array of pseudo professional organizations, created and funded by the state – the trade unions, the Union of Writers, the Youth movement, the Veterans Association – existed but there were no independent organizations or associations that defended the collective interests of a group or its members, and had experience of pursuing their interests through dialogue, compromise, political competition or direct action. Any independent activity or protest was quickly suppressed by the security services. The only public political activity was large collective gatherings that passed resolutions prepared beforehand by a small leadership group. The ritual formalistic public political language bore no relation to the private languages spoken by friends and colleagues.

What kind of a state existed? One based on authoritarian rule by an elite of co-opted Communist-party members, who professed the belief that their socialist society was moving towards communism. Power and resources were held in the same hands. And the holding of power in Moscow, the capital, mattered hugely. Changes at the top reverberated down but in many respects the regions were run like local fiefdoms. When the regional boss was changed, a new team took over. Those in a position of authority saw themselves as the giver and guardian of rights. Officials looked up, not down, and they relied on their group of acquaintances. They reported up, ticking boxes, making sure the 'right' information reached higher levels. They relied on control of the media, and use of the legal system, and security organs, to ensure all remained quiet.

Meanwhile a bureaucratic state apparatus oversaw the running of a huge state-owned economy, a major defence industry, and the distribution of the country's resources. By 1985, a shortage economy was increasingly failing to supply the needs and wants of the population. An extensive welfare state, responsible for everything from housing to healthcare, to employment and pensions, provided a very basic level of support. And the legal system? This was part of the state's system of control. A continental system, it was based on detailed codes, the Criminal Code was harsh, and the task of prosecutors and judges was seen as one of punishing criminals. A benign sovereign could (and did) announce amnesties for prisoners, or issue pardons. At the same time, a telephone call from the local party secretary could change a judge's decision.

What does such a state–society relationship mean for the individual? First, the individual stands alone in relation to power and authority, in an unmediated relationship, without a group representative. What then does s/he rely upon? A connection with the leader or powerful people is the best option. Reliance upon one's own small group of family and trusted acquaintances comes next – they may help, assist, or find someone whom one can petition. Using the legal system is also an option – or the finding of a way to get round it. And very occasionally, a one-off protest may bring results. This was a society and politics that since the 1950s had produced its loyal supporters, and a small number of dissidents (whose objections to the regime were based on very different, sometimes conflicting beliefs and convictions), and citizens who were fearful, and others who had simply opted for as interesting or satisfying life as they thought they could achieve.

It was into such an environment that Gorbachev introduced the toxic words 'glasnost' (publicity or openness) and 'perestroika' (restructuring) in 1987.

The emergence of a new order

Glasnost brought the unprecedented opportunity for media and hence public discussion of the Soviet past and present, and new ideas of all kinds. As perestroika progressed and Communist-party rule began to unwind, ideas, hopes, and demands rose to the surface: for memorials to Stalin's victims, for freedom of speech, freedom to travel, a better standard of living, the right to demonstrate, and to register independent organizations and political parties. There was little reference here to the Universal Declaration of Human Rights but there was the beginnings of a new politics, and in 1990 the first open elections to both republican and regional or local assemblies. Among the deputies who won places to the Russian Congress of Peoples' Deputies, there were individuals who had been associated with the original Moscow Helsinki Group, now re-established. In both the political arena and in the embryonic human rights community, its members would subsequently play a significant role. But, for the moment, the battle was between those defending the existing Communist-party order and a heterogeneous alliance of reformers, under a banner, Democratic Russia.

In 1991, following an abortive coup by the old guard, the Communist Party of the USSR was dissolved, Gorbachev stepped down, and the republics of the USSR split into independent states. Russia, the heartland of the USSR, emerged as the Russian Federation, with Boris Yeltsin as a popularly elected president who looked to Europe as a future partner. With Russia now an independent state came the need for a new constitution, but a constitutional conference was unable to agree on a draft. In September 1993 a frustrated Yeltsin attempted to break the deadlock by dissolving the Congress elected in 1990 and, faced with violent opposition on the streets of Moscow, brought in the tanks. The White House (seat of the Congress supporters) was shelled, its defenders arrested. By December a new constitution, which, while strengthening the role of the president, claimed the Universal Declaration as a founding document and bound the government to observe international conventions, had been approved in a popular vote, and elections held to a new smaller parliament and federal council. This was the environment in which the first, officially registered, human rights groups made their appearance.

Chapters 1 and 2 take us through these extraordinary years – from perestroika up to the new constitution of 1993 – the political developments, the everyday context, and the activities of the new human rights organizations. Thereafter we follow the activists on a rocky path from 1993 up until 2013. It is not an easy journey, partly because the political and social terrain undergoes significant and unexpected change, partly because the human rights community is so heterogeneous, and its members branch off in different directions. A large cast of characters appears, some depart off stage, and reappear, while very different topics – from the bullying of army conscripts to violence against women to justice for Stalin's victims – crowd the pages. Wherever possible, I get the activists to do the talking. Bringing the issues and the activists to life both for those who know Russia well, and for those who, for various reasons, are simply interested, is no mean task. I know many of the activists very well, their crowded rooms, the way they argue at meetings, or relate to their clients, as they now call them; I have spent hours travelling in trains with them, bumping over icy roads in minibuses, standing in prison courtyards, drinking vodka late into the night. I can see them, and hear their voices. But what do their words convey to the reader? In places I put in the background but, before we embark on the journey, I want to give the reader a sense of the human rights community after 20 years of life, and struggle. We start with the environment in which, by 2010, the activists were working, then join them at three events.

The new Russia: 2010

Defending human rights was not a safe occupation if your activities offended powerful individuals or violent racist groups. In 2009, a young advocate, Stanislav Markelov, and Anastasiya Baburova, the young woman journalist who was with him, were shot dead in broad daylight on the streets of Moscow after leaving a press conference. In 2009, when the Moscow Helsinki Group introduced annual awards for human rights work, one of the ten awards was to Natalya Estemirova, a leading human rights activist in Chechnya, murdered earlier that year, and another to an activist in detention; in 2010 two of the awards went to individuals who had been severely beaten up, one left paralysed for life.

Yet, as regards rights and freedoms, the situation in 2010 was unusual. On the one hand, key political and civil rights had simply been lost (or never won?). For the past ten years the country had been ruled by a political elite with strong ex-security service elements, which had taken control of key structures (parliament, government, regional governors, security services, the judiciary, and popular media) and economic assets. The marginalization of opposition parties and manipulation of elections inflated the very real support received by president or ruling party, but there was no clear or popular opposition ideology or figures. The architects of this system of 'electoral authoritarianism' seemed, in their turn, to lack any ruling ideology apart from that of remaining in control, advancing their own material interests, and maintaining Russia's status in the world.

Politics, and policy making, had become opaque. A growing state apparatus was enriching its members through corruption. Where a political decision was required, the courts complied. Mikhail Khodorkovsky, the oil magnate who had criticized Putin, and whose Open Russia foundation had been prepared to support human rights activities, had been behind bars since 2003, and his oil empire dismembered by the state. In December 2010 both he and his colleague, Platon Lebedev, faced new charges and, following a mockery of a trial, were sentenced to longer terms of imprisonment. Some oligarchs had fled abroad, others toed the line. Yet judges could refer to rulings of international bodies, and the government implemented decisions of the European Court of Human Rights. Human rights issues were openly discussed, and reported, at the President's Council for the Advancement of Civil Society and Human Rights.

The loss of empire, which had first brought Russians back to the Federation as refugees and displaced persons, and been followed by military action within the Federation (the two Chechen wars of 1994–6 and 1999–2002), had resulted in an uneasy settlement. By 2010 Chechnya was run by its Kremlin appointee, Ramzan Kadyrov, a violent individual, with the assistance of his security forces. The Caucasus, with its very mixed ethnic and religious communities, and open to Islamic movements from outside Russia, remained a region of unresolved problems and tension, while labour migrants from Central Asia were becoming more and more visible in Russia's major cities. A conservative Russian Orthodox Church and Russian nationalists were finding their voices, in public and in the media, which reported a growing number of racist attacks. Patriotic rhetoric coloured official announcements.

Meanwhile, computers, the internet, and mobile phones had transformed communication between individuals, organizations, and the regions of the huge country. Anything could be said on the internet, 'the chattering classes' were writing, talking, and publishing their views on almost everything. As Maria Lipman, an editor, put it in 2010:

The message which all three TV channels broadcast is not that there are no problems, rather that there are many problems. But the key message is that We are in charge [...] initially I [Putin] was wholly responsible, took control of the country, of your lives. Now it's us – now there are two of us.

It is important to recognize that it is simply not true to say that everyone has been silenced and everyone praises Putin [. . .] there's internet, radio, the smaller TV channels. There's freedom to express yourself. Please, speak out, if that's what you want to do. You can be the speaker, or the listener. But the authorities do everything that is needed to ensure that those means of mass communication, where there is still a degree of editorial freedom, do not have any influence on decision making [. . .] you can put out information, but it won't have any political impact.

Not only as regards freedom of speech was Russia a country of contrasts. With privatization running amok, the nineties had been a time of dire poverty for most of the population. Even in Moscow there was little ostentatious wealth, foreign cars the exception rather than the rule. By the turn of the century the city was changing, fast, with its new buildings, boutiques, huge advertisements, fast food outlets, but change had barely scraped the face of provincial Russia, where people were struggling to survive. By 2010, there were pockets of wealth in all the large Russian cities, not just Moscow, and hundreds of thousands of their citizens had travelled abroad. It was 2004 before real cash incomes, edging upwards, approached 1991 levels, and the 2008–9 financial crisis hit both corporations and small businesses, but control of energy resources enabled the government to maintain the rise in the standard of living. The system could be described as a variety of 'state-capitalism' – where financial/business and political resources are often held in the same hands by the directors of a state agency, and independent financial or business assets are held courtesy of the political leadership (or leader).

By 2010 a new middle class was emerging, but income distribution was grotesquely unequal. In 2009, the average income of the top 10 per cent was 17 times that of the poorest 10 per cent, still stuck in poverty. A small and phenomenally rich elite enjoyed a lifestyle that matched its counterparts in Europe or North America, perhaps even more ostentatiously. Moscow prices were London prices, the bars and restaurants, and boutiques even flashier, cars with smoked-glass windows parked on the pavements, skirts were even shorter than in London. But the insecurity surrounding property assets, and the level of corruption, discouraged both domestic and foreign investment, while wealth continued to stream out to safer havens. London was awash with Russian money – which was going not only into houses, country estates, Bentleys, and children's education but also into buying football clubs, newspapers, and bookshops. As Oleg Orlov, of the International Memorial Society was speaking to a small London audience in November 2013 on the campaign against human rights organizations, the *Evening Standard*, bought by a wealthy Russian, Alexander Lebedev, ex-KGB, for his son, Evgeny, carried a news item on how two groups of Russians finding themselves at the same London nightclub decided to outdrink each other – the winners spent £60,000, the losers more than £50,000. Meanwhile, back home, the health and welfare system, barely surviving, was increasingly challenged by the spread of narcotics, HIV, TB, and continued alcoholism.

However, in 2010, human rights activists, journalists, and sociologists were talking or writing of new forms of civic activism or social action, often transient, localized, but nevertheless new. While much of this activity – people collecting money for sick children, helping the homeless, collecting money for imprisoned artists and homeless dogs – was at a local level, events could draw in volunteers from across the country, and receive national media attention. All agreed that this kind of collective action was still limited, and not political. But, as Tanya Lokshina of Human Rights Watch suggested, there were some protest activities, sparked by feelings of outrage, and she gave as an example:

There are very active campaigns in the blog-o-sphere [...] information is published on tenders for state contracts, and you can discover that the governor of the city X ordered two Louis XIV chairs for his office, I am hardly exaggerating, and an internet campaign gets underway in which angry individuals shower the governor with letters, speaking their mind freely, and in the end the order for the chairs is cancelled.

What though of the human rights community that had come into existence in the new Russia? To give the reader a sense of the community as Putin prepared to return to power, we attend three events in December 2010.

Three gatherings in 2010

Our first event is a Constitutional Forum, held on 12 December 2010, Constitution Day. The day-long meeting, or Forum, was organized by a small informal council for human rights, set up by leading Moscow organizations. Its allies were four liberal opposition politicians, hoping to combine forces to oppose United Russia (the governing party) in the 2011 elections for the Duma or parliament, and to campaign against Putin in the 2012 presidential election. Human rights activists and public figures gathered, from across Russia, to start a campaign to restore their rights, as laid down in the 1993 constitution: 'The Russian Federation is a democratic federal law-based State' (Art. 1); 'Everyone shall be guaranteed the freedom of ideas and speech; the propaganda or agitation instigating social, racial, national or religious hatred and strife shall not be allowed' (Art. 29); 'Judges shall be independent and submit only to the constitution and the federal law' (Art. 120). These rights, the organizers argued, were the priorities; without them, the other rights laid down in the constitution could not be guaranteed. Therefore the campaign should focus on: Ensuring the independence of courts and judges; immediate measures to guarantee free elections during the pre-election campaigns of 2011 and 2012; guarantees of freedom of speech and information.

The Forum was held in the huge Cosmos hotel, built for the 1980 Olympics, but itself overshadowed by the soaring hundred metre high obelisk celebrating the Conquerors of Space. The massive hotel, with its lecture rooms and auditoria, lends itself to the holding of big events. In 2001 I had attended a two-day All-Russian Extraordinary Congress in Defence of Human Rights at the hotel. Over 600 delegates of 250 organizations from 62 of Russia's 89 regions, joined by politicians (from the liberal parties), guests, and the media, had assembled in the huge auditorium, then gathered in side rooms for thematic discussions. Funding came from Western foundations. The atmosphere was upbeat.[5] Now, ten years later, at the more modest Constitutional Forum, financed by Mikhail Kasyanov, an ex-prime minister and opposition figure, the mood was subdued. I met many old friends or acquaintances among the 300-odd who gathered in one of the smaller halls, many who had been at the Congress in 2001. The majority were activists from across the country, those who had been defending very different kinds of rights over the past 20 years. While a few representatives of a new, young, twenty-first century generation were present, none seemed anxious to have their voices heard. This was not their scene. There were a few well-known liberal academics. The television cameras were absent. The press was silent. Only the internet carried news of the event. By 2010, Russia, politically, was a different country from that of 2001, and 1991 seemed a long while ago.

The opening session was chaired by Liudmila Alekseeva, now frail, white-haired, bird-like, a dissident from the 1970s who heads the Moscow Helsinki Group, one of the two best-known human rights organizations. Sergei Kovalev, also over 80, a biophysicist with a dissident past, now president of the other internationally known organization, the International Memorial Society, was an early speaker. Kovalev, small, slight, has a deceptively mild and slightly absent-minded appearance that cloaks a stubborn personality, a personality that must have driven prosecutors and prison camp officials into a state of angry frustration. Lev Ponomarev, a democratic activist of the perestroika period, who heads a more politically oriented organization For Human Rights, suggested:

> We set ourselves an objective – Alekseeva, Kovalev and I – the key aim was to obtain legitimate, transparent elections. That's our common aim, wholly political. But we consider it to be one of defending rights. Because, if we don't have legitimate elections, we cannot resolve questions of human rights.

Elections were the issue that dominated the agenda. Kovalev did not mince his words. The authorities, he declared, with a reference to an (in) famous quote from Stalin, 'were again turning citizens into screws, and the screwdrivers in their hands are ever more visible. To live in such a country is repugnant and dangerous, but to leave is even worse – this is our country.' We must, he argued, make tough political demands – for honest, transparent elections, independent courts, and freedom of speech. And, while recognizing the difficulty of the task ahead, seek support from different groups in society, including the creative intelligentsia and the new independent trade unions. It is more than likely, he argued, that we shall be ignored. But at least 'we shall be taking a step towards overcoming the misapprehension that civic activities by human rights activists should not include making political demands. It is very probable that some will have serious (and well-founded) anxieties that making political demands will impede the defending of particular individuals' but that, he suggested, was a question each should decide for himself. [6]

Another key figure was Oleg Orlov, direct, straightforward, a biologist who had become a democratic activist under perestroika, and chair of the Memorial Human Rights Centre. One can imagine Orlov in one of the revolutionary movements of the 19th century, but closer to Bakunin than to Herzen. Much of his activity has been monitoring and reporting on abuses in Chechnya. He took up the theme of political action:

> We, as non-political organizations, do quite a good job of working on issues which are within our mandates – defending human rights, the environment, or resolving social problems – but, despite all our efforts, the country as a whole is moving in the opposite direction [. . .] each of us can list a whole number of success stories – court cases won at the national level; cases won at the European Court; people we have saved; well written reports [. . .] but our individual successes do not lead to the achieving of our common aim, for the sake of which we, after all, carry out our work: namely the moving forward of our country in the direction of democracy, the observance of human rights, social justice, environmental safeguards, and so on. We should recognize this, and ask ourselves – why is this so? And find an answer.

The answer for Orlov, and some others, was that 'it is time that the representatives of civic organizations widened their agenda and, while remaining as they are, put political demands before the authorities'. However, even among the most impassioned speakers, many of whom were from the regions, there were few expectations that the Forum would produce much in the way of outcomes. The politicians, led by Kasyanov, spoke; the academics contributed. Draft declarations and resolutions were circulated for signing, or corrections. A declaration 'Time to Save the Country', to be presented to President Medvedev, contained strong words:

Afraid of its own citizens, the ruling Russian bureaucracy has concreted over the political field, and then begun to tackle public organizations, accusing them of drawing on 'Western money', while producing harsher laws which restrict the freedom of association. Episodic interaction with chosen representatives of civil society has a single purpose – to keep public organizations out of politics. At the same time arbitrary actions against such organizations are increasing; repression and the murder of rights activists, of journalists and environmentalists have become a daily occurrence.

There were statements in support of Khodorkovsky and Lebedev, the imprisoned ex-YUKOS oil magnates, statements demanding free and transparent elections, and one criticizing the government's failure to move against the extreme nationalist groups. But while the participants agreed on the issues, it was a different matter when it came to devising a joint strategy to regain these political and civil rights. The organizers were given the task of working out, by February 2011, a programme of joint action, based on the draft resolutions. But they could not agree, and meetings of the group petered out. The four opposition politicians formed some kind of an alliance but were no better able to devise a political strategy to counter the Putin–Medvedev management of elections in 2011 and 2012.

A School for Activists in St Petersburg

A few days before attending the Forum I was at a School for Human Rights Activists, organized by a Human Rights Resource Centre in St Petersburg. Including speakers and organizers, 100 people attended, perhaps half of them from St Petersburg itself, the rest from small organizations in towns and cities across the country. Several of them were accountants, others lawyers, many of the organizations focused on children's needs, or on invalids, but one of the key speakers was a trade union organizer from Siberia. With an able and well-organized young director, Maria Kanevskaya, the Resource Centre operates a free telephone helpline to assist non-commercial organizations with problems ranging from registration to turning to court. We shall come back to the Centre's activities in a later chapter;

here it is the contrast between its December School and the Moscow Forum that interests us.

It was bitterly cold in St Petersburg, minus 20 degrees, and the slippery paths dug across the courtyards through waist-high snow drifts were treacherous. The basement where the conference and School took place was crowded, but warm and well lit. People had come to learn – about how to use the legislation, how to deal with the tax authorities, how to obtain grants, or to turn to the European Court of Human Rights. There were informative presentations given by young professional specialists, and discussion, and sometimes disagreements (for example over whether the legislation on NGOs needed merely amending or radical changes). People from different parts of the country exchanged information on their experiences. For me, and not only for me, a morning's training session by Vitaly Drozhzhakov, a lawyer and trade union organizer from Krasnoyarsk, which included 'Planning organized campaigns to motivate and attract supporters' was something new. He dwelt on the need to translate individual claims into collective claims, either to be taken to court ('the legal defence of rights'), or pursued by direct action ('the social defence of rights'), for example by organizing a picket. He advocated booking a room for a meeting in a local theatre, preparing leaflets, using the press. But only a few participants from Kaliningrad, who themselves had been involved in demonstrations against the regional authorities, favoured this kind of activity. The majority of those present were sceptical even of the idea of taking collective suits to court. 'What country do you live in?', 'Are you from Russia?' 'What about corrupt judges?' 'Siberia is a different country...' Better to win an individual case, and then use it as a precedent.

While there was agreement between those from Kaliningrad, St Petersburg and Krasnoyarsk that the authorities would use any means to obstruct meetings (from claiming that participants were standing one metre outside the confines of a square to ordering a civil defence drill that set off sirens to drown out speakers), no one raised the issue of defending the right to hold meetings. In recent months meetings held, in various cities, on the 31st of the month in defence of Article 31 of the constitution 'Citizens of the Russian Federation shall have the right to assemble peacefully, without weapons, hold rallies, meetings and demonstrations, marches and pickets' had become the most visible form of opposition to the authorities. And no one raised the issue of forthcoming elections, or freedom of information and the press. Defending the rights of vulnerable groups was to be done within the confines of the existing political system, using the courts.

In a forest outside Moscow

Still with the temperature at minus 20 degrees, I found myself at an old-fashioned Soviet rest-home in a forest 30 miles outside Moscow. The dull brown rooms were not very warm. There were photos of Putin, with happy students and school children, on the walls. The cabbage soup in tureens, the rissoles and mashed potato, and the bed sheets so highly starched that they were difficult to unfold, took me back to a Soviet existence. The International Memorial Society was holding its four-yearly conference to approve the reports and accounts, and to elect new officers. One of the earliest independent organizations to emerge in 1988, the Society in 2010 had branches in Russia (50 in all, with legal status), in Ukraine, Kazakhstan, Latvia, France, Germany and Italy.[7] The prime concern for most of the organizations is erecting memorials to Stalin's victims, their rehabilitation, compensation for relatives, and promoting the historical memory of the Gulag. But Memorial's Human Rights Centre, in Moscow, then led by Oleg Orlov, focuses on the infringement of civil and political rights today, as so do some of the local organizations.

There were three guests of honour. Vladimir Lukin, the ombudsman, a Moscow intellectual, formerly a parliamentary deputy from the liberal Yabloko party, spoke warmly of working together with Memorial both on historical and contemporary issues, and told of how, when offered the post of ombudsman by Putin in 2004, he had turned to Sergei Kovalev for advice. Liudmila Alekseeva praised Memorial's achievements in conflict zones, and welcomed the cooperation between the Society and the Moscow Helsinki Group. Ella Pamfilova, with a parliamentary past, at this time chair of the President's Council for the Advancement of Civil Society and Human Rights, commented in particular on Svetlana Gannushkina's work with refugees. Gannushkina, who heads an organization working with migrants and refugees, and is a member of the Memorial Centre, had been nominated for a Nobel prize (previously winning other awards), while Kovalev, Orlov and Alekseeva had recently been jointly awarded the Sakharov prize by the European Parliament.

Of the many issues raised in the plenary and subsequent sessions, for our purposes three stand out. First, as might be expected, Orlov raised the question of political action:

> without significant changes to the political situation in the country, we cannot achieve our aims [. . .] We have to put our political demands to the authorities, although that does not necessarily mean identifying with political parties. For example we must monitor the elections. Yes, this won't please the authorities, and some organizations will come under pressure [. . .] yes, this is a very sore point, and there are those among us who object that this kind of action creates difficulties for us.

There certainly were. Many from the local organizations, primarily interested in getting support for memorials, and for books of memory, which entails working with the local authorities, had no sympathy with Orlov's views. But it was not just this. Memorial has always prided itself on being 'non-political'. But how does one make political demands that carry any weight, except through alignment with a political party? And none of the existing opposition parties would appeal to all Memorial members, even had they any chance of competing in fair elections.

The second issue was the focus of Memorial's human rights work. Should it be assistance to those suffering from political repression or should it include campaigning for access to information, providing assistance to refugees, to orphans, to the indigenous peoples of the far north, and campaigning for alternative service for conscripts? Opinions differed radically, as did the activities individuals were involved in. Perhaps the only point of agreement was that Memorial members should attempt to get included in the new public inspection commissions for prisons and police stations.

The third issue was that of the need for new tactics to attract supporters, whether among the young, or in society at large. Some advocated enlightenment, or 'rights propaganda'. Others stressed the need to convince individuals who had been helped that they should then help Memorial. A focus on potential donors, on those who could help rather than on those who needed help, on membership dues, and a better PR campaign was advocated by some of the younger participants. A session on historical memory lasted into the night. It was agreed to form a working group to work out 'a systematic approach to the use of enlightenment and education'. Quite a task.

Tracking the path from 1993–2013

How had the activists come to form the kind of community that existed in 2010? Chapters 3–5 follow them up through the nineties. I focus on the human rights that attracted the activists' attention, the way they organized their activities, the influence of Western assistance, of the economic downturn and weak state, and the huge size of the country with its very different regions. The war with Chechnya and relations with Yeltsin feature. In 2001, the new Putin leadership issued an invitation to NGOs to participate in a dialogue on the role of civil society. The resulting Civic Forum, which is the subject of Chapter 6, allows us to take stock of the relationship between the non-governmental sector and the state as the new century opens. In Chapter 7 we look at the place the activists occupied in the perceptions of their fellow citizens, at their own perceptions of their role, and their belief in the importance of education. Chapters 8–9 show them actively engaged in 'concrete action', in defending or promoting a variety of rights – from alternative military service to prison inspectors to the criminalization of domestic violence – but in an increasingly difficult political environment.

By 2010, Russia was home to a rich variety of human rights organizations, some very professional, some very creative. There were achievements and failures, legacies of the Soviet past, increasing professionalization, and a changing international environment. In Chapter 10 we return to the International Memorial Society to see these influences at work. In Chapter 11 a younger generation of activists steps forward, both lawyers and others whose formative years, and for some their childhood, were spent in post-Soviet Russia. Finally, Chapter 12 brings together the state of human rights as our period ends, the new forms of social action, and the political developments that followed the protests over the 2011 elections and Putin's return to power in 2012. By 2013 the human rights organizations were under attack. The nature of the attack and their response sheds light on the political regime, the law and order agencies, and the society that had come into being.

In April 2013 a knowledgeable journalist suggested: 'first they are going for the NGOs, then it will be the remaining independent media, then the internet. The aim is to control any opposing voices or activities.' I put this to a well-known activist, a lawyer: 'Do you agree?' 'Yes, but we'll go down fighting. And it's not control in the Soviet sense. They want to be able to push buttons, if need be, but not to run everything themselves, prevent any other activities.' But Boris Pustintsev, an experienced human rights activist from St Petersburg, replied: 'As Mark Twain said: "I can say one thing with absolute certainty – I don't know what the outcome will be." There are factions/disagreements up at the top, some will be saying one thing to Putin, others another [. . .] they themselves have no clear strategy.' And another echoed this: 'If Andropov were in charge, there would be a clear line, now there's confusion.' But by the spring of 2014 with the Olympics over, and Ukraine in turmoil, the future looked decidedly bleak. By the end of the year, the Kremlin was moving, slowly but seemingly relentlessly, to deprive human rights organizations of very different complexions of support from abroad.

In the Conclusion, I pull it all together and address one further question: what kind of a legacy will they, the human rights activists, leave for future generations – what has been their contribution to history? But, now, back to where it all began – perestroika.

PART 1

THE GOLDEN DECADE

CHAPTER 1

PERESTROIKA TO 1993: SEEDBED FOR HUMAN RIGHTS

There was some kind of melting pot, a crucible, which I would call the democratic movement, and it was impossible to understand who was involved in defending rights, or engaged in politics, or with history, or in journalism. It was all mixed up together, unstructured, there was no specialization, everyone was involved in everything. (Oleg Orlov, International Memorial Society)

In December 1986, following a phone call from Gorbachev, Andrei Sakharov, the famous physicist who had played a key role in the Soviet Union's development of nuclear weapons, returned from exile to Moscow. While his international reputation may have saved him from imprisonment, his criticism of Soviet policy on nuclear weapons and on civil and political issues had brought dismissal from work, and cancellation of his awards. In 1980 he had been exiled, under KGB surveillance, to Nizhny Novgorod, a closed city on the Volga. His return heralded a change in policy towards political prisoners. In 1987 Sergei Kovalev, first imprisoned for his dissident views in 1974, was allowed to return to Moscow from Tver, a city outside the 100 km zone surrounding the capital, a zone forbidden as a place of residence to released prisoners. He had close contacts with Sakharov.[1]

By the time Kovalev returned, long forbidden topics had begun to appear in the press, TV programmes had come to life; people set up discussion groups and then organizations; meetings were held, then small demonstrations, then larger demonstrations; conflicting voices were heard within the Communist party, even at a party conference. In 1989 a group of Moscow intellectuals, which included Kovalev, decided to re-establish the Moscow Helsinki Group. But, as perestroika opened up space for action, it was other issues, not human rights, that dominated the public agenda. The members of the reconstituted Moscow Helsinki Group[2] were busy in very different activities. Liudmila Alekseeva, for example, on her visits from America, and even after her permanent return in 1993, was travelling the country in the hopes of encouraging the new independent trade unions to play the part of Solidarity. The situation ('the ground burning under our feet', as Larisa Bogoraz, a former dissident, would describe it at a seminar organized by the new Moscow Helsinki Group in early 1991) had given birth to ideas, hopes, actions – previously undreamt of – jolting hundreds, thousands, of people out of their accustomed grooves.

By 1990, when competitive elections were held for the Russian Congress of People's Deputies, a cacophony of voices, those previously private voices, had invaded the public space: the soviets, conferences, and election meetings. In June 1991, with the support of Democratic Russia, the party that advocated an end to Communist-party rule, the introduction of market reforms, and had a pro-Western orientation, Yeltsin won election to a new post, president of the Russian Federation, the largest republic in the USSR. By December, following the botched putsch in August, Gorbachev's resignation, and the breakup of the USSR, he was president of a now independent Russia, whose Congress or parliament had adopted a declaration on human and civil rights.

In this chapter, I describe the extraordinary social and political environment – first that of the perestroika years (1987–91), then the turmoil in a new 'democratic' state (1991–3) – which provided a seed bed for the germination of human rights organizations. From 1988 onwards, in some places, independent organizations had sprung up to claim a role as spokesmen on behalf of society, or of some of its members. Some would become human rights organizations but they did not spring, fully armed, out of the crucible of perestroika. The Memorial Society, one of the earliest, became the catalyst for the new democratic movement. While democracy, national sovereignty, the market, and freedom of the media would come to dominate the agenda, in 1987 it was the unfinished story of Stalin's political prisoners and victims that captured public attention.

Stalinist repression and the democratic movement

In 1987 a handful of members of a Moscow discussion club, Democratic Perestroika, decided to organize an 'historical-enlightenment section' to campaign for a monument to Stalin's victims, and to call their group Memorial. This was the origin of today's International Memorial Society.[3] The story of Memorial's early years draws our attention to key factors that played a part in determining the kind of human rights community that subsequently emerged, and its relation to state and society. First, the story, then the commentary.

There were no dissidents among the members of the first Memorial group, although Lev Ponomarev, older than the rest, born in 1941, a physicist, had known Yury Orlov, the founder of the original Moscow Helsinki Group, and had accompanied Orlov's wife to visit him in exile near the Arctic circle. It was the release of Sakharov that galvanized Ponomarev, an energetic and impulsive individual, into action, and into joining the Memorial group. And Vyacheslav Igrunov, from Odessa, who had suffered forced psychiatric treatment for his views, while not a formal member, contributed his ideas. The group's members were largely young professionals, working in the research institutes, who had grown increasingly critical of the restrictions and repression the regime employed. The youngest of them was Elena Zhemkova, a mathematician, a graduate student, originally also from Odessa. Depending upon who is telling the story, the account differs quite substantially but all agree that Yury Samodurov, tall, bespectacled, and emotional, played a key role in collecting signatures, whether on the street, in the theatres, or from well-known artists and writers, in support of a memorial, a museum, and research centre, to be presented to Gorbachev at the nineteenth Communist Party Conference in 1988. Oleg Orlov, then a 35-year-old biologist, had had no contact with dissident circles but he had printed off leaflets in support of Polish Solidarity, before giving up in despair. With Gorbachev in power, he believed something could be done. Colleagues in his institute put him in touch with the Memorial group. Their ideas appealed to him or rather their activity – 'concrete actions' – getting support from people on the street.

By this time similar groups were springing up across the country, and the 'Memorial group' had attracted the attention of some of the dissidents. Orlov remembers Kovalev, Alexander Daniel (the son of the well-known dissident writer Yuly Daniel and Larisa Bogoraz), Bogoraz herself, and Arseny Roginsky coming to one of the regular meetings of the group in 1988.

> We, of course, revered people like this. And now four of them came to our meeting. We didn't know anything about Roginsky. A conversation started, as far as I remember, they were sounding us out [. . .] and after some time Roginsky, and then Daniel, started coming to us. We had a formal system of admissions – Roginsky found it strange and novel – we voted him in as a member, and in this way the old and the new joined forces.
>
> In my view the old human rights movement, at least as far as Memorial was concerned, played a hugely important role. Traditions, for example, of scrupulous attention to facts, collecting facts, publishing facts, keeping excessive politicization at a distance, which characterized part of the dissident community, exercised a very strong influence on Memorial's ideology.

Roginsky, a 40-year-old historian from St Petersburg, educated at Tartu University in Estonia, and continually in conflict with the authorities over unauthorized publications relating to the archives, had been warned in 1981 either to take advantage of his Jewish nationality and emigrate or risk arrest. He chose arrest, and received a four-year sentence on a criminal charge of using falsified documents to get access to the archives. Upon release in 1985, he moved to Moscow and, from 1989 onwards, played a key role in Memorial. An able negotiator and analyst, a born story teller, sometimes referred to as the 'grey cardinal', I see him as the Thomas Cromwell of the community.

During 1988 and 1989, petitions gradually gave ground to protests, to confrontation with the authorities, changing tactics, a candlelit vigil around the Lubyanka, the KGB headquarters, on Political Prisoners' Day (30 October), and arguments over the structure and type of 'movement' that was growing. A Social Council of well-known individuals (created on the basis of popular responses to a questionnaire, which put Sakharov and Solzhenitsyn in first place, and included artists and writers) became a negotiator with the authorities. Sakharov agreed to become co-chair; Solzhenitsyn, still abroad, felt it inappropriate to join. After setbacks, opposition from the authorities, and internal disagreements between more and less radical members, a founding congress of the All-Union Voluntary Historical-Enlightenment Society, Memorial, with delegates from the different republics and towns of the Soviet Union, was held in the spring of 1989. Sakharov became the Society's first president.

But what was the All-Union Society? It had held a founding congress but was not yet registered. It had no real structure. In Moscow, as in other cities, its groups of activists operated out of their apartments, now overflowing with documents, letters, files. Money for a memorial sat in savings bank accounts. There were no formal links between local organizations, who had their own and differing rules on membership. Memorial had played a key part in bringing people out on the streets or to sign petitions in support of Stalin's victims and, through this, to galvanize a 'democratic movement', but what now was its role?

In 1989, after the founding congress, the Muscovites set up a Scientific Historical-Enlightenment Centre, headed by Roginsky, responsible for the archive, museum and library collections, and with a brief to work with similar local groups, engaged in collecting materials, uncovering burial sites, and campaigning for memorials, rehabilitation, and compensation. The organization succeeded in bringing, without official support, a huge boulder from the Solovki islands (site of one of the earliest Soviet prison camps) to stand in the square outside the Lubyanka, the KGB headquarters. However, its members were simultaneously involved in demonstrating against the violent suppression of a peaceful demonstration in Tbilisi, the capital of Georgia, and campaigning for the release of the small number of political prisoners who were still being held. When, in the summer of 1990, after competitive elections, Kovalev, now a member of Memorial, became chair of the committee for human rights in the Russian Supreme Soviet,[4] he brought some of the Memorial activists, including Orlov, into staff positions. They had campaigned for his election. Now they began to work not only on rehabilitation and compensation, but on reforms to the existing penal system, and to travel to the 'hot spots' of ethnic conflict in Karabakh, Erevan and Baku.

In the autumn of 1991, in the wake of the abortive putsch, a law on rehabilitation of political prisoners was passed by the Supreme Soviet but, with the legalization of democratic political activities, most of those in the original 'group Memorial' had moved to other things – become politicians, or political activists in different parties, or set up other organizations – and personality clashes or disagreements over strategy had led to resignations. Kovalev was fully engaged as a deputy. Ponomarev too had moved into politics. Elected in 1990, he had soon found himself busy co-chairing Democratic Russia, the party led by Yegor Gaidar, the economist. He ran its staff office, which received funding without particular problems from businessmen who supported Yeltsin. Samodurov and Igrunov were no longer involved in Memorial. Sakharov had died in December 1989.

Aleksei Korotaev, also a physicist by education, involved in Memorial activities in those early years, and subsequently in different human rights initiatives, put it like this in 2010:

> Because [Memorial] was the first organization and was permitted, it absorbed almost all the civic and political activists who existed at that moment. It became huge – 200 branches across the country, 200,000 or 300,000 members – all that really existed. But then, literally in the course of two to three years, it rapidly declined. Put it another way, possibilities for realizing oneself in either civic or political action opened up and very many people who, actually, wanted to go into politics, left Memorial. Some went into politics, others into business. Society had become freer, you could engage in whatever you wanted [...] I don't think this was bad for Memorial, it became more specialized, began to focus on particular issues, including defending rights.

Memorial's strength had come from its role as a leader in the democratic movement. With that seemingly achieved, and with new issues coming on the social and political agenda, it inevitably lost ground. Even the fate of Stalin's victims became but one of the popular concerns, and within the Memorial Society a division of interests had gradually emerged.

In Orlov's words:

> We didn't initially think of ourselves as human rights activists. In 1990–1 we were still stewing in one cooking pot. It was only in 1991 that a component part of Memorial began to recognize itself as involved in human rights – and say – yes, probably, we are a human rights organization and we ought somehow to register as such. In 1993 we registered ourselves as an independent organization in Moscow, the Memorial Human Rights Centre. And some, but only some, local Memorial organizations began to take up human rights issues. You can't say that this idea appealed to all in Memorial. The underlying theme (idea) for Memorial remains one of historical-enlightenment.

The organization now had a 25-year lease on a building, with subsidized rent, under a contract with Moscow city council. It was in 1990 when the redistribution of property – state property – began. In cities such as Moscow or Leningrad, where 'democrats' had won majorities in the city councils, organizations that had established a name for themselves could sometimes lobby successfully for office space with subsidized rents.

In the spring of 1992 the Society held a new founding congress, as the International Memorial Society, with branches or members in Ukraine, Belarus, the Baltic States, and Kazakhstan, as well as within the Russian Federation. Its charter, now registered, described its 'primary missions' as

- Assisting in the building of a mature civil society and a democratic legal state, thus preventing a return to totalitarianism;
- Participation in the development of a public consciousness based on the values of democracy and law, the overcoming of totalitarian stereotypes, and the affirmation of individual rights in political practice and public life;
- Participation in the restoration of historical truth and in the perpetuation of the memory of the victims of political repression under totalitarian regimes.

The two strains within the Society – the concern with past crimes, and the concern with defending rights today – stand out clearly. Recent political developments were viewed very differently by members. Kovalev defended Yeltsin's decisions to close, with force, the Congress of People's Deputies in the autumn of 1993. Some leading Memorial activists were strongly opposed.

Now the commentary. The perestroika years (1987–91), fast-moving, sometimes chaotic, threw up a generation of civic activists who responded to Gorbachev's calls for reform. While some had a dissident past, most were individuals who had never engaged in politics or public activity, and many were young. Individuals were engaged in different civic and political activities simultaneously; the boundaries between professional, civic and political life were fluid. Young professionals played a key role, joined by members of an older generation, some of whom had been dissidents, or had known of the dissidents. Many retained their professional jobs while engaging in these new activities. They were making things up as they went along, with no previous experience of leading or even participating in an independent organization. Not surprisingly, conflicts arose.

As the political situation changed, some moved into politics, a wholly new profession, some for a short while, others for many years. Conflict between Yeltsin and the Congress of People's Deputies during 1992 and 1993, repeated at regional level between governors and soviets, produced new alignments. Finally, with a new constitution at the end of 1993, the state took on commitments to defend human rights, civil, political, and socio-economic, and to observe the international conventions. Independent non-governmental organizations could register, and pursue the defence of such rights. But their role, even with the new 1993 constitution, was far from clear either to themselves or to the authorities.

When, in the following chapter, we introduce a variety of organizations that would become part of the human rights community, a rich picture emerges. Perhaps all that the new activists shared was a desire to change the way the system worked, to remedy its injustices and, this was important, to engage in activities that they found meaningful. But, before enriching the picture, I want to put this new civic activity in a social and political context. It is hard now to convey what living and acting in those years was like, and mine is the view of an outsider, but it may help the reader to understand something of what it was like.

No food but newspapers

Moscow in 1990 was still a dark city; there was nothing in the shops, no cafes; people were hungry. The state-run economy was grinding to a halt and perestroika had brought no meaningful economic reforms. I did not meet any of the Moscow activists at that time. St Petersburg, then still Leningrad, was the city where I had spent time as a graduate student in the early sixties, and been coming back to ever since. Leningrad was still recognizably Leningrad, with its familiar streets and shops, crowded trolleybuses, waves of tired pedestrians searching for food after work, but now home to activities never before allowed. There was a strange discordance between the old familiar surroundings and the new world of public speech and action.

In 1990 and 1991 there was not much food. We survived on porridge, bread, and black coffee, and sometimes there was apricot juice and cognac in the cafe on the corner near the Institute of Sociology, to which I was attached. The hungriest year was 1991. Food was scarce, monotonous, the salami largely fat, and cheese only a memory. Everyone was hungry, losing weight. In 1990 the old system of distribution had broken down, the means of transport had failed. A television programme specialized in discovering warehouses, filled with rotting produce, of dealers slipping goods out of the state network to private traders. People talked incessantly, anxiously, of the approaching 'market'. Nobody knew what this dark frightening thing, looming on the horizon, was but all repeated the phrases that 'markets are necessary, a market is what societies ought to have'. An old man, waiting at the tram stop began to complain bitterly: 'did you see the prices? When were tomatoes ever four rubles a kilo? And all the traders are dark-skinned. What is happening to Russia?' He grew ever more agitated, stamping up and down in his felt boots, as two old ladies started to tell him that he hadn't seen anything yet, 'once we move to the market...' 'What market?' he asked angrily, 'Was this what I fought through the war for? I'm 86 and I can't even buy a tomato.'

Everyday life revolved round a search for food, and following the media. Suddenly private conversations and social concerns had become public. Editors, journalists, TV and radio staff still had their offices, received salaries, and were freer to do what they liked than their counterparts anywhere else in the world. They were accountable to no one, not to an owner, a political master, nor to the market. The only problem was getting hold of paper. In 1989 the unofficial press was badly typed and xeroxed two-sided offerings, either on that thick blotting paper churned out by a factory somewhere that aimed to meet its target in tons, or on near tissue paper. By 1990 there was a great variety. The anarchists (appropriately enough) were still producing very rough copy, and there were still all the odd fly sheets produced by individuals, as well monthly democratic and patriot papers. In April 1990 there was a makeshift stall outside a metro station that sold a variety of democratic publications, by September the groups had set up their stalls on Nevsky prospect. But more than half the tables were covered with sex manuals and astrology, and they were the most popular. The right was there in force one day, with their data on the Jews dominating Russia since 1917. But none of the political groups were selling out.

I found myself making comparisons with the publications of 1917 and early 1918 – also a time when there was a remarkably free press. In 1990 the offerings were meagre in comparison, even when one included the regular dailies and the new weeklies. In April, with delight, I had bought a copy of *The Black Banner*, an anarchist title that disappeared after the revolution, and in September, travelling out in the train to the forest, bought another copy off the long-haired, ragged, anarchist who was selling his papers. But the content was pathetic, and it is hardly surprising if the middle-aged travellers who bought it used it to wrap up their potato peelings, and turned back to *Izvestiya*. In 1917 there were parties with well-argued ideas and platforms, and a whole stratum of bourgeois society that, by its very presence, underpinned a world of owners and unions, conservatives, liberals and socialists. In 1990 there was none of that. There was a large and hungry literate public, but a wasteland without any well-thought-out political programmes contested and polished in the public arena, or political organizations with a committed following.

A new kind of electoral politics

I was in Moscow when the 1990 election campaigns were underway, attended a meeting in the famous House on the Embankment (of which more in a moment), and joined in one of the big demonstrations by the democratic forces. Here for the first time I saw the Russian, the monarchist, and the blue and yellow Ukrainian flags. Years of orderly parades showed their traces: organized contingents moved off smoothly in answer to requests from well-disposed militia men. But now there were knots of impassioned individuals arguing for and against private property, scruffy sellers of flysheets, and the lamp posts were decorated with details of intermarriage between the politburo families. Good-natured, cautious optimism was in the air.

What kind of electoral politics did the activists engage in, in 1990, and how did the soviets or councils, inherited from the Soviet system, operate under the new conditions? In the spring of 1990 I was met at Moscow airport by a young man in his jeans and faded blue jacket who explained, as we drove in to the city, that although a physicist by training he now worked as a guide for different organizations, and he was fortunate because he could use his mother's car. Upon learning that I wrote on Soviet politics, he invited me to a meeting that evening in his apartment block where the candidates for the forthcoming district and city council elections would meet with the electors. As we drove past the Kremlin he turned into the House on the Embankment, the great grey apartment block built for the party elite in the twenties, with its food store, and its cinema. 'But who is your father?' I asked, taken aback, and was left speechless when he replied 'It's not because of my father, but my grandfather, Yakob Sverdlov.' My instinctive response was to reach out and touch his arm. *Sverdlov*, one of the most famous and respected old Bolsheviks who kept the party files in his head until he died of pneumonia in 1919. *Sverdlov*, whose son married one of the daughters of Podvoisky, the Red Army hero (the Kremlin children all played and grew up together), became an NKVD interrogator, and was himself arrested and imprisoned more than once. Now here was their son, a gentle young man, not interested in politics, 'a terrible dissident' according to his mother who later that evening, as we sat in the big solid apartment with its unparalleled view of the floodlit Kremlin, told me (as she had surely told generations of young pioneers) how she remembered pushing Lenin about in his wheelchair after his stroke.

The room for the meeting, with its Red Corner, its bust of Lenin, portraits of Marx and Engels, and Red Banners, was packed with mostly middle-aged men and women. The candidates were allowed three minutes to outline their programmes and, as is traditional, started by giving their autobiographies. Some never got onto their programmes. A youngish man, who had abandoned a Komsomol career to head a cooperative that bought up apartments and rented them out to foreign tourists, remarked that it probably did not matter since he was unlikely to get many votes anyway; a professor of physics stated that he would not bother to outline his programme since it differed little from others. A middle-aged woman announced that she would press for better housing for residents, for ending the influx of migrant workers, for more provisions, a special fund for Moscow, more money for hospitals, cleaner streets, higher pensions, and price-linked wage increases: all popular demands, and ones that she would fight for as an *individual*, not as a member of a party. One candidate proposed investigation of the Prosecutor's Office, greater rights for deputies and for informal associations, and handing all religious buildings over to religious bodies. An elderly intellectual in an Adidas tracksuit asked all candidates to identify their political position on Article 6 in the constitution (on the leading role of the Communist party). All, with the exception of a military man who thought it inappropriate to comment, thought Article 6 should go. It was however the cooperatives that roused passions. The cooperative chairman was attacked for having abandoned teaching the young for the sake of money, and his argument that the taxes paid by the cooperative to the city government were of more benefit than unimaginative Komsomol activities cut no ice with some present. Both he, and one other candidate – a slightly aggressive, skilled worker with a chequered career of party education, expulsion, and a spell working in the Far North, who advocated enterprise autonomy and a free rein for entrepreneurial talent – stood out as representatives of a younger generation.

If the candidates demonstrated new and old attitudes, so too did the meeting itself. When a candidate asked if he could speak ahead of his turn, because he had to leave early, all semblance of order broke down. The chair ruled against, but a noisy minority (among whom the worst offenders were elderly intellectuals who shouted through their cupped hands) accused him of being formalistic and undemocratic. Many joined in, on one side or the other. The chair tried a vote, and unwisely declared that a spotty show of hands looked like a majority; the candidate headed for the microphone, but was shouted down by those who held that following the original order of speakers was the more democratic procedure; others argued that the order had been decided undemocratically. By then the individual was putting on his coat to leave, but a young candidate (whose action was subsequently claimed to symbolize the intelligentsia's willingness to sacrifice themselves for the people) rushed to the microphone and begged him to take his three minutes instead. Somehow, the dispute subsided, and the meeting continued.[5]

The election meeting was of course far from typical but it shared features with those, in some of the large cities, where challenges to the party leadership brought open debate. In such cases, there were no rules to be followed. I have described it at length to emphasize that 'democracy' requires the acceptance or the observance of perhaps quite arbitrary, but agreed, conventions. The Soviet system had bequeathed only its own rituals and conventions, which were no help at all. Where there was no challenge, the usual rules continued to operate: the local elite provided its own candidates, and they were duly elected.

The new politics in action

Leningrad as it was then, had produced its dissidents, underground organizations and, by the 1980s, a flourishing anti-establishment music and artistic community. With perestroika the intelligentsia came to life and, for a short while, so did some of the industrial workers. By 1989 there was a democratic movement no less active than its Moscow counterpart. Memorial was there too. However, many individuals, a few with a dissident past, who subsequently would create human rights organizations in the city, were at this time wholly involved in democratic politics, standing for election in the new soviets in the spring of 1990. Boris Pustintsev who, as a young man, had served five years for distributing leaflets in support of the Hungarian uprising of 1956, managed subsequently, despite obstacles, to get a higher education and spoke fluent English. Active in Memorial, he balloted unsuccessfully in the 1990 elections. But Yuly Rybakov, an artist who had been imprisoned in the mid-seventies for anti-Soviet propaganda, won a seat to the city council. One of his exploits in the 1970s had been to paint a four-metre long slogan, 'You crucify freedom but you cannot handcuff the human soul' in huge letters, on the wall of the Peter and Paul fortress, visible, when morning came, from the other side of the Neva river. The KGB operatives found themselves in difficulties, the river unexpectedly rose, and they could not remove it; they had to resort to requisitioning coffins from a nearby workshop and stacking them against the wall. Other exploits included painting 'Listen to the Voice of America' on the windows of a shop selling radios and, during the night, painting 'for a free politics' on the sides of trams in the tram depot, whose drivers, quite unaware, then drove them round the city next morning. When Rybakov returned from prison in 1982, disillusioned by his fellow prisoners' lack of interest in political freedom, he concentrated on supporting experimental art. But, with perestroika, he returned to political action, and was elected in 1990 to the city council.

The newly elected Leningrad city council, with a majority of 'democrats' among its 400 deputies, opened in June 1990 with high hopes. The opening sessions were televised live, and straightaway we witnessed the new politics in action, disorganized, often chaotic (more than an hour was needed to reach agreement on who should take the chair for the day), and queues of deputies clamouring for the microphone. Yet there was no real debate, rather the council seemed to be a forum for the making of impassioned personal statements, quite unrelated to the arguments of previous speakers. Factions, and groups, emerged but decision making proved extremely difficult, and levels of frustration were high.

The myth of a powerful group of 200 democrats cloaked the reality that they were 200 individuals, with no real basis of social support, nor a shared programme of action. Under the Soviet system such meetings were rituals to demonstrate unanimous support for government policy from a united people. Now perhaps the only function they could serve was to allow individuals to voice their concerns, and complaints. This was something new, but it stood in the way of, rather than encouraging, effective collective decision making. A basic issue remained unresolved. What was the relationship between the discussion and policy making? Debate in a legislature may, at times, bear little relationship to outcomes but speakers know to whom they are addressing their voices – to their fellow party members or party leadership, to their opponents, or to their constituents. The newly elected deputies, most without a party affiliation, and with few ties with their constituents, were addressing none of these. To whom then were they speaking? And to what purpose? Within six months many were dismayed, and electors disillusioned.

I spent time in the Mariinsky Palace, seat of the city council, an imperial building with splendid rooms beautifully decorated in Wedgwood colours, red-carpeted staircases, and a rabbit warren of winding corridors. I swung between hope and despair. Just to be there, to talk to the organizer of one of the independent trade unions, or to listen to discussions about setting up new newspapers, underscored the ending of party rule. Now there was a chance to do things differently. I listened as the deputies rehearsed exactly the same arguments that (unbeknown to them) the Bolsheviks used in 1918 when trying to decide whether authority should lie with the city council or with the districts. Would they find better solutions? They faced appalling problems.

They set up a human rights commission, which included Yuly Rybakov. The new commission decided to concentrate on the rights of children, on religious freedom, and prisons, but it was quickly overwhelmed with letters and appeals from those who had never heard of the Universal Declaration. In the two and a half years of its existence 35,000 appeals were lodged with it. Most related to the lack of housing – and they were the most difficult to deal with. People could spend 18 years in the queue for a flat, living six to a room in a communal apartment, while party workers and justice officials moved to the top of the queue.

Could one say that your commission was primarily concerned with defending social and economic rights? I asked Ryabakov.

Yes. Really our commission became a kind of emergency service. There was no medicine in the shops, and people were dying, while the medicine was in the warehouses, and you needed to pay bribes to get it [...] it needed someone to go and to argue [...] it was the same with food. Once I had to prevent a riot by smokers. Suddenly cigarettes disappeared from all the shops, and smokers are excitable people. I was going to a human rights meeting on Fontanka when my assistant came running to say that barricades were going up on Nevsky and there was going to be a fight in a tobacconist's shop. I ran there. The crowd was angry [...] I call other deputies, some go off to some warehouse or other to get cigarettes, I stay there [...] after a couple of hours they brought a lorry load and start to sell the cigarettes but during those two hours I had to calm the smokers down, and also the police who wanted to beat them up.

Sometimes the television carried reports on issues that preoccupied the commission. A deputy read out a letter from a father threatening to pour petrol over himself and son, and burn the two of them to death, because of lack of help with housing; another gave an account of prison conditions in the city. There was a devastating series of interviews with mothers whose sons, while doing their national service, had died from brutal beatings by their fellow conscripts or officers. A meeting of some of the women with Yeltsin (wiping his eyes with a handkerchief at one point) was included.

Meanwhile Alexander Nevzorov, the talented young producer of *600 seconds*, a TV programme that set scandal after scandal before the viewer, lambasted the city government and advocated monarchy as the best form of democracy. In one episode the famous statue of Peter the Great, now standing on a mound of live rats, was brought down as the rats began to move, a shot that was repeated at intervals with references to the 'troubled times' that lay ahead of the city. We moved inside the Mariinsky Palace, a place that had become a distorted world of moving furniture, acrobats, flying papers, a skull whose grinning black teeth spelt 'Power', a place where the cleaning ladies sadly dusted the furniture and talked disparagingly of today's council compared with the past, and where Anatoly Sobchak, the elected mayor, a dark silhouette against a window, criticized the deputies. It was brilliant television but hard to take. Nevzorov's strategy of undermining the council helped the conservatives, the party apparatus, and possibly the patriots. There was a subtle campaign aimed at raising social tension, spreading despondency and fear with sensational crime reporting – the camera moving in on a murdered woman lying in a park with a knife in her back, while the young policeman took clippings from her nails, the shots of a grotesque burnt body on the roof of the building accompanied by the journalist asking 'suicide – or, one has to ask, something more sinister?' It heightened the fear, particularly felt by women, that the city had become a wholly dangerous place.

There was still a political battle underway. The Communist party continued to control key institutions and resources and the political future was quite unclear. The political institutions inherited from the Soviet system, now peopled by supporters of the old order and those seeking something new, were struggling. With the end of party rule, and with Russian independence, the situation worsened. If the Leningrad city council was divided, and its relations with the mayor, Sobchak, were strained, at federal level relations were even more fraught. But it was not just that a new constitution was needed, and the deputies could not agree. By the end of 1992 the economic reforms and privatization, launched by Yegor Gaidar, the acting prime minister, had brought no dividends for the great majority of the population, rather they had halved their standard of living.

We saw how the commission on human rights struggled in Leningrad. Kovalev's human rights committee, set up by the Russian Supreme Soviet, which had a staff of seven, and 12 deputies, found itself overwhelmed by an avalanche of appeals or complaints during 1990–3, more than a third of which related to prison conditions. Simultaneously its members were working on legislation (on penal reform) and on drafting a law on a human rights commissioner or ombudsman. But the political environment became increasingly hostile. The committee's focus on civil and political rights met with criticism as the policies of privatization and shock therapy eroded living standards. In the summer of 1993, 74 deputies supported a motion, put before the Supreme Soviet, that the work of the human rights committee in defence of social and economic rights had been unsatisfactory; 38 voted against and 17 abstained.

The market arrives

How then was the much heralded 'market' affecting people's lives? Deputies got salaries but most of the activists retained their jobs in the institutes in which they worked. They simply continued to draw their salaries while spending less and less time on their work. Under the old system most in the Academy of Sciences institutes worked from home, only coming in once or twice a week for their department or section's meetings. So too did many journalists, editorial staff in publishing houses, translators, or university teachers. The salaries were low but so were rents, telephone, heating, the metro or buses, as was food, now rationed and difficult to find. Parents supported their children, part-time or one-off jobs brought in bits and pieces. Looking back, now, it's hard to recreate the early post-Soviet environment where the relationship between work and money was so tenuous. The majority of the population was, in one sense, living off state welfare, and before 1992 it was inconceivable that the state institutions (and they all were state institutions) would begin to dismiss employees or, even less imaginable, close down. Only gradually did the planned economy begin to break down: by 1992 people began to find themselves without work, or without their monthly wages, as enterprises ground to a halt, and inflation sent prices rocketing upwards.

Simultaneously unbelievable opportunities appeared for those prepared to take advantage of them. This continued as the nineties progressed. Some of the young clearly had a future in this new world, albeit unstable, fast moving, and unpredictable. It was a time for the energetic, the wheelers and dealers, the ones with practical ideas, self-confidence and ambition. You really could go to Siberia with rucksacks full of money, buy metals, get them over the border to the Baltic States, and make a million. With language skills, and perseverance, you could get taken on by a joint venture and earn more in a month, in dollars, than your father or mother, professors at the university, got paid in a year. Or you kept on your day time job in the institute (it was not that demanding after all), and worked nights in one of the big hotels, earning dollars. The hotel staff were the most highly educated in the world: doctors of biological science carried the bags, physicists doubled as door men, while classical specialists manned the travel bureaus. And if you had the entrepreneurial talent of Boris Berezovsky, a mathematician in a research institute who built up a business empire with incredible speed and moved into politics, or of the younger Mikhail Khodorkovsky, who put his Komsomol connections to work to create a financial empire, you began to play for big stakes.

By 1992 the market, skewed as it might be, had come. In September 1992 an air ticket half way across Russia cost the same as three scoops of ice cream in the new Baskin Robbins ice cream parlour on Nevsky prospect in St Petersburg. A reel of imported cotton cost the same as a bottle of vodka. Even prices for domestic goods seemed all over the place. An overnight train ticket to Perm, in the Urals, cost less than a kilo of cheese. But while a Westerner might puzzle over paying more for a ball point pen than for rent, Russians were faced with making ends meet in a world where prices were catapulting up and wages and salaries not paid on time. By 1992 real personal incomes had fallen by 50 per cent since 1990. Those on basic pensions, without family support, were the hardest hit. Food prices had risen ten times in the space of a year. Salaries of professional people by about five. Those who could not turn their hands and minds to business ventures were struggling. Individuals hawked cigarettes at street corners, kittens and puppies in the underpass on Nevsky prospect, pensioners and children tried to sell newspapers in metro passages, and the beggars and cripples sat against the walls with their battered caps in front of them.

Networks of friends and acquaintances remained an essential part of existence and, in an environment of scarcity, some relationships were based purely on expediency: coaching children for university entrance, offering medical or legal advice were 'goods' to be exchanged for lifts in a car, farm produce, or an appointment with a hairdresser. This way of operating – by barter and connections – took an enormous amount of organizing, and hence telephones were vital, but there were no telephone directories or yellow pages. Secretaries spent hours on the phone establishing where sugar was to be had, and aspirin, and arranging how to get a child across town to grandmother. Not surprisingly most Russians were very loathe to fix any appointment beyond the following day. Who knew what might need to be done the day after tomorrow? The notion of writing a letter and fixing something well in advance was even more alien. Secretaries often had no idea of their boss's whereabouts or future timetable; it was the rare individual, in any line of work, who had a diary. Appointments and plans that seemed to be firm simply evaporated.

By the summer of 1993 few had found salvation in a new political creed or in orthodox religion. Spiritualism and the paranormal were far more popular. After the TV news an elderly man with a flowing beard and a young woman, both in black gowns and mortar boards, took it in turns to give the horoscope for the following day. In Perm the big Political Education hall built under Communist rule, which seats a thousand, was packed out for the four-day visit of a faith-healer from Moscow. At two sessions a day, 100 rubles a ticket, and another 100 for her poster (so powerful that it should be gazed at for no more than ten minutes a day, but could be stuck under a table top to cure an alcoholic husband), she must have made a million from the visit. There we sat, row upon row, largely middle-aged and elderly women, with our jam jars of water, tubes of toothpaste and hand cream, all of which would acquire healing qualities, and with our photographs of sick relatives. Word had it that the water would begin to boil. It did not at that session, and I was

greatly relieved when my companion, a retired party worker, had the sense
to have a small sleep during the seances. Most who were there were poor
people, who had travelled in from the country for more than one session,
hoping beyond hope to find a cure for their ailments.

The political institutions struggle

I managed to get a pass to attend the session of the Russian Congress of
Deputies in the winter of 1992. Security was tight. In the evening, when
it was dark, all had to leave by crossing the deserted Kremlin courtyards,
out through the postern gate opposite St Basil's, across an empty Red
Square, and then past the pickets, ranged like medieval armies with their
banners and pennants – Democratic Russia on one side, chanting
'Support Gaidar', the Communists and the patriots on the other
shouting 'Gaidar out, Yeltsin out'.

The congress itself was a heavily establishment body. Democratic
Russia might have won seats, but not everywhere. Solid blue and brown-
suited middle-aged men, army and naval officers, and the occasional
woman deputy, often fresh from the hairdresser, in an angora jumper,
and high heels, dominated the assembly. The provincial elite of ex-party
secretaries, factory and farm directors were there in their dozens. A few
elderly intellectuals, stooped and in glasses, with untidy hair (including
presumably Kovalev), a sprinkling of bearded democrats, and Gleb
Yakunin, the dissident priest in his cassock, stood out. The deputies sat
in rows, stretching back in the great hall, with a gangway down the
middle, facing the lectern and behind it the banked podium. At a long
table on the podium sat the speaker, Ruslan Khasbulatov, flanked by his
deputy chairs and telephones. Behind, highest of all, sat Boris Yeltsin, a
computer right and left, with two telephones, solid, impassive,
sometimes checking his watch as debate dragged on interminably.

The format and rituals of the congress were those inherited from
Soviet times; they governed any congress, soviet, factory conference.
We stood in silence for the miners who had died in a recent accident; we
stood in memory of those deputies who had died since the last session;
and we clapped those who were celebrating their birthday today. Then
the congress got down to business. There was no real debate, just a string
of short impassioned statements, sometimes to the point, sometimes not,
and then wrangling over the procedure for taking a vote. In the breaks

the corridors filled with smoke, and groups of journalists, with TV cameras, mobbed individual deputies. There must have been as many journalists as deputies – every regional paper and station wanted its own report. There was a huge buffet downstairs, and a newspaper and bookstalls. The bestseller was Igor Kon's *Taste of the Forbidden Fruit*, the first book on sexology written for the general public, followed by Kipling's *Mowgli*. The deputies from the provinces were busy buying picture books for their children, and posters of Marianna from the Mexican soap-box TV serial.

Very few of the deputies could be called parliamentarians, hardly surprisingly. Most did not hold positions they could argue out; they had individual or institutional interests to defend; some were anxious, at all costs, to make a name for themselves; many were confused and concerned by the collapse of the Union, the economic chaos, and rising prices, but had not the slightest idea of what should be done. Some owed their posts, and flats, in Moscow to Khasbulatov; some found the idea of voting against the president difficult but were anxious to remain in favour with Khasbulatov, or with the president for that matter, and hence the crucial importance of a secret ballot on key questions.

This was the congress when a group of deputies gathered on the podium to complain over what they considered a misuse of procedure and Khasbulatov, in frustration, asked: who will rid me of these democrats? A group of patriots advanced with alacrity. There was pushing and shoving, the odd fist flew. Yeltsin left in disgust. Khasbulatov called for an adjournment, and left the hall too. The thickness of the cigarette smoke in the corridors was choking. How could such a disgraceful thing have happened, people asked? The popular press had a fine time of it: 'Great Deputy Ding Dong in the Kremlin' ran a headline. Many among the deputies, and the population, despaired at their inability to devise and keep to effective political procedures, or to produce a workable political framework. Once democracy and freedom had been won – or granted – on what grounds were 'rights' to be defended? The constitutional conference could not agree.

In the autumn of 1993, following his dissolution of the congress, Yeltsin set up a working party to produce a new constitution. Kovalev, appointed as chair of the president's new human rights commission, was included. The working party drew on the UN documents on human rights. Article 2 of the new constitution states: 'Man, his rights and freedoms are the supreme value. The recognition, observance and protection of the rights and freedoms of man and citizen shall be the obligation of the State.' And Article 17:

> In the Russian Federation recognition and guarantees shall be provided for the rights and freedoms of man and citizen according to the universally recognized principles and norms of international law and according to the present constitution; fundamental human rights and freedoms are inalienable and shall be enjoyed by everyone since the day of birth.

In December the constitution received 58 per cent of the popular vote. Elections were held to a new much smaller federal parliament, or Duma, and an upper house of regional representatives, the Federal Council. By the beginning of 1994 a new political order was under construction. Autonomous organizations now had a legal basis but many, not only the Memorial Society, had been seeded and sent out shoots even before Communist party rule finally collapsed. They, and the way they grew during the early years of the new Russia, are the subject of the next chapter.

CHAPTER 2

HUMAN RIGHTS ORGANIZATIONS: FIRST SHOOTS

In Russia, as we saw, human rights was not the platform on which the democratic and civic activists challenged Communist party rule during perestroika. During 1991–3 the new political parties dominated the scene. But human rights were stealing, gradually, on to the agenda. The Supreme Soviet had its human rights committee, headed by Kovalev. The Leningrad city council had its human rights commission. In February 1991, Larisa Bogoraz, the diminutive and elderly chair of the Moscow Helsinki Group, welcomed speakers and participants to a seminar on human rights, held in a hall in Moscow. The seminar was the first in a series, organized by Bogoraz, which ran for the next three years. The topics ranged from natural rights to freedom of movement, from freedom of speech and communication to social rights, from philosophy and activism to nationality issues and human rights. For many who attended, Muscovites and people from the provinces, elderly and young, the seminars opened up a new world of ideas.

In introducing that first seminar, Bogoraz referred to its aim as one of increasing the understanding of the importance of 'legal culture' – without legality, she suggested, politics, and the way we live, grinds to a halt.

> We hope that you, returning to the regions, will be able to engage in legal enlightenment and education [...] Of course you may ask

whether now, when the earth is beginning to burn under our feet, is a time for education [...] and I do not think that all of life's problems are resolved through law, but law is the mechanism which helps us to resolve the problems.

We are not here, she insisted, to engage in proselytizing (agitation); our gathering together here confirms that, in the main, we share the same views. But did they, and did the new activists who by 1993 were creating organizations in provincial towns and cities?[1]

Liudmila Alekseeva, one of the Group's founders, only managed to attend one seminar. Elderly, but with an inexhaustible supply of energy and optimism and with AFL-CIO support, she was too busy travelling the country seeking out new independent trade unions. The 1993 constitution, Article 30, proclaimed: 'Everyone shall have the right to association, including the right to create trade unions for the protection of his or her interests. The freedom of activity of public associations shall be guaranteed.' As Alekseeva travelled the country, looking for trade unions, she would be approached by people who had set up human rights organizations but:

> when I managed to squeeze time off from my trade union work and to meet with these people I discovered that that they had no idea of what human rights were but had chosen to call themselves human rights activists simply because they had heard of us, of the Moscow Helsinki Group [...] they did not know what human rights were, they had no experience, no money, no organizational experience – in other words, nothing. Just the desire to do something.

Once independent NGOs could register themselves and, post-1993, with a new constitution which had drawn from the Universal Declaration, and with activists abandoning political careers, the number of organizations began to multiply. Memorial had set up its Human Rights Centre in 1993. The Moscow Helsinki Group struggled. It was not clear what its role should be, now that there was a democratic order. Its original 'Soviet' role of reporting the authorities' infringements of civil and political rights had been assumed by a more radically minded dissident, Alexander Podrabinek, who in 1987 started a weekly publication, *Express Khronika*, to carry on that tradition, and remained highly critical of any cooperation with the new authorities.[2]

We look first at several Moscow-based single issue organizations, whose leaders had taken up causes during perestroika, and then turn to those in the provinces.

The Moscow organizations: prisons and the army

In 1992 ten Moscow NGOs created an umbrella organization – The Russian Research Centre on Human Rights – under a director, Aleksei Smirnov, a former dissident. Together they stood a better chance of getting subsidized office space. And they did – in the centre of Moscow. But the idea that they might work together, share resources, and decide common strategies, proved unrealistic. They were headed by strong-minded individuals, who had very different agendas. Among them were the Moscow Helsinki Group, Prison and Liberty led by Valery Abramkin, the Soldiers' Mothers Committees, the Mother's Right Foundation, Rights of the Child, the Independent Psychiatric Association of Russia, and an Inter-regional Human Rights Network. Together these provide a quite representative sample of the very different kinds of organizations perestroika had produced. Most of them still survive today, and still have an office on the same corridor. The Moscow Helsinki Group, in 1996, acquired its own, more spacious, office space and moved out, but that is to run ahead.

Valery Abramkin had spent time in prison for his underground publications. In 1989 he set up an organization to campaign for prisoners' rights and prison reform. One of his key slogans was taken from Dostoevsky's notes on prison 'The degree of civilization in a society can be judged by entering its prisons' and Abramkin himself would have found a place in a novel by Dostoevsky. Quietly spoken, thick glasses, still suffering the aftermath of TB contracted in prison, stubborn yet always courteous, he was respected by fellow activists, by prisoners and by the prison service. The strongest impression gained during the first of his six-year prison sentence, he wrote, was that while almost all his fellow prisoners had been 'correctly' convicted, very few could be considered 'criminals'. 'If, with the wave of a magic wand, it had been possible to swap the prisoners with a random collection of people from outside, no one would have noticed.' And that convinced him that the system, which 'quite incomprehensibly' imprisoned so many people who represented no danger to those around them, had to be changed.[3]

Subsequently renamed the Moscow Centre for Prison Reform, Abramkin's group both monitored conditions and outbreaks of violence in the prison system and, during 1990, worked under the aegis of the human rights committee of the Russian Supreme Soviet to produce draft legislation on penal reform. It was largely because of its effectiveness that, with a sigh of relief, Orlov and his fellow activists in Memorial left the prison system to Abramkin's organization. In the nineties, it put out a weekly radio programme, *Clouds*, for prisoners, printed brochures on how to appeal for a pardon, or parole; it organized collections to provide soap and food for children in prison, who were often hungry, and essay-writing competitions. Exhibitions to portray the plight of prisoners, many sick with TB, and roundtable discussions with deputies, and high ranking officials from the prison service were held not only in Moscow and St Petersburg but in other cities too. By the end of the decade legislation on the implementation of sentences had improved, as had conditions in some of the prisons and penal colonies.[4] I come back in a later chapter to the success or failure of the organizations to influence legislation, here it is the emergence and development of a variety of single issue organizations during these 'golden years' that interests us.

By way of contrast, Mother's Right owed everything to the opportunities perestroika placed before young people, opportunities unimaginable to those of earlier generations. It was a time when chance encounters, and the energy and talent of an individual, could have far reaching consequences. Mother's Right, allocated two square metres of space, and a table and chair, in a room shared with three other NGOs in 1992, is still in the same offices today but now with two rooms, crowded with files, desks, computers, and publications.[5] Its director, Veronika Marchenko, a lively blonde blue-eyed teenager in 1986, had appeared on a TV programme, a discussion club for young people. This led to an invitation from the journal *Youth* to join its youth section. She began work there, while studying in the evenings at Moscow University's journalism faculty.

Our youth section quickly became very popular (the print run of the journal in those years was more than three million), and somehow or other we were invited to appear on the super-popular evening TV show *View*. I didn't utter a single word about the army. But, simply from seeing me on the screen, a woman from the Ukraine, from Nikopol, decided to write me a letter about the death of her son. And that started it all. While I was preparing a publication about the death of Alurdos, the cadet, fate sent me, via the editorial office, the mother of another dead soldier son, from Moscow, Pashkova. I included her story of his death in the article. Then I spent six months getting it through the military censor, a Soviet atavism, breathing its last as, with a red pencil, it deleted any geographic references in my article which would allow our enemies to know where our troops were stationed.

Her article appeared in June 1989 and, within a month, she had received a flood of letters from all across the Soviet Union. It was clear to her that 'hazing' in the army did not consist of occasional tragic incidents. She wrote further articles. Then, working from home together with friends, she wrote to Gorbachev, to demand changes in the law, and began to collect materials for a Book of Memory, and to set up Mother's Right, an organization dedicated to the right of a mother to know how and why her conscript son had died. By the end of the nineties, Mother's Right had produced publications, and had a small network of lawyers working across the country to take up cases on behalf of grieving parents.

The Union of Soldiers' Mothers Committees still has a room across the corridor. This was a grass roots organization of mothers, with committees across the country, which sprang up following changes to the draft in 1988. It quickly became widely known. Staffed entirely by mothers whose sons had been brutally treated or died as conscripts, its often small organizations (of three or four individuals) offered help both to parents and to the boys themselves, either in pleading exemption from the draft, or providing support to those already serving. Their aim was, and remains, to end conscription in favour of a wholly professional army. While both the Soldiers' Mothers and Mother's Right are concerned with the treatment of young men in the army, they pursue different aims, and their organizations are very different. In 1994 they worked together on a seminar project but they soon developed lines of work independent of each other. And the Union of Soldiers' Mothers Committees, Moscow-based, does not speak for all the Soldiers' Mothers

committees. The St Petersburg committee, for example, has a strong
independent voice. All these organizations and their activities ten years
later feature in Chapters 8 and 9.

Abuse within society or state neglect

Appeals for help from people who felt they had no one else to turn to –
whether from the relatives of Stalin's victims, prisoners, or soldiers'
mothers, came flooding in in response to newspaper articles or television
programmes. Not all came from those who were suffering at the hands
of the state. In 1989, a young statistician, Marina Pisklakova, petite
and blonde, who still leads ANNA, an organization that focuses on
domestic violence, moved to a new Academy of Sciences institute headed
by a well-respected and well-connected economist, Natalya Rimashevskaya. She was given the task of identifying the issue that was, at the
present time, of greatest concern to women. She designed a simple
questionnaire, with items such as child benefits. This was published in
the journal *Working Woman*, and readers were asked to respond.

> I received two letters which were not answers to the questionnaire,
> simply two letters describing awful things that were happening in
> their families. I didn't know how to classify them, they didn't fit
> into any of the categories. They simply wrote about the abuse they
> suffered from their husbands.

She turned to a colleague for help in answering the letters because
'one thing I had understood. They had both written "You in the
Academy of Sciences are clever people. You surely know what I can do"
and I had understood that they had written to me because they had no
one else to turn to.' One of her colleagues explained that in the West this
was known as domestic violence whereas in Russia it was still a taboo
subject. Wherever there was an opportunity, such as waiting in the
school playground, Marina began to talk about it with other women and
soon she had those to whom she would offer support, by simply
listening. But she recognized that this was no answer. In 1991 when the
institute sent her to Goteburg for two months, Rimashevskaya advised
her to try and find out more about combatting domestic violence
in Sweden. She did, and received an offer from Ritva Khomstron,

the director of a crisis centre, to come and train her. Why me? she asked. To which Ritva replied that since she had already started on counselling, there was no way back. On her return to Moscow, Rimashevskaya suggested that this should be part of her research work. Ritva came, at her own expense, and together they worked on setting up a telephone of trust, and on training people to counsel callers. Rimashevskaya gave her a room, a telephone number, and announced the number on a popular Moscow radio station. And the calls started coming. It was 1995 before Marina, now with a group of counsellors she had trained, left the institute and registered ANNA. By then the idea of 'crisis centres' had spread across the country, and in 1998 they came together to form an Association, with Marina elected as chair.

Not all these new activists were young. For older individuals too, perestroika could change their lives in mid-career, those who were natural activists but, under the Soviet system, had been unable to employ their talents in meaningful social activities. Activists-manqué, we can call them. Svetlana Gannushkina, who taught maths at the Historical-Archive Institute, was in her late forties when perestroika began. With a well-known psychiatrist as a grandfather, after whom a hospital was named, she had grown up in a family to whom people often turned for help and, as a teacher, students brought her their problems. But it was signing letters of protest against anti-Semitism that brought her, in March 1988, an invitation to the House of Scholars to participate in a discussion of anti-Semitism organized by an instructor from the Central Committee of the Communist Party. This was the time that the conflict erupted in Nagorny-Karabakh between Armenians and Azeris, and an appalling pogrom of the Armenian minority in Sumgait, a town in Azerbaijan, occurred. Svetlana spoke twice, each time for two minutes. Once in reply to a proposal from a Jewish speaker that they should talk about nationalism, anti-Russian attitudes, and the plight of blacks in America:

> I responded that I wanted to talk about the things that disturbed me, that I, of course, sympathized with the blacks and Indians, but I wanted to discuss issues that caused me pain, things of which I was ashamed and for which I felt responsible. And later [when a representative of Karabakh committee] stood up and said that you have gathered here and are discussing your Jewish affairs, while

our people are being slaughtered, I said that of course I understood him but, given that we had gathered to discuss a concrete issue, I couldn't, now, recognize my responsibility for what had happened in Sumgait. The government must take action, and the Azeri intelligentsia should examine its conscience.

However, subsequently, upon reflection, she decided they too should take responsibility, and asked for the transcript to note this. The incident illustrates Gannushkina's qualities as a participant in discussion. Unlike many she is always focused, succinct and, what does not come out here, able to confound an opponent. In response to hostile questioning, recently, from prosecutors on why she should assume Western funders were interested in a stable Russia, she asked the official to consider the following situation: he lived with his family in a small house, with a well-kept garden, on a quiet street but, unfortunately, his next door neighbours, in a large house, with an overgrown and untidy garden, had a large and noisy family; windows got broken, car engines revved up during the night, and sometimes fights broke out. Would he like living next to such neighbours, she asked? Might he not favour investing some effort and means to assist these neighbours and their children in finding a new way of living? While she sometimes relies on humour, she can also demolish an opponent's argument with a series of logical and informed statements, and she has no hesitation in taking on a minister, prosecutor, or the president himself.

Following the discussion in 1988 she was invited to become a co-founder of a new section on national-political relations under the Sociological Association which took up the Armenian–Azeri conflict. In January 1989, during the winter break, she decided to visit Erevan but, at the last moment, changed her mind and went to Baku in Azerbaijan. She returned with 30 interviews with members of the intelligentsia, interviews that revealed a much more complex set of attitudes than those ascribed to them by those who supported the Armenian position. But it was her meeting with the Azeri refugees, driven out of Armenia that, in her words, decided her future fate.

They were simple peasants, it was a heart breaking scene, because they had been driven out, over a pass in December [. . .] they were in a campsite, it's true they had been allowed to take some of their things with them, but there was a woman whose two-month-old baby had frozen and she was in a completely deranged state. These were people who lived in Armenia, spoke Azeri, knew no Russian, they were peasants, and they had no idea where Karabakh was [. . .] When we asked what had happened, the party organizer of the collective farm and the director of the school stepped forward together and explained 'Armenian comrades with machine guns came and ordered us to get out.' They still called them comrades. What a terrible injustice! Why drive out these peasants? The local Azeri boss in his sable hat and leather coat turned up and started to calm them down. He said to them 'You'll understand our position, you are not our people, we should not be looking after you, a territorial division exists. What should we do with you?' No one understood what to do with them. And that led me to take up the issue of refugees.

In this case, it was the absence of any state institution with a brief to deal with a political and humanitarian problem that produced the NGO. The unforeseen ethnic conflicts, followed by the breakup of the USSR, brought the refugees, first those fleeing the violence, then the Russians leaving the Central Asian republics. With the appearance of refugees in Moscow in 1990, their plight became a topic in the press. Lidia Grafova, a well-known journalist from *Literaturnaya gazeta*, together with Gannushkina and others decided they should set up an organization to provide, at the very least, humanitarian aid. This was Citizens' Assistance, again still operating today, and still led by Gannushkina. But she had quickly realized that, with the ending of the Soviet Union, legislation regarding migrants was crucial. She started to look at the legislation, at first, understanding little but 'drawing on knowledge of how mathematical theories work, began to learn the laws' and, since then, has concentrated on mastering the legal issues. The unwillingness of many in Moscow intelligentsia circles to recognize that there were two sides to the Armenian–Azeri conflict dismayed her, and it was this that led her to Memorial. Dmitry Leonov, one of the Society's founding members and a key figure at the time, introduced Gannushkina in 1993 to the human rights group.

They were people, with whom one could talk of both sides. That was important for me, that I was among like-minded people, who were able to think widely, analyse, do research, engage in monitoring, although the word did not exist then [...] and so I joined Memorial [...] Memorial came into existence – from Memory – but then it became clear that human rights were not only infringed in the past, but also today – and the human rights centre appeared.

But while continuing to teach maths, Citizens Assistance was where she spent most of her time. Until 1996 the organization's 'office' was the space under a staircase in the building occupied by the newspaper *Literaturnaya gazeta*. A group of volunteers held weekly receptions to give refugees advice, food, and support. In 1998 the city government provided Citizens Assistance with an office at a subsidized rent. But by now Gannushkina had set up another structure, Migration Rights, as part of Memorial's Human Rights Centre, to offer legal support to migrants and refugees. This has gone from strength to strength, for reasons we explore in Chapter 9.

If most of the early human rights organizations were those concerned to defend individuals against the powerful and unaccountable state apparatus of coercion – the prison system, the army, the security services – both Pisklakova and Gannushkina were focusing on the issue of abuse within society, abuse of individuals where the state stood aside. Those who took up children's rights were often trying to deal with both simultaneously – the abuse children suffered at the hands of their parents and the inadequacy of state provision for those children. By 1991 the underground cellars of large cities, and their railway stations, were home to countless children, curling up to sleep with their dogs after a day's begging, stealing, and sniffing glue. Boris Altshuler, also a physicist by background, set up an organization Children's Rights, also with a room in the Research Centre, to campaign on their behalf. In ten years' time, he would be orchestrating an Alternative Report on the state of affairs in Russia to the UN Committee on the Rights of the Child, but in these early years it was immediate help that the children needed. By way of example, I turn to an initiative that involved active citizens using what still remained of the old state system.

In 1993 there were thousands of homeless children in St Petersburg. Some had run away from alcoholic parents, some been abandoned, others had absconded from brutal children's homes; some came from far afield.

Ranging in age from four or five to 18, they formed little gangs and lived by stealing, begging, collecting empty bottles and claiming the deposit, and by prostitution. They all smoked, some sniffed petrol and glue; some of the adolescents had a mental age of five or six; many could not read. They had head and body lice and, eating whatever they could get hold of, suffered from chronic gastro-enteritis.

Two enterprising women, in 1991, took a gang of children to the mayor's office, to plead for help. The deputy mayor, appalled, lifted the telephone and gave authorization for them to take over a deserted hostel. Some of the children had been found in cellars, some just turned up; several were quite disturbed. The young girls could be taken for boys: their voices were hoarse and rough from smoking, their mannerisms tough, a defence against the world they lived in. By 1993, when I visited the hostel, 45 children, mostly girls, were living in the three apartments that had been renovated. There was a kitchen in each apartment, a play room, a school room, and a sick room. Most of the equipment came from the Swedish charity named after the children's writer, Astrid Longren, and the home was called Astrid House. The municipality paid a daily allowance for food, to be bought at wholesale prices from a base which supplied children's homes and hospitals, but medicine was a problem.

They still all smoked, and that was allowed – on the stairwell. They needed endless care and lots of attention; they needed one-to-one tuition. The little children had a good number of toys – tiny five-year-old Petya, found in rags in a cellar, unable to talk when he came, was sitting watching television hugging a doll to himself. The older children were worse off. They only had one jigsaw – Made in England, a thatched cottage with roses climbing up the walls – and a set of draughts. The home was an open one, the only constraint that the children must be in by nine o'clock. One evening they set their dogs on a mentally-retarded man who happened to walk by. The staff locked them out for the night, saying that people who behaved like that were not welcome. The children were bewildered; they built a little fire to try and keep warm, and stood against the building all night. They were concerned that they had upset the staff, but they were not really clear what the fuss was about. Gradually they got rid of the dogs. The staff's aim was to help them to understand how to live an ordinary life, and to find them foster parents. In order to comply with the law, to safeguard the children, and to encourage a family to take a child, the foster parents were registered as 'employees' of the home, and entitled to receive the food allocation for the child, for provisions bought at the wholesale store. But the future for the older girls looked bleak.

Those who ran the Astrid House would not have thought of themselves as human rights activists, nor would those who were setting up human rights organizations have considered them to be such. Yet the boundary between what they were doing, and Gannushkina's assistance to refugees, or Abramkin's campaigns to help feed hungry children in prisons, was blurred. The individuals mentioned so far, apart from those at the Astrid House, applied their talents and energy to creating non-governmental organizations, and have remained with them ever since. I have had to leave many others, no less deserving of mention, out of the picture. How might we characterize our perestroika activists? Talented, energetic, willing to take risks – yes – and with little or no experience of setting up and running organizations, negotiating with the authorities, or engaging with the outside world. Many paid their first, short visit to a foreign country during the nineties. Many survived by keeping their old jobs or using contacts among those whom they knew; none thought of setting up membership organizations except Memorial, where it occurred spontaneously.

St Petersburg and the provinces

It was not only in Moscow that by 1993 non-governmental organizations, with a mandate to defend rights, had set themselves up and registered. In many cities the pattern of democratic action, in which civic activists and critics of Communist party rule entered the electoral arena, and won seats, repeated itself. Politics and civic action was entwined. Gradually, and for different reasons, some of the activists distanced themselves from politics to focus on setting up human rights organizations.

In 1988 in Ryazan, a garrison town south of Moscow, Andrei Blinushov, a young historian, resigned from his post in the police department. This was in protest against the violence employed by a police riot squad brought from Moscow to break up a peaceful demonstration in support of elections. Active in the new democratic movement, and specializing in relations with the press, news of Memorial inspired him and others to set up a Memorial organization, which they registered in October 1989. But it was politics and the forthcoming elections that occupied most of their attention. Several of their members were elected to the city council in 1990, and set up a commission on rehabilitation and human rights.

> After some minor confrontations the city fathers tried to buy us off with a set of documents, already drawn up, which would give each of us a plot of land in the centre of the town, a large plot with the plan for a detached house, we turned it down [...] but this brought a split in the democratic movement because some of its members and the new NGOs simply could not refuse such a profitable offer [...] Sadly, I must admit, we found ourselves in a minority and formed a small opposition on the city council.

In Tomsk, a university town in West Siberia, a place of exile for those sentenced under Stalin or their relatives, the 'democrats' also appeared, and won seats to the council. Not surprisingly some of them combined their political activities with taking up the cause of those repressed under Stalin. Nikolai Kandyba, a young scientist, but already taking up a variety of cases before the courts, was both active in Memorial and as a deputy.

While Blinushov and Kandyba combined politics with Memorial activities, others participated in the new political parties. Igor Kalyapin, born and brought up in Nizhny Novgorod, city on the Volga famous for its trade fairs, and place of exile for Sakharov, was 20 in 1988, studying radio engineering in the evenings, while working in the Chemistry Institute during the day. A presentation at its academic council by a young physicist, Boris Nemtsov, who, wearing inappropriate clothes (shabby jeans), argued clearly and persuasively that Russia needed a multi-party system, surprised and set him thinking. He joined an informal discussion club. He began to think that the way a society is organized politically has consequences for its development. Orwell's *1984* appalled him, and he joined the democratic movement. Here his talents, and his knowledge of chemistry, reaped results. In no time, using a window frame, he had set up a rudimentary silkscreen printer, which could produce colour prints for leaflets, posters. But it was a decision to introduce the Tsarist Russian flag in the May Day celebrations in 1989 that was a turning point in his life. After

scouring albums of old photographs the night before to find out what
the flag looked like, and then replicating it, he and friends made up a
column, and waved their flags. They were dismissed from their jobs, and
from their institutes; fortunately they found employment, for very little
pay, with a farmer, rearing pigs in the centre of the city, who collected
slops from restaurants and hotels in his Zhiguli sedan car from which
he had removed the seats. Meanwhile they had set up a branch of
DemSoiuz, the most radical political organization of the time, which
held demonstrations, demanding a multi-party system, but they also
printed election leaflets (on their silkscreen) for democratic candidates in
the 1990 elections.

By 1991 the authorities were tired of their activities and brought
criminal charges against them for organizing unsanctioned demonstrations. Their response was to set up tents on the pedestrian walkway
in the centre of the city, raise the Tsarist flag, and camp there. Despite
attempts to dislodge them with jets of water from the street-cleaning
lorries, they stuck it for two weeks, and then, 'one wonderful day',
Yeltsin won the election to the Russian presidency.

A black Volga drove up to the camp, and its occupants, young
men, firmly but politely invited us to come to the prosecutor's
office [...] they took us there, and the city prosecutor said 'The
criminal charges against you have been dropped because
circumstances have changed'. Such an article existed in the Code
of Criminal Procedure. And I asked – 'how have circumstances
changed, is it that Yeltsin has been elected?' And he said 'No, it is
simply that last night I opened the Gospels, and there it is written
"Judge not, and ye shall not be judged" to which I replied 'You
should simply write "the Gospel according to Mathew, chapter
and verse" in your file rather than referring to the Code of Criminal
Procedure'. That was the end of the charges.

Kalyapin never thought of going into politics himself once a multi-party
system had been introduced. It was business that attracted him. In a
different environment he might have rebuilt a branch of industry.
By 1991–2, using scarce computer technology, he and his friends were
seriously in demand, putting together almost all the local newspapers,
including government ones. 'The editorial offices were terribly pleased,

and we earned some money.' However, he was dismayed by 'the thievery, the new cooperatives' siphoning off of resources from the state sector with the assistance of corrupt law-enforcement officials and bureaucrats', who were strangling new entrepreneurial initiatives. Profits were going not back into business but to government officials, and in the first place to those responsible for law and order.

> It became obvious to me that human dignity and civil rights had to be defended as fiercely, thoroughly and professionally as private property. Earlier I had thought that once there was private property and competition, market mechanisms would in time sort everything out. But – no.

Together with other activists, he participated in setting up the International Society for Human Rights which began to take up various, very different issues, including electoral rights, and control of penal institutions.

Kalyapin's qualities of energy and leadership are shared by Igor Averkiev, from Perm, a city in the Urals, also a city of exile, but dominated by the chemicals industry, metallurgy and oil refining. Turned down by the history faculty at Perm University in 1980 on the grounds that his stutter would prevent his following an ideological career, Averkiev did his national service. Again his stutter (which is a very slight) proved to be an obstacle. He was not accepted by either the border guards or the paratroopers and, to his chagrin, had to be content with the sappers. Following the army, the university relented and by 1984 he was secretary of the faculty's Komsomol committee.

> Students began to set up anti-Soviet groups, academically oriented. At that time everything anti-Soviet was socialist oriented [...] our first underground student group decided that before we attempted a revolution we should honestly try to change the regime from within, because revolution is bloody, disorderly. And to do this it was necessary to infiltrate the regime, so we decided I should become Komsomol secretary, and set up a club to discuss the problems of socialism [...] but, all the same, this was not to the liking of the authorities.

In 1985 Averkiev and two others were expelled for not taking their exams in military training (was this required for someone who had served in the army?). He started organizing environmental protests. Following an action which included the collection of 20,000 signatures demanding the closure of a dangerous chemical plant, his flat was raided by the security services. The discovery of the charter of his underground organization was enough to result in a criminal charge, but it was already 1987, a new era, and the charge was dropped. Together with friends he set up a social-democratic organization ('we had already pretty much decided that we were not liberals') and for the next five years pursued a political career. Until 1990 he chaired the local Social-Democratic party, and co-chaired Perm's Democratic Russia; in 1991 he was elected a co-chair of the Russian Social-Democratic party, and moved to Moscow.

But Averkiev too became disillusioned with politics. By 1992, as the policies of privatization and shock therapy began to bite, the Social-Democratic party was divided – should it distance itself from Yeltsin or still support him? Averkiev, by now chair of the party, found himself on the left. Attempts to build a coalition with the miners, accustomed to holding a privileged position in the working class, but now facing budget cuts and demanding that the mines work as before, did not work out.

And I found myself faced by another serious problem [. . .] it was very important to me to be in an organization that had an ideological orientation, had a mission, ideas. It was clear that we, I mean we in Russia, had been left behind. *There was no way a proper social base for a classical social-liberal set of ideas could come into being, and, as we can see today, it hasn't happened. And parties came and went because they were of no use to anyone. It became clear that an ideological party could not send down roots,* and that, if you wanted to survive, a party had to become a pressure group, had to find a niche for itself among the oligarchs. As chair I was spending two thirds of my time on raising money for the party. Yes, that is important, but it became the most important thing, and with it one's dependence grew. I know that you don't engage in politics in white gloves, but I understood that that's not my thing and doesn't interest me.

[Author's emphasis]

He resigned in 1993 and returned to Perm, not sure whether to work on the railways, or to try to organize independent trade unions. Almost by chance, learning of a programme of small grants for human rights organizations, he set up a human rights centre. In his case, we see how post-Soviet developments militated against those who would have flourished as politicians in a more hospitable environment.

In St Petersburg, in 1992, Boris Pustintsev, a lover of jazz (the young man who had received a prison sentence for supporting the Hungarian uprising in 1956), set up an organization, Citizens Watch, while remaining co-chair of the Memorial Society. Citizens Watch, whose board included lawyers, journalists, and deputies, stated in its charter that its aim was:

> to assist in establishing parliamentary and civic control over police, the security services, and armed forces, and to help prevent violations of constitutional rights by these governmental agencies. Citizens Watch sees its strategic priority in bringing the Russian legislation related to human rights and the practice of its application closer to international legal standards.

Citizens Watch, and it is surely not accidental that Pustintsev had the language skills that quickly gave him international contacts, was much more similar to a Western civil liberties organization than any of the other new Russian organizations. The mayor's office, while shocked by the reference to civic control over the security services, still agreed to register the organization. But St Petersburg was a 'liberal' city, with a democratic majority in the city council. In Tomsk too, and in Perm, active individuals like Kandyba and Averkiev had no difficulty in registering human rights centres (Averkiev got a quite spacious office in the old party building); but in many other cities, organizations were struggling to receive any recognition from the local authorities.

Some of the early activists remained in politics. Rybakov, the artist who had headed the Leningrad human rights commission as a city council deputy, won a seat in 1993 as a deputy from St Petersburg to the Duma, and served until 1996. In Moscow, Ponomarev lost his seat in the 1993 elections, only to regain it, briefly, in a bye-election in 1994. Kovalev kept his seat as a member of Russia's Choice in 1996. But many who had served as deputies, or worked in political parties, now concentrated their activities on 'non-political' organizations. Some because they lost their seats, others because they had become disillusioned with politics. As Blinushov commented: 'Our entry into politics was for us, natural, but that only lasted until 1993 – because, already from early 1991, we came up against the realities of politics [...] the ability to compromise with one's ideals when convenient, to betray people [...] we came to understand that politics was not the place for us.'

Rybakov, while he stuck at it till the mid-nineties, was at heart an artist and an activist. Kovalev? That's more difficult to say. While he would not be pleased at the comparison, I am tempted to see him as the Michael Foot of post-Soviet Russian politics. He is still a member of the liberal party, Yabloko. Ponomarev, and Averkiev, were politicians manqué. Had they been born in Poland, Hungary, or the Baltic States, they would probably be leading political parties today. But in Russia, as Averkiev commented, viable political parties were not emerging, whereas NGOs now had a sanctioned place in the new order.

A new constitution

If, in 1988–91, all types of activity – petitioning, protests, civic action, political roles – were tangled together, by the end of 1993 the political sphere had separated itself out. Its new institutions, modelled on many long-term democratic states, were those of strong presidential power, yet with a critical role for elected legislative institutions, and for an independent judiciary. The right to freedom of speech and assembly, and organization, were enshrined in the constitution. Those who had argued for human rights and the rule of law found an audience among the politicians, anxious to find partners for the new Russia both in Europe and in the USA.

Articles on political and civil rights, which we cited at the end of the previous chapter, occupy centre space but the constitution also has an impressive list of social and economic rights. Everyone has a right to 'housing', to 'free medical care', to 'free primary and secondary education', to 'a pension', to 'acceptable conditions of work'. Many of these can be found in earlier Soviet constitutions. Then there are new rights – to 'own property', to 'travel freely', to 'choose a place of residence', to 'a healthy environment'. As we can see, while some of these rights seem clear as they stand, others require elaboration in legislation in order to become 'concrete' or 'justiciable'. As regards the defence of one's rights: 'Everyone shall be free to protect his rights and freedoms by all means not prohibited by law. (Article 45)

However, legal defence receives the major emphasis.

> Everyone shall be guaranteed judicial protection of his rights and freedoms. Decisions and actions (or inaction) of bodies of state authority and local self-government, public associations and officials may be appealed against in court; Everyone shall have the right to appeal, according to international treaties of the Russian Federation, to international bodies for the protection of human rights and freedoms, if all the existing internal state means of legal protection have been exhausted. (Article 46)

Article 46 would become important with the Russian Federation's admission to the Council of Europe in 1996, while the relevance of the Universal Declaration and international conventions for the new political framework was recognized by all. In 1998, the fiftieth anniversary of the Declaration, Yeltsin sent a greeting to a conference, emphasizing the Declaration's importance for the defence of human rights in Russia. Yet, as we shall see in Chapter 4, for activists the question of the relationship to the new authorities remained a debatable one, even for those who had most staunchly defended Yeltsin. Some had distanced themselves, moving out of politics altogether. Business interests had no such qualms. Yet all, politicians, activists, and entrepreneurs were stepping out onto uncharted territory. Organization, whether of a political party, an independent NGO, or a private business, was still something new, experience was minimal. Western assistance was just beginning. How would human rights organizations survive in the new democratic, market environment, and how would government officials and society respond to them?

CHAPTER 3

EARLY DEBATES OVER RIGHTS AND STRATEGIES

In the early 2000s, Putin's epoch, I really appreciated the previous decade, because it had given us ten golden years [. . .] they say that we were a democracy – we weren't. It was simply that the state had become very weak, and society was left to itself. And for us those were golden years because during that period, by some miracle, civil society managed to coalesce, or at least it was born. And I consider that the human rights community in our country is the nucleus of civil society. (Liudmila Alekseeva)

However, as Alekseeva herself had said, many of those who chose to call themselves human rights activists did not know what human rights were, lacked experience, and had few resources. In a moment we shall see what she decided to do about it. But, first, we note that the term *pravozashchitnik* (or 'rights defender') was gradually passing into usage. Originally associated with those among the dissidents who, in the late seventies, had demanded the authorities observe the constitution and international conventions, Svetlana Gannushkina remembers the surprise (and pleasure) she felt when finding herself described, in a newspaper in Azerbaijan, as a *pravozashchitnik*. Surely, she reckoned, this was because she was with Larisa Bogoraz. The term's link with some of the dissidents did not always work in favour of those who began to describe themselves as such. While for some it was a badge of honour, there were many in the general public and among their political opponents for whom it came to mean 'Western sympathizer', a 'trouble-maker', someone unable to compromise. The first Chechen war of 1994–6, and Kovalev's principled stand against the federal government's policy, contributed to this.

Chechnya and the report by the 'Kovalev' commission

In September 1993 Yeltsin had established, by decree, a presidential commission on human rights, and appointed Kovalev (without consulting him) as its chair. This was to take on the role of an ombudsman until such time as the relevant law could be passed. In effect this commission, with a staff of 35, returned to the work of the original human rights committee of the Supreme Soviet. Once the new parliament (now the Duma) met at the start of 1994, Kovalev was confirmed as ombudsman, although there was still no law to this effect. His office continued to receive and try to deal with complaints, to prepare legislation, and to monitor and make recommendations regarding the failings of government or justice officials. But increasingly he and his colleagues became involved in the war with Chechnya.

Following the break up of the USSR, the Chechen-Ingush republic (part of the Russian Federation) had declared its independence. In 1992 it had split into Ingushetia, whose leadership resolved to remain within the federation, and the now named independent republic of Ichkeria (Chechnya), with a popularly elected president, Dzhokhar Dudayev, but home to armed conflict between his followers and opponents. Refugees, many of whom were Russian, were fleeing to neighbouring republics or to Russia itself. In November 1994, Yeltsin took a decision to use all available means to bring Chechnya back into the federation, and did not seek Duma approval. Thus began a disastrous and badly planned invasion by federal troops, which escalated into full-scale bombing of the capital, Grozny, by mid-December. The casualties, among the Russian troops, the Chechen fighters, and the civilian population were appalling. While not a popular war, public and political opinion was divided; media coverage was extensive and open, even disagreements within the military were voiced. The Soldiers' Mothers travelled down to Chechnya in search of their conscript sons. Kovalev, with a small party of Duma deputies, and with Oleg Orlov from Memorial, flew to Chechnya; they spent the New Year in a bunker in Grozny, reporting back on the bombing and casualties.

Kovalev's repeated calls for a ceasefire, negotiations, and planned evacuation of civilians, and his criticism of the Russian government both in Strasbourg and New York angered many. On 5 January he had flown back to Moscow from Grozny, to be granted an unproductive interview by Yeltsin who insisted that the bombing had ceased. At a Duma hearing later that month, a storm of vituperative criticism (as well as some support) greeted Kovalev's proposal for the condemning of the military operation and demands for an immediate ceasefire. Blocked from returning to Grozny, he flew to Strasbourg to attend a meeting of the Parliamentary Assembly of the Council of Europe, and spoke against Russia's admission until the military action in Chechnya had ceased, and Russia was 'closer to being a democracy'. PACE voted to delay admission. Kovalev continued to report on casualties and atrocities (on both sides), sometimes acting as a go between, until a military ceasefire was agreed in August 1995. Agreement on the withdrawal of federal troops and on the shelving, for the present, of the question of sovereignty was finally reached in August 1996.

By this time Kovalev was no longer chair of the president's commission on human rights, Russia had been admitted to the Council of Europe, and Yeltsin had won a second term as president. In March 1995 the Duma had voted to remove Kovalev from office as ombudsman but, given that he was still chair of the president's commission, he and his staff continued to work as before. At the beginning of 1996, as he resigned from the office, the commission brought out its *Report on the Observance of the Rights of Man and the Citizen in the Russian Federation for 1994–1995*.[1] As can be imagined, it was hard hitting, particularly in its coverage of Chechnya, which occupied pride of place in the report.

The President's Commission for Human Rights is unanimously of the opinion that events in the zone of armed conflict in the Chechen Republic constitute the most important and most tragic breach of human rights compliance in the Russian Federation in 1994 and 1995. In the magnitude and severity of the human rights violations, in the sufferings of hundreds of thousands of Russian citizens, and in the brutalities perpetrated against the civilian population, the Chechen events are unparalleled since the era of mass political repressions in the USSR.

Detailed reports of atrocities committed by both sides followed. Actions in Chechnya received the harshest criticism, but the Kovalev report was hardly complimentary about the overall situation. How did its authors conceive of human rights, and which infringements concerned them most?

> The President's Commission for Human Rights finds it necessary to declare that during 1994 and 1995, the human rights situation in the Russian Federation has remained extremely unsatisfactory [...] the provisions of the Russian Constitution concerning human rights and civil liberties remain largely rhetorical; they have not been backed by the force of law [...] The Commission is particularly concerned that in many aspects of civil and political rights and liberties there has been a distinct retreat from democratic achievements.

The report emphasizes the failure to introduce either the law on alternative civilian service (devoting a section to the appalling treatment of conscripts in the army) or the law on the ombudsman, or to implement proposals on judicial reform. The dire state of the judicial system is described, and the report

> notes in particular that there have recently been recurrences of the attitude toward the courts of the bad old days, i.e., government documents and statements by high officials, including those at the very top, have criticized the courts for: handing down unwarranted not-guilty verdicts; releasing detainees from custody; and dispensing excessively lenient sentences. Officials have also denounced courts and judges for being too independent, and have proposed closer contact between the courts and law-enforcement agencies in the war on crime.

Slightly defensively, the authors note that:

> A relatively small place in the Report is devoted to an extremely important problem: the violation of citizens' social rights, although clearly, this is the area that gives rise to the most social tension and these violations affect the absolute majority of the population of the

Russian Federation. The Commission's position in this regard is explained not by a failure to appreciate the significance of this area but by the fact that social problems are studied and analysed by a whole range of other specialized government agencies.

And the report does deal at some length with the problems of non-payment of wages and unemployment, the fall in real incomes, and inequality.

Society is becoming split into quite distinct classes primarily due to a gap in incomes [...] The 'new poor' have become a phenomenon in Russia. This category includes the one-in-four working persons who cannot earn enough from their job to make a living. Above all this concerns workers at enterprises suffering from the debt crisis who do not receive their wages for months at a time, workers in government-subsidized industries, scientists and scholars.

Violations of rights in penal institutions receive particular attention, together with a recommendation that the state create 'an independent, civilian review board to monitor human rights in the penal system'. Other items too have a contemporary ring:

the aggravation of racial and ethnic intolerance and discrimination, sometimes involving high-ranking officials [...] the law on freedom of movement and choice of residence are ignored. The resident permit system [the *propiska*] is being used as a mechanism to discriminate against ethnic minorities [...] Political and nationalist extremism is not properly condemned and resisted by government bodies charged with preventing extremism through the force of law [...] The rights of refugees and forced migrants are not actually protected and their social adaptation is in fact hindered.

A rather different set of issues, but still relevant for today, includes:

The restriction of freedom of expression and access to current and archival information under the pretext of protecting state secrets [...] The Commission is particularly disturbed by the dissemination of disinformation by government and other official sources [...] Under the guise of fighting crime there is a tendency to expand the powers of security and law-enforcement agencies to the detriment of Constitutional rights and guarantees [...] The number of persons charged with unlawful detention, the use of force against suspects and witnesses, and the falsifying of evidence and so on, has almost doubled.

There was then plenty of scope for action. By this time the term *prava cheloveka* (which can be translated as 'rights of man' but which, in the new international environment, was increasingly called 'human rights') was already part of official language, and associated with the Universal Declaration. This did not mean that state officials now welcomed human rights organizations. But it did mean that individuals who wanted to engage in some kind of activity to help the vulnerable or to challenge government behaviour could register themselves as organizations defending human rights. As disillusionment with the politicians grew, the defence of human rights became the ground on which people of very different persuasions set up their tents. Not surprisingly their views on what were human rights and appropriate strategies to defend them differed.

Who qualifies as a human rights activist?

In 1993–5 the human rights commission, headed by Kovalev, received financial support from a Russian–American Project Group for Human Rights. Registered in New York, with a small board of Americans and Russians, one of whom was Kovalev, the Project Group received financial support both from its American members and from the Ford Foundation. Its activities included assistance in the drafting of the law on the ombudsman (bringing the Polish ombudsman into discussions), researching public opinion, and a small-grants competition for human rights organizations in the regions. Moscow and St Petersburg were excluded. Both Nikolai Kandyba (in Tomsk) and Igor Averkiev (in Perm) received grants for their recently established human rights centres. In the autumn of 1995, several of the grantees were invited to a seminar to discuss, together with leading Moscow activists, 'who should be considered to be a "*pravozashchitnik*" in the present situation, which rights should a contemporary activist be defending and against whom or against what'. The discussion produced quite heated exchanges.[2] Six months later, at a roundtable organized by the Ford Foundation for younger activists from Moscow and the regions, some of the same issues, and the disputed points, arose. What were the disagreements over?

At the first seminar, Liudmila Alekseeva led off with the statement that demands for freedom of speech, press, creativity, religious belief, and the right to leave the country had, in the Soviet period, been prioritized by a small group of people, not because they were the most important but because, without them, it was impossible to defend other rights.

> Now we have some kind of freedom of the press, the freedom to organize exists, and the results have been exactly those they should be [. . .] the number of people involved in human rights activities has grown sharply and human rights activity has taken on a new appearance. People have begun to defend, as a priority, those rights whose infringement are the most important to them – and these are social rights [. . .] you can break the window of the person who has offended you, or you can beat him up but that's not defending human rights [. . .] defending your rights through a court, using the law – that's human rights work [. . .] there has been a colossal leap in the legal consciousness of the people. Alas, that hasn't happened with the authorities and government officials, their legal consciousness is still that of cave dwellers, and a great amount of work remains to be done.

Kovalev agreed as regards legal consciousness, echoing Bogoraz's position at the 1991 seminar, and his own earlier publications, where he had defended his entering politics because he believed that cooperation with the authorities could advance the rule of law. He had not been optimistic though: with both rulers and ruled holding primitive, cave-dwelling conceptions of legality, the task was huge, and the human rights movement poorly equipped.[3] Kovalev continued in subsequent years to maintain this position, while perhaps increasingly emphasizing the centrality of law as the mechanism to defend the individual.

> Law is the only path that can lead to the eternal Russian dream of social justice [. . .] The absence of or underdevelopment of legal

norms guaranteeing freedom and individual dignity have been Russia's misfortune throughout her whole history [. . .] either we shall scrabble out on to the main road to the development of humanity or we shall remain stuck in the byzantine-mongol bog of state absolutism.[4]

At the 1995 seminar he did not agree with Alekseeva on socio-economic rights. When two of the participants, Alexander Tarasov from Tver, and Igor Averkiev from Perm, argued the case for consumer rights and economic and social rights, and for public oversight of budget expenditure, he responded 'that this is not, in the strict sense of the word, human rights activity although it is extremely helpful for human rights activists in that it is enhancing the public's legal consciousness'. This was echoed by Sergei Sirotkin, a close colleague: while very useful, this type of activity is not 'the organic, natural, normal and specific activity of human rights activists', and by Konrad Liubarsky (from the Moscow Helsinki Group): 'to argue that at the present moment when people are going hungry economic rights are the most important, and all the rest are trivial, is hardly correct. Not everyone understands the simple truth that in the absence of democracy the cow cannot be milked.'

This, referred to as the classical conception of human rights, got support from some of the new activists from the provinces. 'Which rights should we be defending? In the first place we should be thinking of political and civil rights, and extending them' (Kandyba from Tomsk), but the activists found themselves struggling to cope with increasing numbers of people, with all kinds of problems, who clearly needed help. So the question arose: whom should they be helping, and by which means? Only those who were suffering at the hands of the state? Pensioners were being tricked out of their homes or savings by unscrupulous individuals, wages were not being paid by both state and private employers. Kandyba, recognizing this, moved on to arguing that they should take up the case of any one in need. Alexander Gorelik, professor of criminal law from Krasnoyarsk, while arguing that the state should be the main target for human rights activists, agreed: 'Human rights defence should be defending the rights of those who can't defend themselves regardless of whether it is the state or private persons who are responsible. For example, invalids, children, prisoners, conscripts.' Gorelik, elderly, scholarly, able to inspire students and retain their respect as they made their careers in the law and order agencies, and with a rare talent for composing humorous limericks to mark any occasion, would subsequently introduce innovative practices for law students in Krasnoyarsk. Here he was arguing in favour of human rights organizations' focusing their attention on the courts' illegality or maladministration of justice. Where courts themselves act illegally, he argued, the individual is left in the worst of all possible situations because 's/he has nowhere else to turn'.

But it was the issue of 'politicization' that produced the most heated exchanges. Averkiev argued that a human rights activist must stay out of politics. As a rights' defender he should take up the cases of elderly individuals, regardless of their political persuasions. How should he have acted when a right wing, 'fascist' type organization was illegally refused registration? Should he have said – quite right?

> From a legal point of view it was so primitive, just as it used to be. One of the representatives of the president rang the justice department and said 'Don't register them'. How about that? And Memorial took the line 'For God's sake, so what, quite right too'. If I were a social-democrat, and primarily a politician, then all right I wouldn't care a damn. But as a rights' defender I cannot do that.

The problem, he argued, was that human rights activity in Russia was too politicized. And here he mentioned the association in the popular mind of the Moscow human rights defenders as 'anti-Russian', taking the side of the Chechens, and their involvement in Yeltsin's forthcoming election campaign for the Russian presidency. The Perm human rights organization, which he headed, had written into its charter that it did not have the right to speak on behalf of any political organizations.

Tatyana Kotlyar (from Obninsk, a determined woman who would go on to acquire a law degree and defend, among others, migrants) responded with:

> Defending rights is of course not political activity [...] my response to an individual who comes and asks for help cannot in any way be influenced by whether he is a communist, or a fascist, or whatever [...] if rights have been infringed, it's irrelevant whether the individual is a woman or a man or the colour of his

eyes. But whether the human rights activist can also take part in political activity is quite another matter. If, earlier, I was a member of Democratic Russia or Russia's Choice, I don't see why I should give that up. But I would carry out those activities within another organization, not the human rights organization. Just as I can also study maths or go to drawing classes.

However, the response from the Moscow leaders is tougher. Sirotkin argues: 'Whether we like it or not, the ideology of human rights is a liberal party ideology. Whether we like it or not, neither the Communist party or the esteemed Agrarian party will ever defend liberal values, the ideology of human rights.' And Oleg Orlov, from Memorial, accuses Averkiev of advancing a highly politicized social-democratic view of human rights.

What are human rights? I or Sergei Adamovich [Kovalev] defend the liberal view. And in that respect we shall always remain 'politicized'. In our view, human rights are a particular set of inalienable rights, not social rights which have been won, not those social goods [. . .] and when you say that we should defend those who are being hurt – that's not defending human rights. That's – if you like – social work. The human rights defender concentrates on defending inalienable rights which underlie the creation of state institutions which can support all other rights.

Orlov gave 'the right to reside where one wishes' versus 'the right to adequate housing' as a clear example of the difference between the two kinds of rights and argued, that harsh as it might seem, freedom of movement is the critical one:

Either we want a barracks where we shall be guaranteed a right to housing or we defend human rights and in that case human rights are a harsh, cruel thing. We defend rights but we are not kind uncles who put food in the open mouths of all the suffering [. . .] The social gains that the toiling workers have made [. . .] that lies outside our activity and we have to understand that if we have got the individual out of the barracks and given him rights – it can be very tough. We are talking about two different concepts of rights.

Interestingly enough this issue – of the right to housing – was raised by
Albie Sachs, one of South Africa's leading constitutional lawyers,
at a conference on access to justice, hosted by the World Bank in
St Petersburg in 2000. A group of shanty town settlers had won a case on
housing resettlement, based on their constitutional, and human, right to
shelter, a ruling he supported. Earlier, in exile in London, he agreed,
he would not have supported such a 'social right' as constitutional but in
the new environment in South Africa he had come to look differently
upon 'rights'.[5]

However, returning to 1995, Kovalev agreed with Orlov: 'It was
quite right to ask – what is the concept of human rights? It is simply a
set of basic postulates of liberal philosophy, translated into legal norms,
expressed in another language.'

There is no evidence that the newcomers from the regions changed
their positions. Averkiev returned to the attack at the Ford roundtable,
arguing that what people were looking for was 'justice' – 'fair play,
decency, deliverance from official abuse and arbitrariness'. The Anglo-
American conception of human rights, which the Moscow dissidents had
begun to promote in the 1970s, he argued, was not helpful in Russian
conditions; it was rather an obstacle to defending rights. Most people
turned to him over housing, economic rights, education issues, and he
saw his task as getting the wrong righted, whether through the courts or
by turning to the relevant government department. If a telephone call
from him could get a response from an official, that is what he should do.

But, it was put to him, the result was simply more and more cases.
How would this solve the problem of the authorities' behaviour that,
Veronika Marchenko from Mother's Right suggested, was the main
obstacle to the observance of rights, and with which he agreed. Did not
his approach, which could be described as that of a *zastupnik* or
intercessor, simply reinforce the patron–client relationship between the
authorities and the citizen? How could this be remedied? No one,
among either the Moscow leaders or the new activists, had the answer.
As one of the participants, S. Buryachko, put it at the 1995 seminar:

It seems as though everything has been properly legislated, the
acts guaranteeing our basic rights and freedoms exist, we are
beginning to live under new conditions. At the same time we
notice, in our everyday lives, that a lie is still a lie, that the state

continues to lie as before, whether on the part of its leaders or through its administrative organs.

Sergei Belyaev, a slightly pugnacious labour activist from Ekaterinburg, who had set up an organization, Sutyazhnik (or Litigator), to challenge the local authorities' rulings on a variety of issues by taking them to court, backed by imaginative public campaigns, suggested that the problem was people's unwillingness to act in defence of their rights. No agreement was reached, and Averkiev would continue to defend or advance his arguments in coming years. But no one denied the importance of using the courts. Kandyba from Tomsk suggested that winning cases and getting them implemented would gradually change the poor performance of the justice system. Belyaev saw this more in terms of challenging the courts to implement the laws. And Professor Gorelik, as we saw, had argued for exerting pressure on the judges. This issue, 'the use of law' to change the justice system, comes up repeatedly throughout the period, and we shall return to it more than once.

Moscow Helsinki Group resurrected

In a conversation, many years later, Liudmila Alekseeva suggested that the participants in the 1995 seminar had been very downcast by the 'dismissive' attitude of the Moscow 'leaders' and that she had said to them:

> Never mind, you guys, don't listen to them, human rights activists must defend a whole spectrum of social issues [. . .] now we have more political rights than we had in the Soviet period but social rights are just a complete mess [. . .] human rights activists must defend those rights about whose infringement citizens complain. You are real human rights activists.

But they were small and scattered, with few resources, and little expertise, often ignored by the local authorities. Branches of the Memorial Society existed but their members' concerns were not those of these new organizations, while the Soldiers' Mothers focused wholly on conscripts. This was the situation Alekseeva decided she should remedy, and she hit upon the now moribund Moscow Helsinki Group in search of a chair. Her hopes for a Solidarity movement, based on new trade unions, had evaporated: as the economic crisis deepened, the roots of active worker opposition withered. She ended her link with the AFL-CIO and offered to take on the chair of MHG. The board welcomed the suggestion and her idea of holding a conference in May 1996 to mark its twentieth anniversary.

By this time, as we noted, Kovalev had handed in his resignation from the president's commission on human rights. Most of the staff left too. In May 1996, shortly before the presidential elections, Yeltsin issued a new decree on the commission, giving it a mandate to assist the president in guaranteeing the rights of citizens. His choice for chair of the commission was Vladimir Kartashkin, a conservative professor of law, who during the seventies had slighted human rights as a Western invention. Many of the human rights activists were pessimistic. Kartashkin as a defender of human rights while Kovalev was publicly vilified? While Yeltsin won the presidential election at the second round in July, the Communists and patriots outdid the democratic candidates for places in the Duma in December. Kovalev still won a seat (on the Russia' Choice party list) but Lev Ponomarev was out.

Ponomarev, having lost his Duma seat, and witnessing the disappearance of Democratic Russia as a political party, set up a new organization, For Human Rights, based on many of the original party activists in the regions. Representatives from 60 regions attended its founding congress in 1997. They set up centres to assist citizens whose rights had been infringed; they aimed to exert civic control over the authorities' actions and, where possible, to get their nominees into the regional human rights commissions. They remain the most political of the human rights activists, yet it is not easy to identify a shared agenda, and over our period their numbers dwindle. Ponomarev is outspoken, brave. Some would say intolerant, hostile to others who do not share his views, and not sufficiently careful to check his sources before publishing materials. In the eyes of a commentator who knows the community well:

He could be a symbol of the man of 1989 [...] All the creators of those clubs, those very active people found themselves [in the mid-nineties] without anything to do [...] some of them only knew how to curse the authorities [...] they are energetic people and political activists [. . .] they are real activists and in that sense, important people.

Liudmila Alekseeva too was undaunted by political developments. Nothing, it seems, can daunt her and undermine her optimism. When, over 80, she broke her hip, falling down the stairs at a human rights conference, and the doctors, after a heart scan, advised against an operation, she told them sharply to pay more attention 'to the spirit of the patient, not a scan', and to proceed. They did, and the operation went well. In May 1996 she proposed that the Moscow Helsinki Group should invite all the activists whom they knew in the provinces to the conference.

> And we should suggest to them that MHG, as the oldest human rights organization in Russia, should serve the human rights movement, simply serve other organizations, not deprive them of their independence. I had gained a huge amount of experience from working in America as a consultant to the Helsinki Group [. . .] I had understood that you should create a network, not try to work from the top down, claiming to be the leader, because that's a Russian sickness, each wants to be the boss [. . .] and I took this idea to the Soros committee[6] [. . .] each organization should do what it considered needed to be done, and our job would be to see that they did not die.

This, she argued, could be done by teaching them, bringing them together for seminars, providing them with information. MHG could publish a free information bulletin, 'in which they all featured, so they would not feel that they were quite alone in their town, rather that some kind of a community existed and together they could defend each other'.

The Soros Foundation gave $20,000 for the conference. Yury Orlov, the founder of the original Moscow Helsinki Group, now a professor of physics in America, came, representatives from the former republics and those from the regions attended, in all 35 were present. On the opening day, Mikhail Krasnov, a lawyer from the president's administration, unexpectedly appeared. Alekseeva seized the opportunity to ask him whether he could not arrange a meeting with Yeltsin for Orlov, who had suggestions regarding the negotiations with the Chechens. Krasnov arranged it.

> Preparing for the meeting, Yury Fedorovich [Orlov] said to me 'Liuda, let's write a letter, saying that MHG needs office-space'. I said 'You are going to talk about Chechnya, about important things, and then you mention office-space!' He said, well we could at least write the letter, and see how the meeting went; if it seemed appropriate, he could hand it over. To that I agreed. I wrote that we needed office space inside the Garden Ring, 300 metres with subsidized rent, as was appropriate for non-governmental organizations. And he took the letter.

At the conference those from the provinces had complained bitterly that their local authorities refused to recognize or to engage with them.

> When Yeltsin asked how he could be of help to MHG, Yury explained that the activists from the provinces do not have any access to officials, could not he, Yeltsin, make some recommendations to the regional governors that they should work with the activists [. . .] Yeltsin said he would think about it [. . .] and issued a decree that recommended the governors set up commissions for human rights, modelled on the president's commission, and give them office space with subsidized rents [. . .] Literally, a week after Orlov met with Yeltsin, we were given office space.

Responding to individual appeals, particularly if made by people they knew or, for whatever reason they wished to have on board, was the way heads of institutions (of all kinds) operated in the Soviet Union. Both Yeltsin and Orlov felt comfortable with this. Yeltsin responded with a decree, and with office accommodation (we should perhaps remember that he needed all the support he could get in the forthcoming election). As relevant, he saw himself as the guarantor of constitutional and human rights, and the commission on human rights was there to assist him. The state was responsible for seeing that the laws are observed. From this perspective, independent critical organizations or activists may be an irritation, particularly at local level.

Two weeks later, MHG reported that on 13 June Yeltsin had signed a decree commending the decisions of the conference and expressing his support. This, the announcement continued, together with the general acknowledgment of the Moscow Helsinki Group as the foundation of the International Helsinki Movement, gave the MHG 'a unique opportunity' to promote 'cooperation between government bodies in the centre and the regions, a cooperation which, at present, is virtually absent'.[7] The MHG was asked to send lists of their proposed candidates to the regional authorities for inclusion in the new commissions, which it did. But this produced a split among its board members. Kovalev and Bogoraz were categorically against human rights activists being members of such commissions – they would be bought off, they were inexperienced, and the human rights movement would die. It was decided to put it to a vote. Alekseeva, as chair, made the vote one of confidence in her leadership; if the proposal to reverse the policy passed, she would resign. A minority voted for, the rest abstained, and Alekseeva continued as chair and with the policy. Admittedly it only resulted in a couple of activists being included in the commissions in 8–ten regions but, she suggested, that was at least something – after all people lived in those regions too. In most cases these commissions were staffed by officials.

On one occasion Kartashkin, chair of the president's commission, brought them to Moscow. In Alekseeva's account, when he spoke, everything was all right, but 'when I [Alekseeva] spoke all the officials started muttering – who is this, some human rights activist? I thought they were going to leap up and tear me to pieces. I felt real hatred, not even just coldness, but hatred.'

By now Memorial was renting a building from the city at a subsidized rent, the MHG had good office space and, in 1995, the city authorities had given the Sakharov Foundation (based in the USA) 'a 25-year rent free lease on a 10,000-square-foot, two-storey building located in a handsome park across the Garden Ring Road from the flat' where Sakharov had lived, now housing part of his archives. Renovation funded by Freedom House, the National Endowment for Democracy, and USAID allowed the building to open as the Sakharov Centre in the spring of 1996. Yury Samodurov, originally from Memorial, became its director, organizing educational and cultural events. The Moscow Helsinki Group saw itself as a more practically oriented organization.

It would act as a centre to provide regional human rights organizations with information and literature; would defend them before regional and federal authorities; issue bulletins on the state of current affairs; organize free legal aid for citizens regarding their constitutional rights, and provide educational courses for human rights activists.

We shall hear more of the commissions and we shall meet up again with others among our perestroika activists. But some of them feature in Vyacheslav Bakhmin's assessment of the situation in 1996, as Yeltsin entered his second term of office:[8]

> At that time, it seems to me, structures began to emerge out of the original atmosphere of enthusiasm and a human rights 'soup' of different ingredients – some were of the Kovalev type, or of those who were close to him, for example Ponomarev. These people took a very tough stance against the state, one of non-cooperation, opposition. They saw how the state openly ignored human rights, and it seemed that to achieve anything through the state was very difficult, if not impossible. [...] another, more pragmatic group, carried on working with the state, simultaneously attempting to defend human rights [...] among them you could include Soldiers' Mothers, for whom it was important to achieve something for their constituents. They understood that without cooperation with the authorities they could not achieve anything [...] You could probably put Abramkin [the penal reformer] in this category. MHG – that's more complicated – because it wavered between outright opposition, depending upon Liudmila Mikhailovna's [Alekseeva] position, to cooperation. It was the same with Marchenko [Mother's Right].
>
> And then there was the third group whose members were prepared to work closely with the authorities, and tried in this way, to achieve something for their target group [...] invalids, the elderly, children with Downs syndrome. These were organizations which had nothing against the state as long as the state supported their efforts. They had far more lobbyists inside state structures than the others because all were concerned by the social problems [...] and where the state did not respond adequately enough it was for lack of resources and not because of principled objections to what these organizations wanted.

In several respects 1996 was an important year for human rights. With its admission to membership of the Council of Europe, Russia took on certain commitments (to abolish the death penalty, to sign up to the European Convention on Human Rights, and to transfer the prison system to the Ministry of Justice). A moratorium on the death penalty was introduced (and renewed indefinitely in 2010). All institutions involved in the implementation of sentences, and the remand centres, were transferred to the Ministry of Justice in 1997. In May 1998 the Russian Federation signed the European Convention on Human Rights and Freedoms and, by the end of the year, its citizens were able to turn to the European Court of Human Rights. A further condition for membership was that Russia introduce the post of commissioner or ombudsman for human rights, a post already referred to in the constitution, and in 1996 the appropriate legislation was passed. The creation of such an institution had been the subject of often acrimonious debate since the early nineties, and it was 1998 before the Duma could agree on the election of Oleg Mironov, a Communist party deputy, as the first ombudsman.

The debates within the human rights community would come and go over the next ten years, changing focus as the political and economic situation changed. Both the way demands were framed and the choice of strategies to influence state officials or to get popular support will attract our attention. We can identify three or perhaps four different ways of framing and making demands of the authorities: confrontation, cooperation, and collaboration. Petitioning is the fourth, lying somewhere on the borders between cooperation and collaboration. Confrontation assumes the state is an adversary; cooperation implies state and NGO recognize each other as legitimate independent partners, willing to work together; petitioning implies a subservient relationship, the appeal to a higher authority; and collaboration signifies a willingness on the part of the NGO to follow the game plan set by the state. The strategies adopted are influenced by their members' concerns and the state's actions. It takes two to tango, and who led and who responded, and how, altered the pattern of the dance over the period.

But now we must move out into the regions, with their sharply different social and political elites, peoples, and traditions, all part of a landscape scarred by fighting in the Caucasus, by dying industrial towns, and poverty, where disillusioned politicians, Western aid, and new recruits sought to advance the cause of human rights.

CHAPTER 4

LOCAL DIFFERENCES, TACKLING ISOLATIONISM

Some talk of a human rights movement in the country. But that's fundamentally untrue. Our country is so huge, and there are such differences between regions, there always were. For example, in some, such as Krasnodar, both at the end of the Soviet period and at the beginnings of the nineties, there was active opposition to any activity by human rights activists, they even produced falsified criminal cases against them, and imprisoned them, and that continues today. In other regions, for example, in Voronezh, that never happened and does not happen, and we are not even talking of Perm or Krasnoyarsk. (Andrei Blinushov, Ryazan Memorial)

Among human rights activists, Perm, sometimes enviously, is referred to as 'the nature reserve', a protected zone. 'I was talking to Averkiev', said a visiting activist, 'when the governor rang him on his mobile phone to talk about something. The governor! Unbelievable. Where else could that happen?' Averkiev set up a new organization, a Civic Chamber, in 1996 but continued to head the Perm Human Rights Centre until the early 2000s. Now headed by Sergei Isayev, who worked with Averkiev from the start, it no longer has its offices in the municipal buildings, but rents three rooms and a corridor in an old building in the centre of the city. It is still probably Russia's most active and well-organized centre, dealing with a variety of problems, and recognized by the local authorities. By way of contrast, in Krasnodar, down in the south, the head of the most active human rights centre was beaten up so badly in 2010 that his life was in danger. Here long-term collusion between criminal landowners, police, and prosecutors recently ended in the murder of 12 members of a family, including women and children.

But is local variation surprising in a country the size of Russia? The country stretches across nine time zones, and from the Arctic Circle in the north to the Black Sea and the Caucasus in the south. Its regions, climatically, geographically, in terms of their resources, and their populations (100 different languages are spoken) are strikingly different. Ethnic Russians constitute 80 per cent of a population of roughly 150 million, and the use of Russian as the language of the federation dominates, but several of the republics also have their own language as an official one. Moscow, as the capital, with its population of over ten million, its resources, and power, is the place to watch. Decisions taken in Moscow reverberate down throughout the country. However, at the same time, the different regions and republics, the subjects of the federation as they called (now constituting 83 rather than the 89 inherited from the Soviet administrative map) are remarkably self-contained or isolated 'fiefdoms'. And some of them are huge. Leningrad region, which surrounds St Petersburg, is the size of the UK, Krasnoyarsk krai[1] is the size of Europe. Whether it is true that in the late Soviet period there were Communist party first secretaries, who liked to have their region literally 'tree-fenced' to distinguish it from neighbouring regions, I do not know but it was, and still is, true that regions live their separate lives, remarkably oblivious to what is happening in other regions. There is one's own region, and there is Moscow.

Industrialization and collectivization in the early thirties, then the Gulag labour camps and exile, followed by the German advance into European Russia, uprooted millions of individuals and families, sending them east to Siberia and to the north. Many stayed, and intermarriage of the different nationalities produced multi-ethnic populations in Siberia and the Far East. In the south the different peoples of the Caucasus stayed or returned to their homelands in the 1960s. But by that time population movement was largely over, and the final decades of Soviet rule were marked by immobility – with one exception – the lure of Moscow. People tended to stay in the region in which they were born – or gravitate to Moscow, if they could. Perhaps to St Petersburg, or

Leningrad as it then was. The residence registration system, and the (non) availability of housing was a contributory factor. There were also cities, closed to outsiders or requiring permission to visit because of their industrial profile. Nizhny Novgorod, with much of its industry based on the defence sector, where Sakharov was exiled, was closed in this sense, as was Perm. But there were also the really closed towns, built around a secret defence or research installation, towns with good amenities, lakes and forests, but surrounded by a perimeter fence, with entry and exit checks, where not even relatives could visit, and known only by a post-office number.

Perestroika produced different responses in different places. We have already mentioned the democratic activity in St Petersburg and in Tomsk. In Nizhny Novgorod the young scientists from the research institutes were active players. In Krasnodar krai a conservative, patriotic party elite, competing business clans, and the resurgent Cossacks fought over power. Alexander Auzan, president of the Consumers' Confederation (Confop), offered one explanation for the differences:

> In what sense is Russia a federation? Different regions have different types of political regime. For example, Bashkortostan has one kind of political regime, and Perm krai a completely different one.

> How do you explain that? I asked.

> I think that it's because of the historical culture and in part because of the history of the past twenty years [. . .] I have often said that the civic capital of Russia is Perm. It stood out in the distant past, when it had one kind of serfdom, because it had the Strogonovs and not the Demidovs, there wasn't the barbaric exploitation that happened with merchant manufacturing, it was home to many political exiles who brought their libraries with them. At the end of the nineteenth and beginning of the twentieth century a workers' aristocracy emerged which played an important part during the civil war, then new generations of exiles began to appear. The result was a region with a high level of culture, well-developed industry, and established liberal traditions, pluralist traditions, because the exiles held very different views. In my

opinion that's one of the explanations. But each factor is important. Suppose, for example, the economy was weak, it wouldn't have the influence it does, but it's got a strong economy.

In a city such as Perm local activists may have an influence unmatched by that of organizations at federal level, but, in Auzan's words:

On the other hand there are regions where the civic organizations have no influence at all. They are perceived as an unwelcome opposition, that can be the case even in a decent city like Voronezh [...] I was there once with Lukin, the ombudsman, acting as a mediator in a conflict between the governor and the civic organizations. In Voronezh there are many good organizations. There's the Centre of the Human Rights Youth Movement, and Thunderstorm, a new environmental movement, there are interesting people.

Yes, there are, and we shall meet them in Chapter 11. Unlike organizations in many other cities, they have office space in the centre, albeit crowded, and they can attract deputies to attend discussions on a regional law to increase the potential for NGO influence. The very fact that Vladimir Lukin, the ombudsman, came as a mediator suggests a community with some influence. In 2012 the office was raided by the security services, and some of the leading activists targeted with threatening hate mail.

The further you are from Moscow can make a difference. From Siberia, or down in Astrakhan, Moscow seems very far away indeed. But this can work both ways. On the one hand it provides more freedom for action, on the other an organization can be shut down very easily if the regional rulers so wish. The extent of Moscow's political control over the regions is of prime importance. Under Yeltsin a weak federal government practically lost control over both the local elites and the resources. Once privatization was allowed, the competition over the region's resources started, sometimes in a more orderly fashion, sometimes violently. In Perm, the new privatization committee was headed by a former city party secretary. 'What will you do when you've completed privatization?' I asked him in the early nineties. He smiled 'We are always able to find something to do.' Resources (now private property) and political power again became closely linked, but the holders could change, with a political struggle, or, since 2004, at the behest of the Kremlin. Putin reasserted federal control, and took responsibility for appointing the governors. But the lobbies exist. In the competition for the post of governor of the huge and wealthy Krasnoyarsk krai in 2002 one of the two leading candidates was backed by the nickel lobby, the other by the aluminium interests. One got the governorship, the other was given the chair of the krai legislative assembly.

The resource base matters – both for contributions to the federal budget and for subsidies from the centre – and affects the regional elite's room for manoeuvre. And, most important, regional office holders must sense the way the wind is blowing in the Kremlin, the priorities, and which problems can be ignored. This can offer a window of opportunity to a human rights or environmental group. A recent example was the campaign waged in St Petersburg against the building of a Gazprom skyscraper not far from the city centre. The campaign dragged on, getting attention, and popular support. It was a distraction, and a nuisance. The Kremlin decided that it was better that Gazprom and the city government drop the project.

All these factors influence the role human rights and other non-governmental organizations play or have played in different regions. Here is one further suggestion, from Blinushov:

> In my personal opinion, and I don't pretend that it is the whole truth, a great deal depends on the local leadership of the security services which, in the majority of the regions retains a continuity with those of the Soviet period, peacefully making the transition to a new Russia, but preserving the traditions, perceptions, which were handed down from generation to generation, from one boss to another.

However, while the environment (cultural, economic, political) played and plays a role, the very uneven pattern of human rights activity across the country cannot be explained without reference to the willingness and ability of an individual or a small group of individuals to take up and defend a cause. This, the individual factor, can make all the difference. It was important both during perestroika and afterwards, and as the

Putin regime made life more and more difficult for human rights organizations in the first decade of the new century.

NGO weaknesses in the provinces

Liudmila Alekseeva, we remember, had been concerned by the activists' difficulty in getting acknowledgement from their local authorities. She was well aware that they might be in a minority on the regional human rights commissions. She also recognized that the combination of their stubborn individualism, lack of skills, experience, or any inclination to work with 'colleagues' in the same city, let alone from other regions, weakened the human rights community as a whole.

In some cities a human rights organization might be the only one but in many places, by 1996 or 1997, there were several. In the now pro-NGO environment, and the escalation of social problems, both human rights centres, and single-issue organizations focusing on children, on prisoners, invalids, or on forced migrants, or domestic violence sprang up. There might also be a Memorial organization, a Soldiers' Mothers Committee, or an environmental group. But the picture varied. Whereas St Petersburg had Citizens Watch, a strong Soldiers' Mothers Committee, two domestic violence centres, and two Memorial organizations, Perm had a Human Rights Centre, two Memorial organizations, a weak Soldiers' Mothers Committee, and no Crisis Centre; Nizhny Novgorod had its Human Rights Centre and a Soldiers' Mothers Committee, but neither a Memorial organization nor a Crisis Centre. There might or might not be an organization or individual attached to Ponomarev's For Human Rights.

However, organizations within a town, city or region tended to keep their distance from each other and, even if they worked on the same issues as their counterparts in neighbouring or other regions (for example, Memorial organizations or Soldiers' Mothers Committees), had no connections with them. As was true of the local elites, they looked to themselves – and to Moscow. For them too this had a rational basis: Moscow was the place where the funders were, the Moscow organizations had resources and expertise that could perhaps help them, and Moscow was the place where you could make connections. The realities of travel and communications in this huge country played their part too.

Travel by train or by air, from one regional capital to another, was often only possible via Moscow. Yes, you could travel by train (slowly) from Vladivostok in the east, across Siberia, stopping at Irkutsk, Krasnoyarsk, Novosibirsk, and on to the Urals – Perm and Ekaterinburg – and then on to Moscow. But, if you wanted to go from Perm in the Urals to Nizhny Novgorod on the Volga or to Murmansk in the north, then you had to fly via Moscow. To plan a trip, by train, from Rostov in the south, via Voronezh, and thence to Moscow would add days to a journey. In some sense all lines led, and still lead to Moscow. An overnight bus will take you from Krasnoyarsk to neighbouring Tomsk, and four hours in a minibus will take you on to Novosibirsk, but often it's simpler to bring everyone to Moscow. Remember too that in the nineties neither mobile phones nor the internet were part of everyday life. Telephone communication was poor, and patchy. There was internet communication in the Ford office, and (by 1998) the office staff had mobile phones. But none of that helped a great deal if the people one wished to contact had neither.

Before we look at strategies to link up organizations, either within a city, or across the country, we turn to a conference, organized in St Petersburg in 1998 under the patronage of the president's new commission on human rights, in honour of the fiftieth anniversary of the Universal Declaration, and funded by the British Know How fund. The conference was entitled 'The Human Rights Movement and Mechanisms to Defend Human Rights'.[2] Its proceedings illuminate both the context in which the organizations were operating – a new context, with an overlay of past practices and attitudes – the isolationism within 'the human rights movement', and the difficulty of reaching agreement on how to move forward.

The St Petersburg conference

In the spring of 1998 the Duma (parliament) signed up to the European Convention on Human Rights, a major step forward in the eyes of the human rights' activists. But in May it elected Oleg Mironov, a Communist party deputy, who had supported the war in Chechnya and favoured keeping the death penalty, as the ombudsman. Nor were some other developments encouraging. Sergei Pashin, a well-known and erudite young judge, who had headed a now defunct presidential task force on judicial reform, was under threat of dismissal by Moscow city court for his too liberal judgements, and Alexander Nikitin, a retired naval officer in St Petersburg working for an environmental group, Bellona, had been charged with espionage.

The conference was organized by the human rights commission, headed by Kartashkin, together with support from leading Moscow centres and Citizens Watch, the St Petersburg organization, led by Boris Pustintsev, which was actively supporting Nikitin. The conference proceedings followed a standard pattern. They opened with the reading of a letter in which the president sent his greetings and support for the conference, and referred to the majority of the regional commissions' having well-known human rights activists among their members (which was quite untrue).

Pustintsev then welcomed the participants. He reminded them that the conference had been Kartashkin's idea, and suggested that

we in our activity *help* the state to become law-based, therefore we should not set out from the start to be confrontational with the authorities – dialogue is what is required, and in those instances (not so frequent, alas) when the authorities react favourably to important public initiatives, we welcome close working relations.

Kartashkin took over as chair. As was customary, a commission was elected to work on preparing a draft resolution to be adopted at the end of the conference. Then Kartashkin made a conventional presentation: NGOs have a role to play, he affirms, and he regrets that not all the regional authorities have included human rights activists in their commissions and that, in their turn, some NGOs have been unwillingly to participate; while he regrets the ombudsman's position on the death penalty and alternative service, the president's commission will support him on social and economic rights; the past year, 1996–7, has seen much greater activity by the commission – seminars, distribution of information, including on methods of work. (Any Soviet institution or organization always reported an increase in such activities over the previous year.) But then, he suggests, 'human rights work should be undertaken by all the democratic forces in society', not just by the human rights activists who sometimes insist that they should take the lead. To be fair to Kartashkin, in concluding, he refers to the European Convention, and how this makes possible the taking of cases to the European Court of Human Rights.

Liudmila Alekseeva, as the most eminent human rights activist present, spoke next. She was in a robust mood:

> The idea behind the [human rights] movement remains the same today as it was earlier: to defend the individual from the state and its officials. Its core principles remain the same: a principled refusal to use violence, instead to base oneself on the laws of the land and international documents on human rights, on the Universal Declaration [. . .] Today defending human rights has not become any easier [here she refers to the recent murder of a democratic editor, Larisa Yudina, in Kalmykiya] The constitution contains a rich list of rights and freedoms, but the law doesn't work. Officials, including judges, repeatedly fail to observe the constitution or the laws. [Neither, she points out, did the president in the offensive against Chechnya.]

Given the size of the country, she argued, Russia needs 'tens maybe hundreds of thousands of human rights organizations'. However, things are moving forward – Ponomarev's For Human Rights now has branches in 58 regions, and MHG is working on education. 'And we shall become strong – and the greatest blockhead in officialdom will respond to us, will be taught to obey the laws – after all, that, is the one thing human rights activists demand of the authorities.'

Oleg Mironov, the new ombudsman, followed with a short statement describing his task as being one of restoring rights, improving Russian legislation in accordance with international standards, and raising legal consciousness. No one paid any further attention to him – but then there was hardly any attempt by anyone, over the next day and a half, to respond to points raised by a previous speaker. Most had come with their prepared texts; their task was to present them. There were too many of them to fit into the timetable which, by the second day, had become overcrowded, partly because it included an outing to the palace at Peterhof, and it was not clear how there would be time to get the draft resolution printed out, circulated, and discussed. Had this been a Soviet conference, it would not have mattered because the prepared resolution would have just gone through. But now there were those who wanted it to be done properly, 'democratically', and the participants cared about what they had to say.

The interjections, and proposals as to how to manage the outing, and lunch, and circulation of the resolution took up even more time.

What did they want to say? There was no organization by theme, which made reporting quite difficult. The topics included, among others, restrictions on freedom of information, pressure on trade unions, the rights of those repressed under Stalin, the need to create a new police force from scratch, to reform penal institutions, to ensure open local elections, and the Nikitin case.

Professor Gorelik from Krasnoyarsk was there and restated the need to re-educate the judges, who still thought their task was to fight crime. He cited a survey showing that American 12-year-olds think the task of the court is to decide whether an individual is guilty or not, whereas Russian 12-year-olds think it is to convict criminals. He complained that appeals, on correct legal grounds, were returned by higher courts without explanation.

Valentina Melnikova from Soldiers' Mothers (Moscow) spoke in favour of working with the authorities over, for example, budget issues, and defended their cooperation with the prosecutor's office over an amnesty for conscripts who absconded. She was challenged by Ella Polyakova from the St Petersburg organization, which was dealing with 200–250 conscripts a week. Polyakova's criticisms of the authorities were so hostile that Kartashkin became uncomfortable, and probably so did most participants. A quick survey found that 60 per cent favour dialogue with the authorities; 30 per cent – dialogue on some issues; only 3–5 per cent favoured confrontation. The representative from Ivanovo referred to their having a council of representatives from different NGOs, which 'is not a place for politics, it puts forward suggestions to resolve concrete problems facing the citizens [...] political discussions, slogans, attacks of any kind are forbidden at the meetings by the council itself as pointless and unproductive'. Democracy, he argued, requires opposition, but constructive opposition.

Svetlana Gannushkina's contribution, presented in her absence, was the longest and most professional. She brought up the residence registration, the *propiska* issue – despite the Constitutional Court's ruling it illegal in April 1996, and again in 1998, the mayor of Moscow had simply stated that he would not observe the judgement. The residence restrictions continued to apply, and, moreover, had popular support. But then she turned to the more general issue of attitudes to the law, and raised key issues:

We went on about a law on refugees but when in February 1993 a law appeared we didn't even bother to read it; we reckoned it would make no difference [. . .] we still assumed that the only way to get results was to go to the top person but, when the structures of power and authority broke down, we gradually came to understand that the only way to prevent chaos is to create 'legality', a legal territory, in our huge country.

People still doubt whether it is possible to make laws work in our country. People often say to us — surely you are not such optimists that you believe in the law? It's the equivalent of asking us: do you believe in air? If there's no air, we can't breathe, we simply won't exist. The only space in which mankind can live is one with air. And the state, at present, is so constructed that it can only exist in a law-based space. If such a space does not come into being, Russia as a state will die. There's only one way out: we must create a law-based space.

Our task today, she continued, is 'to change state policy towards migrants and refugees [. . .] and most important of all — to help migrants defend themselves — not to act as petitioners in the offices of all powerful officials, but to demand the observing of their rights, as defined by law'.

However, the theme which, not surprisingly, received most attention was the human rights commissions themselves. But even here there was little attempt to respond to another's comments, and engage in discussion. Pustintsev queried the dubious composition of the president's commission, and spoke of the difficulty of getting information from government departments; Nikolai Girenko, a liberal St Petersburg academic who wrote against racism and would shortly be murdered on his doorstep, argues that the combined efforts of the commissions and rights activists would be insufficient 'to break up Russia's reinforced concrete bureaucracy, or rather its viscous padded version which has to be dismantled, and rebuilt in such a way that its officials obey the law'. Others, from different regions, spoke of the difficulty of getting any representation on a commission. The representative from Arkhangelsk described a two-year struggle, following the June 1996 decree, first to get a commission set up, and then (April 1997) to get one NGO representative on the commission, which was staffed by a professor of political theory, a political scientist, a writer, and representative of the tax inspectorate.

The commission met once, in April 1997, to draw up a plan of work, and then in September had proposed Petrov, the head of the administrative apparatus of the regional authority, as the new ombudsman. With his election, no further need was seen for the commission, whom, she was told, had worked well – in six months 12 citizens had turned to it, and in nine cases their complaints had been satisfied.

Lev Ponomarev was aggressive. Eighty per cent of the commissions, he argued, are 'fictitious' but, then, 'would one expect regional authorities to include human rights activists in the commissions when the federal human rights commission is headed by an official, and includes hardly any?'

This was hardly polite towards Kartashkin, but then from Ponomarev one expected confrontation. We cannot stand aside, he argued. 'The present political system has become one in which "politics" is only practised by the political *nomenklatura* [an appointed elite], together with the new rich.' So we should participate in elections. His organization For Human Rights would put up candidates in 60 regions in the 1999 elections.

The only attempt to respond to some of these comments came from the representative of the commission from Orenburg. He had hoped to meet more commission members at the seminar, and was surprised by the criticism of government officials – he was a government official, and failed to see why this might mean he could not do his job properly. He was amazed to hear that there are 23 rights organizations in Sverdlovsk – should they not unite? In Orenburg there was perhaps one. And he was puzzled by the references to the Nikitin case, and to judge Pashin: he did not know who they are and therefore cannot support statements on their behalf. Perhaps on the bus to Peterhof, palace and park, someone told him. His comments illustrated just how large, and how localized, a country Russia was, and we note that for him Ekaterinburg still has its 'Soviet' name – Sverdlovsk. In ten years' time, the internet and mobile phones would have cast a web over most of the country, and drawn its faraway parts closer together – but that was a decade away.

Towards the end of the presentations, Andrei Babushkin, from Moscow, in a rapid fire delivery, suggested 12 detailed points to be included in the resolution. Babushkin, a dynamic and unusual individual, abandoned the teaching of scientific communism at the time of perestroika to join the democratic movement, and won a short-lived seat on Moscow city council. While still involved in politics today as a Yabloko supporter, it is his

20 years' work with the homeless and ex-prisoners that makes him well known in his locality, and to Moscow officials. We shall meet him again, but here it is his detailed proposals, relating to the work of the commission, to the ombudsman's office, draft legislation on changes to criminal procedure, and recent concrete cases involving activists – to mention only some of them – that we note. Even were time not running out, and lunch and the excursion to Peterhof approaching, there was no way most of them could possibly be discussed and debated (as Yury Shmidt, the well known St Petersburg defence lawyer, points out).

But now we were already into calls from the floor on the need to discuss the resolution before or after lunch. How this was finally resolved we do not know but the transcript includes a two-page 'final document' which includes some of Babushkin's recommendations in shortened form, and others. Two, which had emerged as leading demands from the human rights sector in recent years, were legislation on alternative civilian service in place of military service, and public inspection of places of detention. Chapters 8 and 9 follow their trajectory over the coming years.

The document lays the main blame for the infringement of human rights on the failure of a law-based state to come into existence, and the slow development of civil society. Federal, regional and local authorities, it notes, do not observe the laws and introduce legislation that infringes basic rights. Its recommendations include the ombudsman and the commissions working together to produce federal and regional annual reports, and that the human rights community should participate in working out a Federal Conception of Human Rights for Russia on the Eve of twenty-first century. (This proposal, thankfully I am tempted to say, went no further. But then no one really assumed that it would.)

The conference addressed a letter to the chair of the Supreme Court regarding the Nikitin case, and one to the higher collegium of judges on the Pashin case. The letter to the Supreme Court may have influenced the subsequent decision to drop the charges against Nikitin, but Pashin was dismissed. It was clear to most that their recommendations would have little impact.

During the conference, Valentin Gefter, who works with Kovalev (then still a deputy, but also heading a small human rights research institute) had asked: 'Which of us, state institutions or civil society, is the weaker in defending the rights and freedoms of man?' and claimed that both were equally weak.

Not only are we not moving forward along the road to a law-based state, not only is judicial reform and many other reforms not proceeding, but we are in stops and starts moving backwards [. . .] So what should we do? Somehow we have got to move to a coordinated system of working together.

We note the isolationism of the individual participants, each focused almost entirely on the issue that concerned him or herself, the speaking 'across' rather than engaging with each other and the non-correspondence of the resolutions or final document with clearly thought-out, and agreed, positions of a majority of the participants. These are difficult things to achieve even when one brings together groups of people who share many views in common, so one should not be surprised. But we do want to ask – what purpose then was the conference meant to achieve? And, to return to Gefter, how could the activists begin to work together?

Working together?

At the seminar in 1995 Liudmila Alekseeva had argued that:

The first thing that strikes you about Russian society is that the communists have money, the nationalists have money and for some reason or other the democrats do not. And the second thing – all we Russians, including the democrats, including the human rights activists, lack the ability to work together. Even the best people, the best workers. It's a historically-inherited national characteristic. Perhaps we simply lack experience in civic activity. I see this very clearly because I lived for thirteen years in America. Americans work together better than we do.

NGOs in Russia are often criticized for their inability or unwillingness to work together. One of the reasons surely is their need to compete with others for funding, sometimes from the same donor. Such a pattern of behaviour is hardly limited to Russian NGOs. The search for funding is highly competitive, and there is no reason to think that this free market – where donors have competing preferences and NGOs, institutions, or individuals develop strategies to take advantage of them – produces outcomes that are of the most benefit to the community or indeed guarantee the promotion of a donor's preferences. By the second half of the nineties, there was money, substantial amounts of Western money, funding human rights organizations, and in Chapter 5 we assess its impact. But what about inherited national characteristics? Some Western scholars have written of a 'Russian intelligentsia tradition' in which 'purity and principle take precedence over strategy and action' and we shall meet others, including Vladimir Lukin, elected ombudsman in 2004, and leading activists, who stress 'the archaic attitudes' of the people.[3]

Cultural arguments are tricky. Cultures are multi-faceted, and they can change or adapt to new circumstances. Some Russian cultural patterns that existed at the beginning of the twentieth century surely influenced Soviet rule, in various ways, and themselves, over the years, changed with it. Which new traits were brought into being by Soviet rule, industrialization, and twentieth century developments is a question for endless exploration. There is however plenty of evidence of people or organizations joining forces, and, working together, throughout the nineteenth century, during and after the 1905 and 1917 revolutions, and into the 1920s. People, in all strata, worked together effectively, either to challenge, change or to support the existing order. They worked together during World War II, no less doggedly than did their allied counterparts. Lenin complained, it is true, that the problem with the social-democratic movement was its lack of organization. Sometimes, when driven to despair by an endless discussion that closes with resolutions, forgotten as soon as they have been passed, or ends without agreement on any course of action, his words come back to haunt me. But they do not offer an explanation for today's actions. For that we must look to the attitudes, and patterns of behaviour, that existed within society (whether among intellectuals, state officials, students, the industrial labour force, or pensioners) when Russia set out to chart a new course in 1991.

Here, given that the issue is 'working together', I remind the reader that the many years of Soviet rule had denied its citizens the right to engage in public discussion and move to independent collective action. This found expression, in the post-Soviet environment, in a divorce between public speech (was it even discussion?) and action.[4] The possibility of talking openly about issues, old and new, was entrancing. Conferences! There had always been conferences but now they would be 'real' and Western funders put up the money. There was a strong belief in education or enlightenment – very much part of a Soviet inheritance – and a practice of adopting resolutions to pass to those above, or to the outside world, resolutions which, it was assumed, would now, somehow magically, be significant because they 'really represented' what the signatories thought. The practice of writing of public letters to be sent to the authorities could surely now be used to effect. Often these activities took precedence over running an organization. Understandably. There was little experience of organizing, let alone democratically.

In the summer of 1998, 25-year-old Tatyana Lokshina returned to Moscow with a contract to work in a publishing house. Eight years earlier, upon finishing school, she had left with her parents for Boston, Massachusetts, and had now finished graduate school. But, as she arrived, in August 1998, at the time of the financial crash, the publishing house froze all vacancies. Her pre-raphaelite face and halo of hair would, a century earlier, have brought her work as a model, but in Moscow in 1998 jobs were next to impossible to find. Someone told her that the Moscow Helsinki Group was looking for a person with English language skills for a USAID project. Tanya had no particular interest or knowledge of human rights but her language skills, and her having done a little part-time work in the Sakharov archive at Brandeis University in Boston, brought her the job. She thought of it as a short-term fill in, until she could get into publishing.

> You were given an untrained assistant, and gigantic tasks, and you either carried them out as far as you were able, or they defeated you. If you had some success, then you were quickly moved up. By 2003 I was already the executive director of MHG. Absolutely inexperienced, without a clue of what it was I was engaged in, but somehow or other it seemed to be working, and after all you have no other points of reference, no one is explaining how you should be doing things [...] There was such a strange combination of, on the one hand, some kind of irresponsibility, and on the other unlimited possibilities for you to set yourself targets and do certain things which, in a different context, and at your age, you would never have attempted.

Would it have been the same, I ask, if you had been working in publishing?

No, definitely not. Working in a publishing house is very specific work, it's a craft. It's clear what has to be done, and how to do it.

So why wasn't it like that in human rights work?

Because everything was only just being born, everything was absolutely new, living material that was being born and changing. Now it's very different, today that kind of thing is impossible [. . .] I am not here passing any judgements, I am just stating a fact.

The same situation surely characterized the new world of business, property, and making money. It would be interesting to compare the degree of professionalization, which all agree distinguishes the human rights community today from that of the nineties, with that in the business world. And to ask, not merely what accounts for changes in that realm but whether any older cultural patterns persist across such very different spheres of activity. What else was present in the human rights community? The looking to a leader who, while he or she holds the position, has power and authority. The absence of accepted procedures for removing some one from office. Leaders of organizations, as someone put it, tend to leave office feet first. There was the trust which existed between a small group of long-term friends or acquaintances, and the distrust of others. All these factors came into play. None of these practices would disappear overnight.

Liudmila Alekseeva welcomed a Soros initiative to set up local centres for civic initiatives 'a space where all could meet – organizations and individuals, who share the idea of an open society – from political parties to, say, gardeners'. This might encourage them to work together. However, while sometimes offering office space, and a place to pick up information, such centres did not usually result in joint action by the members, any more than did the Research Centre on Human Rights in Moscow. After all, they might well be competing for funding. To bring them together one needed Moscow's involvement. Liudmila Alekseeva defined the task of the Moscow Helsinki Group as one of attracting funding for large projects in which human rights groups from across the country would participate.

Thanks to my American experience, I withstood the pressure from my fellow countrymen who, in keeping with the national tradition, wanted to create a vertical organization. They wanted to create associations, filials of MHG – no way! Let each organization retain its complete independence and be our partner. I stood to the death on this, quarrelling with everyone, especially with Ponomarev. He is a much bigger fan of vertical organizations.

NGOs from the regions who participated in a project would come to Moscow to attend seminars and training sessions, and meet each other. Depending on the project, the participants would differ. And, meanwhile, MHG would devise educational programmes. This idea, inadvertently, produced the first community-wide website.

In 1996 the Moscow Helsinki Group and Sergei Smirnov (of the Russian Research Centre on Human Rights) were trying unsuccessfully to design an educational programme. Sergei had just graduated as a geophysicist, but his hobby was computers. He and Andrei Blinushov, from Ryazan, who had started reading computer journals on the internet, decided to see what they could find on the web about Russian organizations. The answer was nothing – and then, in Blinushov's words 'we thought, and the idea seemed to us very daring, to try to set up a website, not just with educational materials, but a shared site which would have information about different organizations, where there would be editors too'.

In 1997 they came to the Ford Office with a proposal for an internet project, Human Rights On-line, a proposal that included setting up a website, providing a limited number of local organizations with computers, travelling out to the regions to show them how to use them and how to provide material for the hro.org website. Over time the local organizations could create their own websites and gain local publicity. The website, with its online board, was to be operated out of Ryazan and Moscow. It was the first internet site where organizations from across the country could send in information and keep themselves informed of what others were doing. Today it provides ongoing information on the human rights community (conscription, and arbitrary police behaviour, are the most popular topics), a bulletin of daily happenings, has a large archive, and has organized internet campaigns in defence of individuals or organizations.[5] Since 2000 it has suffered more than one hacking attack, the latest coinciding with the 2012 presidential election.

By the late nineties the ideas of networking, of shared projects or activities, as a way of overcoming both local and regional isolationism had begun to catch on. Western donors were enthusiastically promoting it. Maybe, by creating networks, the isolationism and individualism of NGOs could be overcome, and the NGOs themselves, as members, would carry more weight at local level, and at federal level? As we shall see, some worked better than others. But the most ambitious project, which lasted ten years, was MHG's regional monitoring of the observation of human rights.

MHG and monitoring

In 1997 the National Endowment for Democracy gave MHG a grant to conduct a pilot project: organizations in five regions would send in reports on the human rights situation in their region. In 1998 this was extended to 30, by 1999, with a major three year grant from USAID, the number had risen to 60, and in 2000 all 89 regions responded. USAID continued to support the project until 2009, although with decreasing funding, and the number of participants dropped to around 20. In the words of Nina Tagankina, at the time a member of the Nizhny Novgorod Human Rights Centre, now executive director of the Moscow Helsinki Group:

> At first, they sent in bits, then we sent them details, and a form to fill in; they did not have to fill in everything. We suggested key groups: psychiatric patients, women and children, prisoners, Aids sufferers, groups whose rights, there is good reason to think, will be infringed. And then we sent 'theme reports' to our experts.

When we look at the 20 or so regions which, from 1999, stayed the course and submitted reports, we notice that, in most cases, the same organization with the same leader was in charge. But some strong organizations had dropped out – presumably because they were busy doing other things. And, as Tagankina put it, 'There were those who simply weren't able to monitor the situation throughout the year. You have to have a system – using both the media, and a public reception centre to which people turn with their complaints, and human rights activists who appear in court, write documents, hold press conferences [. . .] The work has to be systematic and multifaceted.'

As funding decreased, centres were asked to send in what they could, and their 'bits and pieces' were included in an overall report. This was a project that provides us with insights into what working together could mean, and the results it can bring. Let us look at it first from the perspective of its young administrators, one of whom was Tatyana Lokshina, and then from that of a participant.

When I began to work in MHG I was astounded by the level of professional irresponsibility. With my university background I had a fairly clear idea of what constituted research. What was being called the Russian monitoring of human rights did not seem to be based, in any way at all, upon a methodology [. . .] then Sergei Lukashevsky, who had just joined the MHG, wrote one up, and I sort of helped along but there was also the question as to how the regional partners would react. There were some organizations which turned out to be prepared to learn, out of interest, and there were others who weren't prepared to lift a finger, because they did not care about research at all. The results were horribly uneven. The all-Russia report which we compiled annually, on the basis of the regional reports, was very different from the regional ones. We had to rely quite heavily on our own monitoring of the media.

Sergei Lukashevsky, who had recently graduated from the Russian Humanities University and, while a student, had worked in Memorial, brought his writing and editing skills to the project. The themes, he suggested, were proposed by the regional participants, several of whom were part of the Ponomarev network, or by members of the liberal parties. But some were quite new to the human rights community.

One of the participants was Igor Sazhin, a young history teacher in Syktyvkar, in the northern Komi republic, whose family had been deported there in the 1930s. Interested in his family's history, in 1996 he approached Mikhail Rogachev at the Syktyvkar Memorial organization. When word came of the MHG project, Rogachev suggested he might like to set up an organization and participate. He decided he would; he would set up a Memorial human rights commission to collect material on the infringements and do this in his free time. But then he began to think: should he not be offering legal advice to those in conflict with the authorities as well as collecting the data? He struggled at first but in 1998, when MHG was paying local organizations for the editorial work on the monitoring project, he was invited to a seminar in Moscow, and Marek Nowicki from the Polish Helsinki Foundation came to explain how to do the monitoring. He went to a summer school in Warsaw at the Helsinki Foundation. The connections made at these meetings, in his words, made him feel part of a community of individuals, who are linked up electronically, not through Moscow, and who exchange information on new legislation (for example on the public commissions to oversee places of detention), on court cases they have won (or lost), on practices such as pressing for bail if remand centres are full. While Sazhin is a member of Memorial, and on the International Society's board today, his connections are not necessarily with Memorial organizations. Andrei Yurov, from Voronezh, who set up a Human Rights Youth Movement, which we meet in Chapter 10, is a close colleague dating from those early MHG meetings.

Starting in 1998, Sazhin and his colleagues began to produce a shorter annual report, based on their report to MHG, to send to the head of the Komi republic and to republican officials, and then moved on to sending quarterly reports.

> We should educate them too. We tried for a year, no response, just an acknowledgement, but then I learnt that they did pay attention to the reports [. . .] and most important this played a PR role, they began to notice us [. . .] Making use of the report at local level in order to change the situation turned out to bring significant results.

But it took them time to realize that they could use information, for example on police behaviour, to lobby for change. The majority of the organizations, he suggested, who participated in the MHG project simply sent their reports in to Moscow, and did not think of using them at local level. When he registered the Memorial human rights commission (in 2002), it had already established a reputation for itself. It is an atypical organization.

We have seven activists who regularly come to the office and work. And about 20 members. Our approach is unusual: the largest membership dues are paid by the members of the board, they pay 1000r [£20] a month.

Do they all work somewhere else? I asked.

Yes. I work in a school, and I earn a bit more by teaching human rights. What I do in the organization is voluntary work [i.e. unpaid]. I believe that if someone doesn't have the ground firmly under his feet, he can't become the defender of someone else. So, already firmly on your own feet, and with an income, then you can join an NGO and help people. So far this works for us.

On our board we have a businessman, two lawyers who are well established, one person who, while not a lawyer, earns pretty well from a law practice, and I, a history teacher. We manage to put together about 10,000r [£200] a month and that's enough to pay for the office, communal charges, telephone and internet [...] yes, there are problems but we are trying to think up new approaches [...] donations through a bank [...] soon we're going to have a donation box. If the population trusts us, they must supply us with some resources. That's my vision for the future. Everywhere in the world NGOs work like that, it's only we who turn for help to the West.

With Sazhin, Lukashevsky, and Lokshina, we have representatives of a new, second generation, those who began to work in human rights organizations towards the end of the nineties. In 2004 Lokshina left MHG to set up an analytical centre, Demos, to report on and analyse human rights infringements, and by 2010 she was working for the American-based Human Rights Watch in their Moscow office, travelling, including to the Caucasus. Lukashevsky replaced Samodurov as director of the Sakharov Centre in 2010.

I come back to the 'generation question' in later chapters, here we are interested in what the monitoring project produced. For the first few years MHG produced annually book-length reports, in Russian and in

English, and accompanying volumes that reproduced edited versions of the regional reports. They varied in content and structure. The report on 1999 contained special sections on the electoral franchise, on social, economic and labour rights, women's rights, children's rights, and mass violations in the Chechen republic. These, in approach and style, vary with the expert (sometimes an academic) who wrote them. The 2000 report is organized into sections, starting with the Inviolability of the Person, and continuing with Observance of Fundamental Civil Liberties, moving on through political rights, and social rights, to the status of the most vulnerable groups, and again the hand of invited experts is visible. As can be imagined, the reports by the regional organizations vary wildly.[6]

Liudmila Alekseeva suggested that: 'Working on the monitoring project helped weaker organizations become stronger. That was the first thing. And second, it was joint activity. We did it together, we met to study how to do it, then did it, then met to assess the results. And that played an important part in creating a community.'

Yes and no, would be my response. Certainly, as we saw in the Sazhin case, it played a crucial role in getting an organization off the ground, and established in its locality. But there were others that came into existence because of the foreign funding and faded away once financial support shrunk, and, despite the claims from some regions that their report is a collective effort, one has to be sceptical. St Petersburg is of course not typical but here, within a few years, a council of human rights organizations was producing its own annual report, while another organization, Strategiya, participated in the MHG project. The project did not leave behind it a network of organizations engaged in collectively mapping human rights infringements, either in a locality, or across Russia. However, the seminars and discussions in Moscow, and the part played by Marek Nowicki from Poland, played an important part in bringing younger participants together, and creating lasting personal networks. I look at his contribution in the next chapter.

At the presentation of the first set of books, the results of the MHG monitoring project in 1999, Arseny Roginsky, from Memorial, in his congratulations to Liudmila Alekseeva, brushed aside the issue of human rights − what she was doing, he said as he embraced her, was furthering the emergence of civil society. At the time, I was puzzled. But this was its contribution, and an important one, to the idea of a civil society, where independent voices and organizations, separate from the state, and from across the country, talk to each other about infringements of rights, and sometimes work together to try to hold the state responsible.

MHG today has a small and efficient staff – Nina Tagankina, from Nizhny Novgorod, as its executive director, and Daniil Mescheryakov, from Irkutsk, as project organizer – and a well-organized website. It continues to seek funding for projects that involve local organizations. A coalition against discrimination proved very popular. At twice-yearly board meetings, according to Tagankina, 'Liudmila Mikhailovna decides our basic strategy [...] and on strategies for action [...] there was Campaign 31,[7] we sought some funding for that.' Donor preferences obviously played their part. Today, faced with the 'foreign agent' law, MHG no longer accepts foreign funding and, in this instance, it has surprisingly broken ranks with long-term allies in the human rights community.

Liudmila Alekseeva, in many ways, was still the voice of the Russian human rights community in 2013, widely revered by local organizations, and recognized by officials as someone who cannot be ignored. (She received a greetings telegram from Putin on her eightieth birthday.) A visit from her to a meeting in a provincial city raises the profile of local activists. According to Lokshina, 'Russia is a country of authorities and well-known names' she remembers people coming from the provinces to see Alekseeva – 'they simply wanted to touch her hand. It was very important then.' In her Moscow apartment her large clumsy telephone, which she manages with extraordinary dexterity, rings constantly – it could be the police chief (about a future demonstration), or 'a very unpleasant deputy', a journalist, Lukin the ombudsman, or the young National Bolsheviks. Somehow she has time for everyone, before ordering a delivery of pizza for an evening meeting to discuss how to move the judicial reform process forward.

CHAPTER 5

WESTERN ASSISTANCE, AN EXTRAORDINARY CONGRESS

> Despite all the minuses, civil society and the country would be
> different today had it not been for Western assistance. Very many
> aspects of today's activity – from words people use, to
> technologies, to practices – were introduced with the help of
> donors' money, and hence you can't underestimate its importance,
> despite all its minuses.

Vyacheslav Bakhmin's words are echoed by others, both activists and
funders, with different emphases. By the second half of the nineties, and
throughout the first decade of the new century, Russian NGOs were
receiving substantial Western financial assistance. Did such aid have a
significant or marginal impact, contribute to or do little to encourage
the development of democratic practices, fair and tolerant societies? This
has been the subject of a lively debate among Western scholars.[1] All I
offer here are some reflections on how it influenced the Russian human
rights community, both positively and negatively, before looking at an
Extraordinary All-Russian Congress to Defend Human Rights, held in
2001, which provides a snapshot of the community at the beginning of
the new century.

The background

What prompted the funding? It was, as we saw, a time when human
rights had moved high up the global agenda, and both Western NGOs

and the voices of the Helsinki Committees found a response from their governments, and from private foundations. Women's rights, media rights, prisoners' rights, refugee rights all had strong advocacy groups in the West, anxious to take the message to Russia, an unexplored territory. Activists could claim a shared identity based on the universal doctrine of human rights. It was an exciting but bewildering world both for funders and for the new rights organizations in Russia. The funders and advocacy groups shared a widely held view that Russia was engaged in a difficult transition to a liberal market economy, with a democratic politics. Quite what that meant, and whether American, Italian or Swedish experience might be the most relevant to Russia, was rarely discussed by donors or recipients. Its closed existence under Soviet rule meant not only that Russians had very little knowledge of the West, but that Westerners had very little knowledge of Russia.

How did the new activists respond in the nineties to the availability of Western money? Russian organizations, it seems, had the opportunity to choose from a rich variety of sources.[2] But it was not that simple. All grant-making organizations have their own preferences, rules for applying, reporting procedures, etc. Most required applications in English. Some required Western partners. The paperwork could be overwhelming, and the questions sometimes incomprehensible. In the mid to late nineties, even Moscow organizations struggled to understand what applying for a grant, let alone receiving one, involved. Donor preferences for short-term projects and their unwillingness to fund everyday running costs had consequences. Russian organizations had to try to hide such costs within 'projects', and lived from month to month, unable to do any long-term planning. They dreamt of grants that included support for rent, communal services, and staff salaries (institutional support) as well as for project activities. The Moscow Helsinki Group, despite receiving large US government grants for projects, struggled to find money to cover office running costs and rent.

Vyacheslav Bakhmin knows the world of both the activists, and the Western foundations for whom he worked during our period, probably better than anyone else. In his words, while the foundations' programme staff 'think about the results, all the same, the trouble is they think in terms of projects [...] people struggle from one project to another, and don't manage to achieve anything.' And Tanya Lokshina, with experience in different organizations, is convinced that: 'one of the worst mistakes made by Western donors was not to create a mechanism for providing normal institutional support [...] you work under the constant pressure of writing up short-term projects, thinking up complete nonsense.'

The funding world was awash with Western consultants, experts, and NGOs who, whatever their knowledge or interest, were anxious to tap into this new source of income. In the 1960s a banner 'There's money in poverty' decorated the Economics Faculty at the University of Wisconsin; now 'there was money in Russia'. Western government grants almost always included their experts in projects, while the European Commission's approach to grant making (Western partners are obligatory) gave birth to 'the Brussels bandits', consultancy firms that bid for the projects put out to tender by the Commission. They set up, on paper, partnerships between Russian organizations they often have no knowledge of and highly paid Western experts or consultants with little or no knowledge of Russia. Western experts sometimes play a very positive role, and some partnerships, including those funded by the European Commission, for example the joint work done by Russian and Western lawyers (EHRAC and Memorial) in taking cases to the European Court of Human Rights, or that of ECRE/Migration Rights, to which we return in Chapter 9, have been and still are very fruitful. However, the waste or misuse of money under the EC system, and indeed under some of the big government programmes, is a frequent complaint. 'Millions have been poured down the drain under the Rule of Law programme' sighed an experienced lawyer, while Bakhmin commented:

Monsters like TACIS and USAID, and the European Commission – they often distribute huge amounts of money not only ineffectively but in a way that damages the development of civil society [...] they themselves have to hand out this money because the system is such that if they do not do it today, they won't be given it in future, they have to account for it, and the reports are often a sham.

As can be imagined, it was important and difficult for the different donors to keep track of others' activities, and there could be duplication or dismay at some of the projects funded by others. By 2000 those with offices in Moscow had set up a Donors' Forum (of both government and foundation funders), which met regularly. Undoubtedly helpful in creating an awareness of each other's programmes, the interests and approach to grant making of its members were sufficiently different to preclude anything like a common strategy. To some extent the private foundations, or at least MacArthur and Ford, tried to spread the load between competing grantees (MacArthur supported the Sakharov Centre, Ford the Memorial Society). If, however, representatives of the private foundations might consult, and sometimes agree, on a strategy towards an individual grantee or grantees, the Western government funders (from USAID to DIFID, SIDA, or the European Commission, to mention only a few) pursued their funding strategies independently. The need to follow the preferences of a foreign ministry or state department, to implement the results of political bargaining in Brussels, or the personal preferences of a president of a foundation, meant a field of players whose individual interests took precedence over any team work.

A new player could enter the field, announce a new programme, and suddenly a particular field would be awash with money, and grantees old and new scrambling to take advantage of it. Western funding, attracted by an organization's record, tended to follow a (successful) organization and this could lead to 'overfunding'. (One human rights activist had the honesty to say that, by 2010, his organization had more than enough financial resources.) Rather differently, an activist might agree to take a project on board with seeming enthusiasm, but unless s/he was the right individual, in the right place, at the right time, the strategy would leave little more than a paper trace. Funders, government or private, like to see results, and this encourages grantees and programme staff to report them when a more honest (and useful) assessment would be to explain why a project failed or produced very little. Russians (and not only Russians) are good at ticking boxes, writing reports that bear little relation to reality. Ironically, Western funders' blueprints for grant proposals and reporting techniques encouraged grantees to place their imaginative ideas in a Soviet framework of unrealistic planning, fudging of reports, and creative accounting. (But, let us be careful here, some of their Western partners, with no Soviet background, were adept at such practices themselves.)

And what of Moscow versus the rest?

The larger, better known, Moscow-based organizations stood a much higher chance of obtaining funding than those in the provinces, and

Soros, Ford, and MacArthur were prepared to give them institutional support. This had positive and negative consequences. It allowed organizations, in a world where no membership income existed, to establish themselves and think in two- to three-year terms. However, the downside was that donor and grantee became tied into a relationship in which the donor was loathe to pull the plug on an established organization while the grantee came to rely on its major sponsor. Not surprisingly, accusations of close or cosy relations between funders and particular Moscow organizations sometimes soured relations within the NGO community. NGOs in the provinces complained repeatedly of the favouritism shown to Moscow organizations, and of their elitism. They grumbled that Moscow activists got large salaries (by and large untrue) and resources to which they, the poor relatives, had no access (often true). The competition for grants, in the words of one activist, created market conditions, in which the big sharks ate the small fishes. There were no anti-monopoly barriers, or agreements.

It is enormously time consuming to deal with hundreds of applications, and very difficult to monitor results – and in Russia, given its size, particularly difficult.[3] Both Ford and NED set up small-grant programmes to be run by Russian organizations, with respected members of the Moscow human rights community making up their expert committees. Applications – for perhaps $5–10,000 – were submitted in Russian, as was reporting, and there were seminars to bring the grantees together. While these programmes, which lasted for perhaps ten years, undoubtedly helped local organizations, they could only offer support to 30 or so organizations a year, and the funding was for small projects. The really enterprising organizations began to apply directly to Western donors. They wanted support for offices and staff, publications, projects, events. Whether in Moscow or in a provincial city, the strategy for an enterprising organization was to get several grants, from different donors, and some succeeded. By 2001, at the end of a golden decade, all the Moscow organizations whom we have mentioned so far were obtaining funding from different sources, and there were active human rights organizations scattered across Russia who were getting direct grants from Western funders – in St Petersburg, in Murmansk and Syktyvkar in the north, in Ekaterinburg, NizhniTagil, and Perm in the Urals, in Tomsk, Krasnoyarsk, and Irkutsk in Siberia, and Khabarovsk in the Far East. South of Moscow Ryazan stood out, and Lipetsk, then, moving down the Volga,

Nizhny Novgorod, Kazan, and Yoshkar-Ola had active organizations, and further south Mordova, Voronezh and Rostov. In the Caucasus there were outposts in Dagestan, Ingushetiya and Chechnya itself. Many of their activists came to know each other, and their leaders met at seminars or the Warsaw summer schools, of which more in a moment.

We met the representatives of some of the successful provincial organizations, which had existed from the early nineties, in action at the seminars and conferences in Chapters 3 and 4. In Nizhny Novgorod the centre split in 2000 into an Inter-regional Committee Against Torture (headed by Igor Kalyapin, the young activist and entrepreneur) and a Human Rights Union. Others, such as the Human Rights Centre of the Mari-El republic, the Public Committee for Human Rights of the republic of Tatarstan, and the Human Rights Centre of the republic of Mordova (under the leadership of Guslyannikov, the first elected president of the republic) had come into existence two or three years later. We are talking about organizations that had perhaps three paid staff, an accountant, and a few volunteers. Most were small, most relied on a circle of known friends or acquaintances, few were widely known, and they were learning new skills. Most of these organizations still exist today, most with the same leader, maybe a new profile, and more staff, and they keep their books much better. A few have faded or ceased to work on human rights issues. And, in recent years, new organizations of a rather different type have appeared. We shall meet them in Chapters 11 and 12.

What do we note so far? The availability of Western grants, in an environment in which Russian donors, or philanthropy more generally, still hardly existed, and certainly not in relation to human rights, enabled human rights organizations to establish themselves, and to carry out a range of activities that benefited the vulnerable and victims of ill treatment. At the same time, the jostling competition for grants set organizations apart from one another. It was rare to find someone, such as Stanislav Velikoredchanin who, while heading an organization Christians Against Torture and Child Slavery in Rostov, saw his role as one of helping very different organizations find their feet, and apply to one of the small-grant programmes. The first Soldiers' Mothers Committee I visited, in 1996 – three elderly women in a room, with a telephone, near the local recruiting office – had been helped by Velikoredchanin to get a small grant but postage costs were swallowing up their pensions. If they requested slightly more, they enquired of me, hesitantly, would it be thought they were asking for a pension increase for themselves?

And this brings us to the question of the role grants played in an environment in which people were struggling to survive. On the one hand, Western money brought a whole stratum of active individuals looking for a survival strategy into civic activities which, otherwise, would only have come on the agenda years later. This can be seen as a positive development, but it meant they could have shallow roots. In Bakhmin's view: 'there's a whole stratum of organizations working on quite incomprehensible topics, and what they write is incomprehensible too.' Furthermore, and he is speaking in 2010:

> There are those organizations [. . .] in particular, those related to gender issues — organizations focusing on sexual minorities, and even on trafficking [. . .] if it hadn't been for Western funding, they would not have appeared. They would have emerged in the future, as society developed, as society came to realize that such problems are important too.

However, a grant-making strategy ahead of its time may leave traces to be picked up later. To give two examples — the monitoring of police precincts, and a social marketing campaign — both faded or came to nothing ten years ago but now have reappeared, in new form. Support for those advocating the criminalization of domestic violence has taken nearly 20 years to bear fruit, but that does not mean that support was originally misconceived. I suspect that support for LGBT activists who, by 2012, were being targeted by hostile Duma deputies and vigilantes, and who face a rough time over the next five years, falls into the category of planting seeds for the future. But here hostility and media attention has put the issue of sexual minorities firmly on the public agenda.

The enthusiasm for funding civil society was not always to its advantage. Yes, the Russian environment was one where charitable giving did not exist, and one in which, as rich Russians emerged, they took care to avoid funding activities of which the Kremlin disapproved. However, in their desire to provide assistance, Western funders largely neglected the issue of encouraging the development of domestic fund-raising strategies, including charitable giving, membership dues, public campaigns. Charity Aid Foundation's work is a notable exception and charitable giving and volunteering are now part of the scene. But too many of the human rights organizations grew accustomed to thinking of Western grants as their single source of income, and lack the mindset or skills that would allow them to focus on raising money from their fellow citizens, wealthy or not. An exception is Veronika Marchenko's Mother's Right but, when I cite this, the reply from other activists is that the wealthy are scared, and ordinary citizens not interested in the issues they address, whereas the death of conscripts is 'a popular issue'. That itself is debatable. More important is how little attention Western donors paid to helping Russian organizations, even in or perhaps because of the unfavourable environment, to learn to look for money and support within the country.

Some provincial activists put it more strongly to Denis Volkov, a sociologist who conducted an interview survey in 2010:

> some of them say that when the authorities used to listen to them, and there was foreign funding, there was no need for popular support. In the words of one respondent 'the distance between the man on the street and the activists is the same as that between him and the governor'.[4]

It also gave ammunition to political opponents and, given the popular antipathy to the West, fed the belief that, if supported by Western money, activities were suspect. As Aleksei Korotaev, with experience dating from the early days of the Human Rights Project Group, put it: 'All the same a wary, hostile attitude towards everything that comes from the West lurks in Russian popular consciousness. It is too deeply rooted to be eradicated quickly. In that sense anything that is associated with western money immediately is given a minus mark.' In the nineties, the salaries, although miserly by Western standards, could appear substantial (an activist receiving $100 a month – the salary of a professor!) – 'they are living off Western money, they earn more than we do, they are not being fed for nothing, they must be doing something bad.' By the end of our period, this abnormal balance was no more, and Western money was shrinking fast, but the popular response to the 'foreign agents' law in 2013 indicates that the receiving of Western money was still viewed with suspicion.

It was not only Western money that could undermine the activists' credibility. In Korotaev's view:

The orientation towards Western foundations and working with them has had a major influence upon the way activists talk [. . .] and this language is absolutely incomprehensible outside the community [. . .] an idiotic situation has arisen in which great ideas are expressed in words that are simply incomprehensible to the majority of the citizens of this country [. . .] and when we approach the average [Russian] donor here, we have to speak a language that they understand and not a Western language.

Short on experience of organizing, promoting their ideas and working together, their dependence on Western funding compelled activists to take up the ideas, strategies, and language used by human rights activists in the donor country. Sometimes this worked for them, sometimes it fell on stoney ground. An exception was the 'education' offered by the Helsinki Foundation in Warsaw. And, by the start of the new century, and as it progressed, knowledge and expertise in chosen areas was increasing, new tactics and strategies were being adopted. We shall see them all in evidence in later chapters, but here we look at Marek Nowicki's contribution.

The influence of Marek Nowicki

Marek Nowicki, a physicist, originally a Solidarity activist, then a Helsinki Committee supporter, had set up a Foundation in Warsaw, with a brief to teach and train human rights activists. This included summer schools for Russian participants, where the teaching was in Russian, and which introduced them to human rights both as a subject of study and as ways of monitoring and defending rights. Nowicki was an inspiring teacher. I can attest to that. A small, slight man, smoking as he talked, walking round the room, he made his listeners think, while at the same time suggesting different ways they could advance or defend human rights. His excellent Russian, and his knowledge of Russia and the environment in which they were living and working, made him a role model for many. Sadly he died, of cancer, in 2003.[5]

Igor Sazhin, the young history teacher from Sytyvkar whom we met in the previous chapter, is in some ways a classic product of the Nowicki schools. There, he said, for the first time he met people, such as Wiktor Osiatinsky (professor from the Central European University)[6] who actually think and write about the concept of human rights; he came to understand that human rights are an issue everywhere, that in the West too they come under attack, that the problems of ethnic minorities, attitudes towards women, discrimination, exist everywhere, and their defenders survive because people support them financially. He met people from all over Russia, and remains in close contact with some of them. And, also important, Marek Nowicki showed him how to teach human rights in a way that brings them alive. Sazhin is, I suspect, a talented teacher in his own right, but his debt to Nowicki is apparent.

Olga Gnezdilova, a young lawyer from Voronezh, who participated in a Moscow Helsinki Group project, monitoring places of detention, using methods devised by the Poles, is another young activist who attended a Warsaw school, in 2002.

It was very useful [...] they talked of how Poland had overcome its totalitarian past, how they reformed the court system, and the prison system. Experts talked about the transition, about how human rights are affected, all that was for me was important because we faced similar problems. The fact that they had managed to solve these problems suggested that we too could overcome the past.

Olga appears in action in Chapter 11, and also Maria Kanevskaya whom we met in the Introduction. Maria, while still a student at the St Petersburg MVD University, aged 20, in 2002 took part in 'a special course for 28 leaders of NGOs from Russia, in Russian, at the Helsinki Foundation in Warsaw. We listened to Marek Nowicki's lectures till ten in the evening.' She met Marianna Sadovnikova from Irkutsk, who headed an NGO that worked in the juvenile colonies, and 'Pavel Chikov from Kazan, Irina from the NGO The Individual and the Law in Yoshkar-Ola, Maria Sereda from Ryazan Memorial'. Towards the end of the course, the participants were invited to submit projects for a small-grant competition for which the Foundation had funding.

And Marianna, with whom I shared a room, said 'Set up an organization quickly, I'll write up a project, and we'll bring Irina in', and during the next three days, brainstorming, we wrote up the project. We knew we would win because all the others were simply writing their individual projects, and ours was a joint project. And of course we won.

For another young woman from St Petersburg, someone with no particular interest in human rights, and a quiet, reflective personality, a chance encounter at the Helsinki Foundation was life changing. Born into a professional family in Leningrad in 1975, Katya Sokiryanskaya studied languages at the Herzen University: English and Japanese. While still a student, she travelled to the Caucasus for a holiday and, bothered by the sight of soldiers at the border, began to read about Chechnya. After graduating she went to Warsaw, to spend a year learning Polish, and someone introduced her to the Helsinki Foundation, where she worked as a volunteer for several months, including helping with preparations for a school.

> And Marek [Nowicki], very serious but with that smile in the corners of his mouth, said 'You are interested in Chechnya? Which sources do you use?' I said, newspapers, the media. 'And have you seen the Memorial Society's information?' At that time I had a vague idea of what Memorial was [...] but at that School there were two representatives from the Memorial organization in Ingushetiya, one was a Chechen, the other an Ingush [...] they were the first Chechens and Ingush whom I had met in my life. And during the coffee break I went up to them and said, light heartedly, 'now I am going to pester you about what's going on in Chechnya'. To which Usam Baisayev, with his usual sarcasm, said 'Yes, you people from Petersburg, know how to pester', and went on to tell me what the St Petersburg special forces were doing in Chechnya [...] in particular about the village New Aldy, which we later filmed, where on 5 February 2000 the St. Petersburg special forces carried out a clean-up operation and in the course of a few hours 56 peaceful residents were killed.

Over the next few days they explained how Memorial tried to monitor and report on the situation in Chechnya.

> And for me this was a complete shock, I was totally unprepared for it [...] as a product of perestroika I lived with the feeling that

now we live in quite another country, that the totalitarian past is over, and life will become more interesting, freer, with every passing day. And now suddenly I learn that in my country people from my city are carrying out special measures, absolutely fascist measures, like those in Hitler's Germany which we read about in our school books. This shocked me so much that it changed my life.

As a graduate student, she moved from St Petersburg State University to study ethnic relations at the Central European University in Budapest, from where her research took her, in 2003, to Nazran, in Ingushetiya. She found the Memorial group, and stayed with them for five years, travelling to teach at Grozny university in Chechnya until 2006 when it became too dangerous. In 2008 family illness brought her back to St Petersburg, from where she continued to work for the Moscow Memorial Human Rights Centre, preparing and writing reports on the Caucasus, before moving to work for the International Crisis Centre.

Nowicki also came to Moscow, invited by the Moscow Helsinki Group, to participate in the training of those involved in the monitoring project. According to Lokshina, he began to teach them

what defending human rights is, what that crazy word 'monitoring' means, what an activist ought to do in a more or less normally functioning country. At that time Russia looked as though it was moving in that direction [...] what the Poles did was very significant.

Her words are telling. What if Russia was not moving in that direction, was not 'a more or less normally functioning country'? How appropriate then was the Helsinki interpretation of human rights and strategies? Whether a future generation of activists will interpret human rights in the same way is an open question but the Polish model – an emphasis on the UN conventions, on monitoring infringements by state institutions, and on the defence of an individual's rights through the courts – was a key component in the education of many of those who took up human rights in the late nineties. And, as important, the Helsinki schools created links between people across the country.

In Russia itself, the end of the nineties and the early years of the new century were home to endless training seminars and schools on everything from human rights education to how to organize a campaign or write a report for a UN committee. Opinions differ on the value of these programmes, much beloved by Western funders and trainers. Jens Siegert, with 20 years' experience working for the Heinrich Boll foundation in Moscow, is sceptical.

> Criticism can be levelled against the EC, TACIS, and American government programmes, USAID, partly too the Soros Foundation. In the main against those programmes which saw support for civil society in terms of a technical task. There were a whole number of centres which put on courses on how to write applications, organize work, and so on, provided technical information but which lacked any normative, ethical or moral presuppositions which are needed to give an activity some real content.

However, all would agree that by 2010 the degree of professionalism within the community – preparing applications, presenting reports to the UN committees, assessing results – was light years away from that of the early years. In Chapters 8–9 we shall see evidence of this. But here we return to the situation as the new century opened, with a brief visit to an Extraordinary Congress to Defend Human Rights. The congress, funded by Western foundations, where more than 500 delegates from human rights organizations from all across Russia gathered, provides a snapshot of the community in 2001, a community that could be likened to a herbaceous border whose plants and boundaries change over time and look different from different vantage points.

The Extraordinary Congress of 2001

Yeltsin, who had won a shaky victory for a second term in 1996, proved to be a corrupt president increasingly unable to function, but he had left the media, the electoral system, and the non-governmental sector largely alone. In 2000 a popular, tough, young president was in the Kremlin. Putin, the working class boy from an inner city courtyard in St Petersburg, who had decided on a future career in the security services while studying law at St Petersburg State University, won the presidential election comfortably. Able and energetic, he had been appointed by Yeltsin to head the FSB (security services) in 1998, and then to the prime ministership. But, if in April 2000 a human rights activist, a respected dissident, might voice the opinion 'I think we can do business with Vladimir Vladimirovich, he's like a blank sheet of paper', by the summer of 2001 few were optimistic. It was disturbing, walking home on a summer evening to find members of the special services, with their black balaclavas and weapons, surrounding the house of Vladimir Gusinsky, owner of NTV, the best of the independent TV channels, and to learn he had been arrested. He was later released and allowed to leave Russia, after selling his channel. Boris Berezovsky fled abroad. The parliament was becoming more and more subservient. The oligarchs were beginning to look over their shoulders, and pack their bags. Working for a Western foundation that funded, among other things, Russian NGOs advancing the cause of human rights and legal reform, one sensed the atmosphere slowly changing. Ministerial and tax officials were flexing their muscles, making any activity, any small operation, even more time consuming – changing the regulations, changing the colour of the paper – and, with a sigh, I recognized that the informers were back, and the office probably bugged.

Held in the huge Cosmos hotel, the leading Moscow organizations had called the congress in the spring of 2001 because of 'the growing threat to human rights and freedoms'.[7] In their words, court reform had stalled, the free press was under constant attack, government and society was becoming increasingly militarized, demands for a healthy environment ignored, and the war in Chechnya was continuing, accompanied by serious and widespread infringements of human rights and the norms of humanitarian law. Particularly worrying was talk, emanating from on high, of a constitutional assembly to review the 1993 constitution. Their statement:

Taking part in the congress are human rights organizations of different kinds, those defending freedom of speech, rights of forced migrants, of conscripts and many others, and other non-governmental organizations (environmental, womens, youth groups) for whom defending human rights is only one of the aspects of their work, and also the free trade unions.

suggests that they perhaps held different views on how to interpret *prava cheloveka* or 'human rights'. The titles of the seven sections at the congress illustrate the wide range of issues that were seen as relevant: the defence of the constitutional order and a law-based state (signed up to by 89); Chechnya (72); citizen control (66); right of access to, obtaining and distribution of information (37); the defence of independent private enterprises (42); the strategy and tactics of the defence of the social rights of the population (85); ecology (47, agreed after a debate). The issues ranged from Chechnya to heart operations for children, from the rights of small business to penal reform or honest elections, from access to information to environmental damage.

Sergei Kovalev was there, now president of the International Memorial Society, still a deputy in the Duma. The debate over whether human rights activity should be or can be non-political of course took place, and perhaps pride of place was Kovalev's contribution. After listing the worrying developments in the political sphere, he suggested that:

> The human rights community must react more strongly, than previously, to political developments. Politics – that's not our affair? Law is outside politics and above politics? Certainly, but only while politics does not threaten the basis of law and democracy, only as long as the primacy of law is recognized, and there is no attempt to turn law into an apparatus to serve politics. If such a danger arises, then the human rights community is forced to become 'politicized'.

What forms can this take? Kovalev suggested the expert monitoring of infringements and distributing the analysis, non-violent opposition – petitioning, picketing, boycotts, legal cases, and, if necessary, well-organized demonstrations. But none of this should take the place of everyday human rights work, and of working with other non-governmental organizations. Not all, probably not even a majority of the participants, agreed with him. Many of the new rights organizations abjured any kind of direct action, cooperation with the authorities heavily outweighed confrontation, and only a small minority wanted to engage in political opposition.

The organizers suggested that each section should discuss: 'those activities of the authorities, including legislative initiatives, that present a threat to human rights and freedom' and 'the changes that need to be made to laws and other normative acts, defining the rights of different groups of the population'. On this basis, they continued, 'it will be possible to work out both the demands to be made to the authorities, and strategy and tactics for national campaigns devoted to the most disturbing issues' while 'each section should devote time to discuss the problems facing NGOs — the increasing pressure from the state on the structures of civil society.'

And, finally, the organizers emphasized, a key objective of the congress is

> to present society with clear and well-argued evidence of the real threats to rights, freedoms and the lawful interests of individuals and social groups, in order to present a programme of action to counter those threats.

Unfortunately, they suggested, our citizens are not sufficiently aware of the 'rights clauses' in the constitution, and how to defend their rights through legal means. 'We, human rights activists, have considerable experience and must defend the constitution as it is.'

Quite a set of tasks, one might say, and quite unmanageable. Apart from different conceptions of what 'defending human rights' meant, the particular issues the activists worked on (prisoners, children, conscripts, the media, the environment) prompted different responses. Other factors too — the need for financial support, the variation in politics at local level, and political change at federal level — pulled organizations in different directions. Perhaps all they agreed on was that they had a right to exist as independent organizations, and to pursue their activities legally and by non-violent means. Imagine such a gathering in the UK. What would the participants agree on? And a programme of action — should that not be the task of political parties, professional associations, the media? The plenary sessions, and then the sections or panels, produced statements, heated discussion, and long resolutions, but no collective strategy.

Was there agreement on aims? That the government and the judges should obey the laws — yes — but, naturally enough, the participants held very different views on how and where the legislation needed to be changed. And, as regards legislative control of the new powerful corporations, this simply did not enter the picture. It was the state's misuse of its power that held their attention. Strategies? Regarding the state's and the judiciary's observance of the laws, the strongest weapon used so far was critical presentations at international gatherings, reports to UN committees, the Council of Europe or OSCE and, just beginning, the taking of cases to the European Court – but this only scraped the surface. How could government officials be brought to assume that they should implement instructions, fairly and legally? The justice system would have to be reformed, from within, but how to achieve that was far from clear. Campaigning for legislative reform was still in its infancy. And here the politics of the nineties had played an unhelpful role. The successes that had been achieved (penal reform, improvements to the criminal codes, compensation for the victims of Stalinist oppression) had come from having the right people in the right place at the right time, from being able to use political connections, not from being able to exercise the weight of organized political support. By 2000 even the liberal parties that did exist were not particularly interested in the human rights organizations.

Historically it has been groups with sufficient weight or support behind them who have compelled rulers to recognize their rights, get them written into law and then implemented by the justice system. The Russian activists hit the ground running at a time when 'the human rights agenda' was the name of the game but the institutional environment provided little entry into or influence upon political authorities. Meanwhile, with the constitution affirming a huge array of rights, including social rights, the property free for all and the pauperization of the population produced massive violations of basic rights. This would have presented any judicial system with intractable problems. The activists were faced, however, not only by a conservative state apparatus and a continental legal system inherited from the old order, with its detailed codes and emphasis on individual claims, but an environment in which trade unions, pressure groups, independent professional associations or charitable organizations, engaged in the defence of their constituents, or the poor and vulnerable, existed only on paper, if at all.

The equipment the new activists brought with them – a reliance on known and trusted friends, the ability and willingness to survive on a shoe string, enthusiasm but little organizational experience – and the resources they drew upon – Western ideas and Western funding, links with leading individuals, opportunities to experiment – had to be deployed with little support from either public or professional organizations. Many who included themselves under the human rights banner would, in other societies, or at other times, have called themselves supporters of civil liberties, or simply pressure groups with a specific focus (similar, for example, to the Howard League for Penal Reform, or the NSPCC in the UK) or have gone into politics. The human rights organizations found themselves trying to fill in the empty space between the state and its people, taking upon themselves tasks that in other societies are often filled by these kinds of organizations, and political parties.[8]

Could this be called a movement? No. Was it even a community? Yes, in the eyes of many of its members, and it was exhilarating to be part of such a large gathering in the Cosmos hotel. I can vouch for that. I had been sceptical initially, but then won over to provide some financial support. People left for the provinces with the feeling that they were part of something bigger. Surely their voices must carry weight in the political arena, even if the new president, Vladimir Putin, came from the security services? All too soon he would throw down the gauntlet, and they would need to respond. That is the subject of the next chapter.

PART 2

TAKING STOCK

CHAPTER 6

THE CIVIC FORUM OF 2001:
TO TANGO OR TO SIT IT OUT?

'Life', according to Veronika Marchenko of Mother's Right, 'has presented us with Hamlet's question – to be or not to be – while specifying the place and time of the action – the Civic Forum in Moscow in November. Each of us is trying today to find an answer, believing that the tragedy could end differently and we could rewrite it to spite the venerable Shakespeare.'

When carrying out interviews in 2010–11, I asked those who had been activists since the nineties whether any particular events, conferences or meetings, in their view, stood out as having been significant or important for the human rights community. I had expected some to mention the 2001 Extraordinary Congress or a 2004 conference on The Human Rights Movement Today, which appears in the next chapter. No one did. But almost all mentioned the Civic Forum. Why was this? Upon reflection, I think it was because the forum did several things simultaneously. It brought the human rights community face to face with the authorities, and compelled a decision – do we or do we not work with them; it showed what independent organizations had managed to achieve (what they were capable of) and simultaneously their limitations; it brought out their opponents too. In this sense it cleared the mist away. It allowed them, and allows us, to see how key actors within state and society – the political authorities, government ministries, the media, and NGOs – viewed each other in the summer of 2001.

****

In June 2001 a strange assortment of non-governmental organizations or associations were invited to the Kremlin to discuss the question of 'state and society' with President Putin and a group of political consultants. Among the 28 present were those from organizations for 'the development of civil society', women's causes, a media union, the beekeepers' association. A well-known conductor, and a cosmonaut were included. There were no human rights organizations.

Gleb Pavlovsky, an ex-dissident, a political consultant who heads a think-tank, the Foundation for Effective Politics, and was closely associated with the Putin administration, had already flown a kite in the newspaper, *Izvestiya*. Referring to organizations which focus on the environment, consumers, or provide social assistance, he argued that:

> Today this {civil} society is not represented by any parties, or organizations, nor by any lobbies that are well known to all, as it is in any Western or the other post-Communist societies [...] The task is to help them move out into public space, into the main media, into providing real public expertise, including that of advising on government decisions [...] the authorities do not have the right to ignore the existence of civil society, they must, for a start, listen to what it wants.[1]

The Moscow Helsinki Group received a telephone call, telling them that Liudmila Alekseeva should remain in the city on 12 June, because she might be receiving an invitation from the president to a meeting. But this did not materialize. Alexander Auzan, of the Consumers Confederation, had been invited to a meeting in the president's administration to discuss possible participants but, when the staff member said that they would not be inviting Memorial or the Moscow Helsinki Group 'because they broke up the Soviet Union', Auzan remonstrated and, as a result, his invitation was withdrawn.

At the meeting Putin echoed Pavlovsky's comments, speaking of the need, now that the state had been strengthened, of a constructive, continuous dialogue between 'the authorities as a whole and the aggregate of civil society [...] We are used to thinking that total responsibility for what happens in the country rests with the authorities

[. . .] but non-government organizations should share this responsi-bility'. After all, he stated, 300,000 are registered with the Ministry of Justice. And he referred to the fact that 'Very many non-governmental organizations exist today on grants from foreign organizations. That is not to our credit. Of course we support that kind of cooperation with international organizations but it is obvious that our civil society must develop on its own foundation, that's self-evident.'[2] Some of the participants gave this their enthusiastic endorsement in a leaflet:

> We are prepared to apply all our efforts to the further transformation of our Motherland and to share responsibility with the authorities for this. Its citizens need a great Russia – free and flourishing! It cannot be built without an effective state and a great society, and their agreement and joint labour.

How though to give society such a role? Aleksei Leonov, the cosmonaut, suggested that there should be a Civic Chamber, attached to the office of the president, an idea that Putin welcomed. Over the next two months, the press and Pavlovsky's website gave details of various proposals – for a Civic Forum or gathering, in September or October, to elect a Civic Chamber. It was claimed that 500 organizations, part of an NGO network 'We, the citizens!' set up by a Moscow academic, Nina Belyaeva, were preparing for this. A press conference was held by members of an organizing committee, which included both some who had attended the original June meeting and newcomers – Vyacheslav Igrunov, the early contributor to Memorial who had become a Yabloko deputy, and Ella Pamfilova, a well-known non-party politician, active since the early nineties, first as a deputy, then in government responsible for social policy issues. The committee was based in Pavlovsky's Foundation. Such a forum, it claimed, would aim 'to create a European society with a Russian soul' – to carry society's views to the authorities – but members of the organizing committee clearly had rather different views on how this should be done. One spoke of a chamber, one of whose 'important functions [would be] working out a consolidated position of the non-governmental organizations in a particular sphere'; another was more concerned with the forum as an occasion for focusing on ways of developing civil society; Igrunov suggested that 'the process of preparation may turn out to be more important than the gala event itself

[...] organizations must think how to work with their deputies [...] civil society cannot be divorced from political society, and political parties are themselves part of civil society'.[3]

Liudmila Alekseeva was invited to join the organizing committee but refused — how, she asked, could 5,000 delegates, however they were chosen, claim to be the representatives of civil society, and elect a chamber? A few days later she received another call — under what conditions would MHG participate? But, in the meantime, Vladimir Kartashkin, chair of the president's commission on human rights, had spoken on the radio of the importance of cooperation with constructive organizations, but not with those which 'unfortunately continue their destructive activities — those which have not forgotten their dissident past'[4] and contrasted Memorial unfavourably with the Moscow Helsinki Group. 'I responded that we shared the same views, and it was absurd to talk about us as constructive and non-constructive. So, now the next phone call came "Under which conditions would MHG and Memorial participate?" to which I replied that you need to speak to all of us.'

In an unprecedented move, Vladislav Surkov, a key figure in the president's administration, asked for a meeting with representatives of the human rights organizations. It was decided to invite him, the rest of the Kremlin party, and the secretary of the organizing committee, to such a meeting but to hold it in the Memorial offices, given that Memorial had been the subject of criticism. This, on 20 August, was the first of several meetings at which representatives of the two or rather three sides — the president's administration, the organizing committee, and leading human rights organizations — negotiated the conditions under which the latter were prepared to participate in a Civic Forum. Most, but not all, of the leading Moscow organizations participated in negotiating an agreement

Arseny Roginsky, from Memorial, argued:

the Civic Forum is just one episode in the development of civil society in Russia. It can turn out to be an important and necessary step, or a damaging one, or quite irrelevant. There's no guarantee on that score. However if, as a result, some mechanisms are created which will allow for continued dialogue between non-governmental organizations and the corresponding state structures, then the forum's objectives will have been fully achieved.

Journalist: But some say that you are constantly being deceived?

Roginsky: Before you can be deceived, you must first be seduced.
Nobody as yet has seduced us with anything. So, suppose we are
unable to defend our position — so what? The idea of establishing
real mechanisms of interaction between the state and society will
not be realized — that's all — and independent non-governmental
organizations will remain as they were before, and the authorities
will maintain their previous distance from independent civic
initiatives.[5]

But Lev Ponomarev was totally opposed:

It's already clear: the authorities are not interested in any real
dialogue with civil society. They have spat on the statements by
human rights activists on the mass infringements of human rights
in Chechnya, the torture and killings [. . .] Human rights activists
must oppose their politics, and the antidemocratic and antisocial
course adopted by the government [. . .] we do need arrangements
for meetings with the authorities but such arrangements must be
set up on the initiative of the organizations of civil society, we
should not behave like petitioners. We do not have the moral right
to turn ourselves into 'the leading reins' of the state.[6]

The organizing committee was reorganized, and human rights activists
were among the 5,000-strong gathering that met in the Great Hall in
the Kremlin on 21 November. Liudmila Alekseeva chaired the opening
plenary session. Sergei Kovalev was among the participants. But
Ponomarev refused to have anything to do with it, and Alexander
Podrabinek, editor of *Express Khronika*, was scathing:

'The entire country saw how the participants of the Civic Forum
gave a standing ovation to its favourite president, a man stained
with the blood of thousands of innocent victims of his Chechen
escapade. Everyone could observe the trained Cheka agent sitting
next to Liudmila Alekseeva, chairman of the Moscow Helsinki
Group, in a spirit of mutual understanding and unity. What
tolerance and goodwill! Supporters of the Civic Forum explained

their decision to participate by the need for dialogue with the government to create 'grounds for negotiations' [... but] they will keep on criticizing power within the necessary limits and depict equal rights dialogue under the approving glance of the strict Kremlin boss. The Civic Forum has turned into the beginning of the hopeless degradation of the human rights movement in Russia.[7]

What does the Civic Forum (from its appearance as an idea, then the negotiations, the planning, the event itself, and any outcomes) tell us of state–society relations ten years after the Russian Federation emerged as an independent state? And what should be the response from human rights organizations to overtures for some kind of an institutional dialogue from a regime, engaged in a war against some of its subjects, and curtailing the rights of others? Who, when the dust settled, had been right? Roginsky and Alekseeva or Ponomarev and Podrabinek? My task is to tell you as much as I can of the events surrounding the forum, and yours is then to decide.

The state of play in the summer of 2001

By now Putin had been in power for a year. In Vyacheslav Bakhmin's words:

> With the coming of Putin to power a system began to emerge. He's a person who thinks in terms of systems, he has to have everything organized, clear. He started by reorganizing business, then turned to the regional authorities, those were his priorities. He turned his attention to civil society, trying to understand what kind of a phenomenon it was. There was already a substantial number of organizations, many of them had made it into information networks, they were talked about, and he needed to understand what they were; he wanted to deal with them as he had with business, that is simply to create some kind of structure which would represent his interests, and he would interact with it, putting the pressure on when necessary, giving support when necessary.

And from Roginsky: 'We entered the Putin period with some important achievements. In those years [the Yeltsin years] in Russia 70–77,000 organizations which actually do something came into being [...] Looking around, we suddenly felt that we represented something significant in the life of Russia, we felt that we had some strength.' But as the authorities gradually moved towards electoral authoritarianism, removing the oligarchs from the political scene, controlling the Duma, and mass media, the activists recognized that the direction of the wind was changing.

The term 'civil society' had become part of the lexicon of democratic activists and scholars in Eastern Europe in the 1980s, denoting civic activity, independent of the state, seen as a crucial component of a democratic system. It quickly became widely used (and argued over) by their counterparts in Russia post-1991. 'Some aggregate of relationships and organizations, which act independently of the state and are able to influence it' but did this mean it included political parties, or were they somehow separate?[8] Scholars disagreed. Should it include racist or ultra-nationalist groups, or not? Where did the trade unions and the writers or artists' associations, with their buildings, bureaucratic structures, and welfare programmes fit in, if they did? The scholars debated the issues but, by 2001, were in general agreement: if one was talking of the new non-governmental organizations, civil society was weak. According to Kholodkovsky:

Despite the emergence of a substantial number of social organizations (we are talking of some tens of thousands of real organizations) [...] they still don't create the weather in Russia, they are not capable of producing the social atmosphere. Human rights organizations, consumer associations, the Soldiers' Mothers Committees and other similar structures selflessly defend human rights and social interests. They represent the real shoots of civil society in Russia but they are not yet strong enough to be equal partners of the authorities. Civic activity is drowning in an apathetic environment, occasionally achieving local successes but too often not strong enough to pierce the armour of bureaucratic indifference and self-interest.

The main traits of this new 'civil society', or 'third sector' as it was sometimes described (to distinguish it from 'politics' and 'business') were the following. First, while there might be 300,000 non-profit organizations registered with the Ministry of Justice, not only were most of these very small, with a handful of members, but many of them lived for a short while, and then faded away. A truer figure was 55–70,000 active organizations. Most of these were small. The majority were concerned with social issues – with children, those homeless or with disabilities, with invalids, the elderly, ex-prisoners, drug-users; there was a range of environmental groups, housing groups, the gardeners, hunting associations; then came the stamp collectors, artists, theatre groups, youth groups; and the human rights groups, which, as we saw, embraced a wide range of activities. As Roginsky put it: 'Non-governmental organizations are very different one from another. The only thing which they have in common is that they demand of the authorities that they create conditions, under which each of these organizations can be independent of the authorities and can develop.' Moscow led the field by a long way, both in terms of numbers and size of organizations, and their ability to get funding; then came the other major cities, but patterns of activity varied, and an organization might suddenly appear and prosper in a small town. So much depended on an active and committed individual, willing and able to stand up to or get support from the local authorities.

But if, as suggested by one commentator, a highly-developed imagination was needed to be able to talk of civil society, why did Putin pay any attention to it? The reasons, I suggest, were the following. While the majority of the population might have heard only of Memorial and the Soldiers' Mothers, several of the new organizations were visible to a Moscow audience, they received media coverage, and they and their criticisms of the Russian government were known on the international scene. (Kholodkovsky's choice of organizations was not accidental.) The Extraordinary Human Rights Congress in January 2001, funded by foreign donors, had attracted both opposition politicians and media attention. Then in April there was an embarrassing moment at the Civic Dialogue between Russian and German representatives, an official event held in St Petersburg, where the Russian representatives at the session on civil society were the Minister of Internal Affairs, a former prime minister, and political scientists. 'But where' asked the Germans, naming Memorial and others, 'where are the civil society organizations?' The Kremlin was put out, 'What, how can it be, that we don't have a civil society? Organize one quickly!' And Pavlovsky was given the task of taking it forward.[9]

There were other reasons too for Putin's interest. Boris Berezovsky, now fled to London, had set up an International Foundation for Civil Liberties, based in the USA, to fund Russian NGOs. Elena Bonner, Sakharov's widow, had accepted money for the Sakharov Foundation, so had Abramkin for his work with prisoners, and Soldiers' Mothers. There was talk of substantial funding to be forthcoming. By May, Berezovsky was talking of setting up a liberal-patriotic party. *Izvestiya* wrote of Berezovsky attempting to privatize, and Pavlovsky to nationalize, the NGOs.

According to Liudmila Alekseeva

> As a clever man, Putin began by wanting to see what this civil society was. I was told by someone, in private, (I haven't seen the report myself) [...] that before organizing the Forum he asked Gleb Pavlovsky to prepare an expert report on who the human rights activists are, the NGOs, and what they represent [...] and the person who saw the report told me that the section which gave details on how many human rights organizations there are, and what they do, was done very competently, but there was a question − on their motives − why do they engage in these activities? And here the answer was: motivations unclear [...] Because, it's true, people were not motivated for career reasons, or to make money, or even to earn gratitude. The population showed no particular signs of being grateful, and as for the authorities, forget it. Why then do the activists get involved? Pavlovsky could not come up with an answer.

As we have seen, people took up human rights activities for different reasons and, when we widen the picture to include all the non-governmental activists, the reasons multiply. It is difficult to talk of any shared views within this extraordinarily diverse NGO community as to what their relation to the state should be, and what they wanted of the political authorities. And, in their turn, the political authorities? It may be, as Bakhmin suggests, that Putin wanted some kind of a corporatist structure to play a part in a managed democracy. More interesting perhaps is the response of those to whom he turned for suggestions as to how to proceed.

Pavlovsky, and one of his young colleagues, Sergei Markov, advocated creating a structure to represent the sector. They were supported by the leader of a NGO, Maria Slobodskaya, who saw herself as a key figure in the development of 'constructive non-governmental initiatives', which should receive financial support from the government. (In conversation she suggested that organizations, such as Soldiers' Mothers, should be excluded.) But both Ella Pamfilova, and Vyacheslav Igrunov, with a more liberal cast of mind, came on board. The organizing committee struggled. At some point Vladislav Surkov, from the president's administration, architect of Putin's 'managed democracy', intervened – or perhaps simply took over. A gathering of NGOs, without the best known ones, which elected a chamber to represent the community, would not serve its purpose. This lay behind the approaches to the human rights organizations which, by the end of the nineties, had begun to play a role as the nucleus of a wider civil society.

Negotiations

Apart from some of the women's organizations, there were few civic or human rights organizations led by academics who continued to pursue an academic career.[10] An exception was the Confederation of Consumers' Societies, founded in 1989 by a group of well-known academics and of individuals who had established themselves as trustworthy 'queue-organizers' for deficit goods in the late Soviet period.[11] Alexander Auzan, an economist at Moscow State University, whose research focused on consumer markets, was elected president of the Confederation in 1990, and was still in post in 2001. By now a professor at Moscow University, energetic, a good speaker, a clear leader, he had become well known for his civic activities. The Consumers Confederation, in his view, was perhaps the most successful new movement of the 1990s.

> I put it down to the fact that our revolution was not a bourgeois revolution, not a liberal revolution, but a consumers' revolution. It was a revolution, by which I mean a transition from Soviet society, from a shortage economy to a society of demand. The wind of history filled the sails of consumerism. As a result, in the space of a very few years, we, strange eccentric individuals, became popular on the TV and in the press as thousands and then millions of people began to turn to court, watched TV programmes, read advice to consumers in the papers.

He came to know, and he respected, such people as Kovalev but their positions were very different. On meeting with Kovalev in 1993, who told him that what he was doing could not, strictly speaking, be called defending human rights, his answer was that he always bore in mind 'Mark Twain's comment that "books by great geniuses are wine, and mine – are water. Everyone drinks water". Defending consumer rights is a form of civic activity which almost everyone in the country understands, and, maybe it is a step towards understanding other rights.' Kovalev did not agree, but Liudmila Alekseeva became a firm friend. She wanted to know why the trade unions and ecologists seemed to lose their court cases, whereas the consumers won. According to Auzan, it is all a matter of rewriting the legislation so that it works in your favour. If for example 'moral damage' is defined as 'causing physical or moral suffering to an individual', then you can claim damages for poor service – by a dentist, airline, tourist company, for electricity cuts, or for a faulty microwave oven. Judges agreed. (After all, one is tempted to say, they suffered from such things as much as anyone else.)

But before Putin's presidency, Auzan was not really part of the Moscow human rights *tusovka* or 'talking shop'. Abramkin used to organize an evening for human rights activists on 6 January (the Russian Christmas Eve by the Old Calendar) at the Sakharov Centre at which many would gather but I do not remember Auzan (or Marina Pisklakova of ANNA, or any of the environmentalists) being present. Somehow consumer rights did not fit into human rights. By 2000 the Ford Foundation was supporting public interest law projects in many countries, and organized a conference that brought public interest lawyers from Latin America and Russia together in Moscow. A lawyer from the Consumers' Confederation gave a good presentation, but she seemed like a bird from a different world among those from the penal reform, army conscript or refugee organizations, even among the lawyers working on environmental issues or domestic violence. However, by the beginning of the new century, when some of the Moscow human rights activists started coming together on a regular basis, Auzan was among them. In his view

The nineties were a golden period for Russian civil society because the government neither provided any assistance to nor interfered, in any way, with civic organizations, while at the same time the environment encouraged them to develop freely. Yes, we knew each other, but we did not even use the word 'civil society', no one talked of civil society in Russia in the mid-nineties. Recognition of ourselves as a community came once the consolidation of the state started in Russia. [. . .] And, in so far as the state was getting stronger, the question arose – could we in any way influence the process in the absence of some process of consolidation within civil society?

By 2001 a group had formed which included representatives of Memorial, MHG, Zabelin from the Socio-Ecological Union, Auzan, Simonov from the Glasnost Defence Foundation, Averkiev from Perm, and others. This, which entitled itself the People's Assembly, met regularly to discuss topics of common concern, for example the tax code, and made representations to government departments. There was also a group called Common Action, dating from the January Extraordinary Congress. It included representatives from Memorial and MHG, and Ponomarev, Gannushkina, Simonov, Babushkin (Committee for Citizens Rights) and several activists from the regions. Both these 'talking shops' sent representatives to the meeting with Surkov in Memorial to discuss holding a Civic Forum.

Auzan suggests that Gleb Pavlovsky favoured expert communities as the core of civic activity but

> it seemed to me that I knew the expert community better than Gleb because from first hand experience I knew how far my colleagues were from the kind of civic activity that I, for example, was involved in. But the human rights activists could become such a nucleus, and they did – in 1999–2000 – and in a certain sense they still are today [2011].

Why could they play this role? In Auzan's view it owed a great deal to key individuals, such as Kovalev, Alekseeva, and Roginsky, thinking in wider terms than that of defending a particular 'right'. Memorial and MHG stood out as the leading organizations and, around them, not only some of the single issue human rights organizations but also the environmentalists and consumers association came together. Aleksei Simonov, who had set up the Glasnost Defence Foundation in the early nineties, was another key figure, known to all the journalists. And Auzan himself, we should add, contributed a respectable academic reputation, leadership of a large, well run organization, and the much needed ability to chair a discussion, to find points of agreement rather than disagreements, and speak to the point.

At the initial meeting with Surkov, the activists presented their key conditions for participation: no elections should be held to produce a Civic Forum, rather NGOs should send delegates; the sole purpose of the forum should be that of discussing ways to encourage dialogue between NGOs and government departments; on no account could or should such a gathering 'elect' a structure, a chamber, to 'represent' civil society. Throughout this, and all subsequent discussions, the activists stressed that parliament was the place where society's elected representatives met to take decisions, and that an elected forum or chamber would have no legitimacy whatsoever. Surkov was accommodating, but wished to leave the question of a future elected structure open for further discussion. It was agreed that a group of activists, Pavlovsky, and staff from the president's administration should hold further meetings to discuss these points, and the formation of a new organizing committee.

As Alekseeva put it:

> Briefly, Surkov agreed to all our conditions – there should be no elections [. . .] and we discussed it among ourselves and decided that, if they were prepared to agree to our conditions, it made no sense to refuse to participate. Auzan said that if we were in agreement on that then we must be part of the organizing committee, be in all the working groups, and work like horses. Because, for sure, they wouldn't. But we would, and hence the forum would turn out as we wanted. And that is what happened.

Members of the original committee had been busy sending messages out to the regions, advocating the setting up of civil society chambers – to raise the profile of civil society, to help society and state work together. Some human rights organizations, they argued, are prone to see the state as the enemy and that has got them into a dead end 'because now the key infringer of human rights are powerful interest groups, and in this situation the citizen should see the state as his main defender [. . .] while human rights' activists fight against the state and in this way promote the infringing of human rights'.[12] But, it seems, they had lost the ear of the president's administration. Over the next two weeks more than one meeting was held, until on 4 September the key points of an agreement were hammered out at a three-sided meeting between Surkov and Abramov (president's administration), Pavlovsky and Pamfilova (from the original organizing committee), and Auzan, Babushkin and Zabelin from the human rights community.

The key points were: the president's administration should openly declare its role as one of the participants in the forum; a new organizing committee should include representatives of the president's adminis-tration and government, of the old organizing committee, and of the human rights community; regions should present lists of delegates, to be ratified by the organizing committee; the forum should be devoted to ways to enhancing dialogue between NGOs and government; no elections should be held at the forum to leave a structure in place. All these decisions, including the financing of the forum and its budget, should be made public, and openness should characterize all further activities.

Not all the activists were happy. Elena Bonner suggested that while the war with Chechnya continued, any cooperation with the authorities was out of the question; Samodurov (from the Sakharov Centre), Ponomarev (For Human Rights), and Podrabinek (*Express Khronika*) were opposed. Memorial sent out a long document to all the local Memorial organizations, laying out the reasons why the Society's board had agreed to participate but emphasizing that they should take their own decisions.

By 17 September, a much larger organizing committee existed on paper but it was a working group of 21 individuals (seven each from the original committee, from state structures, and from 'the activists') that mattered. The activist members were Auzan, Simonov, Roginsky, Babushkin, Zabelin, Dzhibladze[13] and Alekseeva. For the next two months this working group, at protracted and exhausting meetings, devoted itself to organizing a two-day event that would bring 4,000 delegates of Russia's extraordinarily diverse civil society to Moscow to meet with representatives of the government.

By early October a budget of $1.8 million had been announced. The working group had agreed that the forum would focus on ways to develop civil society in Russia and its interaction with the state: on the mechanisms, priorities for dialogue, and on recommendations to the authorities regarding the guaranteeing of legal, economic and other conditions to allow for the effectiveness and development of civil society institutions. The regions were encouraged to send in lists of proposed delegates. A memo sent out on 12 October stated:

> Civil society is not the authorities' vassal, just as it is not their adversary. It is a natural and equal partner with the state in creating a strong and prosperous society. But an effective state is the natural partner of civil society in its day to day activities [...] We are convinced that a free and flourishing Russia is impossible without a dynamic, developing, responsible and innovative civil society.

Apart from these key actors, others too would play a part. We have referred to the academics, who were busy discussing civil society. They were perhaps the least important. But, at this time, there were still liberal academics who held positions in government ministries, or as consultants to members of the political leadership, and their advice could be helpful. Most of the government officials, the long-term civil servants, whether at federal level or in the regions, had little knowledge of and even less interest in the third sector. The Duma deputies showed no interest in becoming involved, neither did the political parties. The business community was busy with its own problems.

What strikes the observer (and was remarked on by some of the academics) is the absence of intermediaries, in the form of interest groups or political parties, between these new civic organizations and the state. The only interest groups, wrote one, are the elite oligarch groups, while the parties lack any grounding in social constituencies. But what of the media, the 'fourth estate', as it was sometimes referred to? In Moscow at least, it entered the fray. According to Auzan, the fact that Aleksei Simonov was part of the Moscow human rights community was important here. Simonov was a special case because

> Uncle Lyesha, as the journalists call him, son of the wonderful writer and poet Konstantin Simonov, has belonged to the world of literature and journalism since he was in nappies. And he is someone who defended the Communist press in 1993 when Yeltsin tried to close it down, and the liberal press in recent years. So all the journalists trusted him. And we understood that when Lyesha Simonov stood side by side with us, the press, regardless of their view of what we were doing, would not shoot us down.

The journalists welcomed the opportunity to write about the disagreements within the non-governmental community and wrote extensively of the unfolding 'drama' and the event itself. A very acrimonious exchange of views between well-known members of the ex-dissident community at the Sakharov Centre (where Kovalev and Alekseeva defended participation) was reported at some length. But, in general, journalists gave very different voices a hearing – whether those of the activists, Pavlovsky, or Abramov from the president's administration, who was still hankering after 'the setting up of a body whose members will organize discussions on different levels, including at presidential level, but not all in the organizing committee support this'.[14] By the time the Civic Forum opened, the Moscow press and a couple of websites were devoting daily articles to the topic. Banks and oligarchs were approached with enquiries as to whether they had been asked to contribute funding. While they refused to mention sums, it was clear that they had. The most expensive item was travel and hotel accommodation for the 3,000 plus delegates from the regions. The Moscow contingent dwarfed the rest.

By early November 60 of Russia's 89 regions were showing signs of drawing up lists of potential delegates to be forwarded to the organizing committee for approval. Ten were simply silent. Dzhibladze's organization was sending out an information email bulletin (*Grazhdanka!*), which kept its readers abreast of developments. The committee also had a website. By now it had been agreed that after a plenary session participants would attend one or more 'negotiating tables' or discussion sessions with relevant members of the government and their officials. It was Surkov who had suggested that government officials should be brought in. The task of the working group was to decide the themes for these 'negotiations' and who should be in charge of organizing them. In all 21 were agreed, ranging from 'Local self-government and local community' to 'Military reform, military service and human rights', from 'Public health and the environment' to 'The youth movement and youth policy'. All would gather for a final session, chaired by Mikhail Kasyanov, the prime minister, at which the recommendations of each negotiating session would be presented by one of its members.

Pavlovsky and Belyaeva were still talking of the forum becoming institutionalized, in some way or other. Auzan wrote of the disagreements within the working group on this score. The 'political technologists' wanted to organize a structure of representatives of NGOs from the top downwards, a structure that could influence the press and put pressure on the Duma; the activists themselves wanted none of this, rather that there should be 'coalitions, complex working groups, which would meet to discuss key issues', and a system of 'sluices' by means of which government officials and working groups would meet for discussions. According to Alexander Oslon, a sociologist and member of the original committee 'the human rights activists were, are and always will be frosty with distrust. For one simple reason – they are emotional people. But today the distrust level has dropped to such an extent that it is possible to work together.' Is it going to be possible to organize the negotiating tables, the reporter asks? 'As far as I know Putin will instruct all ministers and top officials to be at the disposal of organizers on the day of the Forum.' But, Oslon continued, it is quite difficult to imagine Kasyanov, the prime minister, spending two days going from one table to another. 'In fact, the Forum will not be an easy test for the authorities too, after all for many officials it will be the first time that they meet with this far from straightforward audience. So, I think there will be some opposition from the side of the officials [. . .] We'll see.'[15]

Sceptical journalists raised their voices. Why should one assume that government officials would be interested in attending negotiating tables? A recent roundtable on a draft law to allow public observers into the penal institutions, attended by Duma representatives and members of the prison service, had been ignored by the prosecutor's office and the Ministry of Justice.[16] Perhaps the Forum would change this?

Roginsky agreed with Oslon that 'very complex relations persist', seemingly little things provoke disagreements, for example the singing of the state hymn (the original Stalin hymn that had been brought back by Putin) at the opening of the forum. 'We in Memorial took a position – we won't stand [. . .] but I hope it won't come to this – the hymn after all is for state occasions, and not for social events.'[17] And it did not. The organizing committee decided that Liudmila Alekseeva should chair the opening plenary session, at which Putin would speak first. How embarrassing it would be, she pointed out, if she did not stand when the president did. The idea of the hymn died a quiet death.

The Civic Forum itself

The Forum got off to a bad start. Long queues of delegates moved increasingly slowly through the check points at the two postern gates

into the Kremlin. Whereas in Soviet times the holding of a party
congress always went smoothly, this time (for whatever reason) only two-
thirds of the delegates were in the Great Hall when, 45 minutes late, a
decision was taken to open the proceedings. Liudmila Alekseeva and the
rest of the speakers were in place.

> We had agreed that the speakers would go in turn – one from the
> government, one from the NGO sector. And, given that I was to
> open the proceedings, I got there early, and had the list of speakers.
> The head of the protocol department came up to me and asked to
> see the list. He was not at all happy. 'What is this? First there
> should be these, and then those.' I said to him 'This is the list.
> Go and open the meeting. I am following the organizing
> committee's instructions'.

Putin stepped briskly out of the wings, and we rose to our feet. Liudmila
Alekseeva gave the floor to the president, who, after a short statement of
welcome, passed the baton to the first of the speakers. They included
several members of the organizing committee (Auzan so hoarse from
negotiating during the past week that he could hardly speak), the chair
of the Duma, a Constitutional Court judge, the ombudsman [...] but, in
all honesty, the audience was engrossed in observing Putin, and many
delegates could not resist the opportunity to present him with
documents, leaflets, books, letters and petitions. They brought these
down the aisles to his assistants or security guards, who placed them on
the long table, at which he was sitting, together with Liudmila
Alekseeva. The piles grew. He looked at some. After perhaps an hour, he
explained that, while it was more interesting to be here rather than
engaging with mundane affairs of state, he had to leave to attend to
them. He also, with a smile, said he was surprised by a request from one
delegate for a joint photograph, and by another, given this was a civil
society gathering, asking *him* to remove the chair of a non-governmental
association. His assistants carried the piles of materials out after him.
As Bakhmin commented: 'I was amazed when, from among the 5,000
present in the Kremlin Hall, so many began to bring him petitions, and
he piled them up. He was amazed too, and he asked, what kind of a civil
society are you if you respond to the authorities in this way?'

Does that mean that Putin himself, and state officials, feel comfortable with such a relationship? It is said that in the nineties, on the day Yegor Stroev, the elected representative to the Federal Council, held his weekly meeting with his constituents in Orel, the queue would form, the black Volga appear and Stroev emerge, to go down the queue, listening in turn to the requests, granting some, refusing others. The landowner speaking to his serfs? But Stroev himself had had a long career as a party official, and this suggests that perhaps we should look to a more recent past. The results of a survey, conducted in 2004, led its authors to conclude 'The majority of our citizens, including those who are liberal minded, think of rights as something given to them by the state.'[18] But then of course that was the way it had been under the Soviet system. Was it so surprising that, when re-registering the Ford Foundation's office and its programme, in the late 1990s, the Chamber of Commerce queried the programme on support for the defence of human rights with the statement that it was the Russian government's job to defend its citizens' rights? Yes, indeed, but hence the dilemma – because governments so often fail to do so.

The 21 negotiating sessions that followed were almost all organized and chaired by members of the organizing committee, some of whom took on responsibility for more than one. Roginsky and Orlov were in charge of 'Chechnya [. . .] ways to achieve peace and agreement', Alekseeva, together with Belyaeva, took on 'Civic control and civic expertise', Dzhibladze had two – one on tolerance, another on the legal and economic preconditions for effective NGO activity, while Babushkin and Abramkin organized 'Guaranteeing human rights in the justice and penal system'; Simonov was responsible for 'Open sources of information from the state', Auzan for 'A social contract: society – business – government', and for 'Local self-government. . .', Igrunov, Grafova and Gannushkina organized several on migration policy, forced migrants and refugees. The idea behind these 'negotiations' ('*peregovornye ploshchadki*'), a term consciously chosen to distinguish them from one-off roundtables, was that civic activists and government officials should sit down to discuss issues, and plan ways to maintain such a dialogue in future. Did they work?

All agreed that some achieved something, others very little. For a start, they took place all over the city, and there were delegates from the provinces who either never managed to find the location or decided to go shopping instead. According to Alekseeva:

The part that should have been organized by the president's administration was very badly done. I subsequently said that if we ever again organize a joint event, then let those who work [in MHG] first give you a training seminar on how to organize things so that people aren't waiting up half the night to get their travel expenses. The discussion sessions were all over Moscow, and people were struggling through the snow to find them. Key individuals did not turn up at all the sessions. But the Forum itself was all right. And they observed our agreements. We had warned them that if they begin some kind of voting, I would rise and leave the hall, asking others to do the same. There weren't that many of us – 400 out of 5,000 – but they did not want a scandal, and everything went smoothly.

While attendance by government officials at the plenary had been ordered from above (in the words of one commentator 'from the faces of the officials it was obvious that they were bored out of their minds and only wanted to leave as quickly as possible') participation at the negotiating sessions depended upon one's immediate superior. Liudmila Alekseeva noted that, at the discussion on civic control:

> Very few came – we made a whole list of those who should participate in the discussion but all we got was a deputy minister of justice, and someone from the central electoral commission – and at the negotiations when we had to work out some concrete measures, there were no representatives from the prosecutor's office, nor from electoral commission, just two young women who weren't clear why they were there.

Gannushkina and Grafova wrote to Kasyanov on the failure of either the Minister of Internal Affairs or a deputy minister to respond to proposals for discussions, despite their new responsibilities now that the federal migration service had been abolished. Furious exchanges did occur – for example between the president's press spokesman and Kovalev over the war in Chechnya – and disagreements were marked at the session on army reform but some concrete suggestions, or agreements on future meetings, were presented at the final session, chaired by Kasyanov, the prime minister.

How did the activists assess the event at the time? Roginsky, as always, refused to dramatize it – some discussion had taken place, and it was good that it did not always work like clockwork because that showed it was not a stage-managed imitation of a meeting.

Are the authorities willing to share their power? asks the reporter.

There can't be any sharing of power. Our ambitions do not go that far. Power is power, and as such its holders are authorized to take decisions. Our responsibility is to make proposals. And to put a well-argued case to the authorities, if their decisions seem to us to be wrong – that is what is called 'public expertise'. And to track how they are implemented – that's called 'civic control'.

To talk about equal rights is very naïve, he continues, 'Half the officials a few weeks ago had no suspicion that non-governmental organizations existed', and some of the organizations see themselves as clients of the state in order to obtain all sorts of benefits so how could they be 'partners'? But, he suggests, the use of phrases 'equal partners, negotiations, dialogue, civic control' has introduced new terms into the political rhetoric.[19]

He expanded these comments in an article for the Memorial bulletin: 'there is a large group of non-governmental organizations which view their relationship with the state in the old categories – the authorities are the source of all and any "goods", the organizations relate to the authorities exclusively in the role of petitioners'. The Civic Forum got press attention, including a lot of hostility, and scepticism. Why? Human rights organizations are seen as oppositionists, and the press sees itself as the intermediary between the authorities and the people, and therefore is not happy with the 'new role' of human rights organizations. And the political parties too were upset. 'But what is interesting is that the journalists' criticism of human rights organizations for participating meant that they were actually upholding the idea that NGOs must be independent.' His conclusion 'In some sense, what did not happen at this event (i.e. the creation of an organ which usurped the right to speak for civil society) is as important as what did' was one shared by many.[20]

Liudmila Alekseeva referred to a radio broadcast, where she was asked to choose one of the following three statements: 'the Forum was a sincere endeavour on the part of the authorities to have a dialogue with society', 'The Forum was a wish to build society under the authorities' control', and 'the Forum was simply an empty bureaucratic idea'. 'When I was asked which answer I would give, I said: "I can't give you one answer because, the Forum was all three rolled into one". To some extent the authorities recognized that a civil society already exists in Russia and wants to have some active contact with it. But are our authorities capable of partnership or are they in thrall to a grasping-domineering instinct – only time will tell.'

And Vyacheslav Igrunov, surprisingly perhaps for a democrat and a liberal, favoured continuation of such meetings once a year:

> After all such meetings are not, as it were, meetings with workers and collective farmers, but with the most active citizens, who bring with them 'the pulse of life'. A meeting with them could help both the president and the government to recognize new problems, to feel life's demands.[21]

The critics and the aftermath

A publicist, Leonid Radzikhovsky, wrote a damning critique as the forum opened. Reminding the reader of the old Russian tradition of meetings where 'the people' directly tell the Tsar 'the whole truth', a tradition mocked by both Dostoevsky and Gogol, he refers to 'the inappropriate meetings from the tsarist Duma to the Congress of Peoples' Deputies'. Nothing exciting could be expected from the Civic Forum, which would also be managed, but why was it needed? The assembling of 'the people', he argued, is seen as necessary because the 'parliament' doesn't work as a representative body whereas 'if it, and its lobbyists, was working, it would seem odd to collect "the people"'. As it is, he continued, the Civic Forum is attracting little interest from society:

> And this suggests we should think about the relationship between the authorities and society in Russia. The democrat and liberal continually moan that we don't have a civil society. Two postulates underlie this statement: a presumption of the guilt of the state, and of the innocence of civil society. First, that civil society, i.e.,

the aggregate of social organizations, political parties, the independent press and so on, is significantly 'better' than the authorities, the state, or officialdom – it's closer to the ideals of democracy and liberalism. Secondly, that the authorities, officialdom, and so on, from every side squeeze this very civil society, do not allow a hundred flowers to bloom, they have even thought up the forum in order 'to take them under control'.

Both these postulates, he argues, are as old as Russian public opinion. Society remains very primitive, and the authorities are a police power, similar to that of Nicholas I; at local level things are still at the level they were in Gogol's *The Inspector General*. Sending letters to Putin regarding the infringements of human rights in Chechnya has no effect. What is needed, he concludes, 'is a parliament'.[22]

Criticism from (liberal) party politicians and parliamentary figures was surely theoretically correct from a democratic point of view. Gennady Seleznev, the speaker of the Duma, pointed out that all draft laws first went through a parliamentary hearing, with experts present, and that the Duma had a council of NGOs to assist in its work. Vladimir Ryzkhov, a young democratic deputy, expressed it more strongly:

the Civic Forum was a profanation [...] dialogue should be through elections, with strong political parties, with local self-government, the independent press, NGOs, with the business community [...] each of which in its town, village, or region – achieves its rights, including through an independent court system – that's what is civil society.

while Sergei Mitrokhin, from Yabloko, quoting an ex-prime minister 'Well, give us your proposals, and we'll stack them up all together in one place',[23] suggested the same would happen for those from the forum. While all this might be true, neither the Duma nor political parties were managing to pursue or defend the rights and interests of the majority of the population, and hence such criticisms left them with questions to answer.

Events shortly afterwards were not encouraging. Memorial and MHG wrote a letter to the president on 26 December expressing their dismay at his decision to dissolve the commission on amnesties. Grigory Pasko, an environmental campaigner, who had been the spokesman for the session on access to information at the Civic Forum, and greeted with applause, was subsequently found guilty of publishing restricted materials and sentenced to imprisonment. A year later, pardoning had been drastically curtailed; nothing had come over proposals to demilitarize Chechnya; draft legislation on prison visitors was stalled, and a disappointing variant of the law on alternative service for army conscripts had been passed.

In 2004 Surkov returned to his idea of a chamber of civic organizations to assist the president and government on policy initiatives, and to disburse grants in an annual competition. Legislation, passed in 2005, provided for the president's appointing 42 members, they in turn choose 42 more from among Russia-wide associations, the 84 choose a further 42 from among regionally-based NGOs. The first session of the Civic Chamber was held in 2006. Academician Velikhov, a respected elderly physicist, was appointed secretary. Several members of the original organizing committee were given seats, as was the occasional oligarch, TV personality, and defence lawyer. None of the troublesome human rights organizations, and not even Auzan, were included,[24] but over the years (the Chamber has a three-year term of office) a few respectable campaigning organizations have been brought in. No claim was made that this Civic Chamber represents civil society.

Bakhmin suggests:

Putin understood [from the Civic Forum], that they [the NGOs] are pretty weak structures, very ill assorted, they do not have any real strength of their own and, more than that, they are oriented towards the government, they ask the government for assistance [. . .] It seems to me that this was some kind of a turning point: he understood that nothing new will come out of this in the near future and there is no real strength in this society. The theme of civil society was taken off the agenda for a while.

But at least the human rights and other organizations were left largely alone until 2006. And Putin recognized that it was useful to have contact with the leading organizations, and that they would speak their minds. He dissolved Kartashkin's commission on human rights and in 2004 set up a President's Council for the Advancement of Civil Society and Human Rights, headed by Ella Pamfilova, to which she invited several of the leading human rights activists, and which we see in action in later chapters.

By 2005 the sky had darkened. In the December 2003 elections to the Duma the barrier for party representation was raised to 7 per cent, and the remaining small 'liberal' parties failed to make it. Kovalev was out. United Russia, the president's party, swept the board, while the Communist party and Zhirinovsky's Liberal Democratic party, both willing to play the part of a loyal opposition, retained some seats. In the spring of 2004 Putin won the presidential election for a second term of office. September 2004 saw a tragedy in Beslan, down in the Caucasus, when Chechen Islamic militants, demanding the withdrawal of federal troops from Chechnya, took more than 1,000 hostage in a school in a neighbouring republic; its storming by the federal army brought the deaths of 334 hostages, including 186 children. Georgia, and then Ukraine, witnessed unprecedented action on the streets, with NGOs playing a part, which brought in new rulers. In December 2004, after mass protests, the election results in neighbouring Ukraine were overturned, and the pro-Western Yushenko returned as president.

These developments brought a tough response from the Putin regime. Regional governors were to be appointed, not elected. And, according to Bakhmin,

> Putin understood that some civic organizations could play the role of some kind of intermediary structures, through which, he felt, certain Western forces could exert an influence on the situation in the country. That made an impression upon him, and the examples of the successful orange revolutions in Georgia and especially in Ukraine, really scared the authorities. And they straightaway began to pay attention to the youth, and the human rights organizations, and civic activists.

As the Civic Chamber began its work in 2006, a new law on NGOs introduced stringent registration and reporting procedures (with the Ministry of Justice and tax officials) which threatened the ability of many to exist, let alone function. Western foundations and Western funding came under heavy attack. In the spring of 2006 a spy scandal erupted: a British embassy official, responsible for a programme of support for human rights organizations, was photographed using a fake stone as a cover for a transmitter to contact agents and download information.[25]

Looking back ten years later, those who had supported participation in the forum reckoned it had been worth it. For Dzhibladze the Civic Forum was the first attempt to control society but 'Then we were strong enough to say to them – Come out of the shadows [. . .] and we had a number of supporters in the government, and in the Ministry of Economic Development.' He reckons that until 2004 civil society organizations grew stronger, better able to work with state and with society but after Beslan everything changed. Auzan views as fruitful the years until the arrest of Khodorkovsky, the oil oligarch who criticized Putin, at the end of 2003, and 'the war by the state against society was delayed for three to four years – we became the object of attack from a stronger authoritarian regime not in 2001 but in 2005'. What else was gained? 'Did we achieve our aims? No, in the sense that civil society does not have the influence it had in 2001. But it was worth doing.' It was one step along the path of establishing conditions for a dialogue between officials and civic organizations: all those terms – equal partners, negotiations, protocols – changed the format of meetings and laid the basis for a new culture, where an agenda, points of discussion, and decisions are noted.

Alexander Daniel, from Memorial, partly agrees:

there was the idea of setting up 'negotiating tables' at different levels [. . .] they proved to be ineffective and short lived, but some still exist and there are public councils attached to some of the ministries. And as regards the Civic Chamber? Yes, it is some kind of a superstructure over part of the non-governmental organizations in the country, but only over some of them. And of course in that structure the state wishes to have the driving wheel, as it does, but I cannot say that it is a wholly useless organization. It does quite a few useful things. And sometimes it demonstrates a certain independence. To put it briefly, it has not become particularly harmful, but at the same time neither has it become particularly useful as an organization.

So, albeit with the wisdom of hindsight, which still leaves questions that are difficult to answer, how would you, as a human rights activist, have replied to Veronika Marchenko in 2001? Would you have participated or refused to engage?

CHAPTER 7

ACTIVISTS AND POPULAR ATTITUDES

In 2004 Aleksei Korotaev, someone with both Russian and international experience, suggested to his fellow activists:

> We talk about human rights in terms of the UN declarations. Victims usually express themselves in quite other ways [...] There's no public demand in this country for what's called 'the defence of human rights' [...] I organize a minimum of two, and sometimes four or five seminars a year on the UN system of defending human rights – the theory, mechanisms etc. [...] and the only real conclusion that I can draw is that no one except the human rights activists, who are happy when I come, is the slightest bit interested in the UN system. It helps them to feel that they are part of some worldwide activity.

If, by the new century, increasing pressure from the Kremlin posed one problem for the human rights organizations, public indifference was another. To many it seemed time to think hard about why they, and the values they championed, were failing to attract a response from their fellow citizens. Tanya Lokshina and Sergei Lukashevsky, who had left the Moscow Helsinki Group to set up an 'analytic centre', Demos, headed an initiative to bring leading activists, specialists in public opinion survey research, sociologists, and the new PR experts together to undertake research, discuss the issues facing the human rights community, and come up with recommendations. This, in itself, reflected the presence of a younger generation of activists. Both Khodorkovsky's Open Russia foundation and Western funders supported the project and further research.

The issues that concerned activists of both older and younger generations included the challenges from the international and domestic environment, the 'war on terror' following the 9/11 attack in the USA, the arrest of Khodorkovsky earlier that year, and Putin's re-election to a second term. Sessions on all these issues featured in a 2004 conference, part of the project, but here we focus on the session devoted to the lack of public support.[1] We start with popular attitudes towards rights and to activists, before turning to the activists' perceptions, and conclude by looking again at the different elements that made up the human rights community.

Popular attitudes towards rights

The ending of Communist party rule had been accompanied by huge expectations that not only would personal freedoms exist (to speak out, to travel abroad) but that living standards would rise, while free medical services and pensions would continue to provide security in sickness or old age. Instead the majority experienced extreme insecurity and impoverishment, while a privileged few enriched themselves. Disillusionment with the ability of a free press and electoral freedoms to produce politicians who would remedy the situation became widespread.

Dmitry Dubrovsky (a young sociologist, teaching human rights at the Smolny Institute in St Petersburg) adds another dimension to the arguments we have heard from Orlov and Auzan.

> Rights were understood not as civil rights, not as something positive, rather they were negative – against the Soviet Union, against authoritarianism, against the Communist party. When all that disappeared, it became apparent that there was no shared agenda [...] Everyone holds the strange view that the movement against the Soviet Union was necessarily a movement for civil rights. But it was not like that. People think the same way about an anti-colonial movement – that it is necessarily a democratic movement, when it is not necessarily anything of the sort. It was

the same in Russia. There was an anti-totalitarian, anti-Soviet, anti-Communist movement but not one that, unfortunately, had any clear conceptions of civil rights. At that moment there was a spontaneously evolving 'democratic' platform, with very wide margins and a confused concept of freedom of speech, because freedom of speech was absolutely critical, as in February 1917. Then the consensus evaporated, and the liberals played a part in this because, upon coming to power, they claimed that the economy would now advance, democracy would catch up and everything would be fine.

Nationwide survey research, repeated annually since the 1990s by the Levada Centre, which asks the respondents 'Which of the following human rights do you consider are the most important?' always shows 'the right to life' leading the field. But it is very difficult to interpret what ticking this box really means, especially in comparison to some other options. By the middle of the first decade of the new century, the following (in this order) continued to be prioritized: 'The right to free education, medical assistance, security in old age, and when sick'; 'the right to well-paid work according to one's specialization'; 'the inviolability of personal life and housing'; 'the right to a state-guaranteed minimum subsistence level'. By 2010 'the right to own property' had just pushed 'the right to a state-guaranteed minimum subsistence level' out of fifth place. The list does not include, for example, the right to a fair trial, but it is clear – as the commentators observe – that the rights of freedom of speech, or of electing one's representatives are rated as far less important than those above.[2]

In 2001 the Levada Centre carried out a nationally representative survey designed by Sarah Mendelson and Theodore Gerber, two American scholars, which included questions on the strength of support for eight specific rights, listed in the Universal Declaration of Human Rights. These were: freedom from arbitrary arrest, freedom of religion, the right to work, freedom of expression/information, freedom from torture, the right to a minimal standard of living, the right to own property, and the right of free association. The responses suggested that rights concerning a minimum standard of living, private property, and a job enjoyed the most support, with freedom from torture following closely behind, and then freedom from arbitrary arrest.

Support for the others was more qualified, and weakest of all was support for free association.[3]

Other surveys in the early 2000s show little interest in the rights of association, or in joining a trade union. Very few people participated in any voluntary or social activity. Most, when faced with an infringement of their rights, do nothing; a quarter of the respondents stated they would be prepared to turn to court; very few would be prepared to participate in a protest.[4] However, according to the findings of a survey conducted for the 2004 conference: 'In fact the population reacts quite sharply to the infringement of these [personal and civil] rights – but mainly when it involves abuse and injustice by officials, the police, or various bosses and leaders'. And when asked 'what would be more important for the future well-being of Russia?' given a choice between civil rights and freedoms or a system of vertical power, 38 per cent opted for civil rights compared with 31 per cent for vertical power.[5] Prioritizing socio-economic demands at a time of impoverishment does not necessarily mean a preference for authoritarian rule.

But these kind of surveys can only tell one so much. How did people think about human rights? In 2003 Igor Averkiev offered an answer, based on the 3–5,000 individuals who each year turned to the Perm human rights centre. Human rights are 'the defence an ordinary person has against the rich and powerful'. Particularly for the elderly, it is not important whether the offender is the state, a corporation, neighbour, or a relative. Human rights are 'my shield against arbitrariness, injustice, stinking injustice, and blatant lawlessness', those actions that affect basic aspects of my life – housing, work, my pension. 'I don't necessarily want to go to court, I should not have to pay for a defence lawyer, any way it's all sewn up [...] If you are a human rights defender, you should assist me', if needs be with a phone call to the relevant person. Although not usually voiced as such, there is an assumption that human rights are for the poor, because the rich can pay for what they want. And, there is simple confusion – 'all my rights are human rights because they are "rights" and I am "human"'.[6]

At the 2004 conference Yury Dzhibladze echoed this with:

> When people react positively to the term 'rights-defence' or 'defending human rights', it may well be because these terms include the word 'defence', and not because they believe in

adopting an active civic stance or because they share these values. It's rather, if you like, that people see the terms through the prism of their paternalistic views. Someone, a human rights activist, cares about them, and would help to mend a leaking roof.

And the sociologists conclude that:

> the main problem is that the average citizen has a superficial conception of his or her rights as such. There is no awareness of the values of rights and freedoms. What are rights, in such a view? They are always something very personal, individualistic. People do not talk of rights as shared values [. . .] in our society the values of collectivism are not recognized. In the minds of our citizens, rights – that's something that they need, that is in their interest [. . .] they are what is due to a person.

The explanation they offer 'for the persistent character of these beliefs' is that 'the majority of citizens, including those who hold liberal views, perceive rights as something given to them by the state'.[7] As I suggested in the previous chapter, they were given by the state in the Soviet period, and many reappeared in the 1993 constitution. Its new civil and political rights, with the emphasis on international conventions, also came from above, not after a long process of protracted bargaining, or even a roundtable where opposing groups hammered out a compromise position (the parliamentary attempt had ended in deadlock). They owed their inclusion to Yeltsin's wish to retain the support of the democrats and to have support from Western governments. The constitution may have won the support of the majority in a popular vote but that did not mean that all understood it in the same way. What then did the population think of the human rights activists?

Popular attitudes towards human rights activists

'A normal person should be doing three jobs, so as to be able to feed his family, and not be concerned with defending the Chechens.'[8]

Yury Levada, the father of public opinion research, referred to the post-Soviet Russian citizen as 'passive, patient, and sly' – in other words as very little different from his Soviet counterpart. And indeed the daily struggle to feed a family, or get medical care, the disillusionment with democratic politics and its assumed benefits made the survival tactics of the Soviet period as relevant as before. Trust and rely on those whom you know; use personal connections in the first instance, find a patron; if there is an organization that will help solve your problem, try it, but don't expect too much; be wary of engaging in collective action, at most in a one-off mass protest to achieve a concrete result. Two examples, both of behaviour, and of attitudes towards activism are quoted in the research report by Elena Rusakova.

> If a person comes up against a real, actual threat (for example, a son is conscripted into the army), and attempts to defend him, this is viewed as absolutely normal behaviour (and the individual is not seen as a human rights activist) [...] But if someone is continually involved in this activity, that is in helping not only 'her own' – she becomes seen as 'strange', is viewed ironically, with puzzlement.

Yet this surely is not a good example because the Soldiers' Mothers were taking up the cases of other people's sons, and this was viewed sympathetically. More revealing is the following: religious lessons are about to be made compulsory in a school; several of the parents object but none are prepared to respond to the suggestion from one that they should write a joint letter to the director of the school; no, they each prefer to deal individually with him.

The sociologists draw attention to a social norm – it is unwise to tilt at windmills. 'People straightaway begin to relate to someone who is prepared to participate in civic activity, public activity, even if they react positively to them, as a "marginal individual".' A human rights activist will probably be categorized as someone who could not make it on a professional level, maybe as someone without a profession, a dilettante. Young people refer to them as 'strange', 'cranks'. Quite kindly, they may be described as the 'holy fools' of today. In other words, the sociologists suggest, there are strong norms of acceptable or sensible behaviour and 'for the majority of the population (but not for all!) an active civic position – is an infringement of an established norm of behaviour'. If the activists are described as 'helping people', then the respondent is more positive. However, it depends upon whom. Where a justice system is serving the majority of the population badly, there may be little sympathy for those who defend minorities against discrimination – 'why are they fussing about them, when judges treat us all so badly?' [9]

But, most people simply do not know what human rights activists do. Those with higher education might manage to name Memorial, the MHG and Soldiers' Mothers, but others have difficulty in naming even Memorial. The respondents in the 2004 interview survey claimed to know practically nothing of human rights organizations, but they 'knew' the following: first, if human rights organizations are defending rights they must be state agencies, funded by the government; second, some provide free legal aid, but they are obliged to do this and cannot charge for it; and third, there are some organizations, staffed by 'dissident-types', who fight for ethical issues and justice, and they will disappear when they have achieved their aims. In general, the assessment – where it was proffered – was quite positive. The Rusakova research suggests that the public response to the activists, while perhaps not so positive, was ironic rather than hostile. After 2004 the emphasis in the media on their receiving Western funding, and then the spy scandal saw a more negative response, but this was short lived. Some thought of the activists as politicians but as 'unsuccessful politicians', and were hard put to distinguish between them. A much more widespread attitude was that 'it's not clear what on earth they are doing' and there was little interest in knowing more.

All the above refers to the general public. When level of education is introduced, the better educated know more, and respond more positively. It is a pity government officials were not asked for their views. In an interesting experiment, conducted by the Independent Council of Legal Expertise, judges, prosecutors and defence lawyers, when asked for theirs, came up with a very negative picture of 'highly politicized individuals who, instead of producing concrete information, talk in general phrases, they can behave with little tact, interrupt or argue with judges' but, when presented with a list of individuals whom they did not know to be human rights activists, 'gave them positive ratings as good defence lawyers'.[10] People who had been helped by a human rights organization, not surprisingly, were grateful but, as we saw earlier in Auzan's comments, that made them no more willing to then help the organization, financially or otherwise. And, as someone commented, 'It's mostly poor people whom the activists help, and they haven't any money, and the rich aren't interested.'

The activists' perceptions of the problem

All agreed that they lacked popular support but they did not necessarily agree on the reasons for this. Most of those present at the conference in 2004 probably assumed that they shared a common creed (the Universal Declaration of Human Rights) and that this set them apart from their fellow citizens. But Igor Averkiev threw down the gauntlet by arguing that, while 'human dignity' was an inalienable part of being human, part of the problem was the Declaration itself:

> The spirit and the letters of the Declaration – that's the only thing that we can, today, understand as human rights. I don't feel very happy with this but today there is no other paradigm. Therefore when today we talk of human rights we have in mind the UN conception of human rights, regardless of how we relate to it [...]
>
> While this is a problem for Russia and other post-totalitarian states, we are only illustrations of a more general crisis. All that is connected with worldwide, historical and other questions relating to human rights is experiencing a crisis today. The crisis of liberalism as an ideology is clear. And it is clear that human rights and liberalism have at the very least a strong historical connection. Human rights have always been endowed with a kind of sacredness. In the twentieth century the UN gave it this with its association with its being higher than the state, a 'super-value', part of international law, etc. And today the UN is in crisis, and international law is experiencing a crisis [...]
>
> I am absolutely convinced that the problem of human dignity [...] is an eternal value, some eternal feeling of a person. And the arbitrariness of power, not only of the state, but any power – that's also an everlasting problem. In that sense human rights are part of objective reality. We are now involved in the problem of finding a new paradigm. It is a global problem – but we are facing it too.

Few took up Averkiev's arguments. The discussion revolved around whether their ideas, based on the Universal Declaration, were perhaps too advanced for the greater part of the population or whether it was their inability to get them across that was at fault? Yury Dzhibladze wanted activists to use key concepts from the Declaration:

> It seems to me that people do react to the word 'the dignity of man' and we should sell ourselves by using that [. . .] today people feel that no one pays any attention to them, the authorities and others denigrate them and so on. 'Dignity' is an inalienable part of human rights, it's the basis of human rights.

Despite a tendency to talk in UN language, Dzhibladze was one of the few at the 2004 conference to suggest a practical reason for their needing to share a language with the people.

> In order to be heard, and not simply cry in the wilderness, we must have backing. That is we can only have a conversation with the authorities from a position of strength. Strength – not in the sense of bringing the people out on to the streets, although that's a possibility at a particular moment. Rather we need the people themselves, citizens, so that we have the strength to engage in dialogue with the authorities.

He, in contrast to many, as we shall see in Chapter 8, saw his mission as one of influencing policy through negotiations with the authorities. Part of the problem was that activists were speaking to different audiences – international NGOs, Western donors, government officials, journalists, and, as they came increasingly to call them, clients, and this required different ways of talking. Some favoured, and probably all agreed, that they must use different materials for different audiences. Lukashevsky argued: 'Given that there are many target groups, and society is so multifarious, a different strategy has to be adopted for each', and the sociologists recommended that:

> The rhetoric used by activists must vary depending upon the type of recipient of information. At a minimum there's the man in the street, the expert community, and the authorities. Each of them requires their own type of information. Expert and scientific texts may work for experts and the authorities, but citizens need much simpler, popular, materials.

Korotaev suggested that the community was a broad church – it included all sorts – politicians, supporters, hands-on defenders, and those promoting values.

> That's normal [...] For an understanding of what we as a community are, as a whole, our products must be packaged differently for different target groups [...] forgive me for the cynicism. But among ourselves we must agree and have a clear understanding of our shared strategy, implemented through very different types of activity.

Others were more willing to blame themselves for not addressing the issues that mattered to people, or for writing in a way that appealed to Western donors and international agencies, but not to the Russian public. In 2008, at a conference funded by the European Commission to mark 60 years of the Universal Declaration, Dzhibladze, in answer to his own rhetorical question 'What must we do to return these words [universal inalienable rights] written 60 years ago, to the centre of life of societies and the world?' suggests: 'we have a non-trivial task before us – the translation of human rights and the declaration on human rights into everyday language [...] we must turn these high, maybe abstract, values into everyday practical principles useful for people'.

While Arseny Roginsky, a couple of years later, would claim:

> Activists cannot translate their [ideas] into the Russian language. That doesn't mean that we must translate 'right' as 'justice'. But all the same, they should get closer to the Russian language, they don't think about that and they are not able to do it. Those who write reports are oriented towards their main audience which is European or the world community. But I think they will learn, in time.

However, in the discussion in 2004, Lev Levinson (an analyst and activist) took the criticism further:

> One of the problems is the exclusive nature of our human rights community. Effectively human rights activists have long since become some kind of an elite group which has monopolized the

rights to human rights [...] whereas we should be widening human rights discourse and sharing the field with others who are prepared to work in it. I mean not only the trade unions but many others.

This takes us back to the debates in the mid-nineties. What had changed? Then the activists had engaged in quite bitter arguments over 'who is right?' in their interpretation of human rights. In the debate between the Kovalev group and activists from the provinces in 1995, the differences between the supporters of the classical civil and political rights conception and those arguing for the inclusion of socio-economic rights came out quite clearly. By the beginning of the new century the latter had won their place on the agenda, and even Kovalev, by 2010, was suggesting that partners should be sought among the new trade unions. But if there was an acceptance that we can agree to disagree, did not this make the task of getting their ideas across even harder? The activists themselves were talking in different languages. Compare the following statements. The first by Valentin Gefter, who was chairing the session at the 2004 conference, and spoke, in his conclusion, of the baneful influence of traditional Russian attitudes:

> The language itself, which we use, and in the first instance to a wide circle of Russian citizens, is not theirs, it includes other concepts and slogans, which do not relate to many of life's priorities [...] that immediately brings us face to face with the age old Russian problem (part of our history and mentality) [...] the non-correspondence of 'human rights' and 'interests, both group and individual' [...] We have talked a lot about this but [...] we haven't reached an understanding of what to do about it, except for the need to exert ourselves by engaging in enlightenment, in working on these remnants of a pre-legal and egotistical consumer consciousness.

A group of activists from the provinces who had discussed the issue of finding a common language during the break, spoke very differently:

> If we accept that our strategic aim must be that of *forming popular opinion, working together with the people, and directing public opinion,*

then we must make social rights one of our most important priorities [...] *Only in that way shall we be able to involve the broad masses in our work.* And only then can we engage in education, explain that the monetization of benefits, or a wage lower than the minimum required for subsistence is the result of our not having civic democratic freedoms.

[Author's emphasis]

One can imagine some of the Moscow intellectuals shrinking at this classic piece of 'Soviet speech' but, upon reflection, was Gefter's any less 'Soviet' in its view of the enlightened working to eradicate 'the remnants', not now of a bourgeois consciousness, but of a 'pre-legal and egotistical consumer consciousness'?

Diversity within the community

In the experts' opinion:

The professionalization of the community [...] simultaneously promotes differences among the activists, divergent activities, and competition within the community which, while it still recognizes itself as one, cannot respond effectively and in unison to external challenges. What is needed is to work out a clear, agreed, position, a statement of priorities – of tasks – something that is very difficult because of the horizontal nature of the community, which itself is a matter of principle.

But was it the professionalization of the community, and its lack of vertical structures, that were responsible for the disunity? We have seen how, as disillusionment with the new political sphere grew, as poverty spread, and as neither local authorities nor the justice system were able to cope with the multiplying appeals for help or for the observance of rights, hundreds of very different organizations appeared. The activists' self-description – human rights activists – owed something to the international popularity of human rights at the time Communist party rule in Russia collapsed but also to the fact that the 1993 constitution affirmed a huge array of rights, including social and economic rights. Here was an ideology that could create a broad church. The church however barely held together. Schisms occurred, heresies were denounced. This was not surprising, given the catholic nature of the doctrine – human rights – and the different concerns or interests of those who advanced them. Some were inspired by the desire to press for reforms of the justice system, to defend new-found freedoms, to effect legislative changes; others to act as some kind of political opposition. Many were primarily concerned with defending or improving the lot of vulnerable people. Those who took up the plight of street children or of the migrants flooding into Russian cities, or thought the bombing of Grozny, the capital of the Chechen republic, unacceptable, were not inspired by international declarations. They were responding to things that they found abhorrent and that they thought should be addressed. Ideas of decency, of the treatment of one's fellowmen, of children's needs, of recompense for past atrocities, of abjuring violence – all rose to the surface. And this is one reason why there was such a variety and disagreement within what came to be known as the human rights community.

Was it even a community? Perhaps what is most striking is that such very different organizations should have conceived of themselves as belonging to one. Svetlana Gannushkina on one occasion suggested: 'human rights activists fall into two groups – some are interested in defending "people (humans)" and some in defending "rights".' Arseny Roginsky of the International Memorial Society suggested:

Take the idea of human rights – a very powerful idea but absolutely incomprehensible [. . .] It is clear that an individual must have rights, and the rights should be observed [. . .] but the idea is such a huge, such a difficult one, it gets dissolved into hundreds of different organizations. They all claim to be defending human rights, they can't stand each other, they are very different [. . .] some work professionally, others do not. It's a difficult idea.

This is true not only of the Russian activists. Large UN conferences have ended with violent disagreements between the participants, even when the theme is a single issue one, for example racism. What we can say is that the more catholic the interpretation, or the rights that are included, the less likely will be united action and, in this respect, the Universal Declaration creates problems.

Without doubt, what we can call the Helsinki interpretation of human rights, promoted by those who had been involved in the Helsinki movement in the USSR and Eastern Europe, and by Western governments, and then picked up by Western funders and NGOs, inspired many. A commitment by the state to its constitutional obligations, with priority for the citizen's political and civil rights, and an independent judiciary to ensure that these rights are observed, were key elements in this position. The desire to promote the rule of law, understood as a situation where the state could be held accountable by the courts, had lain behind the work of the original human rights committee of the Supreme Soviet, and had played its part in influencing the wording in the 1993 constitution and the creation of the institution of ombudsman. Russia's signing of the European Convention on Human Rights, and the ability to turn to the European Court of Human Rights, whose brief did not extend to social and economic rights, seemingly strengthened such a position. Gefter, at the 2004 conference, declared:

> We lack conviction and honesty when we say that defending human rights is *not defending the rights and interests of one or other group*, however badly they may be infringed, or however discriminated maybe their representatives, but *rather the defence of Rights for their own sake.*
>
> [Author's emphasis]

And Tanya Lokshina restated this position in interview in 2011:

> A human rights activist is not a defender of victims. There's a principle difference between the defender of a victim and the defender of a right. The human rights activist is not only and not primarily defending a particular individual who, for example, was tortured in a remand prison or who was not given access to a legal counsel. He is defending values and mechanisms. The [principle] of Rights must be guaranteed. Hence each concrete case is simply just one small step in the promotion of a principle, that of law.

She continued: 'In defending a concrete individual, you must focus on the supremacy of law, and not on the individual as a victim.' 'Do you think most people think that way?' I ask.

No, some think like that, others think differently [. . .] one of the
apparent weaknesses of the human rights community is [. . .] not
only the inability to articulate this but also that many activists see
them themselves as defending victims [. . .] and begin to take the
side of their victims, and to support them as a defence lawyer
would, or an aunt, mother, grandmother.

The activities of the Soldiers' Mothers Committees, Abramkin's Centre
for Prison Reform, of Marchenko's Mother's Right, the domestic
violence centres, or Memorial's campaigns for compensation for Stalin's
victims owed little to concerns for the supremacy of law. As we
suggested, the prime concern of many was to help those suffering from
abuse or neglect, whether at the hands of the state or other citizens, and
to hope that gradually their actions would have an effect on the
behaviour of those who abused the power they held. But because so
much of everyday activity in Russia was subject to legal regulation,
infringements so frequent, and politicians so unresponsive, the activists
increasingly looked to legal means to fight their cause. The courts
became the site for contestation. Larisa Bogoraz, in that first human
rights seminar in Moscow in 1991, had urged the participants to engage
in spreading 'legal consciousness'. She would have been pleased to see,
15 years later, how many of the activists were using the law to defend
rights but it was not a belief in the supremacy of law that had brought
them into defending human rights.

Olga Shepeleva, a young lawyer from the Nizhny Novgorod
organization, who had studied at Columbia, New York, and would
subsequently move to Moscow to work on public interest law, clearly felt
frustrated by the discussion at the conference.

We have talked a lot about diverging paths, methods and
strategies, about which rights to focus on, social or civil, about
whether the population's perception of the phrase 'defence of
rights' is a problem of language or a problem of the value of human
rights in Russia, we have talked about the general crisis of human
rights, and about what is a human rights activist – a missionary or
a fighter but [to take this any further] we must understand and
answer the question: *what are human rights activists actually doing in
today's Russia, what are their aims and tasks?* [. . .] *Offering particular*

services to the population, or something else? Once the aims are clear, and hence why human rights activists are needed in Russia, strategy and tactics can be determined: will activists negotiate with the authorities, and how will they negotiate, do they need public support and in what form, and so on. I want to ask: why are we here?

[Author's emphasis]

Surely the problem was that they *were* involved in all kinds of different activities, prompted by different aims, and concerns. Perhaps all they held in common was the commitment to using legal, non-violent means of defence, to the peaceful pursuit of reforms, and a belief in the importance of education or enlightenment. Most, but not all, had distanced themselves from the discredited political arena. At the 2004 conference Lev Ponomarev urged the participants to think of creating the wing of a political party, or to set up their own, which his movement For Human Rights was in the process of doing. This fell on deaf ears, as did Averkiev's argument that 'if someone is defending social rights, then he should have the appropriate technology [...] if he wants to be a missionary, and blaze a trail, he must be morally above reproach, and without doubt be charismatic [...] if he wants to tackle the question of rich and poor, come out against privatization, etc., then he should honestly state that he is part of the new left.'

Dzhibladze disagreed:

We must explain that we speak the truth, offer other information. That means [talking about] 'dignity' and 'truth'. And about 'social justice' [...] which people also want, and not only here, but throughout the world. But it's absolutely not necessary to stick on labels of 'left' or 'right', to create some kind of parties or something of that sort.

But what if the human rights community *was* home to those of different political persuasions, and different views on social justice?

The sociologists, tentatively but not very optimistically, suggested that the new, and educated, middle class should be thought of as a target group, but that the human rights community needed to extend its links with different social groups. Oddly enough they wrote of the need 'to restore the trust of the population in the human rights community' which would require 'the energetic defence of social-economic rights as well as prisoners of conscience, civil rights, and the victims of arbitrary actions of the authorities and the law and order agencies.' But these were all activities the community was involved in, and no evidence was produced that suggested that the activists had been more popular or trusted in previous years. Yet this was something that the activists felt. 'We have lost society, that's the truth. How to win it back, I don't know', according to one activist. And they felt the need for 'our national idea'; the divisions were 'an obstacle to any consolidation of the human rights community and to the working out of a common (shared) idea'. The experts thought the same. 'Many human rights experts view the inability of the human rights community to work out a common position, based on shared priorities, as responsible for its weakness today.' But how could they do so? And, as important, why should they do so? Shepeleva's question still hung in the air. On the one hand they prized their autonomy, and their ability to design their own different strategies, on the other they hankered for a community, a collective consciousness, a solidarity. Not surprisingly agreement on how to proceed remained elusive.

In summing up the discussion at the conference, Gefter suggested that 'Unfortunately we have barely managed to talk about which concrete, recognizable types of activity we should engage in, in order that they don't contradict each other, except for those relating to enlightenment'. And that brings us to education.

Education, education, education

At the 2004 conference Korotaev, asking to be forgiven, claimed that the reason so many participants advocated education or enlightenment was that

> We are the direct descendants of the Russian populist intelligentsia which considered its function to be that of educating the 'dark people' [*temnyi narod*] and leading it to a shining future. We should not deceive ourselves, that's the only reason why we are interested in what the people think, certainly it's not because of what they think.

Some probably were offended and, I would add, a belief in educating the masses was very much part of a Soviet mind set too. At the conference the experts recommended focusing on human rights education for students and school children because they had grown up in a post-Soviet environment, were open to new information, and not burdened with worry over everyday issues. And, indeed, they had been a target group since the early nineties.

In 1991, a group, mostly schoolteachers, members of Memorial, began to gather school children and students to talk about Stalinist repression, they then set up a Youth Centre on Human Rights. They moved on to visiting schools, and organizing discussions on human rights. The leader of the Centre was a teacher, Vsevolod Lukovitsky, and Elena Rusakova, a social psychologist, was an active participant. The Centre's members undertook these activities in their free time; they did not set up an office. Beginning with a small grant from Soros, they began to prepare materials for teachers, and for school children, and in 1998 produced a textbook that received Ministry of Education approval. By this time they were in demand as teachers of new role playing and interactive methods of teaching human rights. One city that they visited, as trainers, was Perm where an NGO, the Centre for Civic Education, headed by Andrei Suslov, a young historian from the Pedagogical University, a specialist on Stalinist repression, was teaching human rights. Suslov's group too produced a textbook, drawing on the Lukovitsky materials, and over the next few years held three-day seminars for school teachers, either in Perm or in the region's towns. Perhaps 25 teachers would attend, 250–300 over the course of the year.

The early years of the new decade witnessed conflicting tendencies. On the one hand, the Youth Centre for Human Rights fell out of favour with the authorities. A revised version of their textbook failed to get ministerial approval in 2000, making it difficult for teachers to use it. In 2001, with youth organizations coming under scrutiny in the search for 'extremists', the Centre's name and its juridical address as the Memorial offices was sufficient to send the police to Memorial to look for young extremists. Lukovitsy and his colleagues set up a new organization, with a suitably neutral name, the Humanist Research and Methodology Centre, but found that schools, regional educational authorities and pedagogical universities were less and less willing to work with them. The Centre joined in a successful campaign against compulsory religious and military education in schools in 2003–05, but subsequently learnt that it was on a blacklist circulated to local institutes that run programmes for raising teachers' qualifications. A firm that prepares electronic materials for schools withdrew an order on being instructed that it was not allowed to work with the Centre.

Meanwhile, in 2000, a Project of Human Rights Education Capacity Development for Russia, designed within the framework of the UN Technical Cooperation Programme on Human Rights was launched. Key activities were the training of teachers of human rights in the higher education sector and in the secondary schools, the introduction of new methodologies into the school curriculum, and the creation of mini-libraries of human rights materials. The establishment of a human rights network of educators, across Russia, one that brought together teachers, NGOs, government and the media representatives was emphasized as a goal. The UN Committee on Human Rights and the Ministry of Foreign Affairs assumed leadership functions, and the Fulcrum Foundation, the Russian NGO that ran the small grants programme under Mikhail Timenchik's leadership, took responsibility for designing and administering project activities.[11]

Pedagogical universities, local education authorities, and NGOs in a number of cities were selected to provide courses for teachers, students, and school children; an essay-writing and project competition brought the winning school teams to make presentations in the Constitutional Court; course materials were published and distributed. The project ran for three years. In 2002 UNCHR included it as a case study in a global review of its Technical Cooperation Program, and received a recommendation for an expansion of the project, once an impact evaluation survey by outside experts had been undertaken. A Russian colleague and I were asked to do it. We struggled, not because of an unwillingness by the participants to assist us (although the teachers' response to questionnaires was very poor), but because, as we suggested in our report, 'any assessment of the impact of teaching on children's knowledge of and attitudes towards human rights [over a short period] is very difficult'. We tried, with questionnaires, and control groups, to tap this, and drew attention to a two-year impact study conducted in Romanian classrooms whose findings illuminate the difficulties in making such assessments. The impact of training on teachers and students is similarly difficult to assess, especially if there is no base line data; all we could say is that many teachers had been introduced to new teaching skills and approaches. Our recommendation that a new project, with stable funding for no less than three years, and with new guidelines, should be based on the existing network, led by the Fulcrum Foundation, did not materialize. The total lack of interest in the project shown by the official from the Ministry of Foreign Affairs, when we interviewed him, alerted us to this project being one from an earlier Yeltsin era, in a different political climate.

What did it leave behind? It's difficult to tell. As Rusakova suggested, and we were well aware, any large project will bring in many who are only interested as long as funding exists. The Lukovitsky group carries on its work in regions, for example Kaliningrad, where the ombudsman offers protection, but when she was away on vacation, their teaching of human rights teaching came under attack. St Petersburg? That is more difficult, Rusakova suggests, because there the group faces competition from a rival group. As we might expect, Perm is a region where human rights teaching is pursued actively. The Perm Centre expanded its activities during the new century, with its members travelling to several cities, including to faraway Astrakhan in the south and Arkhangelsk in the north to hold seminars hosted by the institutes engaged in raising teachers' qualifications. In 2007 the Ministry of Education announced a competition for a manual for teaching human rights to 16–17-year-olds (maybe in response to an initiative by Vladimir Lukin, the ombudsman), to be available for schools with a humanities specialization. The contract was won by a group from the Moscow Academy for Raising Teachers' Qualifications, which included specialists from Perm, and produced an impressive manual. The Perm Centre has a very full list of relevant human rights educational materials on its website.[12] But Suslov feels that, with the political changes at federal level, there is less interest both from education authorities and from teachers. A decline in interest in the history of political repression is particularly marked.

There is no set course in the school curriculum on human rights, and the course on 'citizenship education' has been axed, but a teacher can introduce one, or part of one, under social studies or sometimes under law. It will depend upon her ability to negotiate this with the school director and whether she can include such a course under extra hours (for which she will be paid). Both Suslov and Rusakova would agree that a great deal depends upon the individual teacher, and on teachers' attitudes in different parts of the country. 'How do you explain this?' I ask Suslov. 'I think, first and foremost, it is related to established political traditions [...] from the Soviet period.' He gives as examples the way teachers in Astrakhan obeyed an instruction to turn out to vote for a particular candidate, and how in Cheboksar an order to bring the school children out on a demonstration on 4 November, the new Russian holiday, where they stood for several hours in freezing temperatures, was seen as perfectly normal. In Perm, he suggests, it would have produced a scandal. The authorities would not think of issuing such an order, and the public would not respond so obediently.

> Soviet traditions continue to exist everywhere. And in their new wrapping they reproduce themselves even in those regions, in an environment, where the authorities do not think of themselves as leaders of a soviet type.

For example, in Perm, 'leaders think of themselves as managers of a new type, using the newest management techniques'. At a meeting that he had recently attended, the 45-year-old head of the regional education authority announced to the 48 heads of the district education departments that the governor wanted the heads of all government departments, down to district level, to use personal blogs, using a particular technology – Word Press. Apparently not all were doing it correctly, and regularly, at least once a week. The following day, the head of the education authority continued, the regional government was going to assess the performance of all departments and, in order that they, education, made a good showing, all blogs should be up by 10 a.m. Those who had four to five hours travel to get home that evening, should ensure they were at work, early, to achieve this.

Suslov's colleague commented to him 'So, the raikom [party committee] returns'.

> I think that is the case. Despite all the external appearance of something new, it's the party-Soviet-administrative tradition [...] dressed up in the clothing of 'new management'. He who is in

command thinks of himself as supremely knowledgeable, and therefore requests from society have little significance [...] each region depends upon its own petty tyrant. Here it is blogs, somewhere else it will be something else. And everyone will do exactly as the boss prescribes [...] in the absence of democratic traditions and institutions.

The interview survey of NGO representatives in several cities, carried out by Denis Volkov of the Levada Centre, adds another dimension to this:

Those who have been 'elected' recently on party lists, according to our respondents, are not only uninterested in working with civic activists, but are not interested in doing the work of a deputy [...] any criticism which contains 'real demands' is always viewed as an attack. People appointed by the governors, mayors, or by the deputies, answer not to the electors, but to those higher up. One of the respondents explained the logic of those in power as 'You did not put us in office, and therefore your views are of no particular interest to us'.[13]

But to return to the teaching of human rights. In the early years of the new century, human rights schools, whether for adults or children were still popular, and supported by large amounts of Western funding. While a few remain, others simply closed. According to Suslov:

There's a feeling that all those campaigns, connected with human rights education, with conceptions of tolerance or anti-discrimination have worked badly. Perhaps it would be worse if they had not existed. Take xenophobia – it works both ways – because as regards some officials and parts of the media there are successes. Officials watch what they are saying.

Now there are new projects, financed by the Council of Europe, which again aim to introduce teachers to human rights materials. A project run by a Norwegian Centre, Wederland, in partnership with the Moscow School of Civic Education,[14] will, over a period of three years, introduce cohorts of 15–20 teachers and youth workers in Rostov on Don, and in Stavropol, to teaching materials and involve them in designing courses. I attended the first training session, in 2013, in Rostov. What had changed? It was a pleasant surprise to find that the 'Norwegian' trainers were a young Belarus and Pole, with native or very good Russian, and that among the materials were those by Suslov's centre. It was disheartening that, in a field in which there are good Russian experts and trainers, the Moscow School had not consulted with those among its own alumni. The project looked sensible, and well organized, and the young teachers participated. It has the support of energetic faculty at Rostov State University. But neither the UNCHR project nor one, run ten years earlier in Rostov by an enterprising lawyer and teacher, seemed known to the participants. Whether this project will succeed in introducing something new into school curricula, and influence students' and teacher behaviour, will depend upon the future educational and political environment at local and federal level.

Both Sergei Lukashevsky (the Sakharov Centre) and Robert Latypov (Perm Memorial) believe that to teach human rights you have to move away from courses on human rights. The Sakharov Centre now has a programme of seminars, discussions, films on issues that interest students – and they come, 50 to 60 will turn up. As Lukashevsky explains, the topic could be:

> hegemony over the Arctic – the conflict of interests between different states, environmental issues, the rights of the indigenous peoples of the north. And this takes us to a whole number of Sakharov themes – peace, progress and human rights [...] Unfortunately, few come to historical topics. At the moment, that is not popular, whereas ecology is right in the mainstream, few are interested in political issues, but the fact that it's difficult to breath in Moscow is of interest.

In Perm they approach the issue of education rather differently. They organize schools for journalists, for moderators, on PR, or speechwriting, in other words on subjects which attract those who want to improve or learn new skills. Then they will introduce themes such as freedom of speech or access to information, or the historical past, as part of the material for teaching the skills. The schools are free, on a Saturday, four sessions, and may attract up to 50 young people in their twenties, of whom 30 will last the course. Robert Latypov, the young leader of Perm Memorial, whom we shall meet in Chapter 10, suggests:

> If someone like Ponomarev learns of this, he will be amazed, but maybe he will understand that we are going in a different direction [...] we understand that you have to move forward, try new methods, be interesting [...] even talk about values [...] and in such a way that you get some results.

Lukovitsky of the Youth Centre has taken a different path. He is now also active in a new teachers' trade union. Originally simply designed as a consultation service for teachers facing local problems – for example, the selling of a school building in the centre of a city to a developer – demands came for a trade union, and a newspaper, *1st September*, supported by teachers' contributions, not by the Ministry of Education. Again, there are marked differences in the response from different regions, but the union and newspaper have become sufficiently popular among the 30–35-year-olds to support the setting up of a publishing house.

But now we move on to the activists engaged in 'concrete' action, their attempts to influence legislation and its implementation.

PART 3

ACTIVISTS IN ACTION

CHAPTER 8

ARMY AND POLICE REFORM

In 2010 Boris Pustintsev recalled a conversation:

> Five years ago Blinushov, Dzhibladze and I had an argument.
> Blinushov agreed with me. Dzhibladze was complaining that
> the human rights community was stewing in its own juice, our
> aims and our ideas were unintelligible to our citizens, they felt
> no need of us, we, surely, were working badly with them, we
> ought to reach out to the public. I said 'Yury, you are either a
> politician or a human rights activist. If you want mass support,
> go into politics. Human rights activists will never have mass
> support. Yes, we support the rights of those who do not even
> recognize that they have those rights [...] Human rights
> activists are doomed to a sad and solitary existence. It's like that
> everywhere. Even Amnesty International has never enjoyed
> majority support.

We can imagine the conversation continuing with Dzhibladze arguing
in support of campaigns to influence politicians and legislation,
Pustintsev in favour of strategies to educate those who implement the
laws (the police and the judges), and Blinushov favouring local action to
support vulnerable groups or political rights. While there were not hard
and fast dividing lines between these activities, it is helpful to
distinguish them. Furthermore, while enlightenment was believed by all
to be important, taking up individual cases was an indisputable marker
of an activist. Many, but not all, would have agreed with Grigory

Shvedov, a young Memorial activist and editor of *Caucasian Knot* (whom we shall meet in Chapter 10), that 'there are organizations which act as lobbyists, prepare methodological materials, or engage in enlightenment – I would not call them human rights activists if they do not give help to concrete individuals'. And there are those who on these grounds reject the term for themselves, for example, Sergei Lukashevsky, director of the Sakharov Centre.

> I really do not consider myself to be a human rights activist because, to my mind, an activist is someone who takes up the case of actual individuals. I have never been involved with individuals. I have applied my intellectual abilities to benefiting either the history of human rights or current human rights activity.

Arseny Roginsky, and Irina Flige of St Petersburg Memorial, would agree with him. But all three would be thought of as members of the human rights community. Even among the 'applied activists', if we can call them that, few, I suspect, shared the view of Igor Kalyapin, from Nizhny Novgorod, that, if someone drew a gun on an individual whose case he was defending, he should stand between him and the assailant. In short, activists held different views on appropriate strategies, and how best to promote or defend rights. Some favoured local action, which could include working with law and order agencies; others advocated taking a particular issue nationwide, or to an international audience; others, one of whom was Dzhibladze, wanted to work in the policy making arena.

> I thought that NGOs should learn how to influence the taking of decisions, in the political process, not in the sense of being involved in politics (today we are politically engaged) but then I thought in terms of legislation, of policy decisions, and public control [...] So my idea was to create a Centre which would attempt to bring together the world of activists and the world of experts, on the one hand and, on the other, to change the activists so that they acquired the skills of analysis, of formulating their recommendations [...] and then finding partners in society, the media, and so on so that they became – and this is the critical word – influential.

But what if the authorities are not interested in dialogue? In Grigory Shvedov's view:

> I would not describe lobbying for legislation in our country as human rights activity. In another country it may be. In our country it's the labours of Sisyphus and an individual who is engaged in the labours of Sisyphus can command either respect, or a smile, but in no way would I call him a human rights defender.

And Pavel Chikov, a young lawyer from Kazan, when I ask him in 2011 whether he is interested in changing the legislation or in the way it is implemented, responds:

> Implementation. Because the legislation is more or less all right. What's bad is that those who implement it – the judges, police – are so very dependent upon their superiors. It is a vertical hierarchy, in which instructions on how to implement a particular normative act are not made public, and a normative act can always be interpreted in different ways.

But if the problem was not so much one of legislation but rather its implementation, which were the best strategies to achieve this? Clearly, for the realization of rights, both legislation and implementation are important, while the appropriate response and strategy may vary from one policy area to another. The activist community changes tactics over the period, both as a consequence of its increasing professionalization, the entry of younger generations, a changing environment, and the shrinking of political opportunities. We find ourselves watching a flickering video of the way the state – its leaders, institutions, and courts on the one hand – and society – its organizations and citizens – responded to each other as the post-Soviet years progressed.

I focus on a few, very different, issues, all on the human rights agenda from the early nineties. Military conscription and/or the introduction of alternative civilian service, and the reform of the police, feature in this chapter. Public inspection of closed institutions (remand centres, prisons, etc.), the introduction of juvenile courts, the criminalization of domestic violence, and the rights of refugees and forced migrants follow, but in less detail. A more complete picture of the activists in action would include many more (remember the Extraordinary Congress of 2001) – those defending media freedoms, the environment, the indigenous people of the north, invalids, to name only a few – but those I focus on are sufficiently different for the reader to get a sense of the human rights community in action, the different strategies adopted, and factors that worked in their favour or against. The way demands are framed, the resources activists can draw upon, both skills and material resources, the choice of strategies, and of targets, and the critical importance of being able to take advantage of political opportunities all play a part.[1] At the same time, themes already raised reappear: the size of Russia and regional differences, the ways in which Western assistance could aid or distract, the influence of legacies of the past, including cultural practices, and of a changing domestic and international environment. The International Memorial Society, with which we began at the time of perestroika, comes back into the picture, before we move on to a new generation of young lawyers.

Political opportunities – influencing policy

First, how did the policy-making environment change over the period? According to Tanya Lokshina:

> When I started work [in 1998], despite the awful mess that existed there were specific individuals who were in the Duma, there were individuals in the president's administration, with whom one could and had to discuss things. If a great idea relating to a piece of legislation or how to implement it occurred to you, you knew which keys to press. Now, and it's a paradox, a professional community exists, in which numerous able, progressive young people work, good lawyers and analysts, who have very attractive ideas, but to whom should they take them? I mean at the federal level.

In the early nineties, by combining their efforts, elected deputies and human rights activists with access to the president or to key individuals pushed through legislation on compensation for the victims of Stalinist repression, on improvements to prison conditions, the freedom of the media, and non-governmental organizations. The signing of European conventions and legislation on an ombudsman followed shortly afterwards. By the beginning of the new century open political quarrelling had been replaced by negotiations between former and new party politicians and business leaders; bureaucratic ministries competed with each other and with the oligarchs for resources. Very few from the human rights community were deputies, or even members of political parties; a few still had allies among the deputies or even ministers. Some, as we saw at the Civic Forum, would have nothing to do with the political elite coalescing around Putin, while others favoured maintaining a dialogue with rulers, whether at federal or at local level. They wanted their proposals for reform to be heard and, if possible, translated into policy. Discussions, organized by individual ministries, where government representatives would meet with those from civic organizations, began to replace meetings with Duma deputies.

During Putin's second term as president, the Duma and the upper house, the Council of the Federation, with their memberships determined by the Kremlin, did little more than rubber stamp legislation presented to them. As the legislative bodies faded, and the regions were brought back under control by the federal authorities, the ministries reasserted themselves even more strongly. The Civic Chamber, the appointed and self-recruiting body of NGO representatives set up in 2005, gradually established itself, and its commissions sometimes commented critically on legislative proposals. But throughout the Putin and then the Medvedev presidencies, policy making retreated increasingly into the closed chambers of the president's administration and the prime minister's office, and few had access there. In 2011 Valentina Melnikova, of the Moscow Soldiers' Mothers Committee, suggested:

> We don't know who the president's advisors are. A more closed structure than the administration does not exist. There's the head of the administration – Naryshkin, there's the well-known comrade Surkov, responsible for domestic politics – but who else? Who prepares instructions to be circulated, who reports on the current situation? Those who now hold posts under Medvedev are Putin's people [. . .] and how decisions are reached, I do not know. And when I put the question to sociologists, they also admit that they don't know.

Igor Kalyapin echoed her words: 'It's a mystery to me, how things are worked out up there [. . .] nobody knows how and when and which decisions are taken by those at the top [. . .] but it's clear to me that there are some people who try to steer things in the right direction.'

In 2003 Putin abolished the commission on human rights, headed by Kartashkin, and created in its place, in 2004, a Presidential Council on Human Rights, the members of which he appointed after consultation with Ella Pamfilova, the ex-politician, who was its chair. Several leading Moscow activists were included: Abramkin, Alekseeva, Auzan, Gannushkina, Orlov (for an initial period), Simonov and, from St Petersburg, Pustintsev. The twice-yearly meetings with Putin provided an opportunity for both sides to raise issues that they considered important – from legislative proposals on NGO activity or juvenile courts to developments in Chechnya, from cases of individuals being held in prison to ongoing harassment of activists. Under Medvedev, the council, now a Council for the Advancement of Civil Society and Human Rights, grew in size (Dzhibladze and Gefter were included in 2009), met more frequently, and held some sessions in regional capitals. In 2010 Pamfilova resigned, tired of harassment by the Kremlin-sponsored youth movement, Ours, and was replaced by Mikhail Fedotov, a well-known and respected 'liberal' politician and ex-diplomat.

What opportunities, if any, did this policy-making environment offer to human rights organizations anxious to see legislative change? Not many, we suggest. It was a backbreaking struggle to get an item on the agenda, and its future progress was quite uncertain. With good reason the literature on social movements emphasizes the importance of gaining entry to the political field – through supporters in the political elite or a political party – if a movement's aims are to be realized. Over the period, points of entry for the human rights community dwindled but Dzhibladze was someone who, in the late nineties, believed it possible. From 1999 through to 2005, when the scope for NGO action began to shrink, Dzhibladze's Centre for Democracy and Human Rights was organizing training sessions, signature protests, preparing reports for international conferences or institutions, and seeking contacts with Duma deputies and ministry officials. Dzhibladze, himself an assistant to a Yabloko party deputy until 2003, became well known as a spokesman for the Russian human rights community at UN or European gatherings. One of the campaigns he participated in was that for alternative civilian service.

Conscription and an alternative civilian service

The Soldiers' Mothers Committees, which we met in Chapters 2 and 4, had focused since 1988 on illegal conscription (i.e. of those who should have been exempt), on defending those who absconded, on the treatment of conscripts and, as the Chechen war began, on stopping the sending of conscripts to fight in Chechnya. Their aim remained the ending of conscription and the introduction of a regular contract army. Dotted across the country, the committees had few resources except their members' commitment. But by the late nineties they were becoming more professional. 'You remember what we were like in 1993? Largely shrieks and tears [...] and now we have learnt to work with the legislation – when I go to court, I take all the laws with me.' (Liudmila Zinchenko from Chelyabinsk in 2001) And ten years later, according to Valentina Melnikova, leader of the Moscow committee with whom many of the regional committees worked:

> The qualifications of those who work in our committees, and the correct way in which we advance our mission of introducing a professional army, gives us 100 per cent authority [...] we are, in fact, defence lawyers [...] we must translate the problems people face into a language government institutions understand, and present them with legal demands which they have to satisfy.

While assistance to individual conscripts or those threatened with conscription was their major preoccupation, the leading organizations would challenge new rulings. For example, a change in the wording from 'he whose brother was killed or died while a conscript' to 'he whose brother died while executing his military duties' no longer gave exemption if the brother had committed suicide. Parents who had lost one son were desperate not to lose another. And the figures were not negligible. For example, out of 251 boys who, in one year, did not return home in the Komi republic, 102 had committed suicide. The Minister of Defence issued annual figures on non-combat deaths which, annually, were in excess of a thousand.

The role of the Soldiers' Mothers was brought home to me by a visit to the committee in Omsk in 2000. I had written ahead to ask for a meeting. I arrived early at the small office in the corner of a dusty courtyard, an office shared with the Afghan veterans who, under their blind leader, were discussing NATO policy towards Bosnia. I asked for Tatyana Ivanovna.[2] After a while she appeared, tired, beckoned to me to sit down the other side of her desk, and asked 'so which regiment is your son serving in?' I was left speechless, choked. My heart lurched. For a moment it was one of my sons, who was serving as a conscript, and Tatyana Ivanovna was all that stood between him and the abuse he might face.

The Soldiers' Mothers wanted an end to conscription but, in the meantime, human rights groups had begun to argue for the introduction of alternative civilian service for those who, on religious or ethical grounds, objected to military service. This was specified in Article 59 of the constitution but there was no corresponding legislation. Judges could not adjudicate claims. By 2000 a campaign, 'For a democratic civilian service', supported by 50 different NGOs from 30 regions, was underway. Key issues were the length of service (conscription was for two years) – should civilian service be for two or more years, and who should supervise it?

Following the Civic Forum, there was an agreement that the General Staff would work together with the Coalition (as it was now called) to prepare a draft law. The secretariat of the Coalition included Moscow activists – Sergei Krivenko and Liudmila Vakhnina from Memorial, Dzhibladze – and activists from the regions, including from the Kaliningrad and St Petersburg Soldiers' Mothers committees. The secretariat had managed to establish good relations with the Ministry of Labour and this stood it in good stead when the General Staff began to refuse to engage in consultations. The Coalition got publicity, appealed to a deputy prime minister, and succeeded in having the drafting of the law officially transferred to the Ministry of Defence, the Ministry of Labour and to the Coalition. It was critical, in the campaigners' view, that civilian service be supervised by the Ministry of Labour, not by the military.

The draft law received its first reading in April 2002, 300 amendments were proposed for its second reading. But suddenly the wind changed. The Minister of Labour was summoned by Putin. A new group of deputies was given the task of preparing the draft for the second reading, which introduced tougher conditions (four years of service) and, suddenly, at short notice the law was passed in mid-June.

But employment remained the responsibility of the Ministry of Health and of Labour, the individual could live at home, was entitled to holidays and, with the shortening of military service (in 2008) to one year, alternative civilian service was cut to one year nine months. In 2011 90 per cent of the 879 applications for alternative service received approval.

Here we can talk of success, albeit partial. Without the campaign, which coincided with a favourable political moment (the emphasis on dialogue between ministries and civic organizations), and which attracted the attention of leading ministers, such a law would not have made its appearance. But we note how Putin's intervention influenced the outcome.

A professional army?

In the early nineties, there were military experts who had put forward proposals for a professional army but, over the next ten years, it fell to the Soldiers' Mothers to keep the issue alive. In this they were aided by journalists who regularly took up the topic of the draft, and the public opinion polls that suggested that, while the army still enjoyed quite high levels of trust, by the turn of the century the majority of those polled wanted to see reforms that would end both the poor conditions and the abuse the recruits suffered. Over 80 per cent of boys did not want to serve, and those who sympathized with them outweighed their critics. Majority opinion moved in favour of abolishing conscription.

In 2002–3 SPS, the small liberal party still with Duma deputies, presented proposals for a contract army, and in 2003 a federal programme was announced that proposed splitting the army into two parts – a contract part where all would be equivalent to officers, have decent pay, and civil rights, and a conscript part, which would be separate, only for education and for one year; upon completion the conscript could, if he wished, sign a contract. The border troops became contract troops and were transferred to the FSB, the security services.

Meanwhile Putin publicly recognized that draft offices did not always behave as they should. Thus emboldened, we might say, Sergei Krivenko, a member of Memorial's board, now leading the Coalition, joined forces with the London School of Economics, and a young administrator, Andrei Kuvshinov, originally from a Novosibirsk organization in the Coalition, to design a three-year project, Citizen and Army, and apply for funding to the European Commission. The successful grant application, subsequently extended for a further year (2006–10), and then for another four years to include other CIS countries was administered by the LSE. Perhaps 20 of the original Coalition members participated. The Moscow Soldiers' Mothers, under Melnikova, cooperated initially but soon distanced themselves, while some committees from the regions continued to work both with the Coalition and with Melnikova. Dzhibladze set up his own, different, project with Dutch funding.

Members of the Citizen and Army network continued to advise conscripts on their rights at consultation points; they collected data on infringements, and sent reports to the prosecutor's office and to government departments. They also now took up the issue of contracts.

> Krivenko: With the aid of this project we managed to reach the highest levels, we had meetings with the Ministry of Defence, attended a roundtable which Lukin, the ombudsman organized, and Pamfilova's council. Our network Citizen and Army, became recognized, as was Melnikova's committee. The project helped us to become a socially significant actor – it gave us financial means and resources [...]
>
> Lukin is a fine individual but his office is pretty opaque. It was a major undertaking to get through to him, to get him to take up the issue, organize roundtables, write reports to the Ministry of Defence, get questions asked at meetings with the president. It was the same with Pamfilova. Last year [2010] we managed to organize a big event on military reform under the auspices of the [president's] council, and passed all the papers to the president.
>
> M.: And what were the main achievements of the project, apart from those of getting recognition at a high level?
>
> Krivenko: The provision of real assistance to concrete individuals: conscripts, soldiers, and those doing alternative service. We developed a network of organizations, right across the whole country, one which really worked for conscripts and soldiers. And on this basis we collected the data which we could present to the Ministry of Defence, and make recommendations.

Despite the Coalition, Melnikova, and Marchenko (from Mother's Right) all wishing to see an end to conscription, they work for this independently of one another. Veronika Marchenko, quite simply, prefers to work on a narrow issue, 'dead soldiers', and to do it her own way, which includes winning cases before the European Court, and using striking posters. (See plate 7) In Krivenko's view, Mother's Right 'is a very good human rights organization but, quite simply, Veronika does not work with other organizations'. Relations between Melnikova and other organizations are more complicated. There is a difference in approach between Melnikova and the Coalition in that the battle cry of the Soldiers' Mothers committees 'always was – "No conscription!" [...] and when we write our reports and present them to the president, we don't give them a heading "Conscription is not needed! It should be ended!" which is what they want.' Not, Krivenko argues, because the Coalition favours conscription but because a full frontal attack will get less support.

Melnikova's committee focuses on abuse within the army, and on taking up individual cases. She is sceptical of the achievement of allowing conscripts to have mobile phones: simply another opportunity for extortion by officers, as could happen with the new contract system. In one regiment in the Far East, conscripts were forced to sign up for contracts and, once they had signed, and began to receive pay, it was stolen from them through a deal done by officers with a criminal gang, which was allowed on to the base. Appeals began to trickle out to the Soldiers' Mothers but they were refused access to the base. They managed to persuade a Duma deputy, a general in the Ministry of Internal Affairs, 'to use his right to have an audience with the Minister of Internal Affairs and the Minister of Defence'; the matter was investigated and those responsible brought to justice. But the introduction of contracts was, quite simply, a failure. The General Staff stole the money and falsified the figures. In 2007 Putin learnt of what was happening, tore strips off the assembled generals, sacked the Minister of Defence, and appointed Anatoly Serdiukov, a civilian from the Tax Authority, to sort it out the mess. According to Melnikova:

Serdiukov was in a state of shock, he did not try to hide the fact. The whole system of finances in the armed forces was so tangled that it was quite impossible to track where the money was going, and half was being stolen. And then he came under attack [from] generals who are still serving, and generals who have retired and hold some position or other and do not do anything [...] it's simply corporate theft, a kind of metastasis in the system.

In 2008 Serdiukov was being accused by the army lobby of abandoning the officers, of destroying the army, and acting as an agent of imperialism. Melnikova and her colleagues sought Ella Pamfilova's advice, who arranged a meeting for them with Serdiukov and eight of his first deputies – 'three of us were from Moscow, then there were our members from Sochi, Volgograd, Nizhny Novgorod, 15 of us in all, those who were prepared to meet with the minister, those who think strategically [...] and it became perfectly clear that our position was close to his'.

A smaller meeting with the chief of the General Staff followed, then with Putin, then Medvedev. But despite Medvedev's proposing a five-point plan to restructure and reform the armed forces, the move to a professional army still awaits resolution. The shrinking age cohort, and move to one-year service, has, according to the generals, left the army no option but to return to two–three years for conscription. However, according to Krivenko, 'both the president and the prime minister want a professional army. They recognize that that's the way to solve the problem. The armed forces receive new equipment, the conscript barely masters it in a year, and leaves.' But then, argues Melnikova, that is the issue to concentrate on, not legislation on alternative service. In her view, part of the problem (apart from corporate greed, and in 2012 Serdiukov himself was sacked for corruption) is the persistence of a 'Soviet ideology',

> that we are surrounded by enemies, that the army must be large, that our borders are the longest and therefore we must have the biggest army, that we should not begrudge any expenditure, have a huge number of soldiers, everyone should serve. I've been hearing this since 1989.

Perhaps because the day before we met she had been at a meeting of the public council attached to the Ministry of Defence (one of those that was set up after the Civic Forum), where the issue of ethnic conflicts in the army had been the topic for discussion, she was anxious to talk about the still prevailing 'Soviet' type thinking.

In the Soviet army they used to refer to soldiers from Central Asia as bad soldiers, those from the Baltic republics as fascists, Azerbaijntsy were goodness knows what, Georgians were rich, but in fact all of them were poor [...] And now, it began somewhere around 2000–1, those who retain that Soviet way of thinking argue that if we are fighting in the Caucasus, it is because they are enemies. And then they accuse soldiers from there of being aggressive [...] there's a large number of different nationalities in the army – Tatars, Bashkirs, Karachaevsty, Cherkessy, Dagestany, Ingushi [...] According to our Dagestan committee, half the boys are accused of aggressive crimes, and the other half are victimized by the officers, continually humiliated.

At the Ministry of Defence meeting she argued that encouraging officers to distinguish and characterize different nationalities produces the problem, and was supported by the military commissar from Dagestan,

I reminded the deputy minister of defence, who was there, that all the departments which deal with relations within the army are under his jurisdiction, and I requested that he should include instructions or rules to be included in all the officers' training that they should change the way they speak, that they should adopt a language of unity. Complete silence followed. Ideologically for them that's an alien idea. They are used to differentiating on the basis of nationality.

According to Melnikova, conservatism and nostalgia for the past is ever present.

They continue to insist they must engage in 'education' [...] and what Ida Kuklina [a member of Soldiers' Mothers and of the president's council] has described as 'going forward while looking backwards' continues. They can't any longer say that they are not in favour of reform but, all the same, they try to recreate the past. That's why there's such support for Stalin's greatness, why we hear that we won the Great Patriotic War, and when people begin to ask – at what cost – then they start shouting that we are against the victory [...] it's not all embracing, but it's a constant theme.

If I attend any conference I always find people who produce that
Soviet rhetoric. Bolshevism is not dead yet.

However, in her view, not all is gloomy. And her comments illuminate
both the policy-making process and the channels open to activists.

Military experts who in the early nineties supported the idea of a
professional army and then fell silent recently have found their
tongues again [. . .] and the experts are our officers, comrades.
Moreover Sergei Karaganov heads the group, and he is chair of that
council on foreign security policy that was originally set up by the
newspaper *Nezavisimaya* (*Independent*), and which includes a
number of military experts [. . .] and they have maintained a line to
Putin, and that's all a great help because while you may criticize
Melnikova, you will steer clear of Karaganov because you know
he'll have an answer, he's a very educated man [. . .] we use all the
channels we can [. . .] suddenly we hear that there's going to be
some military conference or other, we haven't been invited, so we
ring up and ask – how can you hold a conference without us?

So which bodies matter in Melnikova's view? The President's Council for
the Advancement of Civil Society and Human Rights, certainly, because
not only are 'the members well-known individuals but they represent
organizations, they are well qualified, and the council is attached to the
presidency, its function is to prepare proposals, or recommendations
relating to concrete issues for the president'. She agrees that the Civic
Chamber also includes some good individuals, and that, by being a
member, it is easier to establish personal contacts with ministers or with
the president's administration.

And does Lukin [the ombudsman] help you? I ask. Yes. He is
much improved. When he was first appointed and made his first
report on human rights in the armed forces, he wrote such a lot of
nonsense, that we, of course, took him apart. But he has really
improved.[3]

Talking to Melnikova brings out, very clearly, the way in which the
Duma has faded as a policy-making body, and how personal relations,

and meetings, with leading politicians and ministers are critical for getting items on the agenda or tackling individual cases. The issue of army reform also demonstrates that organizations find it difficult to cooperate with each other. The animosity (perhaps too strong a word) between Melnikova and Polyakova (the chair of the St Petersburg committee) that we came across in Chapter 3 is still present. Marchenko and Melnikova occupy offices opposite each other across the corridor but they do not cooperate. Krivenko, from Memorial and the Coalition, would bring them together if he could but Melnikova is highly critical of the 'Memorial' group 'while relating very positively to Memorial's work on Stalinist repression and Chechnya'. Too many people, she says, take up themes on which they are not experts. And if we meet in five years' time?

> I think we shall have already shut down our organization, at least I hope so. I am terribly tired. And Russia won't survive another five years with its present army [. . .] But much will depend upon the [new] six-year term of office for the president. The state machine moves faster under a four-year term [. . .] but, in any event, human rights activity has become more effective. There are failures of course – as regards prisons, the police – but in principle people have learnt a lot, people have learnt to turn to human rights organizations and, sooner or later, you find someone who will help.

So what do we conclude here? The Coalition did seize a political opportunity, when it arose, and the law of alternative service is thanks to its efforts. By providing professional reports, its members have succeeded in keeping abuse of draftees on the political agenda, and they have helped individual soldiers. But without the Soldiers' Mothers one senses that the uncovering of abuses would remain largely hidden. Armies guard their own secrets. The army lobby comes out as still very strong. And the General Staff's misappropriation of budget funding suggests a president who, despite his KGB background, can either be hoodwinked or is simply unable to control corruption. Neither Putin nor Medvedev proved able to take the movement forward to a professional army but, surely before long, the demographic decline of the 18-year-old cohort will compel a change in policy.

Now let's look at the police.

Tackling abuse by the police

According to Igor Kalyapin, the radical activist with entrepreneurial talent from Nizhny Novgorod, who now heads the NGO, Committee Against Torture:

> It is not that the Kremlin wants to have a corrupt police force, policemen whom people fear and who may even kill them. It's a side effect of a system of rule which lacks any mechanism of accountability, or of political competition. The authorities would be happy to put [police behaviour] to rights, as long as it did not involve changing the basis of their power. And if there are activists who are working on it, who are not aiming to become the centre of some political activity, then why not work together with them?

As the new century progressed, the issues of police brutality, including the torture of suspects, and of corruption at all levels, increasingly appeared in the news and internet media. Shocking cases attracted attention. In 2009 a young lawyer, Sergei Magnitsky, who had uncovered large-scale tax fraud by criminal gangs and high ranking police officials, was arrested on charges of tax evasion. Held on remand for 11 months, subjected to abuse and refused medication, his death caused an international scandal. Abuse in the police stations, and bribery at all levels seemed endemic. Medvedev talked of reform, and in 2010 declared that a new law on the police was needed. But when the law was passed, in February 2011, the most significant change was a name change: the *militsia* became the *politsia*. In what can only have been a momentary mental aberration, Medvedev referred to the law as a historic document.

The police force is a federal agency, under the MVD. Throughout the later Soviet period, and the nineties, the issue of decentralizing everyday policing (partly funded by regional authorities) came up more than once but the law of 2011 retained the existing system while transferring all funding to the federal budget. As with much else, the 'power vertical', the dominance of the centre over the regions, remains the principle of state organization. However, as Brian Taylor points out in an illuminating article, the Russian police system shares much in common with other police systems: 'The status quo has both a bureaucratic and cultural advantage, and is not only a communist tradition but a long-standing Russian one. It also is far from unique in comparative terms, including for large, multi-ethnic federations.'[4] Similarly, the idea that the police's function is to serve the state rather than citizens, despite the wording in the new law which 'states the police's responsibility to "defend the life, health, rights, and freedoms" of inhabitants of Russia (citizens or otherwise)' is, he suggests, commonly found in authoritarian, middle income countries. Institutional rivalries – particularly between the MVD, prosecutors, and the security services – feature in both authoritarian and democratic systems. (At a seminar for Russian and American prosecutors in St Petersburg in 1998, their shared antipathies and suspicions, in particular of the security services, were apparent.) However, as Taylor demonstrates, two elements in the Russian environment have had a major influence on police behaviour since the ending of Communist-party rule. One, inherited from the past, from the Soviet 'command economy' type of rule, is the quota system, the setting of planned targets for police forces to meet. Here I quote Taylor:

A series of indicators were passed down from the center. The targets were often absurdly precise (a certain number of firearms arrests per month, a specific number of traffic violations, another target for passport infringements, etc.) as well as impossibly high (such as clearance rates over 90 per cent). [...] As before, the quotas are often both very precise and completely unrealistic, and particularly divorced from local conditions. [...] Often these indicators are set with respect to the previous year. So, for example, if in one small village the police were supposed to arrest three people for selling narcotics, the next year they might have to arrest four. What if all dealers in this small village are already in jail, and there is no one else left to arrest? In the best case this village police officer might make a deal with his boss to falsify the report, but it might also be necessary, for example, to coerce someone arrested for petty theft to plead guilty to drug trafficking.

And, as Taylor points out, once an officer has met his quota target, he can enrich himself. The new economic environment of wealthy individuals, struggling entrepreneurs, car drivers, and illegal migrant workers provides plenty of opportunities for poorly paid policemen. Kalyapin soon experienced the corruption.

> Moreover [the law and order agencies] behaved quite unscrupulously. And they have become less and less controllable by anyone. As a result, instead of the development of a civilized state with a market economy, we have something pretty deformed and scary. Those who are in a position of power are not directly involved in economic matters, but they receive most of the profits, while escaping from any control by law, or by society.

Taylor argues, convincingly, that

> In the Soviet period, the demands and interests of the Party–State took precedence over societal concerns, so law enforcement was predominately a repressive organization. That repressive component of behavior has lessened but persisted, while the predatory (economically self-interested) element has grown but is not entirely new. What remains the case is that protection of citizens is often a secondary or even tertiary concern of law enforcement personnel.

Given such a situation, what are the options open to human rights activists to effect changes in police behaviour? Perhaps not surprisingly, in the 1990s, while the human rights centres took up individual cases, there was no attempt to create a coalition to press for reforms. The task, I suggest, was simply too daunting – and, importantly, ideas on how to reform a police service, on what it should look like, what its tasks should be, were thin on the ground. The nineties too were a time of rising crime – robberies, muggings, murder – when the incompetence of the local police caused as much concern as their abusive practices. Over the period, changes within the police – more corruption, accompanied by abuse (there is no way we can assess whether police brutality rose or fell), and, by 2010, the increasing use of violence against demonstrators, brought a new level of concern. Changes within the human rights community – the emergence of a new generation of young lawyers, a more professional approach when advocating reforms –

and changes in the Kremlin's attitude towards Western funders and to active opposition combined to produce a shift in tactics within the human rights community. Taking on the police began to replace working with the police.

Working with the police

Let us follow the path trodden by Citizens Watch in St Petersburg. In the 1990s, Boris Pustintsev, and some of the domestic violence crisis centres in St Petersburg and other cities, advocated working with the police to educate them.[5] By the late nineties the crisis centres were running training programmes for serving police officers, and Citizens Watch had established good contacts with the city police authorities and with the MVD University. Activities included publishing and distributing European materials on police codes of conduct, organizing visits for police to observe practices in other countries, training sessions for recruits, and introducing a course on human rights and policing at the university. Pustintsev's view was, to change police behaviour, work had to be done at grassroots level, as well as at the top. After the Civic Forum in 2001, he was encouraged by the 'dialogue' that continued under the ministry but, as everywhere, much depended upon the relations that a human rights organization, or its leader, could establish with those in authority at regional level. Pustintsev worked tirelessly at this. Among my photographs are those where I and others stand respectfully beside Pustintsev and the regional police chief in police headquarters, or with the rector of the MVD University behind his huge untidy desk piled high with heaps of papers. But if those at the top decided such activities were not helpful or simply not needed, their subordinates concurred. And that is what happened in 2006.

Police projects, whether those of Citizens Watch, or a more ambitious programme, under Moscow's INDEM foundation, headed by Georgy Satarov, had been carried out with MVD approval. Satarov, one of Yeltin's assistants in 1994–7, is a well-known figure in Moscow political and intellectual circles. A member of the liberal establishment, his foundation engages in studies of, for example, corruption or judicial reform. Its website still refers to The Centre for Justice Assistance, a joint venture inspired by the Vera Institute of Justice in New York, and funded by Western money. This undertook a major project in Nizhny

Novgorod, aimed at reducing time spent by those awaiting trial in remand centres, and another, called First Contact, where law students, in a select number of police stations, provided advice and took complaints from citizens. While both projects came up with results that showed how policing could be improved, and citizen satisfaction increased, once the Western funding finished, no attempt was made by the authorities to continue them or replicate them elsewhere.

It was the same with a project, organized by Citizens Watch, also with the Vera Institute of Justice, and with criminologists and statisticians in St Petersburg, which aimed to devise a way of assessing police precinct performance in the eyes of citizens. Surveys of public attitudes to the police had multiplied (which revealed low levels of trust but little else) but did not allow for precinct ranking. The project team struggled but a good workable survey instrument did emerge (one that identified encounters with the police both within and outside the respondent's precinct), and a precinct ranking that could be used by police authorities and community groups as a basis for action. Presented at an international seminar on police accountability, in the summer of 2001, organized by the Vera Institute together with Citizens Watch, it was welcomed by a community-policing official from the St Petersburg police department. The ranking of precincts tallied with the police assessments, and, he suggested, it would be helpful if the team could conduct surveys of encounters for particular groups: victims of domestic violence (a headache for the police), and ex-prisoners. Participants from other countries stressed the importance of including groups that fall outside surveys based on residence, and that may be particularly vulnerable: migrants, hostel residents.

For the first time it looked as though the police were responding but none of the city's top police officials attended the seminar, despite their promises to do so. And no further use was made of the survey instrument. But then, by this time, the regional leadership was expecting changes. In 2003 Rashid Nurgaliyev was moved from the security services to become the minister in charge of the MVD, a position he held until 2011, and changes followed at regional level. Citizens Watch, and INDEM, continued their projects but by 2006 a new law made it difficult, if not impossible, for state officials to participate in projects funded by Western foundations, and amendments to the NGO law[6] brought organizations such as Citizens Watch under scrutiny from tax officials, Ministry of Justice officials, and almost certainly the FSB. With a new police chief, and new rector of the university, any projects that had Western funding were closed.

As an example of the way local officials might interpret the new tougher legislation on NGOs, Citizens Watch's experience can serve. In 2007 the new Federal Registry Service undertook an inspection (*proverka*) of its documents and financial accounts. It found three faults: a staff member had travelled abroad under a project where such travel was not included in the budget (despite the project's allowing for changes to be made in budget expenditure); Citizens Watch had invited individuals from outside St Petersburg to attend seminars whereas it was a 'city' organization (even though, if the proposed activity was 'for the good of the city', this was permissible); by distributing publications, funded by the British or the Dutch ministries of foreign affairs, they were engaging in PR on their behalf (with no regard to the content of the publications?). These findings were accompanied by a letter requesting Citizens Watch to provide all its correspondence for the past three years; its failure to do so would result in a charge of not complying with the inspection request, and hence closure. Its board, after heated discussion, voted four to three to comply with the request but simultaneously to challenge its legality in court. Among their board members was Yury Shmidt, one of Russia's best-known defence lawyers. They lost at the district court hearing, but an appeal to the city court was successful. Perhaps more interesting, when Pustintsev, at a meeting of the President's Council for the Advancement of Civil Society and Human Rights, mentioned the inspection to the deputy chair of the Federal Registry Service, he was accused of making the details up. However, when Pamfilova, the chair of the council, confirmed she had seen the documents, the deputy chair fell silent. Three weeks later the service was abolished, and registration handed to the Ministry of Justice.

By this time human rights organizations, of different kinds, were coming under investigation by the tax inspectorates. Elena Zhemkova, of the International Memorial Society, spent hours either preparing submissions, or sitting in tax inspectorate offices, while their lawyers challenged (and won) a series of court cases. The charges could be very imaginative: 20 elderly Gulag survivors, to each of whom the society had presented a Memorial mug at a commemoration ceremony in a provincial city, had not included this in their income tax returns [...] Domestic violence crisis centres in some provincial cities received visits from the

FSB, enquiring about their foreign funding. Among respondents to the survey of NGO activists in several cities, carried out by Denis Volkov, there were regional human rights activists who stated:

> They are squeezing us again, pretty tightly. These checks by the prosecutor's office or the department of justice [...] I think that it's the policy of the top leadership, the president, prime minister [...] we had a visit from people from the security services, who checked us out [...] earlier we never had anything like that.

And:

> At the present moment they are using both legal and other types of pressure: people are called in by the departments for the struggle against extremism, trade union accounts are blocked, tax inspections of a number of donors are suddenly instigated, and so on. Government agencies, of different kinds, clearly receive instructions from somewhere to use whatever means they can to block some action, to stop a strike or some kind of protest happening, to break up an organization, to scare people.[7]

Much depended upon the local environment. Some human rights organizations went under but the better established survived, while distracted by having to spend time and energy on preparing documents for the tax and justice ministries. At one point in 2009 the prosecutor's office in Moscow decided to get involved, and several – but not all – Moscow organizations received an unannounced visit from an official, requesting access to their files. This initially caused consternation [...] but then nothing more was heard of the requests.

In 2013, as we shall see in Chapter 12, the inspection was more thorough and much more threatening. However, now back to the police.

Challenging police abuse

Human dignity shall be protected by the state. Nothing may serve as a basis for its derogation. No one shall be subject to torture, violence or other severe or humiliating treatment or punishment. (Article 21, constitution)

By this time several human rights groups were actively engaged in taking up the cases of victims of police illegality or torture. The most visible among them were the Nizhny Novgorod Committee Against Torture, headed by Igor Kalyapin, which takes cases, and not only from Nizhny Novgorod; Agora from Kazan, headed by Pavel Chikov, whose network of lawyers in different parts of the country takes up cases involving civic activists; and Public Verdict, a Moscow-based organization, headed by Natalya Taubina, which also has a network of lawyers, takes up citizens' cases, and engages in research and advocacy. All these organizations have won cases before the European Court.

Police abuse is the Committee Against Torture's primary concern. When Kalyapin joined the newly created Nizhny Novgorod Human Rights organization in 1993, his business interests occupied most of his attention. In the nineties these led to conflict with both the police and criminal gangs, and to such a degree that for a short while he moved with his family to a neighbouring region. By the turn of the century, having come to the conclusion that it was important to pursue one issue, and to pursue it professionally, he made human rights activity his main occupation, while continuing to survive as a small-scale entrepreneur. His aim is to demonstrate to people the importance of the values of freedom of speech, independent courts, 'liberal values', by taking up a concrete problem that is of popular concern. The issue he chose to focus on was the illegal use of violence by the law and order agencies. This led to his setting up the Committee Against Torture, linked to but independent of the Nizhny Novgorod Human Rights organization, and commissioning a study from sociologists in St Petersburg on the prevalence of police brutality and torture. The survey came up with the finding that one in five Russian citizens experiences such treatment at least once in their lives.

> People have experienced this, either they themselves or their relatives have suffered, and they know about it. It's laughable to talk about human dignity or liberal values, human rights, in a country where representatives of the state behave in such a way towards their citizens. Freedom, I mean freedom from torture, which is listed in Article three of the European Convention, it's a freedom which everyone recognizes and the majority are prepared

to defend. From this point of view, our activity, our committee's activities, resonate, they are intelligible to all.

For Kalyapin, this is a means of getting a more important message across:

> For me it's the most effective way of explaining that if we want the police to operate, not in their own interests, but in ours, then we must control them. Don't entrust that control to the president, don't entrust it to United Russia, that won't work. We, citizens, must create some kind of mechanisms, learn to use them, and then we shall be able to control that agency.

This means demonstrating that ordinary citizens can pursue their rights if they learn how to do it. His organization aims to show people that any citizen, with some legal knowledge, can in the great majority of cases carry out his or her own investigation of an incident of police violence, collect the evidence, bring a criminal case against the police officer, get a criminal conviction and compensation for damages.

Between 2003 and 2011 the organization, now with a staff of more than 30, won 77 cases against police officers for torture. Perhaps half of these involved officers in Nizhny Novgorod, others were from regions or republics where the committee has set up its sections (Mari-El, Orenburg, Bashkortostan, Chechnya). In an emergency situation (a major incident involving several law and order agencies), they organize a 'mobile group', from among their lawyers, and from other human rights organizations, which flies in and works intensively there for a short period, before handing responsibility to two or three to conduct the case.

In contrast, Public Verdict, set up in Moscow in 2003, was a new venture in more senses than one. A group of Moscow activists that included Roginsky, Alekseeva, Lokshina, and Dzhibladze approached Mikhail Khodorkovsky, the oil magnate, for support for a new organization that, in Taubina's words, could provide

> legal assistance, pay for a defence lawyer for individuals who wanted to bring a case against the law and order agencies for the infringement of their rights, in the first instance against the police, in some cases against the prison service, prosecutors, investigative agencies, and, rarely, the security services.

Leading defence lawyers, Genri Reznik and Yury Shmidt, and Tamara Morshakova (a retired judge from the Constitutional Court) participated in the discussion, as did board members from Khodorkovsky's foundation Open Russia.

In September 2003 Khodorkovsky invited Natalya Taubina, and Pavel Chikov, the young lawyer from Kazan, the capital of the Tatarstan republic, for discussions (effectively interviews), and gave the go ahead, and one year's funding for the new organization, Public Verdict. Taubina became the director, Chikov the chief legal counsel and head of the legal department. Two months later Khodorkovsky was arrested on tax evasion charges. Public Verdict started its work in February 2004. It was the first serious, new, human rights organization to be funded with Russian money – and, sadly, so far the last. Until its closure in 2006, Open Russia continued to fund other smaller projects in the field, and Dmitry Zimin's Dynasty foundation has, for example, supported the Memorial Society. But Public Verdict was something new – designed and funded solely by Russian sources. It has established itself as a well-respected organization, with quite a high profile, but now, alas, almost wholly funded by Western sources.

Before we look at what it does, a word on its director and chief legal counsel. We have met Natalya Taubina before, the young assistant to Aleksei Smirnov in the crowded offices of the Research Centre on Human Rights who, in 1993, headed a small grants programme, and became known in the Moscow human rights community as a pleasant and capable administrator, knowledgeable in dealing with Western foundations. No one would be offended by her becoming director of the new organization – and this was important in a community where personal and political differences, and competitive personalities, are all too common. Younger, and perhaps older, activists refer to 'the Taubina, Dzhibladze, Lokshina set' – as experts at getting funding, dealing with Western funders and NGOs, and writing reports for international audiences – and they do, indeed, share a set of skills and years of working together on related projects, despite being very different. In 2011 Public Verdict was renting a spacious modern office in an office block built by the Turks, who have a penchant for marble staircases and shiny black surfaces. None of the human rights organizations could have imagined themselves in such a setting in the 1990s, and today it is only Public Verdict, the Memorial Society (with a new office, complete with lecture facilities, storage for its archive, library and museum, funded by Ford and Soros), and the Sakharov Centre (with its old but large building) that have a feeling of space. Overcrowding is still the norm, three, four individuals behind their loaded desks, in a small room, up the staircase of a shabby building.

Pavel Chikov is one of the leaders of the youngest generation of activists. Tall, energetic, self-assured, with a degree in international law from Kazan State University, he won a scholarship in 2000 to complete an MA in Public Administration at Dakota State. Upon returning to Kazan, and while working on a postgraduate thesis, he, together with six other young lawyers and a computer specialist, formed a group under the aegis of the Kazan Human Rights Centre, and spent the next two years simply studying different aspects of the system of law enforcement.

> We carried out about 20 projects, that is we interviewed police officers, studied sentences – talked to 700 police officers, to 2,000 individuals who had been charged, studied 3,000 sentences [. . .] We decided to study the law enforcement agencies because the friend with whom I started to work together was a former member of the crime squad of the department for organized crime. He was a serious policeman, with six years' service. He was my fellow student, and he told me a lot about how bad things are in the police. And there wasn't a single organization among the human rights organizations which focused on law and order. And then we came to know Igor Kalyapin, from the Committee Against Torture, and he got us interested in what he was doing – public investigation of torture cases. And once we had finished the research aspect of our work, we began to take up cases, that was in 2002.

For a couple of years they participated in the Moscow Helsinki Group's regional monitoring project, while conducting cases, and by 2003 had won their first convictions of police officers for torture or murder. This brought him to Khodorkovsky's attention, and he left for Moscow but, before leaving, he and colleagues helped to create partner organizations in two or three other regions, organizations based on the Kazan model. Chikov spent two years in Moscow at Public Verdict. He organized the legal department and supervised the work of three lawyers.

I gave it everything I had, for a year and a half I was working 14 hours a day, it was so interesting, just imagine what it was like. When people from YUKOS [Khodorkovsky's company] came and said – we want you to set up 100 organizations across the country, modelled on the Kazan human rights centre, and you'll have as much money as you need. That was a challenge, and interesting, and I was 25 years old [...] and I was to have absolute freedom to do it as I wished. Of course I knew, straightaway, that it was impossible to set up 100 organizations, and I said so – but they replied – set up as many as you think is objectively possible, that's what we want.

He pressed ahead, but his setting up of an association of regional partners made his position at Public Verdict difficult. He left, and by 2006 was back in Kazan. There he decided that Agora, their new organization, should focus on defending civic activists, not concentrate simply on police behaviour, although 'if the police have beaten up an activist, it's a hundred to one that he will turn to us'. Chikov likes administration, likes being in charge, and draws from a well of energy and talent. While their paths and ways of working have since diverged, Chikov and Kalyapin see each other as close colleagues, and respect each other.

So, what does Public Verdict do – and what has it achieved? For a start, it provides legal assistance. There are three lawyers in the Moscow office, perhaps 20 in the regions who participate, and ten regional organizations who cooperate. When taking up a case of police abuse, they pay either one of their lawyers or a local lawyer to act as defence counsel. They provide psychological 'rehabilitation' where it is needed, and, with the client's agreement, publicize the case. In Taubina's words:

So that, on the one hand, the public becomes aware that you can fight against that kind of behaviour, and it is important to do so, because that's the only way we can change the situation. And, on the other hand, we try to attract the public's attention to the problem of the infringement of human rights by law-enforcement agencies.

By 2010 they had won 60 cases, and got convictions for 100 police officers. A hundred cases were ongoing; perhaps 50 new ones coming in each year, from maybe half the regions of Russia. They had taken a few to the European Court. They had no particular channels of communication with any of the law and order ministries but

> from time to time we interact with them over some activities, organized by the president's council, or the Civic Chamber. We do have meetings, initiated by, for example, the department for relations with the public of the MVD, but when they suggest that, before we go to the press with cases of infringements, we should notify them, and they will punish the guilty parties, and issue a press release, we do not agree.

In some regions, their partner organizations work quite constructively with the regional police authorities, and organize seminars for prosecutors and criminal investigators. In 2010 they were heading a coalition working on police reform but, before we turn to this, a word from Kalyapin. He is ambivalent about the changes that Putin's system of vertical control have brought.

> Surprising as it may seem, I would not say that today's authorities, the Putin regime (despite all my irritation and my unwillingness to recognize it) is a poorer defender of human rights than was the Yeltsin regime. I was involved in these issues then [...] I can't say that human rights were better defended then, that the laws were more often observed than today – no, they were not better then, maybe even worse.

The near anarchy and corruption of the Yeltsin period have left their scars. But now, he argues:

> there is a clear hierarchy of state officials, and that hierarchy is compelled to relate its activities to the laws. I am continually amazed by the fact that the corner stone or, more properly, the basic instrument with which we work is the courts. We object to the work of the investigative officer, who is in charge of a case of torture, before the court. More often than not we win these cases. About 70 per cent of our claims are granted by the court. That's the basic instrument with which we compel an investigating

officer to do what he should, by law, be doing. Despite all that is said about corrupt judges, about how the system is fit for nothing – it actually works.

Does it work better than in the nineties? I ask.
Better. The court system works better than in the nineties. I can say that without any hesitation.
And how do you explain that?

Kalyapin's answer is that the seeds of judicial reform that were scattered in the early nineties, including by Sergei Pashin (who probably would not agree), have had some results in making judges act more independently. In Chapter 11 we take up the working of the court system from the perspective of the young lawyers who engage in human rights issues, and in Chapter 12 from that of the ombudsman. As we shall see, there are improvements but the verdict on significant improvements in court performance is still out.

In contrast, Kalyapin suggests, the MVD, prosecutors, and FSB are in the final stages of decay.

These structures have become some kind of a cancerous growth, which is eating away at the organism. They work for themselves, they don't work for the state, or on behalf of society, or of the country. For a long time they have been engaged in 'self service', each works for itself, and in so doing attacks the state. I am not even talking about society, I am talking about the state. They are destroying it. And since they have already swallowed so much of it, they are already beginning to bite each other. Today's pie isn't big enough for them. They don't get enough from the budget, so they are fighting over various corrupt territories from which they can feed.

And, do you think the political leadership is not aware of that? I ask.

I am absolutely convinced that it is aware of it. Simply, such a situation suits some in the elite [...who think] the country is doomed to fall apart anyway, so the only thing I can do, as a highly placed government official, is to get something for myself and my children, who are studying somewhere in England, and for whom

I've bought a property somewhere on the Spanish coast [...]
Others, one can say, try honestly to do something to salvage the
situation, because from time to time some positive signals
percolate down from the top.

Later in the interview, I ask: 'Will the new law on the police bring no
changes?'

No [...] it's some clumsy attempt at rebranding, in today's jargon.
It's a change of costume, very clumsily done, of no use whatsoever
[...] I doubt that there is a single person in Russia who is naïve
enough to think that the police is somehow better than the militia.
Why did they spend so much money on it? I don't know. Who is
Mr Nurgaliev trying to deceive when he says that corruption and a
lack of professionalism is a thing of the past? [...] We, unlike Mr
Nurgaliev, come into contact with the traffic police, with those on
the street and in the police stations, and people see that the police
have not got any better, only they are being paid more.

And this brings us back to the issue of police reform.

Reform of the police

Public Verdict has a wider brief than either Agora or the Committee
Against Torture. The commissioning of research, preparation of reports
on particular issues, the maintenance of a comprehensive website, and of
bringing out publications, all occupy its Moscow office staff. It is not
surprising to find it, by 2010, heading a Working Group (Coalition) of
Human Rights Organizations on Cooperation with the Ministry of
Internal Affairs and the Promotion of Reform. Originally established
in 2008, among its 14 members were many with whom we are
familiar: Agora, the Committee Against Torture, Citizens Watch from
St Petersburg, the Perm Centre for Civic Education, The Committee
for the Defence of Human Rights from Krasnoyarsk (Gorelik), the
Memorial Human Rights Commission from Syktyvkar (Sazhin),
the Institute for Human Rights in Moscow (Gefter) and others. The
Coalition or Working Group bears a resemblance to the Coalition for
Alternative Service but there is a difference. Its member organizations

are much better established, experienced, and work on a variety of issues. Some had worked together previously (in 2004) to produce a detailed report on human rights violations by law enforcement officials, based on data provided by local organizations. This began with the statement:

> The police, as a general rule, act in violation of Articles 2, 3, 5, and 8 of the European Convention for the Protection of Human Rights and Fundamental Freedoms (Rome, 1950, hereinafter, the European Convention), namely, the right to life, prohibition of torture, inhuman or degrading treatment or punishment, the right to integrity of person in relation to deprivation of liberty, and the right to respect for private and family life and home.

The report was divided into sections ranging from 'The use of physical and psychological violence during arrest, detention, and questioning of a suspect', or 'The unjustified use of firearms and physical force in arresting drivers for traffic offences' to 'The use of force, in the presence of police officers, by their former (resigned or removed from active duty) colleagues, or by police off duty', to 'Torture, and causing the death of the victim of police abuse'. Some of the cases are horrific.[8]

When, in 2010, Medvedev announced that a new law on the police was needed, the group sprang into action. Indeed Taubina would argue that it was through their efforts that police reform came onto the agenda, and that journalists in Moscow seek out Public Verdict for expertise and information. I suspect she is partly right but it is difficult, if not impossible, to weigh the contribution made by the NGOs and the impetus given to police reform by a case such as Magnitsky's, and the Krasnodar scandal mentioned in Chapter 4. The ability of the members of the Working Group to work together, and to prepare professional documents, showed how far the human rights organizations had come in the past ten years. What we might call the Lokshina, Dzhibladze, Taubina bequest had paid off. But the group did not include experts from within the police, nor from the MVD Institute. Satarov had managed to include them in his earlier projects but, now, it seemed, the activists were on their own.

The working group prepared a detailed concept paper on the reform of the MVD.

On 19 March 2010 this plan was presented to a joint meeting of
the working group, the Presidential Council on Civil Society and
Human Rights, and the Civic Chamber's commission for public
oversight of the activities and reform of law enforcement and the
justice system. The plan's basic concepts were developed using the
experience of similar reforms in a number of European countries.
In April and May 2010 public discussions of the plan were
organized in thirteen Russian regions in which hundreds of law
enforcement officials, journalists, and representatives of political
parties and NGOs took part.[9]

(But some suggested that law enforcement officials were largely absent.)
From there the group moved on to consider the police in particular, to
issue a response to the draft police law (when it appeared in August
2010), and to provide their alternative. Their main thesis, and concern,
was that it made no sense to try to reform the police without the reform
of the Ministry of Internal Affairs, and police relations with other
agencies. (They did not say so but surely meant not only the prosecutors
but also the FSB.) They expressed dismay that the draft bill simply
ignored this issue. While welcoming the wording on 'basic principles of
police work: the priority of human rights, and an absolute prohibition
on torture', the group argued that:

> The bill does not provide information about the future structure
> and composition of the police. It does not identify which other
> agencies, besides the police, form part of the 'single, centralized
> system of federal executive authority that performs the functions
> of formulating and implementing government policy and
> normative and legal regulation in the field of internal affairs'.[10]

By October 2010 they were insisting that, while the authorities might
have produced a new police bill:

> It will be impossible in practice to transform the police into a
> professional institution that acts in the interest of the citizens,
> ensuring public order and public safety and fighting crime, unless
> a number of wide ranging and well thought out measures are
> drafted, adopted and implemented.

Public oversight of police activities, independent monitoring, a new system of evaluating police work, and investigation of cases of violations, they argued, were crucial.[11] But, and this is what we emphasize here, their advocacy had no effect whatsoever. They were voices calling in the wind, as far as Medvedev, the MVD, and the Duma were concerned. In February 2011 the bill was passed without any amendments. All that the Working Group could do was to state that it would monitor the consequences of introducing the new law, and propose amendments, and that its members wished to see a civilian appointed to head the police.

A year later in April 2012, following an appalling incident, in Kazan, of the torture of a suspect in police custody who subsequently died, Public Verdict approached the leadership of the Investigative Committee of the Russian Federation (responsible for criminal investigations) with a proposal that a special department should be set up to investigate crimes committed by law enforcement officers. For example it should not be left to the law enforcement agencies themselves to investigate such cases. The chair of the committee agreed to look into this. One of the final sessions of the president's council under Medvedev was devoted to the issue of police reform. As Taubina reported, it had been scheduled and put off more than once. Representatives of the MVD, including the deputy minister, who sat throughout the six-hour meeting, came with their prepared statements, and the council's working group presented a draft proposal for discussion. The draft stated:

> The reform of the Ministry of the Interior was of a predominantly internal departmental nature and non-governmental intervention was, in the main, purely formal. The predominantly formal nature of the non-governmental participation in this process has not helped increase the public's trust in the police.

The council produced a comprehensive list of recommendations (presumably prepared in advance), which was approved by a vote, and signed by Fedotov, the chair. It begins:

> To create either under the president or the prime minister a working group to prepare a system of performance rating for police departments; to carry out pilot projects; to work out mechanisms

for independent organizations to check citizens' complaints against the police, taking foreign experience into account.

The list is a long one. In addition to items on budget transparency, complaint books, badges, telephone calls, computer data, it includes the proposal for public councils at ministerial and regional level which should have 'real control functions' and be ratified by the Civic Chambers. And it suggests that a law on 'public control' more generally is needed.[12] But there the matter rests.

In this case the activists' campaign had no impact on legislation. It was clear that the political authorities could simply ignore this kind of pressure when they wished, and, what may have started as a Medvedev idea that something could be done, was quickly quashed by the vested interests of the law and order ministries.

> Activists of some experience speak of how, at a certain point, you reach the ceiling of your potential [to change matters], you understand that you are dealing with the consequences of a problem but not with what is causing it, because that remains exclusively within the authorities' jurisdiction. The level where government decisions are taken is today effectively closed to civic activists.

And that, according to Volkov, has had a demoralizing effect upon some of the activists.[13]

So what did they achieve here? They placed the issue on the public agenda, and they helped individuals. We have no examples of lasting local initiatives. The police are an institution similar to the army, one where the generals control the lower units but, unlike the army, their work with citizens means the cases of abuse are more visible. Clearly more than monitoring or public control is going to be needed to change police behaviour.

CHAPTER 9

PRISON INSPECTORS, JUVENILE COURTS, DOMESTIC VIOLENCE AND REFUGEES

At the end of the nineties, and during the early years of the new century, the idea of uniting all the human rights activists in one umbrella movement, with a coordinating centre, still held sway [...] Today, while all recognize that they share common ground, and it seems quite natural to form coalitions around particular issues, the human rights community is much more professional, much more segmented, each works professionally in his own field, advancing concrete ideas. The expert potential of the human rights community has grown significantly.

Many would agree with Sergei Lukashevsky, the young director of the Sakharov Centre, although, in December 2010, as we saw in the Introduction, leading organizations did come together to lambast the Medvedev–Putin regime for not observing the constitution. In the previous chapter we saw an activist community, still composed of competitors, becoming increasingly professionalized, with its experts able to prepare reports and recommendations for the president, ministries, or international bodies. But its impact upon policy, while never great, became negligible as the policy-making environment offered fewer points of entry and fewer allies. Attempts to introduce either the public inspection of prisons or juvenile courts illustrate, perhaps even more clearly, the increasing opaqueness of decision making in the Kremlin and the subservience of the Duma and the law and order agencies to the tandem's i.e., the Putin-Medvedev leadership's instructions. Here, though, we see justice ministries and courts from a rather different perspective, a wider range of actors appear, and the local environment plays an important role. It may be impossible for local initiatives to change the rules as regards army or police behaviour but as regards the treatment of prisoners or young offenders there were those willing to try. And, in both cases, as was the case with domestic violence and refugee and migrant rights, to which we then turn, changes in the social and economic environment and in popular attitudes make themselves felt.

Which then were the resources the activists could draw on, who were their allies and opponents, and what were the outcomes?

Public inspection of places of detention

A group of human rights activists and deputies had been lobbying for a public inspectorate of prisons and closed institutions since the early nineties. Briefly, in the heady years following the 1990 elections, enterprising activists made use of their new powers (or rather the disorientation within government departments) to visit and inspect prisons, detention and remand centres. The energetic Andrei Babushkin, with a group of fellow deputies from the Moscow city council, instituted a practice of taking judges to visit the remand centres (where accused are held awaiting trial). By 1994 the deputies had either lost their seats or their standing but throughout this period activists could gain access to prisons, remand centres and detention centres. With the transfer of the Prison Service in 1997 to the Ministry of Justice, and with Yury Kalinin, a reform-minded deputy minister, in charge of a service suffering badly from a shortage of money, visitors brought publicity and sometimes material assistance. However, according to Babushkin, this had its downside:

> Very many activists had very little professional knowledge, weren't properly prepared, and committed errors which were then used against human rights activists. For example, they arrived at a children's colony [. . .] the children asked, could they help them to

get housing? They said they could. And a copy of our sentences? We'll help. And send us chocolate? We'll send some. In other words, they took on obligations, not really thinking about how to carry them out.

Meanwhile he and Sergei Pashin (the liberal judge) wrote a draft law on prison inspectors which was taken up by Valery Borshchev, a Democratic Russia deputy in the Duma. A delegation visited England to look at the Inspectorate of Prisons for England and Wales, an independent body whose chief inspector is appointed by the Justice Secretary. The draft law presented to the Duma proposed a federal inspectorate of 50 members, appointed by the ombudsman from a list of candidates (only two from any one organization, whose charter must include the defence of rights); the inspectors would have the right to make planned and unplanned visits, to issue reports and make recommendations. The Prison Service supported the proposals; the police were less happy, particularly as regards inspectors being able to talk to prisoners. President Yeltsin was unenthusiastic, largely because the ombudsman, Oleg Mironov, had been a Communist party deputy. However, in 1999, the bill (supported by the Communists and the liberals) passed its third reading and went to the upper house, the Council of the Federation. But the upper house, consisting of regional representatives, promptly rejected it: they objected to a federal inspectorate as opposed to regional inspectorates.[1]

Borshchev, still a deputy, began work on a new bill that would devolve the inspectorate to regional level but, after the new president had made it known that he favoured a federal system, the bill failed to pass a first reading. At the time of the Civic Forum in 2001, its supporters organized a roundtable to discuss the draft. Members of the Duma, the Council of the Federation, and the Prison Service attended but no one came from other government ministries nor from the prosecutor's office. According to a journalist:

Giving public inspectors a legal status as monitors of the observance of the rights of prisoners was seen as the first step towards overcoming the closed nature of institutions, in which human rights are infringed most frequently. Civic control is needed in the army, children's homes, psychiatric hospitals, old peoples' homes. But, as it has turned out, the authorities oppose any control by society.[2]

Work on a compromise solution dragged on throughout 2003. Hopes were raised that both the president and the chief legal administration (of the president's administration) would now support it and, in September, after the president's spokesman had referred to its needing further work, it passed a first reading. But there it hung, unmoving, until 2007. Borshchev and the other liberal deputies were out of the Duma, there was no one to push it. By 2006 NGOs, and human rights NGOs in particular, were under attack, struggling to survive under the new NGO law. The proposed law on prison visitors was surely dead in the water.

However, in 2007, one of the committees in the new Civic Chamber revived the idea and invited Borshchev, Babushkin, and Valentin Gefter as experts to assist with work on a new draft. Whether the initiative came from within the president's administration, or whether the idea originated within the chamber and received approval from the administration, we do not know. The important point is that, by Putin's second term of office, policy making lay in the hands of a different set of actors. The Duma as a forum for real debate between political opponents, and an initiator of legislation, was no more; the Council of the Federation was no longer composed of elected regional representatives who would defend the regions against the federal centre; the ministries now looked up to the president for guidance in their dealing with society. Leading NGOs could no longer rely on access to a minister or a deputy to argue their case. Now, under the new 'managed democracy', the president and his ministers put forward policies, which passed through the appropriate bodies, and became law. Society, or its active members, had a part to play as expert aides to state institutions, as constructive partners. Hence the Civic Chamber of co-opted and appointed NGO representatives and figures from the academic and cultural world. Hence the setting up, under some of the ministries, of public councils for discussions. (Melnikova from Soldiers' Mothers was on that under the Ministry of Defence, Borshchev on that of the Prison Service, Pustintsev, for a while, on that under the Ministry of Internal Affairs.) Over the next few years such councils, or chambers, multiplied. At the top was the President's Council for the Advancement of Civil

Society and Human Rights, ministries (at federal and at regional level) had their councils, regional authorities were encouraged to set up civic chambers. But the composition of all these bodies, and the rules covering their activities, rested with the relevant part of the executive branch (president, minister, governor, ministerial official) – fair enough, one might say, given that their task was to *assist* the institutions of government.

What did this mean for the new draft on public inspections? An inspectorate was replaced by regional oversight commissions, which would have the right to visit the prisons, and other closed institutions.[3] The commissions were to observe (through visits, investigating complaints, speaking to prisoners, and staff) whether rights were being upheld, to make recommendations, and to assist organizations and staff in ensuring that rights and freedoms were observed. Both planned and unplanned visits were envisaged. The regulations were detailed, and oversight or supervision was to lie with the federal Civic Chamber.[4]

The draft legislation quickly went through all the appropriate stages and was signed into law by Putin in 2008. By 2009 commissions had been set up in 61 of Russia's regions. According to Babushkin, perhaps 100 of the 500 or so commission members appointed in 2009 were human rights activists. As Alla Pokras, from Penal Reform International, pointed out:

> Practically any organization can claim to be a human rights organization because in their charters one of their aims is stated to be: defending their members' rights. There are all kinds of organizations – the Red Cross, Crescent Moon, the Brotherhood of those who fought in Afghanistan, the veterans of the MVD. It is those kinds of people who outweigh the numbers of human rights activists. It's a conscious policy.

Should we think of the 2008 law as an achievement? Liudmila Alekseeva sees it as an important step in introducing public control over state institutions. Babushkin argues that there is something positive to it. His Moscow organization, For Citizens Rights, has half a dozen partner organizations in other towns or cities, and they all try to get a member or members onto their local commissions. In some instances local activists may be able to publicize conditions or practices in local places of detention, including police stations, in a way that previously they could not. But, in 2013, Babushkin was among 38 signatories of an open letter to Academician Velikhov, secretary of the Civic Chamber, complaining that, despite requests, the Civic Chamber did not require information from potential members on their qualifications, and hence took uninformed decisions on membership of commissions.[5] The Chamber's failure to acquire a reputation for integrity and independence means that dissatisfied activists interpret its decisions as politically motivated, and in some cases they may be correct; others however are more inclined to blame simple inefficiency within the Chamber's committees.

Pokras too, despite her criticisms, sees the law as a step forward, and in 2013 became a member of the Moscow city commission.

> Without a doubt, it's positive, although, of course, members cannot do much, because they are few, and there's a lot of work. Few want to do it unpaid. It's difficult to find the money to travel to places – and some of the colonies are in faraway places. Even if we're talking about Moscow, transport is very pricey [...] but in general and as a whole it is a positive step forward.

And she continues:

> Yes, these commissions can do something. Take the case of Magnitsky, yes, the Commission under Borshchev carried out an investigation after his death [...] But Magnitsky's lawyer did not turn to him before – because he didn't know of the commission's existence [...] when you are involved in something, you think that everyone knows about it, but, in fact, go out on the street, and ask and no one has heard of it.

In those cities where groups were already active, the legislation, by legitimizing their actions, will encourage greater oversight. There will be others where little is done.[6] The ombudsman's report for 2012 refers to instances in the Rostov region, in Irkutsk, Sverdlovsk and the Komi republic where, following the denial of access, the commissions turned to the ombudsman and then the prosecutor to gain it. These are all regions where one would expect to find activists exercising their rights.

Similarly in St Petersburg. The Kolpino colony for boys outside St Petersburg had witnessed serious unrest in 2008. In this case some prison officers were blackmailing boys – either they paid them monthly amounts in cash, or they would receive bad references and fail to get parole; some who refused were beaten. Others were not given time to appeal a court decision on transfer. The Kolpino case received sufficiently wide publicity to warrant a visit from a commission from Moscow, which found that 14 of the older boys had been hurriedly dispatched to a hospital for infectious diseases. A subsequent visit by a group of St Petersburg human rights activists, several of whom subsequently became members of the oversight commission, brought results: the governor was removed, and a new one appointed. In 2011 they were apprehensive that the Civic Chamber might refuse to reappoint those who had been too active in monitoring abuses, but they kept their places.

A Commission in action: Perm

However, how might an active commission work? Here I turn to the account given by Sergei Isayev, the director of the Human Rights Centre in Perm, and chair of the new oversight commission. It is hardly typical. The Centre's members had been visiting the prison colonies since 1997. In 2004–5 they signed agreements, first with the Prison Service, then with the police, which covered public oversight, lectures, and charitable assistance. They had been monitoring the detention centres under the police long before the new legislation, and also worked with prosecutors and police on rules for staff to observe. In recent years, in response to complaints received, they had paid frequent visits to the famous White Swan penitentiary for long-term and violent prisoners in Solikamsk, a town in the region. In Isayev's words:

> And this system of mass monitoring, of our being constantly there, produced a fall in complaints and, from its having a reputation for being the worst bully in Russia, breaking people, things have quietened down.
> At the last collegium of the krai prison service, whose meetings we have been attending for several years [. . .] the key report by the assistant head of the service was on human rights. Usually they

invite guests, the krai prosecutor, and us, and the police, and sometimes representatives from the Federal Prison Service but the latter are such block heads, absolutely uneducated, it made me furious last time – some colonel or other with the views of a diplodocus.

Once the new law came, they were active in putting forward candidates for the commission which, in its first term of office had 15 members, from 11 organizations. Eight remained in the 2011 list. Of these one is from Memorial, Igor Averkiev is there, and two others from his organization; three are from the Human Rights Centre (one nominated by another organization to observe the two-only rule).

As a consequence of both our and Margolina's [the ombudsman] efforts, the use of special operations [i.e., the use of physical force by specially trained troops] has dropped by half – an amazing result. Yes, physical force is still used, as it was, but the ideology of the prison service has begun to change, they've understood that they need to use educational measures.

Perm, we have already suggested, is, in the eyes of the human rights community, a nature reserve. Nowhere else in Russia, with the exception perhaps of Krasnoyarsk, can one envisage such a degree of cooperation between its human rights centre and the law and order agencies. Interestingly enough, this produces different responses. Some think of the Permiaki, and this always includes Averkiev, as role models. Olga Gnezdilova, the young lawyer in Voronezh, suggests:

Really they are geniuses, not only for our generation of human rights activists, but for future generations because they have worked out all kinds of innovative approaches [. . .] we talk about problems, propose some way of solving them, but we aren't able to show why this is appropriate, or necessary, or to present and promote our solutions as well and effectively as the Permiaki do. It seems to us that our task is to talk about the problems, and the authorities ought to pay attention, but we haven't yet learnt how to work together with them.[7]

Others consider that the Perm environment – the relationship between progressive governors and NGOs – has been so unique that the activists' innovations are simply not replicable elsewhere. And, in contrast, there are those who consider the Human Rights Centre works too closely with the authorities to qualify as a defender of human rights.

But to return to the public inspection commissions. Pavel Levashin, a young lawyer who worked in the Perm centre, was a member of the 2009 commission. He started his working life in the prison service, but was invalided out, and one of his tasks in the centre was to deal with a weekly batch of perhaps 30 letters received from prisoners. Perm krai has more than its share of colonies and prisons – perhaps 60 in all – Pavel was responsible for letters from 20 of them.

And what are the letters mostly about? I ask.

The issues are basically the same whether the individual is in or out of prison – there are housing problems, issues of disciplinary sanctions, complaints of conditions, pensions [. . .] for example, an individual falls sick or already has invalid status, he is entitled to a pension for that, regardless whether he is in prison or a free person.

But once a year he has to be reassessed, and then the problems arise. The prison administration has to collect documents, organize a medical commission, and send the reports to the pension department – and the documents get lost. Rather differently, sometimes the prison administration uses the prisoners' money to pay for building works or something else, and says the money has not arrived in their accounts, so they can't make withdrawals. Perhaps worst of all are the issues to do with passports. My heart sinks. An individual's passport should accompany him or her from police station to temporary detention to remand centre to court to prison colony but sometimes it gets left behind at the police station [. . .] and the search to track it down becomes Kafkaesque, after a fruitless two-year search, 'we got an invalid a new one [. . .] that was quicker, because he needed to get his invalid status registered and for that he needed a passport. You need a passport for anything.'

On their visits, the commission attempts to engage with the staff.

We arrive at an institution and, as well as carrying out an inspection, when time permits, we try to have a conversation with the staff about human rights [...] and straightaway it's obvious how unenthusiastic they are, and they begin to argue – why are we defending the rights of prisoners, and not their rights – that's their favourite response. We have a simple answer: what's preventing your turning to us? Prisoners write to us about their problems, and that's why we defend their rights. If you say nothing [...] how can we help you?

There was the case of pay for night shifts, for which officers received no extra pay, standing for six hours with an automatic, with only a single break for a meal. 'We learnt about this from a woman officer, once she retired, it took us three years of writing to all and sundry, but we finally won – and now they are paid extra.'

So what do we conclude here?

Without a decision from on high the campaign for prison visitors would have got nowhere. As it was, the new version brought the commissions under the Civic Chamber's aegis. The tendency, which we noted in 1996, of local authorities' staffing Yeltsin's new human rights commissions with amenable members will surely be repeated in many places; there will be commissions that do almost nothing but report results. A very Soviet practice. Given distances, the time and cost involved in visiting far away institutions presents a challenge even for enthusiasts. However, there is now an opportunity for activists to prise open the shutters of closed institutions, and highlight abuse or inhumane conditions. Whether they will be able and willing to do so will vary enormously from one locality to another.

Juvenile justice

In the nineties, Valery Abramkin's organization, the Moscow Centre for Prison Reform, which we met in Chapter 1, led the field as regards penal reform for both adults and children. By 1998 he had succeeded in bringing leading figures in the Prison Service on board. At the opening of an impressive exhibition on prison conditions held in the Polytechnic museum in the centre of Moscow, he held a joint press conference, with the head of the Administration of Prisons, to present the case for reducing prison numbers. The exhibition subsequently toured several cities. He collected donations, in the hungry years of the late nineties, to provide children with food and soap. He would hold roundtables – with Duma deputies and justice officials – to discuss the need for reforms to reduce the levels of imprisonment, and he did not mince his words.

> Let's take a concrete case – a hungry kid stole a few packets of dumplings [...] and the investigator signs the order for his arrest, the prosecutor sanctions it, and the judge refuses to change the detention order – don't they know what will happen to him? Don't they understand that they are not sending him to a remand centre but to the scaffold? From whence he will return, crippled, or he may die. That's not so rare. Don't you feel anything in your hearts, giving a kid a death sentence for a packet of dumplings? I want to know – how do you explain such cruelty? [...] And if, yet again, you don't hear the questions, then I'll tell you – actually it is you – judges, investigators, the prosecutors who are answerable for the extermination of people in the gas chambers of the remand centres.[8]

In Russia the age of criminal responsibility is 14 for serious, 16 for less serious crimes. By the turn of the century roughly a third of all convictions related to a violent crime, and the percentage continues to rise; but the great majority of those in the prison colonies are there for theft, and many for stealing on a small scale. With the demographic decline of the age group, numbers have fallen sharply. And, since 2006, with prompting from the Supreme Court and a new Minister of Justice, judges and prosecutors (at least in St Petersburg) only use detention on remand in exceptional cases, and only as a sentence for serious crimes. But compared with European countries (although not with the USA or England and Wales, where the use of custody is high, and the age of criminal responsibility can be as low as ten) the Russian record is still one of punitive sentencing. One of the reasons for this is that juveniles are subject to a Criminal Code designed for adults.[9]

In 1997 a group of academics published a paper on measures to reduce youth crime, a paper that reflected the emphasis in the international conventions on defending the rights and interests of the child. Its authors proposed 'the step by step creation of a complex justice system for young people' in which new legislation and specialized officials (investigators, prosecutors, judges) would focus on preventive measures and the defence of children's interests. A wide variety of alternative measures should ensure that deprivation of liberty, whether before trial, during a trial or afterwards, should only be used as an extreme measure. The proposal drew heavily from the United Nations and European Conventions to which the government had signed up. The conventions specify that detention on remand and as a sentence should only be used in extreme cases, and that sentences should be short. Alternatives to judicial proceedings should be the norm for a child but, where courts are necessary, they should be juvenile courts.

Boris Altshuler's Rights of the Child (Moscow), although with a wider brief than child offenders, draws heavily upon the conventions. Others active by the late nineties included NAN, a Moscow organization, originally concerned with drugs and alcohol addiction among teenagers, which moved on to advocate juvenile justice reforms, and the Moscow branch of Penal Reform International, which sponsored projects bringing local colonies together with NGOs to work on new strategies to assist young offenders. In the regions, Chance, an Ekaterinburg organization, was providing legal aid to those in custody; the Krasnoyarsk Human Rights Committee, headed by Alexander Gorelik, professor of criminal law, had, together with the krai prison service, agreed a programme of preparation for release for young offenders. A restorative justice programme, organized by Rustem Maksudov of the Centre for Judicial Reform (Moscow) was spreading out to the regions. And by now there were local judges, anxious to see reforms.

The Conventions

As a signatory to the United Nations Convention of the Rights of the Child, the Russian Federation reports to the UN committee at five-yearly intervals. With Russia's signing, in 1998, the European Convention on Human Rights, and the Convention for the Prevention of Torture, the issues of overcrowded prisons, inhumane treatment and harsh sentencing for adults and children began to be repeatedly raised by UN and Council of Europe delegations. The conventions provide the activists with a clear set of targets, which they can set before the authorities, and which they can refer to in their submissions to the UN committees. By 2005 they had joined forces to submit a detailed and professional alternative report on progress and lack of progress to the UN Committee on the Rights of the Child.

Among the committee's key concerns have been the absence of youth courts. In its reply in 2005 to the UN committee, when asked to list its priorities regarding children's rights, the Russian government listed a series of educational and social issues, merely noting that a draft law on youth courts would in due course move up the legislative agenda, and that some experiments in restorative justice were under way. The UN committee welcomed the appearance of several regional ombudsmen for children's rights. However it urged the Russian Federation, 'as a matter of priority', to expedite a reform agenda, which should include the introduction of juvenile courts, the development of an effective system of alternative sentences to include community service, restorative justice, and the provision of training for judges and law enforcement officials. But by now activists were losing faith in the UN committee, and the politicians saw no reason to pay attention to its findings. Juvenile courts in place of adult courts were just such an issue, and it is this aspect of 'juvenile justice' that we focus on.

Juvenile courts: local experiments, key actors

In 2000 the Supreme Court at last turned its attention to the question. It recommended that courts of general jurisdiction appoint a specialized judge to deal with cases involving young offenders, and referred to the need for such judges to have not only a legal training but some psychological, pedagogic and sociological background. It emphasized the requirement for judges to play particular attention to international norms and standards when dealing with young people (Ruling No.7, 14 February 2000). This may have been in response to experimentation at local level. Enterprising individuals – activists, academics, judges, and social workers – were joining forces to introduce changes, and this draws our attention to the opportunities for local action and to key players.

In 1999 a UNESCO-supported project was launched in Moscow, St Petersburg, Saratov and Rostov on Don. The project, drawing on French experience, introduced social workers as court aides: they were to assist judges specializing in youth cases by working with the offenders before and after trial. Despite the project showing positive results – fewer children held in remand, fewer sentenced to custody, and less recidivism – only in Rostov, where it had the support of Elena Voronova, the chair of the regional court, did it take hold. By 2008 all 61 district courts had a specialized juvenile judge; 15 of these were assisted by a social worker; three districts had a model juvenile court, based on Montreal practices. Judges specify the particular programme to be followed by the youngster, and include reporting back to the court. Recidivism fell. Others began to follow the Rostov example. By 2009 juvenile courts were operating in eight other cities or districts – though not yet in Moscow, St Petersburg, or Saratov.

In Saratov the judges objected to working with social workers because 'there is no document in which you are mentioned or registered so who are you, actually you aren't anyone, and we cannot even refer to you.' (social worker). In St Petersburg, despite strong support from at least one district court judge, the project faded given the unwillingness by the city government to fund dedicated social workers. In Moscow the commissioner for children's rights, Aleksei Golovan, announced in April 2007 that agreement had been reached with three Moscow district courts that, as of June, they would be working out 'juvenile technologies' yet the initiative was successfully blocked by Olga Egorova, chair of Moscow city court. Support from the chair of the regional court is clearly essential. But other agencies are important too.

In Krasnoyarsk, where in the early nineties Gorelik had taught law students to answer prisoners' letters, and to set up legal clinics across the city, a youth project followed. Staff and students from Krasnoyarsk State University, with support from the regional leadership of the prison service, work with children on police record, and with small groups of inmates both before their release and afterwards. Much depends upon the willingness of the head of the region's prison service, and the law and order agencies, to embrace innovations, and in this case Gorelik's reputation and connections were critical. As a professor of criminal law, in post for the past 30 years, he had taught most of the judges, prosecutors, and police officials who now occupied senior posts in the regional justice system. They still looked up to him. And it was fortunate that the general who headed the krai prison service, General Shaeshnikov, was a reformer at heart.

The Kansk colony, 300 km from Krasnoyarsk, which I visited in the early 2000s and again in 2009, now has living and work facilities, educational programmes, and leisure activities that few children in the world outside can hope to experience. They run their own TV news programme, have computer workshops, use one of the town's skating rinks, engage in friendly sewing competitions with the local girl's college. In 2003, as part of a project with Krasnoyarsk University, a group of the boys lived in a holiday camp, just outside the city, with a group of students, who introduced them to the opportunities and the hazards of life in a city. The students first spent time in the colony, getting to know the boys, and each was delegated the task of buying a set of T-shirts, jeans, and trainers that a student might wear. They spent a fortnight together.

A few months later they came together again, at the holiday camp. On a day for visitors, for a prank, some of the students had put on drab colony clothes and, when all linked arms to sing their signature song, official guests at the concert were quite confused as to who were 'the criminals'. One of the solo guitar performers was Vanya, now 18, shortly to be released. Unable to join the others a few days previously, Gorelik had suggested that he could be collected from the colony by a law student, Katya, who had a car, and that I, and Alla Pokras from Moscow's Penal Reform International, make use of the opportunity to visit the colony.

We sped across the flat countryside, arrived at the colony, and were shown round. The head of educational programmes, from the krai prison service, happened to be visiting and we went together to thank the governor, before taking our leave. Katya appeared, insisting we must hurry, and Vanya was ready. The krai official was horrified – such a prisoner had to be accompanied by at least two armed guards and a dog. Katya replied that there was no room for them in her Toyota, and Alexander Solomonovich [Gorelik] had told her to bring Vanya. Who ordered this? demanded the official. The governor placed a letter before him, a letter from Gorelik asking the general's permission for Vanya to come, if he arranged transport, and Shaeshnikov had scrawled on the letter: Permission given. The official was still very unhappy. It was time to lighten the atmosphere: I think, I said, two Russian women and one Englishwoman will be able to cope with Vanya. But, said the official, Katya must drive straight to the camp, and not go into Krasnoyarsk with Vanya. No, replied Katya, I must first take our visitors back to the city – those were Alexander Solomonovich's orders [...] I leave it to the reader to imagine who won. Apparently by the time Katya did deliver Vanya to the camp (apart from anything else we were stopped for speeding, and Katya was requested to accompany the police officer to his office for a lengthy interview to sort it out), the colonel in charge was apoplectic with worry.

I visited the colony again, in 2009, after Gorelik's death. His younger colleagues have taken on the work he started, and created new programmes. Government policy aims to have fewer colonies for children, to be renamed educational centres. If their regimes become more imaginative, more like that in Kansk, that is all to the good, but some will be even further from home for the children. And, more important, however good the facilities, locking up children should be a measure of last resort.

To return to juvenile courts: pressure from the activists, with the assistance of legal experts from the Academy of Sciences, finally resulted in a draft law. This passed its first reading in the Duma in February 2002. However, with the receipt of a discouraging letter from the president two months later, and again in 2004, it made no further progress. There the matter rested until, suddenly, in the spring of 2006, the president's administration suggested it was time to move forward. In March a roundtable on 'The Establishment of Juvenile Justice in Russia: Experiments, Problems and the Future', was held in the Duma, chaired by Ekaterina Lakhova, of the Duma committee on women's affairs. She suggested:

> We have addressed this problem more than once: we discussed it during the previous session of the Duma [...] we have held parliamentary hearings [...] Bearing in mind that sufficient experience has been gained in the Rostov region, where juvenile technologies have been gradually introduced and have yielded results, we would very much welcome the setting up of a system of juvenile justice.

In 2006 the roundtable was followed by further meetings, organized by both Duma committees or ministries, to discuss the proposals and projects that had been ignored for the past four years. Both the Supreme

Court and the prosecutor's office suddenly discovered that they were in favour of the introduction of a juvenile justice system. Lakhova suggested that the law on juvenile courts might pass during the present session. However, nothing further happened.

In Moscow Oleg Zykov of NAN, by then a member of the Civic Chamber and of an inter-ministerial government commission on juvenile affairs and defence of their rights, was tireless in keeping the issue of juvenile justice, and in particular juvenile courts, before the federal authorities. In the spring of 2008 the inter-ministerial commission, headed by Rashid Nurgaliyev, the Minister of the MVD, sent letters to both Boris Gryzlov, chair of the Duma, and Vyacheslav Lebedev, chair of the Supreme Court, reminding them of their undertakings to hasten the introduction of the appropriate legislation on juvenile courts, and referred positively to the regional experiments. These letters were not answered. A letter from the Civic Chamber to President Putin, urging progress on the legislation, also went unanswered.

In the summer of 2008 NAN, with support from Canadian colleagues and CIDA (Canadian government funding) organized the First All-Russian Conference on Juvenile Justice, held in the prestigious President's Hotel in Moscow. However, Vladimir Pligin, chair of the Duma committee on constitutional legislation and state structure, is said to have stated that he saw no chance of the legislation passing a second reading without support from the president's administration, and this was not forthcoming. Many consider that Larisa Brycheva, head of the state legal administration of the president, has been responsible for blocking its progress. But by now there was a small but vocal group within the Orthodox Church campaigning against what it saw as a foreign system, 'juvenile justice', whose advocates wished to destroy the traditional Russian system of bringing up children within the family, and to deprive parents of their rights. It is difficult to see how the reformers' efforts could be interpreted in this way, but a noisy campaign, with appeals to Putin, took off, and the term 'juvenile justice' acquired a negative connotation.[10] Perhaps this persuaded the president's administration to take juvenile courts off the agenda. Without access to the inner circles, the reformers could not glean even this information. But they recognized the need to drop the term 'juvenile justice' and talk instead of 'juvenile technologies' (which include mediation, and restorative justice projects, as well as juvenile courts).

In 2010 a working group of judges from different regions presented a report on the state of play to the Council of Judges: ten regions had adopted specialized procedures for dealing with juveniles, but opinions could differ even within a region. There were those opposed to juvenile courts, those in favour of juvenile courts for young offenders, and those that favoured a 'children's court' to deal with all matters involving a child.[11] The Supreme Court issued a memo, which reported favourably on the number of different experiments or models introduced at regional level but then, in 2011, merely re-emphasized the importance of judges using the clauses in the codes that allow a more child-centred approach; it suggested that experienced judges who had undergone training in psychology, pedagogy, and criminology should hear cases involving children. Early in his presidency, Medvedev visited two juvenile colonies in different parts of the country, one was the progressive Kansk colony in Krasnoyarsk krai, and hopes rose. But his appointment of Larisa Brycheva to the chair of a new working group on court and legal reform was seen as a setback, and by the time he left office, juvenile courts were no nearer the statute book. Medvedev could have moved the agenda forward, but was unwilling or unable to take on the conservative elements within the legal establishment.

In some sense this is both the most encouraging, and the most depressing, of our policy areas. Valery Abramkin, the penal reformer, known to ministers and prisoners alike, died in early 2013. How he would assess his legacy, I do not know. At federal level, we observe political indifference, and the conservatism of the federal judges and prosecutors. Yury Kalinin too, the reform-minded minister, gradually lost interest. Voices calling for juvenile courts have recently been drowned out by the conservative Orthodox campaign. The media has shown little interest in the topic but a TV talk show, in which I participated in 2013, staged a debate between experts, deputies, and officials for and against lowering the age of criminal responsibility and introducing tougher punitive sanctions for young offenders. Was this depressing? On one level, yes, because it is always depressing to hear the *Daily Mail* position advanced with vigour but, on another, surely encouraging – not only were there well-informed and able speakers arguing for a reform agenda, but it was debate of a kind that could serve a purpose in the UK. Unfortunately towards the end everyone was talking at the same time. But society now engages in discussion,

however unpalatable some members' views and however restricted the
TV coverage.

Furthermore, while the activists may have failed to persuade the
politicians, Supreme Court judges and prosecutors that they should
bring the treatment of offending children more in line with the
international conventions, at local level there is experimentation and
some startling successes. The Kansk juvenile penal colony can compete
with the best in Europe. This is a policy area in which local actors can
make a difference. Innovative reformers who include judges, local
government officials and university professors as well as human rights
activists have worked together to introduce changes that benefit
children, and to effect changes in the way local institutions (courts,
prison colonies) work. A penal reform community has emerged, and
some of the regional reformers have linked up. Not surprisingly, by
2010 Perm and Krasnoyarsk were learning from each other. The
importance of key individuals stands out, particularly those in a position
of authority – the chair of the regional court, the head of the regional
prison service, the ombudsman, possibly the governor. And, the size and
spread of Russia makes itself felt: developments in a Siberian region may
remain unheard of in the far off European parts of the country or down in
the Caucasus, or simply attract little interest.

If the defence of young offenders or prisoners' rights required the
reform of existing punitive legislation, as well as the introduction of
new, there were other areas involving rights where the absence of
legislation was a central issue. We look briefly at two – domestic
violence, and the rights of migrants and refugees – both of which, as we
saw in Chapter 1, were put on the agenda by energetic individuals in the
early nineties. As case studies they also illuminate the problems faced by
activists working in a country the size of Russia, provide examples of the
role Western funding or expertise could play, and suggest different
criteria by which to measure achievement.

An association of crisis centres

In 1995 Marina Pisklakova had left the Academy Institute and
registered ANNA, with its group of ten trained counsellors. Two other
domestic violence centres had appeared in Moscow, one more focused on
medical issues, and centres were emerging in several cities. She managed

to get funding for an office, and to enlist the help of the Family Violence Prevention Fund from California in designing an educational programme for use by centres across the country. The aim, of what became a fruitful partnership, was to bring the issue of domestic violence to public attention by publishing data on the (estimated) thousands of women who died each year at their partners' hands, producing posters, approaching police, doctors, and social work departments. When they could get to Moscow, the organizers of the new centres came to ANNA for advice, and this prompted the idea of their forming an Association. Western funders, including the Ford Foundation, were enthusiastic. Surely some kind of linkage between the larger Moscow organizations and local organizations, both as a means of communicating ideas and information, and of gaining recognition of domestic violence as an issue, was needed? By the end of the nineties the representatives of 35 crisis centres, meeting in Moscow, had formed an Association, with its charter, and officers. Marina Pisklakova was elected its first chair, under rules that provided for a two-yearly rotation of the chair among members of its coordinating council. She felt strongly that this was appropriate. ANNA continued its existence under her leadership.

But what happened? 'A strange situation arose [. . .] the office of the Association began to compete with the centres for grants.' There were conflicts within the coordinating council. The rotation principle failed to work. Marina passed the chair on to her successor from Saratov, but she then failed to pass it on, as agreed, to the director of the Barnaul centre. Intrigues started. Members of the council brought their complaints to Pisklakova about certain staff members but refused to voice them publicly. 'They couldn't administer the Association in an open fashion. Its members were not prepared to act democratically.' Marina is a clear leader. I remember at a conference of the Association – perhaps it was in 1999 – being impressed at how she, as chair, managed to reconcile factions partly based on personal differences between their leaders. She played a pivotal role, and her marrying an American and making California her home base for several years, with frequent trips to Russia before returning for good, surely allowed the problems of personality to rise to the surface. By 2006 the Association had fallen apart. Its remaining centres came together at a conference to discuss what had gone wrong.

We understood that Russia is a very large country. Centralization from Moscow simply does not work [...] we need regional networks. And we resolved that we would just be an informal network.

But could the strategy of rotating the chair have worked? Possibly, if the aims and interests of the Association and the individual centres had been clearly distinguished. As it was they came into conflict. The centres existed regardless of whether the Association was there or not; they designed their own programmes, which differed depending upon the locality and their members' expertise, and they needed to find funding for themselves. Some of the original centres have survived, but not all. Difficulties in obtaining funding, and a tax squeeze on foreign grants, have driven many under, not only those that came into existence because of funding opportunities.

When IREX started a programme, organizations appeared with their grants, but when organizations come into existence because they have heard there is some funding – and create a crisis centre – then they don't survive. It's the wrong kind of motivation [...] the money ends, the initiative ends.

(The same happened with a programme, under which a group of talented and committed academic lawyers introduced students, at a series of summer schools, to working in legal clinics or embryonic legal aid centres. Suddenly money appeared for 'legal clinics', dozens appeared, most died when the money disappeared.)

Whereas the original centres were set up by psychologists, doctors, journalists, and women from very different professions, today those who work on domestic violence issues tend to be social workers, psychologists, and lawyers.

It's become more of some kind of a professional niche. Then it was activism [....] volunteers are vital because then an organization will survive. Motivation is what matters [...] After all, it's not difficult to start without money, there's greater motivation when people are prepared to start without money, and then get themselves organized and look for funding.

And what of the relationship with government officials? I ask.

In the beginning they could not understand who we were, but were prepared to work with us on training sessions. But on every occasion when they worked with us, it was out of good will on the part of the individuals themselves, not a response from the system itself. However much of what we introduced has now been incorporated into the system as whole.

The fact of the matter is that our situation compared with the traditional human rights organizations is simpler [. . .] maybe not, it's surely the same as regards the rights of prisoners. Where they [state officials] see that our activities bring benefits, they take them on board. But we can't say that we have managed to shift the system as whole – there is still no law. We've got to the point where we ourselves are writing a draft.

As early as 1995 a draft law, recognizing domestic violence as an offence, was under discussion, and supported by the Women of Russia party, but it never got a first reading and, after many years and 48 redrafts, was rejected as unworkable by the crisis centres themselves. In its absence, ANNA has for many years advocated working with doctors, and with the police and courts, on the basis of existing legislation, but by 2012 it looked as though there might, at last, be support for legislation that would make domestic violence a criminal offence. However, their greatest achievement, in Pisklakova's view, is that:

The term domestic violence is now recognized [. . .] it no longer sounds strange. Most people know what you are talking about. We can talk about it quite freely, in official circles, as a social problem. And there are now 22 government shelters in different cities and towns [. . .] there's one with 35 beds in Moscow but that's nothing in a city of 12 million. There's a system of government centres, which are obliged to offer assistance, and that's very important. Because we, as independent organizations, can't directly bring the police in whereas government centres can.

'But', she emphasizes, 'our main achievement is, probably, that the term now has a different resonance. The fact that we could present our first alternative report to the UN [...] that the movement continues to develop [...] even if we won't continue our existence, the term will resonate. There's no way back now.'

Domestic violence was never going to be high up the Duma or government's list of priorities. The fate of the draft law is not surprising. But Marina's conclusion – that their most important contribution (apart, one might say, from the women's lives that they have saved) is to have put domestic violence into the public domain, and received some response from social welfare departments – makes their situation now more similar to that of their counterparts in some Western countries. It is a major achievement. Social attitudes are changing, and the activists will continue to appear, and to press for action. This is an issue involving a fundamental right – to life – and to security from violence. Foreign funding will become less and less important, and one can envisage local philanthropists beginning to respond. At some point one can expect a government response.

A successful network – Migration Rights

Migration Rights, in contrast one of the most successful networks, comes under the aegis of the Memorial Society's Centre for Human Rights. Organized very differently from the Association of Crisis Centres, it allows us to see the factors relevant to success, but it too now faces challenges, albeit of a different kind. And, in its case too, it finds itself today in a situation more similar to that of some of its European counterparts.

Once Svetlana Gannushkina had joined the Centre in 1993, she began to think how best to develop a programme of legal assistance, as contrasted with humanitarian aid, for forced migrants and refugees. At that time, the refugees were Armenians fleeing from Azerbaijan, Afghans from war zones, and Russians from some of the Central Asian republics. While (inadequate) legislation gradually appeared, issues regarding citizenship (including for children subsequently born in Russia) still remain. In 1996 Gannushkina set up an organization that she envisaged as consisting of a number of counselling points in different parts of the country, with a coordinating centre in Moscow. A connection with ECRE (the European Council for Refugees and Exiles) brought its London office on board to work with her to design a programme, to cost it, and to write grant applications. Ford supported the original work on this, and then provided partial funding. This was an example of where the expertise of a Western NGO proved invaluable, a viable and effective network appeared, and the coordinator continued to find further funding, in this case from the European Commission, and until recently from UN High Commissioner for Refugees.

The aim of Migration Rights is 'to provide an effective and accessible system of free legal aid for each forced migrant'. The migrants (or refugees) may come from countries of the former Soviet Union, from the Caucasus, or from Africa, and recently from Syria. The network has a small coordinating centre of four to five full-time staff in Moscow, led by Gannushkina, and 57 counselling points in 45 regions, mostly staffed by two lawyers. They provide legal aid services, and work to improve or challenge local legislation. Approximately 20,000 clients are provided with advice each year, 2,000 are helped to prepare cases, and 1,000 defended in court. The lawyers report on their activities to Moscow, the results are distributed, and the lawyers come to Moscow for conferences or training sessions.

> One of the ways of increasing mutual understanding between the Network and government departments is by the participation of representatives of the Federal Migration Service, the Ministries of Internal and Foreign Affairs, the Prosecutor General, and of other departments in the seminars for the Network's lawyers [...] As a rule, departments are interested in this kind of cooperation which, undoubtedly, allows for the finding of answers to the many complex questions with which migrants struggle. Furthermore, lawyers from the regions have the possibility of engaging, directly, with representatives of federal structures. Taking into account the pressing need to make certain amendments to and improve the existing legislation [...], the Network is attempting to attract the attention of the State Duma to this problem.[12]

The slightly head-mistressy tone of the statement on the website makes it clear that government officials are expected to attend, properly prepared. In the early years of the network, perhaps 30 lawyers would attend a seminar, there were no government representatives, and the discussion was quite excitable. In 2010, ten years later, perhaps 100 of the network's lawyers gathered to discuss specific issues – new or continuing problems faced by their clients, lack of clarity in the legislation, government policy. The new Moscow representative of the Office of the UN High Commissioner for Refugees, and the head of the Federal Migration Service were present. The latter came in for tough questioning. Gannushkina is very clearly in charge and on top of the issues, as are most of the now experienced lawyers. Perhaps half of them are themselves migrants from the former Soviet republics who learnt, the hard way, what it was like to arrive as a migrant in Russia in the nineties. The interchange and discussion was real and focused.

Why does this network work? For a start, all the participants are concerned with the same problems or issues but, as we have seen, this does not guarantee success. ECRE's involvement, support from the UN High Commissioner on Refugees? The crisis centres too benefited from help from Western specialists. The way the network is set up – essentially one of local units all of whose work is as a unit in the network – is more relevant. The centre finds the money for the consultation points. We also have to include Gannushkina's ability to head an organization, to inspire unwavering loyalty from a small staff, and the admiration of many of the participants for her willingness to speak out, and to work tirelessly on behalf of individuals and of migrants as a whole. But all this is achieved by a punishing schedule (perhaps four hours sleep a night), which also includes the running of her other organization, Civic Assistance, and assisting individuals – Uzbeks in danger of being deported, a Chechen in a French prison, a journalist from Belarus [. . .] Her phone rings endlessly. If someone is in trouble, they will almost certainly be advised to contact Gannushkina.

In 2003, Putin abolished the government's commission on migration policy. In 2009, after Gannushkina had raised it with Medvedev, the commission (on which she sits) was reinstated, but by 2011 she was complaining that it was moribund. Her membership of the President's Council for the Advancement of Civil Society and Human Rights (until she resigned in 2012) probably helped in dealings with government officials. And, I suspect, her relations with the UN High Commissioner's Office are not irrelevant. Membership of ECRE, and her international awards, may help with getting major funding from the European Commission, but Russia's joining of middle income countries now affects funding under UN programmes. Migration Rights' fortunes will depend, to a great extent, upon political developments and the international environment. Millions of migrants from Central Asia, the Caucasus, and China now move annually into Russia in search of either seasonal or permanent work, or as a staging post in a journey onwards. The numbers of those awaiting decisions on registration or repatriation are in the tens of thousands. Immigrants, taking low paid jobs, moving into crowded housing estates in the big cities, have become a political issue.[13] Politicians in Russia, as in the UK and other European countries, recognize its value as a vote winner. In the Moscow mayoral elections in 2013 the contenders took it up. In the autumn, the murder of a young Russian in a Moscow suburb was followed by a mass pogrom, with the participation of nationalist Russian organizations, in a trading centre where many migrants gather and work. The police did little.[14] Putin, in his Constitution Day address to the nation in December, dwelt at some length on the need to find new measures of coping with illegal immigration.

Suddenly the issues facing Migration Rights, and politicians' responses seem horribly familiar to a European reader. To convince politicians and the public that migrants and refugees should have meaningful rights in Russia will require an array of allies and new strategies. It will not be easy to attract funding to support such activities. But, just as is the case with ANNA (now involved in projects in the Caucasus), Migration Rights has skills and expertise it could share with others, and not only in the countries of the former Soviet Union.

CHAPTER 10

PAST AND PRESENT: THE INTERNATIONAL MEMORIAL SOCIETY

What have we learnt from the last two chapters?

First, that Grigory Shvedov is right – achieving legislative reform is a Sisyphean task and beyond the means of the human rights community. Its increasing professionalization, level of expertise, and use of new technologies gives it no *political weight.* To persuade political authorities to pursue policies that, for them, are of secondary importance or simply of little interest, you need weapons, among which the support of powerful interests or of a broad social constituency, depending upon the circumstances, are the most useful. But the activists lacked any substantial popular support, still less that of the powerful, while international approval became of less and less interest to the Russian government, and Western financial assistance a target for attack. However, without their efforts legislative change would have been even more modest. They succeeded in providing assistance (often life-saving) to the vulnerable, in introducing or keeping issues on the public agenda, and in professionalizing many of their activities. Some became known internationally. I come back to these issues in the Conclusion.

Second, we have observed the surely not surprising influence wielded by the army leadership, the MVD, and the prosecutor's office, all of which after a shaky few years in the nineties, reasserted their status while maintaining their accustomed patterns of behaviour. The culture of established institutions such as these, in any society, is very strong; only radical reform from on top will bring changes lower down.

Igor Kalyapin, our activist from Nizhny Novgorod, sees it in these terms:

> But, in the main the huge mechanism, controlled by a primitive hand-held system, which we call the Russian state machine, is going down a slippery slope, and no one is seriously concerned with society's interests, or freedoms, nor is anyone seriously concerned with the elementary functioning of the state machine. Sadly things are moving backwards fast. And our political leadership constantly produces and plays on a variety of patriotic slogans, while saying, Russia, move ahead!

Pavel Levashin, the young ex-prison officer, sees it from the point of view of young recruits:

> Until the generation which, in Soviet times was accustomed to using force to decide any issue has completely disappeared, nothing will change. What can you ask of a young trainee who has only just joined? He simply can't oppose the system on his own. People such as that, whether in the MVD, in the internal troops, or in the prison service, simply aren't kept on [...] Staff only start defending their rights – labour rights, pensions – once they have left or retired [...] an individual simply can't take on a system that has solidified over years and years.

In February 2012 Artemy Troitsky, a well-known cultural critic, activist, and Moscow University lecturer, suggested to a London audience that, with the exception of the few years of perestroika, nothing had changed in the relationship of state and society since Ivan the Terrible. Such an assertion tells us more about perceptions than realities but, if we are to understand the behaviour of institutions, both old and new – government offices, law and order institutions, enterprises, the media – or of the activists themselves, and citizens' attitudes towards them, we must try to untangle the way the past influences the present. Can we, as Beissinger and Kotkin have recently asked, determine why? Two decades after the ending of Soviet rule, 'certain institutional forms, ways of thinking, and modes of behaviour appear to have persisted' and others, disappeared? Rigorous arguments, they suggest, demonstrating how and why particular institutional forms or cultural carry over despite 'significant ruptures' or regime change are few.[1]

In the conclusion to this chapter, and to the volume as a whole, I come back to the influence of the past (and which parts of the past?) but, as regards the *institutions* which featured in the two preceding chapters, the answer is relatively simple. The ending of Communist party rule brought a few years of uncertainty over the future but no significant changes to the internal hierarchical running of the institutions. Much carried on as before, while the move to the market, with its scope for bribery and corruption, had an impact on codes of behaviour, both for the impoverished lower ranks, and for the generals, ministry officials, for anyone at the top of a hierarchy, who could now live in a style undreamt of previously.

There were improvements to the prison system, but its key features – high rates of detention, long sentences and harsh conditions – were still there. Yes, these were a bequest from the Stalinist Gulag. But why did they persist? It was not just institutional self-interest and a lack of interest on the part of the political leadership or judges. It was also that the long period of Soviet rule produced a public used to its exclusion from participation in decision making ('I never thought', said one the respondents to a survey, 'that anyone would be interested in my views on how to respond to juvenile crime') and that acquiesces in the continuation of harsh policies. The absence of a tradition of political and social activism allowed the conservatism of the government and judicial apparatus, which became ingrained in the Brezhnev period, to go unchallenged. The new political elite (which included democrats and liberal entrepreneurs) did little to change this.

Government officials find it very difficult to conceive of a role for NGOs and, in their turn, many of the organizations value a partnership with government above that of acting as critics. This allowed a creative authoritarian leadership to emasculate parliamentary politics or control, and to promote 'dialogue', on its terms, with NGOS through the Civic Chamber or with the Presidential Council for the Advancement of Civil Society and Human Rights. Some of the most respected human rights activists in Moscow accepted places and remained on the Council until 2012. After all, this enabled them, sometimes, to achieve a positive result, and to keep issues on the public agenda. 'Speaking to the president' carries not only a symbolic weight, but a real weight with officials, while at the same time it reaffirms a traditional relationship between the ruler and his subjects.

However, at the same time, there were those who did not shrink from criticizing president, ministers, or government officials, and there were independent local initiatives that brought results, including from within the court system. Both were new elements in what we can call a traditional Soviet landscape. In Chapters 11 and 12 we shall see many more. But, first, let's return to the International Memorial Society, whose trajectory over the period illustrates many of the issues we have been discussing.

The International Memorial Society

Accounts of the Society's early years exist, and others will surely write in detail of its activities in later years. My intention is more modest – to show how both inherited and new ways of doing things, and different factors, played a part in its evolution during our period. In the perestroika and post-perestroika years the Society's members across the country were primarily concerned with justice for the victims of Stalinist persecution, but by 1993 its Human Rights Centre, dealing with present injustices, was active. By the late nineties, the Society was known in human rights circles, in Germany, and in some regions, but its work on memory had dropped off the public radar, and its reports on Chechnya appealed to only a small audience. Its public impact was negligible. In Alexander Daniel's words, writing in 1999, a common response would be 'Memorial? Really? Does it still exist?'[2] Yet in 2001 its participation in the Civic Forum was recognized by the Kremlin as critical for the event to take place; it continued to receive international awards from the Polish government and elsewhere in Europe. In 2010, as we saw in the Introduction, the Society's leading members, both from Moscow and the regions, were engaged at its four-yearly conference in discussing and disagreeing over a wide range of activities. They took an active part in the Constitutional Forum of the same year, yet, as the other leading NGOs, they were caught by surprise by the protests against the election-rigging in 2011. In 2013, despite its Human Rights Centre receiving an instruction from the prosecutor to register as a foreign agent, the Society was awarded a presidential grant. On 1 March 2014 its board, without hesitation, issued a statement that the sending of Russian troops on to Ukrainian territory was a crime. What then *was* the International Memorial Society, and what role had it come to play in the human rights community and wider society?

As the nineties progressed, the Society's active organizations across the country worked on historical memory – books of memory, memorials – and in a few places on contemporary human rights issues. There was, however, little cooperation between organizations, or between the local organizations and the Moscow centres, let alone with those outside Russia. But, given its status as an international organization, should it not then act as one, link up its organizations, and thus be able to gain a louder voice? Could not the Society's organizations elect members of a board, which would meet regularly, discuss strategy, and launch collective projects? To its Western funders this seemed an obvious strategy (as with the crisis centres) and, by 1998, discussions over a new Ford Foundation grant to the International Society included the idea of 'strengthening the organization as a whole'.

In 1998 the Society elected a board that included representatives of active local organizations, and from Ukraine and Latvia, and thereafter the board has met regularly, and held the occasional meeting in one of the regions. Joint work on rehabilitation and compensation for victims of repression, and more frequent board meetings, gave its regional members more of a sense of belonging to a national, if not an international organization. Yet attempts to encourage its board to develop and implement a shared strategy, which would unite its organizations, and widen its appeal to a broader public, have brought meagre results. Why?

The fate of an attempt to unite its membership through a newspaper provides a clue. In 1998, the Society advertised for an editor of its periodical. Grigory Shvedov, a young graduate, an historian-philologist with an editorial qualification, applied for the job. He was someone who had thought Memorial no longer existed. The outcome of his interview (at which he was shown something consisting of 'a few pages, stapled together, printed on a large and very fine printer'), was, at Roginsky's suggestion, that they began to publish a newspaper aimed at a wider readership. The new monthly publication, *30 October*, initially included both materials on historical repression, and on Chechnya, and on organizational matters, but it became clear that there was one readership for historical repression (the newspaper has a circulation of 5–7,000), another for a human rights journal, and that purely organizational matters, including the protocols of the board meetings 'which was a unique feature of Memorial's openness' should be circulated as a bulletin within the Society. The human rights journal subsequently failed to find funding, and the bulletin died for want of a staff member to compile it. In Shvedov's view, the majority of the Memorial organizations are not capable of working together to create a regular electronic news that would strengthen relationships within the Society.

But what after all is the Society? In Roginsky's words, it is a confederation of autonomous organizations, a horizontal organization.[3] The board cannot make decisions that bind a local organization. (Participation in the Civic Forum, we remember, was a matter for each local organization to decide.) In other words, the Society is much more similar to an Association of independent organizations than it is to anything else. While it may get funding for a project in which some of the organizations will participate, they live their lives independent of the Moscow Centres or the board. As Roginsky saw it in 2011:

> The Memorial organizations will carry on doing their thing, as they understand it, quite independently of what is happening in Moscow [...] our real help for them, the help of the centre, has consisted of lobbying in different places, at national level, those demands which they put forward. We have often failed, but we have also achieved a great deal [...] Memorial exists not thanks to the fact that it has a good board, a good strategy or a good centre [...] the Memorial network holds together thanks to an idea, the very simple idea of historical memory, an idea that is not easy to realize in practice.

This is partly true, but only partly. Without doubt, the commitment to historical memory gives the Society its basis, its roots, but even by the late nineties its members were engaged in many other issues too. By the turn of the century local organizations had developed very different profiles. Ryazan worked on historical memory, but also produced the website hro.org; by the end of the decade its young members had taken up orphans' rights. The Perm Memorial Society, unusual in that it has a large membership, understandably declining but still around 4,000, has a line in the regional budget for its office and the publishing of books of memory. (Another indication of the unusual situation in Perm.) No salaries are paid. Active since perestroika, its elderly leader, Alexander Kalikh, set up a youth organization as a legal identity in the late nineties, an NGO that could apply for grants, pay its staff, and finance projects. It has its youthful volunteers, who help the aged, but it also organizes educational and human rights projects, and supports alternative service. A separate organization runs the Perm-36 Gulag prison camp restoration project. By the early 2000s, St Petersburg had three Memorial organizations, the newest of which worked on racial discrimination. Vyacheslav Bituitsky of the Voronezh organization participates in the Migration Rights network. Igor Sazhin, in Syktyvkar, heads a new kind of human rights centre. Organizations in Ingushetia or Dagestan are engaged in dangerous work, monitoring kidnappings or murder. By the end of the decade a few organizations were linking up with one another. The St Petersburg Research Centre was working with the Memorial organizations in Ryazan and Krasnoyarsk on a digital Gulag museum. But we saw how, at the Society's conference in 2010, its members found it difficult to decide which of the issues, if any, should have priority.

The Society's Moscow centres have very considerable achievements to their credit. The Human Rights Centre, working with EHRAC in London, has won more than 100 cases before the European Court of Human Rights,[4] Migration Rights is internationally known, as are the Centre's reports on Chechnya. An everyday history competition for school children,[5] scholarly publications on the Gulag based on meticulous work in the archives, compensation for those who suffered under the Gulag, the building of the Society's own archive, publicity for the Katyn massacre in Poland, all are part of the Society's activities. But these reflect the very different interests and concerns of strong-minded individuals who came together, almost accidentally, many years ago, and remain in a sometimes uneasy but respectful alliance with each other. They are held together by a shared past, a shared building, and shared views that one has a right of access to information, both about past and present, that facts are important, as is a law-based state accountable to society. The struggle for historical truth and for rights today are, in Alexander Daniel's words, indivisible. The collection, verification, and analysis of facts underlie both. Writing in 1999, he suggested that the failure of attempts to agree on a 'political position' (remember the disagreement over Yeltsin's actions) had convinced all that, except for a belief in the importance of democratic institutions, these were the only values shared by all. A decade later, he emphasized the conviction that the authorities must come to realize that independence and criticism is not the same as political opposition, 'and political opposition is not a state crime'. Both Daniel and Roginsky make a strong and attractive case for the necessity of linkage between past and present rights, with Roginsky adding the argument that knowledge of history is required for us not to repeat past mistakes. However, it remains the case that the members of the Human Rights Centre, engaged in monitoring human rights abuses, have tenuous ties with those working on past repression, while the elderly children of those repressed under Stalin who make up the Society's Moscow branch have little time for the Human Rights Centre. Not surprisingly, some liken Roginsky, the chair of the Society, to a tightrope walker, skipping lightly and dangerously along a wire that holds two poles together.

There are other factors that work for or against the Society's members acting as a united body. The search for funding has led its organizations and centres in different directions, while its international and national reputation has encouraged foreign organizations or individuals to seek it as a partner in human rights projects for which they can access funding. This has led to members becoming involved in new and very different activities. Sergei Krivenko, a member of the Memorial board, headed the large Coalition project on alternative service. Grigory Shvedov, quietly spoken, able, while continuing to run *30 October* and remaining a member of the board, prefers working on his own to navigating the cross-currents that, from time to time, cause turbulence within Memorial. Working from a café, with wifi, comfortable chairs and good tea, his laptop permanently open, a great deal of his time is occupied by *Caucasian Knot*, a professional news and information internet publication serving a Russian and international readership, for which he has created a network of contributors. In 2004, with Memorial as the lead Russian organization, he took on a project on social marketing led by two American academics, Theodore Gerber and Sarah Mendelson, and funded by USAID. The project had as its aim one of introducing activists in three cities – Ryazan,

Perm and Rostov on Don – to social marketing techniques, techniques that would enable them better to identify issues that engaged the local population, and then to devise a campaign that would resonate.[6] The project, which included several NGOs in the different cities, including the Memorial organizations in Ryazan and Perm, received a mixed reception, with some local activists either objecting to an approach that sees the identifying of popular interest as the critical starting point (for example, the losses among Russian soldiers fighting in Chechnya rather than the human rights excesses) or their simply being unable to identify and agree on a clear target, and design a campaign to focus on it. The Perm activists succeeded in identifying children's rights as a popular issue (hardly difficult), and ran a campaign that raised its profile; in Ryazan the younger activists, after a split within the group, raised public awareness of the losses in Chechnya by a poster campaign; the southern participants never got their act together. In this we see Memorial acting as a lead organization in a very different type of project from its traditional ones, and one that had its critics within the Society.

Perhaps a good sign? The appearance of a younger generation? Whereas an interest in his family history had brought Igor Sazhin in Syktyvkar to Memorial, Grigory Shvedov was simply looking for an interesting job, not thinking of joining a cause and, in this respect, the Society reflected the changes that were taking place in society and would influence the human rights community. The post-Soviet world was already a fixture for a younger generation. Their parents' world of a certain future – education, profession (often that of one's parents), career path, pension – was no more. Parental influence was still important but it was up to you, perhaps as you watched your parents grow poorer and poorer, to make out in an environment of opportunities, uncertainties, and risks. It was often a combination of chance and circumstances, and the desire to make use of skills, that took young people into human rights where their skills, usually from a training in the humanities, were needed. With the odd exception, they grew up, thinking about other things, and would have been most surprised had anyone suggested they should get involved in human rights. Katya Sokiryanskaya, from St Petersburg, who by chance met activists from Chechnya in Warsaw, is a case in point. Robert Latypov who recently replaced Alexander Kalikh, now over 70, as chair of the Perm Memorial Society is another.

Latypov, quite tough, straightforward, was born in 1973 into a working class family in a chemical town, Berezniki, in the Perm region, a town built by prisoners and deportees. To his and his parents' surprise he made it to university. 'Many of my contemporaries either ended up in prison, or became drug addicts, or alcoholics.' It was tough going but he graduated in 1995, specializing in medieval history, and was called up for military service.

> It was absolute serfdom. I did not want to be there [. . .] and I also had to talk to the conscripts about their duty to serve the Motherland, to observe their military vows conscientiously, when I myself did not want to. And that double-standard, those awful feelings when I had to do it, it made me sick at heart.

Once demobilized, he vowed that whatever he did with his life, 'I must be free and the work must be interesting'. That took him first to work as an excursion guide at the open-air local history museum but on a visit to the Kalikhs, parents of a friend from university, he was asked whether he might like to help with a volunteer camp at the Perm-36 Gulag prison that was being restored. He agreed, for two weeks, but was so appalled at the low standards of the excursion guides that he joined the museum staff to work as a guide and on related projects. He stayed for two years and, in 1999, moved back to Perm city to work in Memorial's youth organization.

Had he not known of Memorial before? Yes, his friend Kalikh had told him about it but he was not particularly interested, and his diploma work had been on the ethics of the aristocracy.

> When we were studying [at the beginning of the nineties], history went through a crisis. The year before us had a course on Marxism-Leninism, we did not. But we still had political economy, in which the dominant place was held by a Marxist view of economics. We had barely picked up our textbooks when the lecturers said we did not need them, and they did not know what to teach us [. . .] we found ourselves in a 'time out' because we did not know whether the Soviet system would come back or not, and how were we to study history? Nothing was clear.

This meant that the theme of political repression was also not a straightforward one [...] We wanted to understand and decide for ourselves what our values were, what we held dear. Was a great empire and the memory of it, or were the fates of those who were of that empire, who suffered, and who lived far from easy lives, dearer to us? I still had to go through the army before I could sort this out for myself.

Latypov thinks of himself as a member of a second generation of Memorial or civic activists. Their values have been influenced by those dissidents who joined Memorial, and the perestroika activists, but 'the world has changed, and therefore views of human rights also change [...] to be a hostage to a traditional, classical, conservative view on such matters means that you can simply lose out, cease to be of interest to anyone'. The main characteristic of his generation, he suggests, is the ability to raise uncomfortable questions, remove the taboos from certain subjects. A new generation will, he hopes, do more than this, 'will start, not simply living, but transforming the environment', in particular by working directly with business and the local community, without having to refer everything to the still over-active state. And, as previously mentioned, he advocates teaching human rights in new ways. In the following chapter, I pursue the question of generational change, but note how different were the concerns and interests of Memorial's younger members – Grigory Shvedov, Igor Sazhin, Katya Sokiryanskaya, Robert Latypov. In this, they reflected the Society's complex personality, there since the early nineties, and still very evident today. How they might lead this most unusual Society forward is far from clear.

With many competing interests present, it is not surprising that board meetings can be home to sharp disagreements and, as in 1993, the issue of cooperation with the president – today as regards membership of his Council – produces dissenting voices. However, just as Chechnya brought its members together, so too, presidential actions in the new century, directed against civil and political rights, have had the effect of holding the Society together and, ironically, of giving it a louder public voice. Despite internal disagreements, its board can be depended upon to issue a statement on a key domestic or international incident, to speak in support of a well-known or little-known political prisoner, and to take a public stand on, for example, Ukraine. From this perspective, the Putin leadership has done it a service. Roginsky's words, as Memorial celebrated its quarter century, were not celebratory:

> We have existed for 25 years and we cannot yet say that the country shares our view of the past. We cannot yet say that human rights violations do not take place in our country, to say nothing of the infringements of freedom and democracy. Part of the responsibility lies with us, and it is obvious that we have made mistakes, or not been sufficiently active or focused enough [....] we have nowhere won victories, but, without us things would be worse.[7]

And, he adds, by 'us' he means all those 'islands of independence, engaged in responsible civic activities'. The Society has not only held together, retained its international reputation, in particular in Germany and Poland, but it can and does speak out to and for a much larger number of its own citizens.

Cultural constraints

Does it seem to the reader, thinking back over the activists in action, that they behaved in a particular Russian or Soviet way? Can we see legacies of the past at play? I come back to this in the Conclusion, but this is the place to introduce the explanation offered by Mendelson and Gerber for the limited success of the social marketing project. They suggest that an important factor was: 'a predominant activist culture that discourages and inhibits activists from looking beyond their own circle to the public, relying on empirical data, or planning goal-oriented action' and they attributed 'the resistance we encountered among some activists, particularly older ones, to the lingering hold of intelligentsia culture in Russian civil society'. The activists' weakness as campaign strategists, their concern with 'purity and principle over strategy and action', had its roots, they argue, in a traditional Russian intelligentsia culture. In the repressive Soviet period, which made goal-oriented politics 'futile', critical intellectuals, drawing upon Tsarist intelligentsia traditions, focused on 'providing living examples of principles that contradicted those of the regime'; they formed tightly knit groups where 'authenticity' and commitment to principles took the place of action-oriented politics. And this Soviet-era 'intelligentsia culture', has, they argue, had an enormous influence upon the human rights community because of the leading positions held by former dissidents.

Yes, at times and in places the activists spent a great deal of time talking among themselves (the 2004 conference could be an example) and many of them were not good at organizing campaigns, nor in thinking how to evaluate the results of their activities. An evaluation of a programme by an outside independent consultant was often viewed with suspicion or simply ignored; the views of those they knew and respected were what mattered. The notion of a conflict of interests was alien. But such attitudes and practices were not a peculiar attribute of the human rights activists. They were widely shared. A small group culture and distrust of outsiders was the norm for citizens of all persuasions, not only the intelligentsia. An inability or unwillingness to engage in action-strategy in the post-Soviet environment was as marked, if not more so, among young students, rank and file trade unionists, journalists, or conformist teachers as among critical intellectuals or ex-dissidents. Of course there were the exceptions – those members of the Soviet intelligentsia who applied brilliant action-strategies to building business and financial empires – but the traits identified were very common. And they can all be traced to aspects of life in the late Soviet environment.

To suggest a key factor in determining the actions of the human rights activists was Russian intelligentsia culture, absorbed and crystallized by the dissidents, who 'led' the community, both over-simplifies the Russian intelligentsia, and the dissident community, and exaggerates the influence even of those dissidents who were active in the post-Soviet years, and who themselves had very different attitudes towards action in the new environment. Kovalev, who Gerber and Mendelson cite as exemplifying the priority awarded to principles over action-strategy, was an activist who entered the political arena, and worked (successfully) on getting legislation adopted. Abramkin is another example. The most traditional dissident, in their terms, was perhaps Alexander Podrabinek, who carried on *Express Khronika*, and would have nothing to do with the new regime but he, effectively, took himself out of the growing human rights community.[8] There were those who talked, and achieved very little, but such individuals were as common among the politicians, academics, artists and others, as among the ex-dissidents. Kovalev, in contrast, remained in politics, as a deputy until 2003, and is still a member of the Yabloko party. He continually argued that human rights activists should engage in politics, if possible as elected deputies.

It is true that this divided and diverse community chose for some of its leaders those with an aureole of past suffering for their convictions, had public reputations, and were prepared to engage with the present. Alekseeva was such a one, and we saw how local activists revered her. Kovalev was another. But it was not that by their actions (or beliefs) they fashioned the community or the way activists behaved. It was far too diverse a community for that. And even within Memorial, Kovalev, upon being nominated for re-election as president in 2010, pointed out that he almost always found himself in a minority when it came to board decisions. In contrast Alekseeva's views take precedence in deciding between projects or stating MHG's position but the way MHG works – autonomy for the local organizations who participate in the projects – means that they go their separate ways. What we can say is that one of the prevailing attitudes in post-Soviet Russia was respect for leaders. Kovalev's re-election was never in doubt, and it is difficult to conceive of MHG without Alekseeva. Many of those who set up organizations in the early nineties, regardless of their age or background, still head them today. If we are talking of culture, then here is an example of a widely-accepted practice under Soviet rule: leaders rarely resign from or are voted out of office.[9]

In 2010, Kalikh and Latypov persuaded the 450 delegates at the Perm Society's annual conference on Political Prisoners' Day to elect Latypov as chair of the Society itself

> I thought there would be problems with that – after all Aleksander Mikhailovich [Kalikh] has led the organization for 22 years, and he is very well known and authoritative – but it was all right, I had been in Memorial for ten years and many know me. But what was most important – I proposed that Aleksander Mikhailovich should be awarded the title 'Honorary Chair', and then everyone agreed and voted unanimously for me.

I was reminded of a comment by Tanya Lokshina: 'The culture of the human rights movement in Russia is a culture of authority. Not only in

Moscow but in the regions too. In Perm Averkiev is tsar and God.' But in almost any profession, people in a position of authority tend to remain in post. An English observer is struck by this. In the academic world, in the world of culture or art, the directors and heads of departments stay in place long after they would have been replaced (often to their own relief) in similar institutions in the UK or USA.[10] There are rarely rules, or conventions, on limited terms of office. Whether such cultural habits were perhaps reinforced for an older generation by the threatening new market economy, and whether they will survive generational change in a new economic environment is an interesting question. The Memorial board, dominated by its Muscovite core, has seen little change since 2002. The heads of the most active organizations, all excellent people, stay in place. Meanwhile young members (and some of them may be nearly 30) may decide to move on to other pursuits. And that brings us to the youngest generation.

PART 4

TWENTY YEARS ON

CHAPTER 11

YOUNG LAWYERS STEP FORWARD

A new generation has come on the scene, which talks less and does more, its members are much less enthusiastic about politics, they have grown up with the realization that the democratic revolution as a democratic project has failed. But there's a huge field where you can apply yourself in concrete civic activity.

To achieve what? I ask Sergei Lukashevsky of the Sakharov Centre.

Not to achieve something, but in order to help specific individuals or resolve concrete problems. A particular problem has attracted an individual's attention, for example the problem of torture by the police, and s/he starts to get involved, gets drawn in, but without having any political ambitions.

When we compare the human rights community at the end of the first decade of the twenty-first century with that of twenty or even of ten years ago, the most striking difference is the presence of an army, or at least a battalion, of young lawyers, educated in the post-Soviet period, connected through the internet, by mobile phones, and with the European Court of Human Rights as a court of appeal. From the mid-nineties onwards the demand for defence lawyers (in both civil and criminal cases) from individuals, businesses and organizations grew, and with it the attractiveness of the profession and the opportunities it offered for making a living. Law faculties opened up everywhere. While many (the majority?) of the young lawyers go into the commercial sector (as do their counterparts in other countries), some are drawn to human rights issues, and the existence of the European Court is an attraction.

In 1991 there were lawyers, active in the democratic movement, who subsequently became well known. Genry Reznik and Yury Shmidt stand out as defence lawyers taking on cases of national significance. Tamara Morshakova, a judge on the Constitutional Court, has remained active in human rights circles since retiring. Sergei Pashin, the young author of the original court reform project under Yeltsin, participates in the training of activist lawyers from the provinces under the aegis of an NGO, an Expert Legal Council, headed by Mara Polyakova, herself originally a prosecutor. But the view within the human rights community, during the nineties, and probably that of the lawyers themselves, was that they were acting as aides to human rights' activists, not that they themselves were activists. There were exceptions, for example Karina Moskalenko, a feisty defence lawyer who set up the organization The International Protection Centre, but Professor Gorelik, from Krasnoyarsk, whose Human Rights Committee was staffed by law students, did not consider himself an activist. And the young Sergei Belyaev, whose organization in Ekaterinburg, Litigator, took local authorities or government departments to court, publicizing the campaigns, was seen as somehow different. His approach was, in many ways, ahead of the curve.

Ask activists today, whether in the provinces or the Muscovites themselves, and commentators, to name the most effective human rights organizations and almost all will mention Public Verdict (Taubina, Moscow), the Committee Against Torture (Kalyapin, Nizhny Novgorod), and Agora (Chikov, Kazan). Neither Taubina or Kalyapin are lawyers but their offices are peopled by young lawyers. Some who work with Kalyapin were Chikov's contemporaries in Kazan. They all work with networks of lawyers in other cities for whom human rights activity is a particular field in which they can use their professional skills. Several of them have studied abroad. They answer the advertisements that now appear on the hro.org website – lawyers are required by the great majority of human rights organizations. As Lukashevsky put it:

> The idea of the European Court appeals to them, and an individual begins to get involved, increases his or her professional competence, and begins to think of this as a career path and

professional advancement. There are many more of them now [. . .] It's a field in which you can work, become a professional, and achieve something, maybe not change the system but achieve concrete successes. Criteria exist, if it does not work in Russia, then you can turn to the European Court. And in Russia too you can achieve a great deal in concrete cases.

Today, in the Memorial Human Rights Centre, you will find three young lawyers, sharing a crowded room, busy behind their loaded desks and papers. It is a scene similar to that in the crowded London Liberty offices. A young lawyer in Memorial may have studied human rights law at the University of Essex. They stay two, three years, with Memorial and then move on to another job, perhaps abroad, in London or Strasbourg. Yet, at the same time, the justice systems with which young lawyers in London and in Moscow are engaging are very different, the only common ground they share is the European Court of Human Rights. It is not just that the Russian justice system is a continental system, based on detailed criminal and civil codes, and codes of procedure, a system where the state prosecutor has a greater role and influence, the judge has more authority but less scope for discretion in imposing sanctions, and the jury system has only recently been introduced. It also has features, some inherited from the Soviet past, that badly call for reform measures, for example the power of the chair of the regional or district court to appoint or dismiss the judges, the failure of the higher courts properly to review appeal cases, and their responding to political or financial pressure. Many of the complaints or appeals lodged with the ombudsman relate to the (illegal or inadequate) behaviour of court or justice officials. This is a topic in itself, far from straightforward. In the words of President Medvedev, himself an academic lawyer, at a meeting of the President's Council for the Advancement of Civil Society and Human Rights in November 2009:

An acquittal, in essence, means that the judge is contradicting the opinion of the investigator. It's often quite difficult for the judge to do that. I am not talking about the cases where a judge has come under some kind of criminal pressure; it is simply that it is difficult for a judge to do that from psychological, even professional, if you like from corporate considerations.

Ironically, perhaps, the failings of the justice system, including the judges' behaviour, contribute to the young lawyers' opportunities to intervene – and to win cases against corrupt or law-breaking government and justice officials, not only in Strasbourg but in Russian courts. Given too the extensive legislation on both socio-economic or welfare rights, and perennial issues – the non-payment of wages or pensions, or the provision of housing – there is considerable scope for intervention by lawyers who specialize in particular fields, be it migration rights, employment law, media law, or the right to a fair trial.

In previous chapters we have met some of the new generation of lawyers – Pavel Chikov from Kazan, Maria Kanevskaya from St Petersburg, Olga Gnezdilova from Voronezh – here I want to look at them and others of their generation a little more closely. Is it right to see a generational cleavage within the human rights community, and how might this spell change for the future? But, first, a brief introduction to the European Court, international bodies, and domestic courts.

Seeking redress: international and domestic institutions

By 2008 30,000 of the 112,000 cases pending before the European Court of Human Rights were from the Russian Federation (which has of course by far the largest population of any of the countries), and the number submitted was growing (from 10,500 during 2008, to 14,000 in 2009). The court was struggling to cope with its caseload, even simply to dismiss the great majority as inadmissible, and attempts were underway to get new procedures ratified that would enable it to work more effectively. By 2012 new submissions from Russia had dropped to 10,700 and, in 2013, of the 111,350 cases pending only 20,700 were from Russia.[1] But the figures suggest a strong desire, within Russia, to turn to Strasbourg for justice. Many of the human rights organizations, both those dating from the early nineties – the Memorial Human Rights Centre, Mother's Right, Litigator, Moskalenko's Centre – as well as the newer ones win cases.

As of 2012, 1,262 judgments had found at least one violation of the Convention by the Russian government. More than 100 of these concern serious human rights violations in Chechnya, and cases from the Second Chechen war are still before the court. In nearly all such cases, the court has held Russia responsible for enforced disappearances, extrajudicial executions, torture, and for failing properly to investigate these crimes. A significant number of judgments relate to the 'absence of effective remedies', the wrongful use of custody in remand cases, prolonged detention, and inhumane conditions in remand prisons. But there have also been judgments relating to damage to health from the environment, delays in hearing, and the non-payment of compensation. While the Russian government has generally paid the compensation awarded by the court, it has not always done so, and it has failed to implement measures that would prevent the recurrence of similar cases, or hold the perpetrators accountable.[2]

The Chechen wars (1994–6, and 1999–2002) produced perhaps the most horrendous crimes – the indiscriminate bombing of civilians, the murder, kidnapping and torture (on both sides) of armed combatants and civilians. But the continued use of detention, torture and murder by the Kadyrov regime in Chechnya itself, and the spilling over of conflict into neighbouring republics in the Caucasus, sometimes associated with Islamic militants, marks out this region of Russia. Activists and journalists work at their peril here, and almost total impunity continues to prevail.

While many journalists have died violent deaths in Russia since 1991, it is not always possible to establish whether the victim was targeted because of his or her investigations and publications or for political or business interests. There has been a shift, during recent years, away from total impunity to prosecutions of those committing the murders (but not necessarily of those behind it). The same is perhaps occurring when the target, an activist engaged in protest activities, is either murdered or savagely beaten up by unknown assailants. Until a few years ago it was almost unknown for anyone to be arrested and charged with murder or assault in such cases.

A variety of sources, some specialized, provide a more detailed picture of infringements. These include, for example, reports by the Memorial Human Rights Centre on the situation in Chechnya, or by the Glasnost Defence Foundation, the Center for Journalism in Extreme Situations (CJES), and a new database, http://mediaconflictsinrussia.org, on media rights and freedoms, and violence against journalists. Many of the Russian NGOs and the International Commission on Jurists, which includes two Russian lawyers, make submissions to the UN Committee on Human Rights or to the UN Committee on the Rights of Child when

Russia is the subject of a periodic report. Human Rights Watch, an international NGO which has a Moscow office, staffed by Russians, issues hard-hitting reports on topics ranging from the situation in Chechnya to the fate of migrant labour to the implementation of decisions by the European Court of Human Rights. The EU Centre, a think-tank supported by the European Union, has included human rights in recent reviews, while Western governments and private foundations, which support human rights organizations, publish periodic reviews of their grants. Rather differently, EHRAC (the European Human Rights Advocacy Centre), based now at Middlesex University, which works together with the Memorial Society to take cases to the European Court, issues regular bulletins on the results. The Russian Justice Initiative, also an NGO based on cooperation between European and Russian lawyers, but now denied registration in Russia, takes cases from the Caucasus to the ECHR. Reports from all these organizations are aimed at both an international (Western) audience and at a Russian one.[3]

Most infringements will of course never reach the European Court, and socio-economic rights do not fall within its purview. The majority of young lawyers are taking their cases to the Russian courts, starting at the district level, either defending a client or turning to the prosecutor with a request for investigation and a prosecution. Then, as in other systems, appeals may be launched; cases travel up to higher courts. The Constitutional Court rules on cases of constitutional significance. A different channel, open to the citizen, is to turn to the ombudsman, and many of the appeals are claims against the behaviour of court or justice officials, but I leave the ombudsman's reports, which range widely over the state of human rights, for Chapter 12.

The young lawyers in action

It is absolutely clear that during the Putin–Medvedev period jurisprudence became the key instrument. They, and others, insist on the extreme importance of law, despite the fact that they often break it [. . .] but they created a new rule, whereas in the nineties many questions were decided quite differently [. . .] then a well-known name was enough for a human rights organization to carry weight, now that's impossible.

Pavel Chikov, from Agora, Kazan, was only ten years old as perestroika got underway. For him, and others like him, students or children, the democratic movement was something other people were involved in; the new politics and the Chechen war were not part of their lives. Ivan Pavlov, in Leningrad, was slightly older. Upon finishing the prestigious mathematics school number 239 in 1987, he had intended to go to the Military Academy, but having suffered a traumatic injury at the time of examinations, went instead to the Electrotechnical Institute, which took the 17-year-old graduates of the maths school without entrance exams. He had no interest in the democratic movement.

> At that time politics did not interest many students, including me. The country was changing before your eyes, and you were more concerned with your own fate than with that of the country. You saw how full of lies the system was, how the old system had exhausted itself, and a new system had not yet come into existence, and it was not clear whether in fact it would. Of course you had your doubts. You had to get involved in business, earn to keep yourself alive.

Upon graduating, with a specialization in information technology, Pavlov transferred to St Petersburg State University to do a law degree.

> And, in principle, it was a very good thing that I had already got a higher education before doing a law degree because it gave me some experience of life, not just knowledge. Because I think that you cannot become a proper lawyer by doing a law degree straight after school.

While he was studying and working as a legal assistant in an advocates bureau, he came to know Yury Shmidt, the defence lawyer, who brought him on to work first on the Nikitin case, and then, after graduation, to work in the Far East on the Pasko case.[4] Clearly an able lawyer, he and Shmidt disagreed over the subsequent publication of materials relating to the case, and parted company. Once back in St Petersburg, in 2001 he set up an NGO to focus on the right of access to information. In 2008, the organization was inspected, just as Citizens Watch had been, but Pavlov successfully challenged the findings in court, and then set up a Foundation that parallels the NGO and would allow work to continue should either be closed.

His Freedom of Information Foundation, with a staff of perhaps 20 full-time and part-time staff (legal experts, information technology specialists) focuses on various projects. The three most important are educating the public on how to access information from the government, so that they can track government activities and budget expenditure (for example on dealing with damage from heavy snow falls, or on housing maintenance), actively litigating freedom of information cases on behalf of citizens and organizations, and shaming regional authorities and federal ministries into providing accessible information on their websites. His Foundation is, according to Pavlov, a new type of human rights organization because its members use new technologies to advance human rights, they work for today's citizens, and they want to achieve concrete results. For example: 'In 2005 54 of the 83 federal executive agencies had no websites.' In 2008 a law was passed that obliged them to open them, and Pavlov's organization has been active in chivvying the laggards to comply.

> And each year we monitor the official sites so as to create an atmosphere of competition, so that they want to move up our ratings [. . .] Ministers, for example, use the results of our ratings in their reports for the government or the president [. . .] Our EXMO (Expert Monitoring) system enables one to evaluate sites – it's all on the internet – and in the course of a month our experts interact with the officials.

Pavlov's organization is equally concerned to persuade citizens that access to information is a human right, and that anyone has a right to know how the budget is being spent. And how do you achieve this? I ask.

> It's our most difficult task, to reach the individual citizen, so we carefully analyse the situation in the city [. . .] then we hold seminars, we have a site on which anyone can raise a question, we work with a number of single issue organizations which, for example, defend the rights of residents [. . .] we explain how to make claims and, if they are refused, then our lawyers help them to take the case to court [. . .] ordinary people turn to us, perhaps 100 a year.

For Pavlov:

> It is the lack of openness on the part of the state, and of society, that is problem number one [...] People are usually closed, non-communicative. They work in a particular sphere, they see everyone as a competitor, they fear that if they divulge what they know, they will lose a certain resource. There are two different approaches to communication – one means a closed, the other an open society [...] but neither are the non-governmental organizations, including the human rights organizations, open institutions.

If there was openness, then, in Pavlov's view, the economy could flourish. History is responsible. 'It's the inheritance from the whole previous history of our state [...] not only the Soviet period. Russia never was an open state.' Its thousand-year history, he argues, has been based on the oppression of man 'and it is very difficult to jettison the slave-like mentality which, unfortunately many still possess'. Add to this, he argues, the disillusionment that people felt upon seeing all the lies the authorities told in the nineties, just like in the Soviet period, and you have a very unresponsive auditorium.

Pavlov's concern with 'open access' as a human right also extends to access to archives, which has lead him to work with Memorial. He acted for the St Petersburg Memorial Research Centre in 2009 when, following a police raid, it turned to court to charge the prosecutor's office with illegal actions during the search and to retrieve its hard disks, a case that, to the surprise of all, it won. And in 2013, ironically enough, he was in the Memorial office, querying the legality of an inspection team's requests in relation to the 'foreign agents' law, when he received a call that a similar inspection team had arrived at his office.

I am left slightly puzzled. Pavlov has little patience with an older generation of human rights activists who, he suggests, argue that it will take years, generations, before attitudes of subservience to the state will disappear. Presumably he would take issue with Pustintsev's statement:

> Human rights and the rule of law is genetically coded. It is based on the experience of previous generations. [...] All right the process started under Alexander II [...] but for 70 years

[since 1917] we were in a scorched waste land – where were
human rights? It will need a few generations before the Soviet
attitude towards one's own rights and the rights of others will
be eradicated.[5]

New technology, Pavlov argues, itself imperative if Russia is to
modernize, makes an 'open society' possible. Yet he believes that an
age-old serf mentality is all that Russia has ever had? Why, one wonders,
does he hold to a view that is not only historically very questionable but
weakens his argument that social and state attitudes can change? Is new
technology a magician's wand? In Pavlov, as in Chikov, we have an
individual who combines a lawyer's background with another area of
expertise. For Pavlov it is information technology, for Chikov it is
management, and they both pay special attention to internet PR. Both
attract considerable Western funding, and in 2011 Pavlov's American
wife worked for one of his funders.[6]

Agora, Chikov's organization, based in Kazan, works rather
differently. It is a loose association of 30 lawyers, scattered across the
country, and a few key individuals who will travel to places to work
with a local lawyer, using Agora's model strategies. Their main
communication channel is the internet, but they meet up from time to
time. They began, as we saw, by focusing on abuse of citizens by the
law enforcement agencies, but they now leave that to Public Verdict
and the Committee Against Torture. In 2010 they set up a small
Moscow office.

We focus on legal assistance for civic activists, human rights
activists and journalists. We provide legal aid for them if they are
being prosecuted or face violence or whatever in connection with
their public or professional activities [...] Agora is a security
service for Russian civil society. That's what we are best known for
in Russia. We defend anarchists, the antifascists, oppositionists,
NGOs, journalists, defence lawyers [...] and others. Our lawyers
defend those involved in Strategy 31, the group War [a
St Petersburg radical art group] are among our clients [...] Also
Natalya Vasileva who said that the decision in the second
Khodorkovsky trial was not written by the judge – she's our
client. People come under pressure from the authorities as soon as

they make that kind of statement, and we immediately take on their defence. That's our key priority.

In 2013 Chikov's wife, a defence lawyer, acted as defence counsel for one of the Pussy Riot trio and won her case on appeal.

They start by identifying an issue (for example the use of the law on extremism against activists) and work out a strategy for defending those who are being targeted (in the extremism case there were 15 individuals). They accompany the defence of individuals with a PR campaign, which involves not only using their own information agency (set up to attract advertisers and provide a source of funding), but also getting attention in the popular internet press. If gazeta.ru (a popular internet news site) is writing about Agora, Chikov argues, you do not need hro.org. They have initiated 15 separate cases against the Ministry of Finance – whether the judges group them together or not does not matter – the journalists will write of them as 'the 15 cases'.

> We make as much media coverage as possible [...] put a lot of resources into that, try to change the situation as a whole, by attracting attention to the cases, getting them onto the public agenda [...] and a judgement sets a precedent. You cannot work quietly with our court system because ours is not a common law system.

But, all the same, Chikov argues, precedence is playing more of a role because summaries of Supreme Court practice, its statements, and judges' rulings are acquiring more and more importance. 'Because the laws lag behind actual behaviour, judges compensate by using the evolving court practice, particularly in the case of the persecution of activists. When the authorities begin to think up a new method, we straightaway expose it and get actively involved.'

Chikov is not modest about their achievements – they have worked out a strategy that enables us 'to get involved in a case within 24 hours in any part of the country'. He doubts that in the near future any other organization will be able to offer their level of defence. The only place they do not work is the North Caucasus. They had 50 cases before the European Court when we spoke.

'Do you think you can change, transform the court system or achieve less harsh sentencing with your strategy?' Yes, Chikov answers, it works, and of all that they have tried this is the most effective. But he is concerned about the future. We are not talking about a campaign by bare foot lawyers.

> To remain an activist you have to be able to earn, one way or another, enough to live on. That's a basic problem today because the foundations are leaving Russia. A good lawyer costs good money.

Chikov's focus is Russia, and using a combination of legal opportunities and the media to gain publicity, and perhaps eventually transform the legal system. Pavlov too thinks in terms of Russia but, for him, the target is state and society. Maria Kanevskaya, who we met in the Introduction, chairing a School for Human Rights activists in St Petersburg and, in Chapter 5, attending a Marek Nowicki school in Warsaw, focuses on providing legal assistance to struggling NGOs working on economic, social or civil rights. She clearly likes managing things.

Born in 1982, she attended a French-language school in St Petersburg, and then entered the law faculty of the MVD University, where her father taught philosophy. She was a very active student, winning essay competitions, and through participation in an informal study group on international law, came to hear of human rights. She entered a French competition and, on her eighteenth birthday, received an invitation and the airline tickets to participate in an international 16-day course in Geneva on human rights law. She became an inveterate attender of schools and trainings.

> Between the ages of 18 and 23 I attended more than 15 conferences, courses of one kind and or another. Once I worked out how much my studying human rights had cost Western society – all the travel, and the different programmes.

Her first project concerned young offenders, then she moved on to providing assistance to refugees. The fact that all six members of her organization were from the MVD University made cooperation with government officials easier. However in 2007 her organization was shut down, ostensibly on the grounds that it was issuing educational certificates without having registered status, but really, in her view, because of the receipt of grants from the Dutch government. She lost her case in court, and her confidence and faith in the court system. And, at that moment, she says, she understood that anything was possible in Russian courts. Boris Pustintsev, who with Ivan Pavlov had attended the hearing, urged her to fight the verdict but she did not have the courage.

In 2008 she set up a new organization, The Human Rights Resource Centre, whose aim is to provide legal and institutional support to NGOs (especially young NGOs) and citizen initiative groups in four federal districts of Russia. She set up a hotline by signing a contract with a mobile phone company under which, for a monthly fee, calls to and from NGOs across Russia to the centre's lawyers are free. In 2011 Kanevskaya in Petersburg, and lawyers in Saratov, Krasnoyarsk, and Novorossiisk were available on the hot line from 11 a.m. to 5 p.m. If one of them was engaged, the call switched to one of the others. In 2011 they were receiving from five to 20 calls a day on issues ranging from how to register an organization, how to challenge a ruling or inspection, how to take a case to court, etc. Their website provides further information, and they organize (as we saw) schools to help a wide range of small NGOS with their activities, including taking cases to the European Court.

Kanevskaya became a member of the city's Human Rights Council, an informal body of an older generation of leading activists, in 2010. But when, in December of that year, the city council was to elect a children's ombudsman, and the Human Rights Council nominated one of its members – Natalya Evdokimova (an ex-deputy, and well known in the city) – to stand against the official candidate, Kanevskaya decided to put herself forward as an independent candidate. She campaigned for two weeks, using PR assistants, and lobbying methods that she had learnt from a three-day seminar; she rang all 500 organizations that her organization had helped, contacted key deputies, and got two votes more than the official favourite. This should not have happened. Someone quickly pressed his voting button, but the damage had been done (and Evdokimova came third, and was now out of the competition). A second round had to be held. It was better organized and, as expected, Agapitova, the official candidate won easily. A representative from the United Russia party apologized to her: 'we liked you, maybe another time, but we have a strict hierarchy, and we only support candidates put forward by Matvienko [the governor].'

The Human Rights Council was sharply critical of her for having stood and, according to her, 'harangued her for an hour and a half'. But amiable relations were soon restored, and she participates as a member. In her view: '[the older activists] don't really understand that one should put more in the hands of young people. Some are positively against having younger activists as members [. . .] And if they won't, then they have no future.'

There are other organizations in St Petersburg, run by younger people, some which have been active for ten years or more (Anti-Discrimination Memorial, an offshoot of Memorial, which works on ethnic and racist discrimination, and has now suffered under the 'foreign agents' law), others that are newer (LGBT groups), and Egida (labour rights, discrimination at the workplace). Their members, while respecting the older activists, are not convinced that their time is best spent by participating in the council. But nor do they see Kanevskaya as a natural ally.

A generation gap?

In St Petersburg a generation gap, at least to an outsider, is very visible, perhaps because here there are young leaders. In Moscow, home of the heavyweight organizations, it is different. But the 2010–11 interview survey, conducted by Volkov in six cities, found that:

> Only a few leaders make an effort constantly to attract new staff members, train them, and encourage them. There are very few which from the start set themselves the aim of ensuring generational change within the organization, providing guidance, bringing young members into the process of decision making. In the eyes of young leaders, the old organizations often appear closed, hierarchic structures where the leader takes all the decisions.

The survey also revealed that the most able young people were leaving the provinces for Moscow or to go abroad. Youthful initiatives can fail because their organizers lack experience or reputation but overcoming the generation gap, Volkov suggests, will be critical to the future of civic activity.[7] But is it just a gap between the original perestroika activists, many of whom are now in their late sixties or seventies (and Kovalev and Alekseeva are both over eighty), and these, the latest recruits to the human rights community? Chikov thinks not.

> Crudely, I would distinguish three generations of human rights activists: generation one – the dissidents, two – the managerial-experts – people like Taubina, Dzhibladze, Lokshina, Kalyapin [. . .] it's not always age, it's a way of thinking [. . .] and the third, those who appeared in the Putin period (I think of myself as a member of this generation) [. . .] they are highly professional in what they do. They are among the best lawyers, the best PR-shiki [PR professionals], the best journalists – first and foremost they are highly skilled in their professions.

Although only a few of the perestroika activists had a dissident past, Chikov's characterization is telling. Dissidents and perestroika activists shared a Soviet past, a set of common experiences. Most abandoned their professions (which ranged from those of physicists to historians to film directors) to set up human rights organizations that, as both they and younger activists recognized, they often ran very incompetently. In Chikov's view: 'It was a terrible problem – these elderly people, who didn't know how to manage money, didn't know how to write reports, they simply couldn't adapt to these requirements.' Tanya Lokshina, as we noted, was shocked by the way the MHG was run. Today, she suggests, things are very different.

> Working with the European Court – that requires working on a different level, not with an activist but with a professional approach; [working in a human rights organization] is now far removed from volunteer work, and we are not talking about those pitiful salaries which I remember so well. An effort is made now to support young professionals, there's a recognition of professional expertise, of what should be done to organize the work. Then there was none of that, it was simply a [tusovka] get-together.

But what of Chikov's second generation, the managers, which would include Lokshina?

With the exception of Kalyapin, they do seem to constitute a bridging generation in that they focused on professionalizing the community and its activities: teaching skills, and strategies, whether collecting data, writing reports for international audiences as well as Russian, organizing a campaign, or managing grants from Western foundations. Taubina's skills as an administrator brought her the post of director of Public Verdict in 2004, but by 2010 Dzhibladze, now that campaigning and organizational skills had professionalized the human rights organizations, found himself looking for work. In the words of a fellow activist:

> He's an ideal rapporteur, he's a very good expert, he's an excellent organizer or coordinator of any discussion, particularly, in an international context where Russians are participating. In that capacity he is practically irreplaceable. But he does not have an organization.

Known, smilingly by other activists, as the Minister of Foreign Affairs for Human Rights, his future probably lies somewhere in the international field.

Both Tanya Lokshina and Grigory Shvedov, as we noted, were simply looking for an interesting job where they could use their professional skills. They have this in common with the newer recruits. Shvedov, Chikov agrees, has strong traits of the third generation about him: a focus on effective, innovative strategies, thinking ahead of one's opponents, and achieving results. 'The ability to continue to develop, grow, as circumstances change.' To support yourself, and your activities. And would not Kalyapin, the entrepreneur, also qualify? After all we are talking about attitudes and behaviour, not age. Chikov hesitates and compromises: yes, and Kalyapin's office is staffed by young, third generation lawyers. Perhaps though, when we talk of generations, it is better to recognize that there are always exceptions, and Kalyapin is an unusual activist – a radical democrat at the time of perestroika, then a successful entrepreneur who gradually moved to working as a volunteer for a human rights organization before setting up his own, and is both an effective manager and a tireless activist. And how might Igor Sazhin, up in Syktyvkar, fit in? In his own words:

My attitude to the authorities is as towards something sacred, whereas the attitude [of the young people he teaches] is quite different [. . .] their approach is wholly pragmatic, but on the other hand they believe that they can change something. I also think that you can change something but at the same time I think that change can come from on high [. . .] I still believe that there can be such a thing as a good ruler. But that doesn't interest them [. . .] For them justice is very narrow and concrete, it involves them and their surroundings [. . .] The world, in principle, in their view, is unjust and cannot be just.

It is striking that while the first, now elderly, generation of activists is heavily Muscovite, and many of them were scientists, our young activists, both those who bridge the generations, and the young recruits, are either lawyers or have a humanities background. There are no physicists, biologists, or mathematicians among them. Taubina, Lukashevsky, Shvedov, and Lokshina are from Moscow. Others, the younger ones, come from St Petersburg, the Urals (Perm), Tatarstan (Kazan), the south (Voronezh), the north (Syktyvkar), the Volga (Nizhny Novgorod) and Siberia (Krasnoyarsk). Moscow may have reasserted itself as the political capital of the country, but as regards human rights organizations the scales have tipped the other way.

What else has changed? First, in many ways today's young activists are much more like their contemporaries in the West. Particular events or meetings awakened their interest in rights or human rights, and led to their becoming involved. For Pavlov it was being put on the Pasko case, for Chikov, talking to his friend from the police, for Latypov in Perm it was attending a summer camp, for Sokiryanskaya it was meeting a Chechen and an Ingush in Warsaw. For Drozhzhakov, the trade union lawyer from Krasnoyarsk, it was the treatment of Chinese workers by his employer.

He began bringing potential workers to Russia, under any pretext, took away their passports and then used them for any kind of work. People lived without any rights, wherever they could, ate what they could scrounge, weren't paid. I did not like it, and took it up with my manager, began to help the Chinese, and a conflict of interests arose, because I, the organization's lawyer, was working against the organization. I managed to get it shut down but then I was without work.

He moved into trade union work, first as a legal inspector, and then, as we shall see in Chapter 12, into actively defending workers' rights.

The Human Rights Youth Movement – MPD

Some of the youngest generation attended the Nowicki schools, and/or the schools organized by the Human Rights Youth Movement, an organization set up by Andrei Yurov in Voronezh in the 1990s. This offered summer schools, where young people could learn how to use, for example, flash mob tactics, and then as members of this 'movement' that had branches in Ukraine, Belarus, and reached out to Europe, to work as volunteers on projects in their localities. Maria Kanevskaya, for example, practised volunteer work in St Petersburg, based on MPD training. It is difficult to assess its impact, or how many of its youthful members retain any interest in human rights today. It still exists, Yurov is now honorary president, and Dmitry Makarov, based in Voronezh, but frequently travelling, is perhaps its best-known representative, and now its director. But what does MPD actually do, except to react to events, for example the Bolotnoye process, or bring out a statement on the Syrian conflict? I pursued the question with Maria Sereda, a young activist in Ryazan:

I don't really understand what the MPD is.
    No one understands that. It's some kind if a thingamajig, a civic nesting box. In the first place it's some kind of a sub-culture, some kind of a space, whose legal status is unclear, with some bits of an organizational structure [...] it's some kind of a changing milieu, into which people come and go [...] many leave very quickly but go into human rights organizations, as people with good professional skills.

Everyone knows of the MPD, but finds it difficult to describe. One of its offshoots is the Voronezh Interregional Human Rights Group.

Work at regional level

In 2000 the MPD was running a programme, Start, which included a series of evening lectures on different human rights themes, followed by volunteer activity. Olga Gnezdilova, a third year law student, attended, and joined a letter-box project in which law students answered prisoners' letters (copying Gorelik's initiative in Krasnoyarsk). After graduation, she acted as coordinator of the project, and joined the Interregional Human Rights Group, set up by Yurov and registered as an independent organization in 2000.

Similar to the Human Rights Centre in Perm, the Human Rights Group's lawyers focus on a number of issues, ranging from prisoners' rights to the freedom of association in the surrounding Black Earth region, or providing for example, legal advice to NGOs threatened with closure. These multi-issue centres, popular in the nineties, are now fewer in number, partly because the human rights community has become more specialized, partly because only the strong ones have survived. The Voronezh centre manages to attract some independent funding from Western sources, and participates in Moscow Helsinki Group projects, but its five lawyers earn a living while working part time for the centre.

Voronezh is a pleasant southern city, with wide leafy streets, some eighteenth and nineteenth century architecture, parks, and a wide river cutting the city in half. Fortunately, during World War II, the Germans remained on one side. There's a plaque to Mandelshtam, the poet, who died in a camp, and a statue of Platonov, the writer, now stands in its park, not far from the statue of Lenin. The human rights groups, which include a Memorial organization that works both on Stalinist repression and on migrant and refugee rights, share the floor of a crowded building in the centre of the city. I talked to Olga, a young mother, as she nursed her new baby. We sat on a park bench in the sun while her husband, an environmental activist, pushed their sleeping toddler up and down in a push chair.

In 2006, they took up the issue of public access to court hearings, and court procedures. With great difficulty, they got access to and monitored court hearings. The press took up their critical report, the chair of the regional court responded, and now only a passport is required to gain entry to a hearing.

Do you think, I ask, that the court system can be changed by pressure from below?

Vyacheslav Ilich [chair of the Voronezh Memorial society] argues, quite convincingly, that one should begin from below because it's easier to appeal to the district court judge's conscience, and the higher courts are prone to confirm decisions taken further down. But of course the district court judge is also very dependent upon his or her superiors.

They have noticed that when they take students or a journalist with them, the judges make efforts to observe the laws, and they have a greater chance of getting a favourable decision. But she would not claim that they have achieved significant changes.

In 2009 they produced a report on the teaching of religion in schools, and presented it to the Ministry of Education. They do an annual report on the infringement of social and political rights in the region, and make recommendations, for example of the need to introduce an ombudsman, and this has been accepted by the regional authorities.

We try to educate some of the government agencies. We worked with the Ministry of Justice on the inspection of NGOs, because previously they were acting so harshly, issuing warnings for trivial things that they wanted to consider infringements of the law.

They sent the Prosecutor General's office a report on police use of torture. This may have prompted a visit from the Prosecutor General, and a meeting at which some of the police chiefs received disciplinary reprimands. And what do they hope to achieve?

That those rights which are in the European Convention are observed. We take the issue of police torture very seriously, we want every case to be rigorously investigated by the prosecutor, and those who are guilty to receive real sentences, not today's suspended sentences.

And they want freedom of association – for meetings in the main square. Are they interested in changing the law or in its implementation? Her response echoes those we have heard previously:

Changing the legislation is of course an interesting question but, in Russia, the laws themselves are not so bad. The fact of the matter is that here people do not observe the law or bear responsibility for breaking it.

Here we have a human rights organization, working until recently in a reasonably favourable local environment. We note its 'monitoring', taking up issues, attempts to influence local legislation, to educate officials, and to improve court behaviour. And we see how its lawyers contribute to and benefit from participating in projects organized by the Moscow Helsinki Group and Public Verdict. However, in 2012, before the crackdown on NGOs, the shared office was raided by the security services, some groups had discs confiscated, and unpleasant anonymous phone threats persuaded some to take time out abroad. Surprisingly, the organization was not targeted in the 'foreign agents' campaign in 2013.

My aim is to help people

The two characteristics Lukashevsky drew attention to – pragmatism and a desire to help people 'to help specific individuals or to solve a concrete problem' – come out very clearly from conversations with young activists, be they lawyers or not.

Alexander Zarutsky, a young lawyer working in the Memorial office in Ryazan, tells me that 'My ambition to become a lawyer was motivated by my desire to help people who were destitute and had no one who could help them [...] that remains my main motivation to become a good, skilled lawyer.' Legislation, in his view, can be inadequate but the main problem is 'the banal bureaucratic attitudes of officials'. He follows court practice in other regions – for example he will use the ruling in a recent case in which the Memorial Human Rights Centre in Syktyvkar won damages of 70,000 rubles for a citizen for the lengthy non-implementation of a court decision.

The conventions which exist, the European and UN conventions, they have more of a latent, perhaps virtual character. Maybe somewhere they work. I study court practice, including that of our Constitutional Court, and I see that the court often refers to the convention in its decisions. But as far as the everyday courts are concerned, the conventions are not used.

And if we meet in five years' time, what will you hope to have achieved?

That I shall have become a professional lawyer, in the sphere which I specialize in now. I love my work [. . .] My aim is to help people.

Pavel Levashin, the young lawyer in Perm, whom we met in Chapter 9, talks in a very similar way:

I apply all my energies somehow to help people who need assistance, people who don't have any means of resolving their problems [. . .] I don't aspire to change the situation in the country or in our region, but at least I can help with the problems that exist in our region [. . .] if I win say four cases a year which benefit the pensioners, grandmothers and grandfathers, if I at least assist in helping solve the problems in our region, I'll be glad. There are so many problems.

Zarutsky, himself an orphan, was working on a project to help young orphans get housing once they leave a children's home. The region's population of 1.2 million includes about 4,000 orphans who, by law, should receive housing, but local officials use the excuse of lack of funding to take no action. In 2011 he was dealing with perhaps ten cases a month. While he was taking cases to court, other members of the Ryazan office engaged in social marketing, placing photos of individual orphans in the windows of a mock-up poster of an empty building – as though they were building a house for them – and attracted media attention, and donations from people who signed the photo-cards. They raised funding for 20 flats. The campaign was led by Maria Sereda who had participated in the Gerber and Mendelson project on social marketing, mentioned in the previous chapter, and who subsequently completed an MA in Glasgow on marketing and PR for non-commercial organizations. She returned to Russia to teach the techniques to others while participating in campaigns.

Sometimes we need a dry and serious text by Kovalev, and sometimes a comic strip. These are absolutely different things but as instruments, they are used in the same way.

Sergei Adamovich [Kovalev] once said, after I had made a presentation at a conference, that the imprint of the devil is to be found on all that marketing. Sakharov, as regards mass communication, was almost unintelligible, very difficult to understand. It was his principled position that worked for him, because at that time that was what was most important, 100 per cent truth and sincerity. It still has a role to play today but it's disappearing. It has become absolutely clear that, in today's very different world, honesty, on its own, as a rule does not work, you have to think how to present it.

In answer to my asking what she would like to be doing in five years' time, she responds that she would like to be developing non-commercial marketing for the human rights sector.

'And how do you define "the sector"?' I ask

I would consider all organizations which, one way or another, are involved in normalizing [the right of the citizen to interact with the authorities] to be human rights organizations. Using the law is not the most important strategy. Regularizing the relationship between citizens and the authorities, maybe legally, or not by law, but with the help of communication, dialogue, analysis etc [...]

No one likes torture, violence against women, when kids can't go to school, no one can like that. Therefore in practice there is no avoiding human rights. What will in time happen to them in the realm of ideology – it's very interesting to think about that. But fortunately that doesn't determine everyday activity. Fortunately, you have to defend people when the police beat them up [...] I have the sense that that human rights means 'security' [...] human rights is the means of creating a safe, an unspoilt world. [8]

Meanwhile Natalya Brikker, the young office manager of Memorial in Ryazan, likes administration.

In many ways we are a generation of administrators, managers [...] We join human rights organizations because we understand that not everything is right with the world, that something must be done. We are very focused on getting results [. . .] when we can say – yes, our organization achieved that.

Natalya favours cooperation with the authorities.

Memorial does not work together with the authorities but neither do we position ourselves as out and out oppositionists, we always try to find some entry point that will work. Because we are involved in major social issues, such as orphans and invalids, we find that if we position ourselves constructively, well-prepared, we can achieve much greater results.

Members of this youngest generation may well disagree (as do their parents) whether or not one should engage in political protest. In 2011 one such issue was the protest meetings of the 31st of the month in support of Article 31 of the constitution, the right to assemble. Some joined in, others stayed away. The results of the elections in 2011, and then the 2013 inspections, posed similar issues, requiring political decisions but this, and the response of their contemporaries is the topic for the next chapter. Here we conclude by returning to the young lawyers.

Aleksei Korotaev, whom we heard suggesting in 2004 that no one apart from the human rights activists were interested in the Universal Declaration and UN conventions, characterized the situation as follows.

In reality what human rights activists are basically doing today is helping the observance of the law. As for the percentage of their activity that relates to the international understanding of human rights – it would be lucky if it amounts to ten per cent – writing a report for the UN Committee or to the European Court. Everything else is a straightforward struggle to get a right observed. Full stop. The word 'human' does not appear. Simply rights and law. And that is all one can do in order that one day, on this basis, a demand for human rights will emerge in this country.[9]

Or simply a law-based state, but not one necessarily committed to human rights? Might not that be a more important achievement?

CHAPTER 12

TWENTY YEARS ON: HUMAN RIGHTS, SOCIETY AND POLITICS

Politicians, political commentators and human rights activists assumed that the elections to the Duma in 2011 would provide an overwhelming majority for United Russia, the government party. United Russia won, but did worse than had been expected. The tactic, advocated by Alexander Navalny, an aspiring young blogger whose internet campaign against corruption was hugely popular, of voting for anyone except the government party, United Russia ('The Party of Thieves and Fraudsters', as he named it), paid off. Video and photo evidence demonstrated that the 'official' results (in many places) were suspect. Blatant rigging of results occurred in Moscow. Suddenly voters came to life and the first big demonstrations took place in Moscow and other cities. The breathtaking cynicism of the announcement in the autumn of 2011 that Vladimir Putin, the prime minister, would run for the presidency in 2012, while Dmitry Medvedev, the president, would become prime minister, and, moreover, that this had been agreed between them in 2008 surely contributed to the disaffection. Human rights activists joined the demonstrations, which continued until Putin's inauguration in May 2012, but they were as amazed as everyone else. Aleksei Simonov of the Glasnost Defence Foundation expressed it this way.

> Russia has frozen stock still in bewilderment at herself. What has happened in Russia can be compared to the well-known joke about

the centipede. The centipede was asked: 'Tell us please, how does it happen that straight after the 17th leg, you put down your 26nd? And after that, your 33rd?' And the centipede froze because she had never thought about this. For her it was a natural thing to do. She thought to herself: 'How do I do that?' And she wasn't able to move any more. There is a feeling that Russia, like the centipede, in the weeks before New Year froze stock still in bewilderment at herself. She didn't expect that she could do anything like that. She simply did not expect what happened first of all on 10 December, and then on 24 December. She honestly had not thought she was capable of anything like it [. . .]

And the fact is that this bewilderment has been felt both by those who have been the 'victims' of what's been happening, and by those who have been its cause and source. In other words, those who did this and those who watched what was happening were bewildered in equal measure (and those who watched also experienced a certain horror). Because the question is, what will happen next? [1]

Before we see what did happen next – the authorities' response, that of the law and order agencies, and of the human rights community – we look, albeit sketchily, at the way citizens, 20 years after the ending of Communist party rule, were creating new ways of acting together. Sometimes, but not often, this was in defence of their rights, as the ombudsman, among others, noted in his reports.

Society awakens

It did not all begin in December 2011. Protest activities over local issues, street actions involving a few dozen to several thousand people, the factual transformation of the President's Council on the Advancement of Civil Society and Human Rights into an opposition, all these had become a fact of public life by 2010. And, the upsurge of informal civic activity, with people beginning to come together en masse in very different initiatives (from charitable giving to defending historic buildings) was already noticeable in 2010.

These, the comments of GRANI, an NGO in Perm, which carried out an extensive survey of social activism in 20 regions, town and villages, and produced a detailed report in 2012,[2] echo the observations of activists and others in 2010–11. Among our activists Maria Sereda had suggested in 2010:

> Those societies to save cats, young mothers' clubs, they are very important. It has taken twenty years for people to begin to use freedom, not individually, but collectively. Essentially, people have only now begun to understand [...] that if they do something together, they can achieve something that did not exist before.

And she continued:

> I am very aware of civil society appearing, particularly during the past two years, and quite intensively, it's coming up like grass but not in those places where we watered. It's true, it's only social activity [...] People decide for example that if they can get 100 together, and each contributes 100 rubles, they can rent a place where they can have a club and listen to their favourite music in the evenings. We tried to teach people some tools, tried to get them to join NGOs, talked about human rights. And now I have the feeling that until that elementary level of interaction between one citizen and another is reached, all the rest has little point.

Volkov's survey of activists in 2010, which reaches several of the same conclusions as the Perm team, notes: 'For some of the respondents, their motivation came from the realization that they could improve things in a particular sphere, either in their courtyard or town. They and no one else.'[3] People do not wait for a favour from the government but take certain of its functions on themselves. And, in contrast to the attitudes found by Rusakova in her 2006 survey, people act together: Parents join up to pay for sporting facilities for kids, which are then cheaper, or they write a joint letter to the school director on facilities for disabled children.

The GRANI report noted how informal groups, concerned by local issues, anxious to improve the quality of life, for themselves, and for others, had started entering the public space. Their target was not only government departments, and bureaucracy, but 'society itself – its conventions, stereotypical ways of thinking, customs' and potential supporters. The circumstances which prompted individuals to take up or engage in such activities could vary wildly – from problems which arose after the birth of a child (no child care) to the purchase of a new apartment (inadequate repair services), to an accident with an official car that failed to stop. What had seemed to be an individual problem turned out to be shared by others. As Aleksei Kozlov, from Voronezh, put it: 'Through the pursuit of individual interests, a social problem comes to be resolved publicly.'[4]

These local initiatives, sometimes the brainchild of an enterprising individual that attracted interested volunteers, included campaigning against a plan to mine for nickel, collecting Christmas presents for orphans, a search for lost children and helping residents whose roofs had collapsed under a heavy snow fall. Some activities, as noted by Lokshina (in the Introduction), took the form of protests. The GRANI report also draws attention to 'national campaigns': the 'blue buckets' campaign in which, following a fatal accident, participants across the country installed blue buckets on their cars in protest against official cars using their blue lights to commandeer the central lanes on a highway. In Moscow traffic was brought to a standstill. The spread of forest fires in the dry summer of 2010, when the authorities failed to respond, saw local groups spring into action, coordinating their efforts via the internet. And the flooding in the south, in 2012, brought volunteers flocking down from the north to help. Here the internet played a crucial role. According to one of the respondents, A. Loskutov, from Novosibirsk:

> Today the internet is the main means of communication for civic activists, informational support for enterprises and actions is basically provided through networking sites. It's difficult to get on TV, newspapers are no longer that popular, so we are mostly oriented towards the internet.

N. Zvyagina, from Voronezh, put it more strongly:

> Internet – it's not just a tool for civic activity, but a part of one's personality. If you want to be recognized by today's generation,

you have to get into a network and do something on site, otherwise you just fall behind. There are those who exist and act solely through a site, but they are known to the whole country.

All agree that the internet and mobile phones, by 2010, had transformed connections between people across the country and the opportunities for joint action. In 2011, as we saw, the internet campaign run by Navalny influenced the elections. However, more traditional forms of collective action were also beginning to make themselves felt.

Collective protest

Collective protest had made its appearance intermittently during the past ten years. In 2005 proposals to monetize certain benefits (for example bus passes) brought a wave of protests from pensioners. In 2007–9 a variety of strikes or industrial action gained publicity, most notably a strike over rates of pay, lasting several weeks, at the Ford motor company in St Petersburg, and the blocking of the main road by the workers and their families from the Pikalevo plant, in the Leningrad region, when it was threatened with closure. In this case Putin appeared in person as the saviour of the plant, and was filmed tearing strips off its oligarch owner. The reader may remember that Kovalev, at the Constitutional Forum in 2010, had argued for working together with the independent trade unions. Perhaps that is a place to start.

Labour relations in Russia, since the early Soviet period, have been heavily subject to legal regulation. In 2002 a new, enormously long and detailed Labour Code became law. On paper, employees' rights are many and include all aspects of working activity; in practice the non-observance of conditions, including the non-payment of wages, has been widespread. The ombudsman's report for 2010 drew attention to the passivity of the trade unions, repeating the previous year's comments 'in almost no case of complaints regarding employment was there any sign of an active part being played by a trade union on the employee's side'. Union passivity, it suggested, may be partly explained by their having fewer rights under the new Labour Code, but also by the attitudes of the FNPR (Federation of Independent Trade Unions of Russia), the successor to the official Soviet trade unions. One would hope, the ombudsman's report states, that the government would welcome the emergence of new, independent, trade unions but 'on the contrary local authorities often are suspicious of or show poorly concealed hostility to the new unions'. Organizers and activists, and their families, are threatened by 'unknown' persons, and neither local authorities nor the FNPR react to this. And then follows a further comment: 'Employees, whose labour rights are infringed by the employer, are prepared to turn to the president of the country, to the prime minister, almost to the UN, but not to FNPR.'[5]

A group of activist sociologists, who named their group 'Collective Action', produced data on 70 strikes in 2009, the majority of which were 'crisis' strikes: the stopping of work because of non-payment of wages. This is legal, but there were instances of strikes prompted by the employer's refusal to negotiate over wage rates and conditions, which is not permitted. The Pikalevo action, the authors suggest, spurred others to engage in street action, accompanied by a request (demand?) to the authorities to nationalize the enterprise or, at least 'to introduce order' and punish an 'ineffective' owner. But all too often, they add, media reporting is minimal, and the protesters lack organizational skills.[6]

Vitaly Drozhzhakov, the trade union activist from Krasnoyarsk who participates in the phone-in network, works for a union in the food processing industry, which belongs to FNPR. As a lawyer, he relies heavily on the courts but, as he explained at the St Petersburg school, there are other tactics too that unionists can and should employ to defend rights. What is his take on the situation? The old Soviet employers, he suggests, think in terms of working together with the unions 'but our new managers are trained to think that they must put pressure on them'. He and his colleagues create organizations with 30–50 members 'and with such a group we can break down an entrenched practice, not only in Krasnoyarsk krai but in the whole of Russia'. They led a campaign on the correct payment of overtime, met with management, included the prosecutor, who 'let us down, said that everything was in order. We then went to the krai procurator, and contacted the Coca-Cola factory in St Petersburg where there is a good organization, who joined up with us.' And they won the case for all employed in their industry.

In your opinion, I ask, does the trade union defend workers' rights more actively now than five years ago?

Often young people don't have any idea of what a trade union is, and so it's easier to work with them, explain what we are about and what our aims are.

But it's more difficult with older workers, he suggests, because they think

in a Soviet stereotyped way of the union as some kind of a welfare organization, providing passes to holiday resorts, and they ask why we aren't doing that [. . .] Today the unions are probably more active, and people are more clued up, but people come under pressure today, just as they did earlier [. . .] but people now have a quite different attitude towards us. And the employers have begun to take us more seriously. I felt that after the Ford strikes, which didn't pass unnoticed by our employers, they began a more active campaign against the unions.

Volkov's survey also came up with evidence of employers' opposition to union activity, and of changes in employees' attitudes. A prosecutor brought a criminal case against a new trade union chair, and tried to paste a charge of extremist activity on him. A human rights activist suggested that whereas individuals used to come to them and say 'I am in such and such a situation and I don't know what to do', now they say 'I know I am entitled to it but my employer won't give it to me'. Another claimed:

What's important is to know the law and with its help it turns out that you can achieve something. People have changed, you can't hoodwink or frighten them today. The situation is different now, it's changing all the time. I see it from my own experiences.

The Collective Action group concluded that by 2009, while organized collective action was still rare, and pressure and threats from employers usually won out, a small nucleus of perhaps 7–10 per cent of the industrial labour force could now be considered 'activists'. The great majority of workers still prefer individual and informal methods as a way of defending their interests and rights; they may complain but they do not act. The authors echo comments that we have heard from others – on the general population's submissiveness, the low levels of trust, paternalistic attitudes, the lack of a habit of acting collectively and, they add, a commonly held perception that those who protest are either individuals who cannot make it or extremists. Even activists may consider themselves to be odd, demonstrated by a telling comment from one: 'And this is all despite that fact that a year ago I was just a normal person.' It is difficult they suggest, in the face of such cultural habits, to create new cultural codes.

However, at the same time, the Collective Action sociologists are highly critical of liberal intellectuals who see ordinary people's 'primitive' beliefs as responsible for the persistence of authoritarian government. Rather, they suggest, it is the political elite (old and new) that has failed to live up to the prescriptions of a new democratic and judicial order and whose behaviour prompts a pragmatic response from its citizens: play by the existing rules. And attention should be paid to the slogans of those who do protest 'At least observe your own laws', the demands for 'justice' meaning equal rights for all, 'Down with the arbitrary exercise of power' (by employers as well as by the authorities), and 'Put the authorities under the control of the public!' Moreover, they claim:

An even more challenging call is heard more and more frequently 'Rights are not given, rights are taken'. [A well-known quote from Maxim Gorky, the early twentieth century novelist and playwright.] This slogan is of an explosive character for the existing system of power, which is based upon the right of the 'lord' to grant rights to his 'serfs'.

And with this we turn to the ombudsman's reports.

'Rights are not given – rights are taken'

The ombudsman's office issues an annual report, based primarily on the letters and appeals it receives from individual citizens; when a case is of significant public concern, other sources of information are consulted. The report aims to direct the attention of state and society to 'real problems relating to the observance of rights' that have arisen during the preceding year. As Vladimir Lukin, the ombudsman from 2004–14, himself observes, they should not be seen as providing a picture of rights' infringements across the country; rather they offer us an account of chronic failings, and snapshots of particular issues on which the office has decided to focus. A choice prompted, I suggest, by the political situation, and by events that have made the headlines. As a consequence, the reports are revealing – of a variety of citizens' concerns and of the thinking of a liberal section of the Moscow intelligentsia.

First, the chronic failings. The number of applications made to the federal ombudsman fluctuates[7] but, in recent years, the majority (perhaps 60 per cent) have been complaints relating to court procedure in civil cases or to treatment in places of detention; roughly a quarter raise social issues, of which perhaps half concern housing for veterans, orphans, and soldiers. Labour cases fluctuate. Very few are political cases. Each year the failings of the court system, the delay in cases being heard, the (un)equal rights of accuser and accused, and the failure to ensure the right to qualified legal counsel make their appearance. The non-implementation of court decisions, at whatever level, is a constant complaint. The failure of local authorities, including the city of Moscow, to observe the decision by the Constitutional Court (in 1996, and again in 1998) that the *propiska* or residence registration system is unconstitutional, was still being raised ten years later.

In 2010:

> The problems relating to the observation of freedom of speech and thought are so numerous that it is unrealistic to deal with them all in one report [. . .] here we deal with only two, frequently met with in our work [. . .] the persecution of those who criticize state authorities and their representatives, and the restriction of freedom of thought and word by the arbitrary use of anti-extremist legislation.

The 'misuse' of the 2002 law on 'extremism' by judges is a constant target.[8] Judges, and prosecutors, are also criticized for favouritism shown to government officials and politicians. A perennial problem is that of government departments or employers not meeting their legal obligations. The failure to provide housing for vulnerable groups or, for example, the widespread failure of pharmacies to observe the legislation on price control of basic medications, are cases in point. Too often, however, Lukin suggests in 2010, passive and clientilist attitudes among citizens contribute to the failings of the justice system. His office should not be seen as yet another window for 'petitions' rather 'this new state institution is called upon both to defend the legal rights of citizens and the no less lawful right of society as a whole to become, eventually, a civic rather than a paternalistic society'.

Now for the high profile cases, and Lukin's view of the political situation.

In 2008, the year of the sixtieth anniversary of the Declaration of Human Rights, 'a historic document which, as is well known, provided the basis for the constitution of the Russian Federation, which proclaims the rights and freedoms of man as its highest value', the report had dwelt on constitutional rights and freedoms. In 2009 the focus shifted to certain 'systemic' and 'complex' problems. These included the inadequate pension system, the failure of legal mechanisms to ensure appropriate working conditions or wages, 'a mass of infringements and even crimes committed by law-enforcement officers against those whom they are meant to be protecting – namely citizens of the Russian Federation', and the case of Magnitsky, the young lawyer who died in pre-trial detention.

In place of the epigraph 'The law is stronger than the powerful' used on earlier reports, Lukin substituted Gorky's epigraph 'Rights are not given – rights are taken'. His decision was prompted by dismay at the conclusion of two independent experts, in a court case in Novorossiisk, that a poster 'Freedom is not given, freedom is taken' was evidence of 'extremism' and a call to change the constitutional order by force. Both the poster and his epigraph, he argued:

> are intended to alert Russian citizens to the idea that the future of democracy in Russia depends upon citizens and their active participation in public life, and their commitment to realizing their constitutional rights and freedoms within the framework of existing legislation. If such a slogan is extremist, so too are not only the calls by many respected citizens to participate actively in creating civil society, but also the Russian constitution itself.

In his report for 2010 the epigraph was repeated, but this time the preface suggested:

Our popular political culture, inherited from Russia's great, heroic but deeply contradictory history, includes to a significant degree faith in 'a good Tsar' – a monarch, general secretary, president – in other words, in any highly placed boss whom one should petition in search of 'a favour' or 'justice'. This archaic belief is a serious obstacle to creating a democratic law-based state, *a state whose citizens have shed the pernicious habits of requesting rather than demanding legal rights* or of waiting for rights to be bestowed rather than actually realizing them in accordance with the constitution which is, as is well known, a document with direct effect.

[Author's emphasis]

But, we might ask, is Lukin himself a stranger to these 'archaic attitudes'? As Liudmila Alekseeva explains:

When I am approached on behalf of someone who, say, has been remanded in custody on no grounds whatsoever, or something of that sort, I turn to Lukin. He can respond twice as effectively as I can and get something done [. . .] Why is it important that he was a diplomat? Because all his influence stems from his being able to maintain good relations with those at the top, they respect him and support him. Being a diplomat and a clever man, he simply knows when he can convince the authorities of something, and when not. He does not do things that he knows are doomed to failure [. . .] He says honestly that that is something he can't do . . .

Recently I said to him 'Vladimir Petrovich, I am very grateful for your help'. A man was dying in a remand prison, and he got him transferred to an ordinary hospital, not even a prison hospital. How did Lukin manage this? He did not fill in a form, which stated that this, and then this should be done. He rang Ivan Ivanovich, and Ivan Ivanovich rang Ivan Petrovich, and so on, and finally the poor man was transferred. We achieve the observance of human rights more often by using non-legal than by legal means. That's the kind of country we are.

But before we start sighing with dismay we should remind ourselves that it is not only in Russia that people use connections, particularly with those in positions of authority, in order to get things done and to avoid having to go to court. The question is one of degree, and who has the authority to grant what kind of requests.

More than once, in the report, Lukin returns to this theme.

> Many interpret justice not as the observance of the same rules for all, but as a wished for exception to be made in his or her personal case [. . .] Given the existence of working democratic institutions, such as free elections, judicial control, constitutional justice and others, citizens have the real potential to participate, autonomously, in defending their rights and freedoms, not depending for this on the discretion of highly placed state officials.

But what if these democratic institutions are *not* working? What then should citizens do to obtain their rights?

The report criticizes government officials and judges for their response to the peaceful protest meetings organized for the 31st day of the month in support of Article 31 of the constitution. Lukin himself intervened when a list of amendments to existing legislation, which would have made the holding of demonstrations on the 31st of the month even more difficult, was suddenly introduced into the Duma. Most were withdrawn. He attended a meeting in Triumphal Square in Moscow, as an observer, and wrote to the president on what he considered the police's excessive use of force. A violent meeting, with nationalist slogans, that had taken place in December 2010 in the Manezh Square (following the death of a football supporter in which an individual from the North Caucasus was a suspect), brought a rushed statement from the government that the 31st meetings had set an example. Lukin responded that he saw no cause and effect linking the Triumphal Square meetings with the Manezh Square events, which, he concluded, resembled the riots in the Square in 2002 by football fans after Russia's exit from the world cup.

His aim, he suggested, is to be something like an advocate for Russian citizens, defending their rights and freedoms against infringements by state officials, but to do it in such a way so as

> not to exacerbate the relationship between citizen and the state, rather to defuse tensions and encourage patience and constructive

cooperation [. . .] After a violent and noisy conflict all that remains in a house is broken crockery. And naïve hopes that the broken pieces can be stuck together to make a prettier dinner service.

What do we note so far? On the one hand the behaviour of government officials or the justice agencies corresponds with what we have seen in preceding chapters, and again Russia's citizens are unwilling or hesitant to organize to defend their rights. On the other hand, by 2010 they are engaging in a wide variety of 'civic' activities and, in a minority of cases, directly challenging employers, or local or regional authorities. In 2011, but before the protests, Boris Pustintsev had argued:

> People in Russia are absolutely apolitical but even they recognize that they have rights. And that feeds not only into economic protests when they don't get paid and they go out on a demonstration. Look at what happened in the campaign against blue buckets. Totally spontaneously people across the whole country began to defend their right to use the roads in a normal fashion. That could not have happened twenty years ago. It's something new, it comes from the fact that the foundation for a law-based state is already laid. Whatever the authorities do, they will find themselves less and less able to cope with each succeeding generation.
>
> M: Where has that recognition of rights, that legal way of thinking, come from? It does not seem to me that the human rights community has played a major role in that process.
>
> P: I would agree. But it has assisted in the process.
>
> Many rights that we call fundamental rights, and not political freedoms, are already part of the air people breathe. Today they may be conformists, join Ours, the Young Guard, and so on. But with each new generation, given the continuation of even today's level of political freedom, when the country is open, when unlimited opportunities for exchanging information exist, each new generation will feel itself more and more assured of its rights, and willing to defend them. It's an inevitable process.

Maybe. But in 2010–11 it was as though the majority of these new social or community activists and volunteers had simply turned their backs on the state. They were making use of the opportunities, the uncontrolled spaces, and inadequate government services, to improve their lives. The different kinds of social activism – their prevalence, geographic distribution, relationship (if any) to one another – are a subject for in-depth study. I am interested in them here as a backdrop to the role or the niche that the human rights community was occupying by the end of our period. What was the relationship between these new forms of social activism and the human rights organizations? Very slight. Connections between the new activism and worker or pensioner protest, independent unions, and the NGO community, including the human rights organizations, were minimal. As the GRANI report noted, these new activists preferred to operate with the safety net of 'having nothing to lose'; they did not want to spend time and resources on setting up registered organizations; they were more likely to be trusted by the public if they worked on a volunteer basis, spent no money on an office or drew salaries. They might protest, but not, we shall see, in support of the human rights organizations.

The protests and their aftermath

Young and old came out on the streets in 2011–12, including those who had never engaged in a public protest before, but the organizers (where there were any) and the speakers tended to be from new fringe political groups or media/ literary figures. In smaller towns, where there was no political opposition, an NGO leader sometimes played a key role; but in the big cities the established NGOs were largely marginalized. This was not their scene. The participants, with their symbols and slogans (a portrait of Rousseau with 'Let's renew the social contract!', photos or portraits 'Kafka for honest elections!, Gogol for honest elections!', and the writer Dmitry Bykov's brilliant caption 'Don't rock the boat, our rat is feeling sick!') were anxious to show that they were different from those who took part in the 31st of the month demonstrations, or traditional politicians and human rights activists.[9]

In this atmosphere, demonstratively apolitical, but with a political subtext, the key human rights organizations, as organizations, stood to the side. Activists participated in the demonstrations, but as individuals, and both Memorial and the Sakharov Centre made their facilities available for discussions on key themes. Arseny Roginsky, from Memorial, suggested:

It did not occur to us that we should participate with our posters and transparencies [. . .] we should have been obliged to take on some organizational responsibilities. But we don't know whom to lead and whither! We know how to defend ourselves, including in a moral sense, but we don't know how to advance, to lead a movement, which has suddenly appeared in a quite different context [. . .] There was no role or place for Memorial, and other established NGOs [. . .] Wait a little, and we shall have a place again [. . .] they will either cut off the oxygen, or society will become apathetic [. . .] we know how to live in a period like that and can do a lot that is useful. But a period of outbreaks and a mass movement forward – that's not our epoch.

And, GRANI argues, that is what has happened and, paradoxically, despite the insignificant role of the NGOs, it is they who have been seen as the chief culprits, and hence the target of the 'foreign agents' law. And this in its turn has confirmed the new activists in their view that it is best not to create and register organizations.

Following Putin's re-election to the presidency in the spring of 2012, a demonstration in Bolotnoye Square at the time of his inauguration brought a tough response, and 26 individuals were charged with provoking 'mass disorder'. Some were held in detention awaiting trial until late 2013 and early 2014, and some sentenced to imprisonment. Poorly drafted legislation, which included punitive fines for participation in unauthorized meetings, the limiting of public places for meetings, the reintroduction of libel as a criminal offence, and amendments to the law on NGOs were rushed through the Duma. The amendments to the NGO law required an NGO that received foreign funding and engaged in 'political activity' (undefined) and in 'influencing policy [. . .] and public opinion' to register as a 'foreign agent'. In September USAID (the US funding agency) was asked to leave the country. In October, two-year prison sentences for two of the Pussy Riot demonstrators were upheld.[10]

The new NGO law brought vehement denials from NGOs that they were engaged in political activities, i.e. in seeking political power: they were not political parties. All workers' organizations, NGOs, and volunteer-activists kept their distance from 'politicians' and thus, they claimed, from 'politics'. But such a stance, which became more and more disputed, reflects a very narrow and untenable (even for them) concept of 'political'. They were, after all, aiming to influence public opinion and, in its turn, the behaviour of political authorities, both as regards legislation and its implementation. They were engaged in public criticism, protest, and trying to influence the policy agenda. They were, one can say, acting as responsible citizens in the political life of their country.

The degradation of the electoral system, the corruption within government, and the blatant use of power by unaccountable political rulers led them to try to distance and distinguish themselves from actors in 'the political realm'. However, Volkov suggested, even those who try to stay out of politics, find themselves being dragged in by the authorities themselves. And Collective Action argued that times were changing: politics is no longer that which occupies the authorities. 'It is important to emphasize the recognition of what is a new concept of politics for Russian society – politics is a matter for each individual, a shared activity for all who want to influence the fate of their community.'[11]

What was the ombudsman's take on the situation?

Perhaps more than for many others, a characteristic of our country is its very complex and sometimes multi-vectored development. In this respect the past year was no exception. In writing of the year's events, it seems appropriate to remember an old political formula 'One step forward, two steps back'. Probably only future historians will be able, calmly and objectively, to grasp which of the year's events were the most important and significant for the further development of our society, in particular as regards its legal and human rights aspects.

With these words, and reverting to his original epigraph 'The law is stronger than the powerful', Lukin begins the conclusion to his report for 2012. Drawing attention to the increase in voluntary and political activities of some of its citizens, and a conservative reaction both on the part of others and of the authorities, Lukin bewails the tendency to see 'others' as 'enemies', and calls for a willingness to listen to each other, for tolerance.

There is a great deal in the report on particular rights (and some of the sections – on environmental issues, which includes the building of new airport runways, on the slowness of dealing with migrants' requests for citizenship, on the shortage of kindergarten, or of housing for young people – sound strangely familiar to the English ear) and customary themes reappear. 'People do not judge a law by its words but by how it is realized in practice. Our Achilles heel is not so much the creation of laws, but their implementation.' But the report is sharper in tone than earlier ones, taking issue, directly, with new policies or legislative changes.

Lukin mentions that he had to intervene in particular instances, without waiting to receive a complaint. On both the Pussy Riot detentions, and those connected with the Bolotnoye demonstration (where Lukin saw no evidence to justify detaining individuals on the grounds of 'participating in a mass disorder'), he voiced his disapproval. While welcoming some legislative innovations, he was particularly critical of the speed with which poorly drafted legislation was rushed through the Duma (within two weeks) without proper discussion and, at times, he suggests, of 'a questionable constitutional' character. This includes those we listed above. As regards the 'foreign agents' NGO law, his report claims:

the extremely wide interpretation of 'political activity' threatens to embrace almost all the human rights organizations in the country. Such an interpretation allows any criticism of government institutions to be seen as political activity. But, in a democracy, the movement for human rights a priori has an apolitical character and, characteristically, unites people of very different political persuasions. Such people – they are not enemies but allies of their state, striving to assist it in the correction of its errors, and thus to become better and stronger.

To see critics as enemies, he suggests, is to revert to a Soviet template, inappropriate for 'our developing democracy'.

How the badly worded law of July 2012 on foreign agents would be implemented was quite unclear, even after it went into force in November of that year. Ministry of Justice officials expressed their concerns. Nothing happened. However, following a public statement made by Putin in March 2013 to a security services gathering that the legislation should be implemented, prosecutors swept or stumbled into action. Officials from the prosecutor's office, tax inspectorate, Ministry of Justice, and sometimes the security services, appeared, often without warning, at the offices of human rights organizations and NGOs across the country, demanding documents, charters, hard discs, budget statements, etc. After a shaky start, the human rights community showed a remarkable solidarity and, despite minimal public support, stood its ground. Here I describe briefly key features of a strange campaign (whose details await a future historian), and whose outcome was still uncertain by the end of 2013.

The attack of 2013 and the response

The people who live in our country hold diverse religious faiths, world views and ideologies. Yes, we differ from those who determine government policy nowadays. Yes, we think and serve our country differently from them. But these differences do not give anyone the right to put us on any 'foreign agent' registers. We will not allow ourselves to be struck from the list of respectable Russian citizens and law abiding NGOs. Russia belongs to all of us. We have to learn to live together.[12]

Few would have expected GRANI, Averkiev's Civic Chamber, the Perm Human Rights Centre, and its Youth Memorial to be targeted. And, indeed, this case can serve as an example of a campaign that was so badly orchestrated it defies a coherent explanation. Andropov was surely turning in his grave.

Briefly: over the following months hundreds of organizations were paralysed by visits, inspections, and requests to provide four copies of every conceivable document. A group of 13 human rights organizations turned to the European Court with a claim against the law; Lukin lodged a case with the Constitutional Court. By 20 June, organizations (including the Memorial Human Rights Centre, Chikov's Agora, Public Verdict, the four Perm organizations, two LGBT organizations in St Petersburg, a research centre in Saratov, and Golos, the election-monitoring organization) had received instructions to register as foreign agents. By the end of the year the list of those required to register was much longer, and still being added to (Pavlov's Access to Information was a late addition). None had registered, and the only organizations that, having lost an appeal and facing a substantial fine, were dissolving themselves were Golos and the St Petersburg ADC Memorial (which works on racial discrimination cases).[13] While the reason for targeting some seemed clear (Golos, monitoring elections, for example), other cases suggested prosecutors and a Ministry of Justice quite unsure how to act, with local leaders' receiving different signals from Moscow. By the end of the year some of those targeted had won their cases against the prosecutor (the four Perm organizations, for example, one of the LGBT organizations), others were still awaiting hearings, or had had them deferred more than once (the Memorial Human Rights Centre). Websites sprung up, plotting the situation across the country, and offering help to organizations.[14]

Some officials were threatening; others admitted that 'we don't know why we are doing this, what the point of it is, we have more important matters we should be dealing with'. According to some activists, 'Ministry of Justice officials are fed up – it's a law that is so badly worded they don't know how they should apply it.' The Stork Park in the Amur region of the Far East, home to six of Russia's seven kinds of storks, which received assistance from the International Fund to Protect Storks, on being requested by the regional prosecutor to register as a foreign agent, responded:

> We cannot register as a foreign agent not only because we do not have the money for a further audit and reporting but also because we do not consider ourselves to be the agents of any foreign government. We consider ourselves to be agents of nature, or at the least of our storks, and of those who strive to preserve them for our descendants.[15]

If legislation is badly worded, and instructions unclear, officials struggle. The lack of a clear line from the Kremlin meant law and order agencies, and judges, were at a loss and sometimes found themselves at cross purposes. They were as confused as anyone else as to what counted as *'political'*. One can imagine the prosecutor in the Stork Park case cursing under his breath as he received its response. And how should one interpret judges' decisions, sometimes in support of the prosecutor, sometimes of an NGO? Were judges sometimes using their own judgement because there were no instructions from above, or were they responding to local or federal pressure? Opinions differed.

Organizations continued to argue their case before the courts, or to make public statements. I quote only two. Egida, a St Petersburg organization that 'provides assistance to employees and socially-vulnerable people for the collective defence of their social-labour rights and interests, and the raising of the level and quality of life in the north-west region' had disputed the legality of the district prosecutor's attempt, accompanied by two security service personnel, to inspect the organization without an authorized instruction from the city prosecutor. At the court hearing, Rima Sharifullina, the young chair, put her case:

> Your honour! In your opinion, why is there a mood of protest in society? *It's because of the arbitrary acts of officials.* Those are words of the President of Russia, Vladimir Vladimirovich Putin, spoken at his presidential inauguration. Those who hold power, both in his and in our view, must provide *support* for simple citizens. And the actions of supervisory bodies must be *transparent* and *intelligible to all.*
>
> But, your honour, what happens in practice? [...] Prosecutors have begun to accuse us *who wish to see changes in government policy of being foreign agents.* But we are defenders and representatives of pregnant women and mothers [...] How can we be agents and criminals if we are providing the most hapless citizens with free legal aid? [...] If prosecutors have been given some kind of secret assignment to clear the weeds from the allotment, why is it digging up roses? In reality, we are carrying out the work of the prosecutor, *defending our mothers from the arbitrary behaviour of officials and employers. And the prosecutor, by its illegal actions, is attempting to paralyse the socially-useful work of our organization,* while at the same time causing *great damage to the state,* to which we provide assistance. One has the impression that the work of the prosecutor is directed towards undermining authority at *the pinnacle of state power in Russia.* Thank you for your attention.[16]

The judge was unmoved, but Egida appealed and won its case.

The best public statement came from the four Perm organizations, part of which was quoted at the beginning of this section. It began with the announcement:

To everyone who knows us, we declare that our organisations will not register as 'foreign agents', since neither we nor our organisations are anyone's agents, let alone foreign ones. No one could use us to harm Russia, nor would dare to do so. We are free people who are loyal to our country and we have the honour of working in responsible public organizations that have never been party to the struggle for power. For our organisations, being called 'foreign agents' is an offensive lie [...]

If we lose every case in court, and our organisations are shut down by the authorities, we will find other legal ways to do what we consider necessary. We will not desist in our active attempts to defend human rights and to act in the pressing public interest, whether that means fighting corruption, assisting the disadvantaged, defending the rights of the exploited and aggrieved or improving the quality and availability of government services.

By the time the NGO law appeared as an agenda item at the President's Council for the Advancement of Civil Society and Human Rights in September 2013, the council had changed its composition. Several leading human rights activists (including Alekseeva, Dzhibladze, Gannushkina and Gefter) had resigned in 2012 in protest at the rigging of elections. Putin had responded with the proposal that internet voting should produce a short list of candidates. It was indeed a strange (and far from transparent) procedure, many refused to participate, but Chikov, Kalyapin, and Andrei Yurov (from the MPD) threw their hats into the ring and were appointed. From the Memorial Society, whose board voted by a majority for continuing participation, Sergei Krivenko remained as a member.

The need for radical amendments to the NGO law was argued by Elena Topoleva, from the Agency for Social Information, a key member of the Civic Chamber. Putin agreed that perhaps the law needed amending and the matter should be addressed. But nothing had materialized by 10 December, International Human Rights Day, when Putin hosted an informal reception for representatives of the human rights community. According to Topoleva, her suggestion that he should repeal 'this wretched law to mark this special day' brought a smile, and the response that the law was still needed to prohibit engaging in political activity with foreign money. When asked what counted as political activity, he replied that human rights work did not qualify as such. When pushed further – is political activity then the struggle for power? He replied 'Yes, but not only that.' And again he indicated that both sides should work on amendments.[17] Nothing had materialized by the end of the year.

Meanwhile the preceding months had witnessed some unusual developments. Behind the scenes, Fedotov (chair of the President's Council) and Lukin held discussions with representatives of the president's administration on the need to amend the law, and to find Russian funding. If nothing came regarding amendments, suddenly there was money. In the summer, human rights organizations were encouraged to apply for grants from the President's Fund for NGOs, administered by the Civic Chamber, and at the end of August the Memorial Human Rights Centre (awaiting a court hearing on its appeal against the prosecutor's demand that it register as a foreign agent), the Moscow Helsinki Group, Ponomarev's For Human Rights, and Agora had been awarded grants. Then, in September, Putin announced another 500 million rubles (£10m) for human rights organizations to be distributed by a committee, chaired by Ella Pamfilova. There should be no government oversight: 'independence', he declared, was essential to civil society activity. A large selection committee was formed; Vyacheslav Bakhmin advised Pamfilova on procedures, and in December many well-known outspoken human rights organizations featured in the list of grantees, including a regional branch of Golos.[18] A few organizations (including the Moscow Helsinki Group) returned foreign funding, but the great majority continued to receive new grants.

Meanwhile legislation criminalizing LGBT propagation of beliefs, directed towards the young, had been passed. In September Navalny was convicted for fraudulent business practices, but then permitted to run in the Moscow mayoralty election, where he received 27 per cent of the vote. Lev Ponomarev's organization was subsequently ejected (physically) from its office, ostensibly by order of the landlord, but then, in a gesture that caused amazement, given a new office by the mayor of Moscow. The *Arctic Sunrise* Greenpeace crew were arrested and detained. However, in mid-December, under a poorly worded amnesty to mark the twentieth anniversary of the constitution, the Pussy Riot duo (due for release in March), some of the Bolotnoye detainees, and members of the *Arctic Sunrise* crew joined the several thousand convicted prisoners who obtained release from detention. And suddenly, like a bolt from the blue, as the media was reporting the preparation of a new case against Khodorkovsky and his YUKOS colleagues (due for release in August 2014), Khodorkovsky was pardoned on humanitarian grounds (his mother was sick), flown secretly to Berlin, and talk of a further trial was dropped. In January his colleague, Platon Lebedev, was released.

How can one make sense of this? Did the leadership have a game plan? Some believe that the Sochi Winter Olympics were responsible, not only for the pardons of the internationally known figures but for the contradictory and delaying tactics: once the games were over, and Lukin's term of office came to an end in the spring, any critical, independent activities would be targeted. Government funds would support human rights organizations for a couple of years, foreign funding would diminish, and then government support would cease. Others were less sure that there is agreement on how to govern a society that has recently shown its discontent with its rulers, who now, in their turn, are aware that stifling of independent political and civic activity leaves them ignorant of the views of their citizens. Somehow citizens need to be *incorporated* into a managed democracy. But how?

It was not that the human rights organizations received public support (in fact disappointingly little) and hence represented some kind of threat to the Kremlin, but the way the campaign had developed (or rather had not) was very unsatisfactory. If the continued receipt of foreign funding by human rights organizations irritated, perhaps angered, the authorities, the state's mechanisms for dealing with such organizations were clearly inadequate. Should or would different measures be taken after Sochi? Opinions differed within the human rights community but there was a striking and surprising solidarity in regard to the foreign agents law – by December 2013 not a single organization had registered as such.

****

A year later, with a civil war underway in Ukraine, relations between Russia and the west had deteriorated to a degree unknown for twenty years. An analysis of the policies and postures which brought about the armed conflict, and the new cold war, lies outside the scope of this book, but it has had and will continue to have implications for the human rights community.

Briefly, with Putin's popularity enjoying an upsurge from the Crimean adventure, and with western governments' support of the new Kiev government, itself hardly a beacon of neutrality, the tug-of-war over Ukraine endangers not only its peoples and those of neighbouring countries but reduces the likelihood of Russia and the west working together to find peaceful solutions to global problems. The patronizing statements of some western politicians, talk of Ukraine joining NATO and the European Union, and western financial assistance, have only fanned the flames in an environment where the Russian TV carries an unremitting message of Ukrainian aggression, backed by the west, and dwells on the hundreds of thousands of Russian refugees fleeing from the war zone into Russia. Ukrainians, in turn, flee from rebel-held territories or the Crimea to Kievan territory. Denials of military involvement come from the Russian authorities, while the Ukrainian authorities, unable to control hastily formed or volunteer units, deny civilian targeting. Neither sets of assertions are credible. Surely this was a 'war' which more far-sighted and competent politicians – in both camps – could have avoided. Meanwhile the sanctions tit-for-tat which has shaken the Russian banking sector and affected the consumer, accompanied by the falling oil price, bodes ill for the economy. The rising living standards of the past ten years are history for many who have become accustomed to them but, for the moment, a siege mentality, and a sense that for too long Russia was treated with condescension by its western 'partners', is likely to sustain support for the Kremlin leadership.

Still, from its point of view, why not take some precautions – why not demonstrate that 'we are in control'? Those who receive 'foreign funding' and engage 'in politics' are an easy target in this new cold war environment. It is not, we suggest, that the Kremlin sees the human rights organizations as a threat, as the incubators of a future 'Occupy Red Square', but they raise awkward questions and, as independent-minded and outspoken critics of government policy, they challenge the new orthodoxy of control.

The 'foreign agents' law has been amended: no longer is an organization required to register as such, now the Ministry of Justice has the right to include an organization in the list, and this carries with it more onerous reporting requirements. Fines, and closure, threaten those who do not comply. The St Petersburg Soldiers' Mothers Committee which publicized the fate of young Russian soldiers sent to assist the

Donbass 'Russian' separatists was quickly added to the 'foreign agents' list. By the end of December 2014 the Ministry of Justice's list included more than 20 NGOs, and among them were those with whom we are acquainted – Agora, Public Verdict, Citizens Watch, Pavlov's Freedom of Information foundation, and, two recent additions, Lev Ponomarev's For Human Rights, and the Sakharov Centre, and, from St Petersburg, Maria Kanevaskaya's Human Rights Resource Centre. In January 2015 the Committee Against Torture was included. None of these, as the new year opened, had closed. They were continuing to fight their cases through the courts. In January the Supreme Court ruled in favour of the Russian Memorial Society. But the Memorial Human Rights Centre had lost its appeal against being classified as a 'foreign agent', and the International Memorial Society (the voice of the Society) may come under attack in the near future. A variety of poorly-drafted and punitive laws which include listing the passing of information to foreign organizations as treason, the widening of the interpretation of 'libel' and 'extremism', and statements by prosecutors or Ministry of Justice officials that 'political activity' includes any criticism of government policy do not bode well for the future. But, while there is an even stronger sense of a leaf turning, of a chapter closing, I do not feel the Conclusion requires re-writing – so, for the reader who has read this far, here it is for you to judge.

CONCLUSION

In tracking the evolution of the human rights community in post-Soviet Russia since 1991, and assessing its achievements and failures, I have drawn on a wide literature on human rights, social movements, and Russian developments. The different chapters describe and discuss both the character of this new community, formative influences, and its role as society and the political order changes. Briefly, here, I bring the key findings together, with a final look at the legacy of the past, and at human rights as an ideology, before concluding with the activists' achievements and future challenges.

Why human rights?

The catholic nature of the new community, its heterogeneity and very different voices, had its origins in an environment that included institutions (the army, prisons) where cruelty and abuse was widespread, and where now economic collapse, ethnic conflict, and a failing government at both federal and local level worsened the lives of already vulnerable people. The extent of the problems gave birth to a huge variety of concerns, and human rights gradually became the banner under which individuals of very different persuasions gathered to address them. As Liudmila Alekseeva noted, on her travels at the beginning of the nineties, she would be approached by people who had no idea of what human rights were but were anxious to do something. While it was relevant that there were respected individual dissidents who, in the Soviet period, had advocated the defence of human rights and, in the new Russia, initially had access to policy makers, the impetus for the growth of organizations came from the failure of the politicians, new and old, to tackle the problems and to hold either state officials or private interests accountable for their actions. As politics discredited itself, activists sought a role that took them out of it, while the constitution gave backing to their demands. All this in a heady environment in which, for the first time – in any one's living memory – autonomous NGOs had a legal right to exist, and to engage with the state on behalf of its citizens. The inauspicious environment, the pent-up enthusiasm accompanied by a lack of knowledge of how to organize, campaign, to join forces, and the isolationism and localism that characterized the huge country produced an extraordinarily diverse community.

The concept of human rights, a concept that embraces a huge variety of rights, had a purchase in an environment where state institutions flagrantly infringed rights of all kinds. Its claim to be universal chimed with the perception, inherited from the Soviet past, that members of society can share a common view, now strengthened by the belief that this extends across borders to all right-thinking people and governments. Western funding from governments and foundations, international NGOs, and the Polish Helsinki Foundation, all supported or promoted this view of human rights. And there were the UN and European conventions, with rules for their observance, and the international gatherings. By the end of our period, the Russian human rights community, now with a new generation of young lawyers, was as professional as its Western counterparts.

How had Oleg Orlov put it at the Constitutional Forum in 2010?

Each of us can list a whole number of success stories – court cases won at the national level; cases won at the European Court; people we have saved; well-written reports [...] but our individual successes do not lead to the achieving of our common aim, for the sake of which we, after all, carry out our work: namely the moving forward of our country in the direction of democracy, the observance of human rights, social justice, environmental safeguards, and so on. We should recognize this, and ask ourselves – why is this so? And find an answer.

We come back the community's achievements in a moment. Here we take up his statement that, as regards 'the moving forward of our country in the direction of democracy, the observance of human rights, social justice, environmental safeguards, and so on', they could claim little success. Katya Sokiryanskaya, from the Memorial Human Rights Centre, referring to a detailed report on the situation in Dagestan, prepared in 2011 for a domestic and an international audience in the unlikely hope of influencing government policy, echoed his words:

> Although for the past ten years we have helped a great number of people, whose lives have been saved or changed for the good, we have achieved practically no systemic changes.
>
> Do you think that was inevitable or that if you had worked differently you might have done so? I ask
>
> That's a question which we are always asking ourselves. And we often disagree. There are those who say we haven't managed to achieve anything in the past ten years, and that rights' abuses only became more covert and we now have conflict within five republics {in the Caucasus}, not just one, and more acute.

Thinking back to Lukin's reports, it is clear that the activists had not managed to change the behaviour of government or local authorities nor, in significant respects, the workings of the justice system. The non-implementation of legislation was still there for all to see. The state continued to be either intrusive or non-supportive of its citizens' rights who, in turn, too often failed to battle to defend them, preferring to look to patrons or others to take up their case. But does that mean the activists were to blame?

There were those within the community who reminded their colleagues that human rights activists, everywhere, remain a minority voice. Many, however, thought that at least partly to blame was their inability to find a common language with the majority of the population who, hungry and often cold in the nineties, retreated into private concerns and, then, as the new century progressed, welcomed the stability and rising living standards the Putin regime provided. Some saw the activists' links with Western governments and funding as contributing to popular suspicion, others laid the blame on the public's holding on to age-old Russian beliefs or to ingrained Soviet attitudes.

This brings us to the question of the legacy of the Russian or Soviet past, the weight we should ascribe to the past in explaining the human rights community's practices, successes and failures.

The past as culprit

Men make their own history, but they do not make it just as they please; they do not make it under circumstances chosen by themselves, but under circumstances directly encountered, given and transmitted from the past.

So far, so good. But Marx continues with the sentence: 'The tradition of all the dead generations weighs like a nightmare on the brain of the living.' Here I would take issue with him. Traditions, both very old and less old, are maintained, adapted, or discarded, depending upon the circumstances; sometimes the past weighs heavy, sometimes less so, and how and when is something that always has to be investigated. I would argue that to explain persistence or change we must look at the interaction between the institutional environment (inherited and new), known experience or expertise (or its absence), and the introduction of new ideas. If we think back to the late Soviet environment, we see that perestroika and then the nineties wreaked havoc with certain of its practices, left some untouched, and breathed new life into others.

The claim that Russia's long past is to blame, and in particular its political culture that reveres and looks for 'a good Tsar', is a claim that resurfaces when the political rulers resort to heavy-handed measures of control, are supported by state officials, and meet with little opposition from the public. In 2010, we remember, Lukin, the ombudsman, emphasized its importance in explaining the popular lack of support for democratic and legal institutions which would hold the authorities accountable for their actions, 'the archaic belief' in petitioning for rather than demanding rights. Lukin was talking of popular attitudes and practices. But to emphasize the continuation of an unbroken tradition of repressive paternalist rule and a passive population is to oversimplify both the Tsarist and Soviet past. Paternalism, authoritarianism, and clientilism were all present under Tsarism but so were aristocratic and peasant revolts and, as the twentieth century approached, industrial action. Passivity is not a good way to describe popular attitudes. Throughout the nineteenth century there was debate and action, of different kinds, in different social strata, not only among the intelligentsia. Towards the end of the Tsarist period, a rich civil society, with professional organizations and political parties, holding different positions on what was a desirable and just society and politics, engaged in political dialogue and action. The legal system was acquiring a more independent voice. The revolutionary and early Soviet period was marked by violent confrontations, new forms of collective action, attempts to create new state institutions and forms of government.

It is the period, from the mid-1930s on, which shows us a landscape bereft of active civil society organizations engaging with each other and with the state, and whose citizens are beginning to learn to speak an official language while talking among themselves, privately, in small groups – a state-owned and state-organized society. As the end of Communist party rule, and neo-liberal economic policies plunged this society, short on experience of competitive and open politics or autonomous organizations, into a whirlpool where freedom to say anything, freedom to visit the West, where lawless poverty for the majority accompanied undreamt of opportunities for others, people used what they could from the old and the new. Some Soviet attitudes and practices persisted, some in new garb, others competed with new ways of behaving, spawned by the new political and economic environment.

In Chapter 10, I cited attitudes and practices, common to activists and others, those that strike an English observer. It was not only that leaders remained in office. In all walks of life it was usual to find a subservient or respectful attitude to an authority or to one's boss, the using of connections, reliance upon trusted friends or those whom one knew. The heady years of the early nineties saw the voting in of new leaders – a critical step towards making them accountable – but they (whether presidents, deputies, artistic or institute directors) and their appointees (ministers, officials at whatever level) retained control over major resources, and the power to appoint and dismiss their subordinates. Rules were being made up in the political field, not according to some clearly defined plan or criteria, but on the spot, in response to crises and confrontation from opponents. It was the same for the new entrepreneurs, the activists, and the journalists, all were learning new trades – of their own design – drawing on past experience as well as experimenting. Imaginative ways of circumventing rules or restrictions were highly developed. And, in addition, 'Everything that is not forbidden is permitted' was the new 'official' slogan. Whom should one rely upon in the first instance? Colleagues and connections were the obvious choice, both for those making decisions, and for members of the impoverished public.

There was an abundance of imaginative ideas, combined, in the early years, with the pursuit of unachievable targets. The extraordinary freedom to voice one's views, propose one's solutions, set up one's own organization, produced a cacophony of voices, talking across but not to each other. In the Soviet period the private discussions round the kitchen table never entertained the idea of reaching practical conclusions. Now this love of talking, discussion prized for its own sake, not for any conclusions that might be reached, and the lack of organizational experience, worked against the introduction of effective organizational responses to the social or political crises. Talking publicly, so long denied, was a high priority, and education, of all kinds, was a popular pursuit. Ideas, of all kinds, competed for attention.

In contrast there were still conventions (and a hierarchical system) in ministries, the armed forces, in institutes, and enterprises. State officials, and judges, clung on, impoverished, trying to administer society in the ways that they knew. The institutional rules and practices changed little. And, as the federal authorities began to claw back control, while leaving the new business and financial elite its privileged position, the state apparatus picked itself up, and re-established bureaucratic control as corruption (where were the barriers?) pervaded its ranks. Subsequently the richness of the pickings led to even greater corruption. If a bureaucratic state apparatus has been part of the legacy, perhaps the most striking Soviet bequest to its citizens has been an unwillingness to organize in defence of collective or professional interests. Here the antipathy to the pseudo-collective action organizations of the Soviet period, and the ability of their officials to hold on to posts and resources, has played its part. The reluctance to organize collectively to defend a group interest, to engage in any kind of civic activity, or for groups to cooperate on a permanent basis has remained strong. 'Do you not sometimes think that the Union of Journalists ought to take up the cases of journalists and defend media freedoms?' I ask a couple of able young journalists at a seminar on politics and the media in 2013. 'Oh, no, we're not interested in that sort of thing and those issues, we are too busy earning a living.' While, for officials, organized political or collective opposition is viewed with deep suspicion, and leaders are still leaders.

We noted how the inability of professional organizations or trade unions to refashion themselves and take up new roles to defend their members, and the weakness or absence of political parties, left the space between citizen and the state unoccupied. Unlike the situation in, for example, Argentina, or Poland, where, once the military regime fell, political parties with roots in society, and attitudes and activities associated with a democratic past, could again occupy the stage, in Russia any such infrastructure was missing. Without organizations, such as these, playing a leading role in preserving democratic practices, pursuing social justice, and defending their members' or supporters' collective interests, the activists' achievements could only be modest. Political opportunities shrank. Orlov, unwittingly, provides part of the answer to his own question: was it their task to take all these functions upon themselves? Could the community ever have agreed on a social justice programme, which would have necessitated choosing between competing interests, and different conceptions of social justice? No, surely not.

But then was 'the defence of human rights' itself part of the problem?

Human rights as part of the problem?

In such an environment, to make human rights your chosen strategy may be very problematic. Why? Human rights as a moral agenda can have some effect in societies where citizen rights are well established, together with state institutions and a credible, independent, justice system. Here some of them can be grafted on or introduced into legislation, by political means, and defended through the courts. Rather differently, where human rights is part of an aspirational creed for a social or protest movement – a call to the dispossessed (an anti-colonial movement) or part of a dissident culture (in a Communist party state) – it may play a part in undermining an existing regime. But to make human rights one's banner for creating a new order, or the basis for a state-building document, is to create problems from the start. The agenda becomes huge, a constitution is burdened with claims that it will be impossible to satisfy, and it becomes less and less of a ruling document. For that one needs something that focuses on basic political and civil freedoms, and introduces checks and balances that have weight behind them. If human rights are institutionalized in a constitution where the environment lacks democratic institutions, an independent and effective judiciary, and autonomous organizations with experience of collective action, activists are faced with almost insuperable problems – this even without the introduction of neo-liberal market reforms. If the state proves incapable of coping with the problems, the situation worsens. Without well-established rights (that have been won, not given), and are concrete and justiciable, efforts to defend fellow citizens may simply confirm a traditional view that assistance is needed for individuals to obtain their 'state-given' rights, rather than persuading them that they must organize themselves to obtain and defend rights, extort them from the state or the powerful, and fight to keep them by political means. Can a justice system ever compensate for the lack of such action on the part of society? It is not its task to decide what is social justice and that, as Averkiev tried to argue, remained a key concern for many, while they lacked the tools to pursue it. Ironically enough, given his part in the drafting of the constitution, Kovalev was well aware of the dangers. In 1998 he reminded his audience of the demand, in the Soviet period, 'give us a better *obkom* (party) secretary' which became

> give us freedom and justice [...] but you can't be given freedom
> and justice [...] Human rights are embodied in (given form) in
> political practice and the everyday life of people under one
> precondition: they must be rightly understood not only by the
> authorities but by society.[1]

But in Russia, for most of the population, civil and political rights simply fell into their laps, while socio-economic rights had been gifted by the state, without any discussion of priorities or costs. Understanding of rights comes from people engaging in collective action to defend their rights or interests. Could we argue that if placed in a constitution without prior struggle, without experience of collective action, we have the worst of all possible worlds? Why? Because this suggests that such 'rights' do come from on high, somehow exist regardless of collective action to defend them and give them content. It allows the individual to opt out of his or her responsibility to participate in the defence of a set of interests, professional or otherwise. It also allows those who hold power (political, economic, cultural) to see themselves as responsible for rights and their interpretation.

A human rights ideology or rhetoric encourages the defence of many rights – of victims of environmental damage, of prisoners, children, migrants, pensioners, journalists – but it does not rank them in terms of importance. We saw the debates and disagreements within the human rights community over this, with Kovalev and others gradually and reluctantly giving ground on the primacy of political and civil rights. This is where the logic of human rights led them although, I would argue, they perhaps should have jettisoned human rights and stuck simply to political and civil rights. But that was not the way most of its advocates interpreted the concept, and rightly so, if one took the Universal Declaration as the founding document.

Human rights was a beguiling ideology in the way it was advanced by its advocates from the West, governments or NGOs. It suggested not only that the rights of so many should be met but that they could be. What was needed – the target – was that the state should implement its laws properly, and this could be achieved by non-violent, and non-political means, by monitoring infringements and by legal means. The spotlight moved away from conflicts of interests, between the rights of an employer and of employees, between the indigenous peoples of the north and the oil interests, residents and property developers, away from the way in which state property was being privatized, the privileges of the wealthy, the inequalities in access to education or health care, and defending the interests (rights?) of those left destitute, or sick. It distracted attention from the new alliances between business and politics, at all levels, and the increasing level of corruption.

As relevant, it distracted attention from the task of organizing collective action. Some activists did form or join with others to create pressure groups but there was little interest in or attention paid to encouraging unions or professional associations where those concerned came together to defend their interests or their rights. The individual, as an individual, still faced the government official, director of an institute, or employer, who simply had the power to take decisions. For the individual it was rational to turn to court, or to a human rights organization, or to petition an official or, occasionally, to protest, but not to engage in organized collective action to defend rights and interests.

To change laws, and the behaviour of government agencies, requires political action and pressure. One sympathizes with Ponomarev while recognizing that his call for a human rights party was a non-starter. Human rights cannot provide the basis for a party/political programme (who would be the constituency? Everyone?). But even politicians such as Yavlinsky, who might appear at a human rights event, were not prepared to make them an issue. As the political stage emptied of democratic or opposition voices, the activists found themselves having to speak out, while still claiming a non-political mantle. Willing or not, they found themselves taking on political functions, and disagreeing among themselves. Increasingly the leading Moscow organizations came to play a role as a kind of informal political opposition, putting out statements on all kinds of topics, responding to Kremlin decisions or court rulings. But they had no real entry into the political arena.

So should the Declaration on Human Rights have been taken as a founding document for the constitution? The question is intriguing but unanswerable. Without doubt, the inclusion of articles on observing the international conventions (which came to include the turning to the European Court and the abolition of the death penalty), on the introduction of the ombudsman, and the right to alternative civilian service all stemmed from a human rights agenda, and all have been and still are extremely important. However, a constitution is only as robust as the institutions that create it, and those that could ensure checks and balances, or an independent judiciary, were simply not there. If, as Donnelly suggests, human rights is concerned with how governments should rule, then society or the courts must be able to hold the government accountable.[2] But there is a further problem here. Human rights are *universal,* not state-bound – the migrants fleeing across the sea from Africa to Italy, the Syrians accepted by Sweden – have the right to be treated with dignity by the receiving *states.* National governments, according to international conventions, should be applying international standards, but there is no international mechanism or accepted procedure for holding them accountable. (The European Court does what it can, but all would agree it can only touch the tip of an iceberg.) States are still the significant actors, with control over considerable resources, and obligations to those who elected them, and who will or will not re-elect them. At the same time they are unable to control either the population movements (the growing march of the international proletariat) or the global movement of finance capital through the banks and corporations, and the ensuing financial crises, affecting their citizens. Somehow there is a jarring juxtaposition – a world of national states, but states faced with global movements they cannot control, and which make a mockery of any claims to universal human rights. Should then a state's constitution be based on universal rights?

However, to return to Russia, would a less aspirational constitution have been any more effective as a document, ensuring rights were observed, and laws implemented? To my suggestion that one of the consequences of an aspirational constitution, whose clauses cannot be realized, is that disillusionment follows and, in the case of post-Soviet Russia, the belief that constitutions are, as they were in the Soviet period, for decorative purposes only, Boris Pustintsev responded (and the English is his):

The 1993 Constitution, despite all its imperfections, allowed for political gains that the present rulers find hard to eradicate; true, they bite them off, piece by piece, but it's so long and contradictory a process that their efforts are doomed in the end. They strive for a Pinochet-like model: more or less free economy, more or less open frontiers but strict control over political opposition inside the country. Such a model may work for some limited time in a small homogeneous country like Chile, but not in today's Russia.

It was our persistent reference to the 1993 Constitution that in 2009–10 allowed us to break down and bury the 2006 law introducing total control of the Federal Registration Service over NGOs. It was the 1993 Constitution (its provisions of the preference of international agreements in the human rights sphere) that forced many federal ministers to publicly disagree with Putin about the latest anti-children law, a promising actual rebellion within the Putin's team. I have never expected the new constitution to be observed unhindered, but it opened up prospects to the shining snow-white peaks that might never be reached but, nevertheless, formally have obliged the main actors to move in this direction. So our opponents have constantly to digress from their actual goals and to divert their attention, to resort to cunning and maneuvering and, inevitably, at every turn lose momentum. The events since December 2011 have demonstrated that the number of people disagreeing with the thesis that constitutions are for decorative purposes only, is on the rise. If it was not for the 1993 constitution, Russia would be much less dynamic today and much more hopeless.

I find myself persuaded. But is now perhaps the time for a new approach, and the rewriting of the constitution?[3]

What if Western governments and foundations had not made human rights a priority in their grant making? Again, this is a largely unanswerable question. In Chapter 5 we identified various pluses and minuses associated with Western assistance, most of which were not specific to human rights programmes but also accompanied educational, media, public health or environmental programmes. But were there consequences specific to 'supporting human rights'? Or, to put it another way, does it seem from today's perspective that a focus on other things would or might have brought greater benefits to the pursuit of human rights in post-Soviet Russia? Today I would argue that the emphasis on human rights encouraged an overoptimistic belief that, armed with knowledge of human rights and professional skills, the community could persuade or compel government institutions to implement or observe human rights. But, as argued above, a human rights ideology has little influence in a situation where the political and judicial system are failing to hold either powerful interests in check or the state accountable. However professional the activists, they need to be underpinned by organized collective interests and political support to have any real influence.

So should Western funders have not focused attention, in equal (or greater?) measure on supporting trade unions, professional associations, student groups – or on political parties? All, except the German party foundations, backed away from supporting parties, because that meant direct involvement in politics. In theory, yes, I would argue, we should have supported such activities. Until a society has developed an infrastructure of organizations, defending their members' own interests, in competition with others, arguing over 'which rights', and attempting to get their preferences onto the political agenda, it is premature to start trying to pursue individual human rights. But, as one donor put it, you have to work with what you've got. As Liudmila

Alekseeva discovered in 1993, union activity was fading away, and the
Russian professional intelligentsia, of all generations, was desperately
trying to cope with its impoverishment by all available methods, but not
by organized action. And, apart from the AFL-CIO, in the early years,
I am not aware of any Western unions or professional associations,
anxious to participate in projects in Russia to create memberships,
organize collective action, and defend their members' interests.
'Collectivism', as Communist party rule collapsed, was out of fashion
on both sides of the former iron curtain; 'individualism', the free market,
and 'human rights' were in.

The failures, then, of the human rights community were largely not
of the activists own making, rather that they strove to realize an
unrealizable task. And, in so doing, they achieved a great deal, and not
only for those suffering from abuse or discrimination.

Achievements

What had the human rights community achieved during the 20 years
since the new constitution of 1993? Again, back to Orlov in 2010: 'Each
of us can list a whole number of success stories – court cases won at the
national level; cases won at the European Court; people we have saved;
well-written reports.' Yes, they had saved the lives of many, won
damages or compensation for many more, succeeded in winning justice
for others, and convictions for the perpetrators. Yes, they had learnt how
to monitor infringements and produce well-written, documented,
reports both for the Russian authorities and international organizations.
They had become as professional as their colleagues in the West. Leaders
in the community had a place at discussions with the federal authorities,
including the president. Using international conventions, the European
Court, and Supreme Court rulings were all part of the professional
baggage of a generation of young lawyers. New forms of communication,
professional skills and expertise characterized many of the organizations.
Compare the 1998 conference in St Petersburg (in Chapter 4) with the
2009 campaign on police reform (Chapter 8) for a sense of the changes
during the past ten years.

There were other achievements too. Although the activists' success in
influencing legislation was very limited, without their efforts there
would not be the ombudsman's office, the laws on alternative civilian

service, or the monitoring of closed institutions. And, no less important, they had managed to get domestic violence, racial discrimination, and police brutality on to the public agenda, even though they had not managed to get political support to translate recognition into policies.[4] Victims of Stalinist and subsequent persecution had received compensation, or at least memorials, and the Gulag had not disappeared from public discussion.

There is no way of knowing the influence their activities have had either upon those who, feeling emboldened, decide to stand up for their rights or upon those, officials or judges who, accustomed to ride roughshod over plaintiffs, now hesitate. How the countless educational programmes (Chapter 7) may have influenced, however tangentially, the way today's young professionals think, remains an unknown. However it is indisputable that, through the activists' efforts, both at the Civic Forum in 2001 (Chapter 6), and subsequently in the struggle to defend their existence under the NGO law of 2005, and in 2006, they managed to maintain the right of autonomous organizations or associations to exist. Some of the human rights organizations themselves went under but the principle of independent non-governmental organizations not only remains official policy but is taken as a given by countless people who have no interest in human rights. Whether the clampdown, starting in the spring of 2013, will drive a further wedge between outspoken human rights organizations and those who work loyally with the authorities remains to be seen but the right to exist as an independent non-governmental organization is part of today's culture.

Aleksei Korotaev, one of the original activists, in comparing the community's influence in the nineties and today, sees it as significantly less.

All the same, what we can call the human rights community was sufficiently visible, active, and in some instances able to exert influence upon some of the authority's actions. In any event there were some points of access to the authorities. Now, most would define the human rights community as marginalized, on the edges of the life of society and the country, squeezed out of today's developments, although it's difficult to determine what the basic line of development is. But in any case it is clear that there's very little demand for the human rights community and its values today.

And Grigory Shvedov, from a younger generation, sees

> No renaissance within the community [. . .] the large organizations
> are declining, people are leaving [. . .] I don't see any growth, apart
> from the legal sphere, which has great potential.
>   Why are they leaving? I ask. Because of the political situation?
>   No, I don't think that the political situation is the main factor.
> It's simply that, probably for a number of different reasons, people
> aren't coming in.

But should they and we be depressed by this? Not necessarily. We have
argued that for human rights organizations to exert any significant
influence upon the behaviour of state or private institutions, there has
to be an underpinning of democratic control over government, an
independent justice system, and active civic and professional
organizations. While democratic government is still not on the agenda,
and extremely unpleasant nationalist organizations exist, there is now a
much more professional and able but discontented sector of the business,
political and intellectual elite that wants to move to a less corrupt, more
legitimate system of government, one that would tackle Russia's
traditional economy, secure property rights, challenge corruption,
encourage investment, and move Russia forward. There is a growing
stratum of professionals (economists, lawyers, software experts, PR
managers, journalists), working in policy areas, and some on human
rights issues. Some divide their time between Russia and the West, as do
leading academics, but the lively intellectual elite, many of whose
children study abroad, is primarily engrossed in Russia's problems.
Neither its members nor the wider society have illusions that the West
has ready-made answers for them.

    This is then a pluralistic, quite open society, with skills and
potential. Its young lawyers, and the issues they work on, using their
legal and communication skills, bring them face to face with the
authorities. They cannot but be drawn into political action. Can we
find instances — in other societies or in history — where lawyers,
working from below, play an important role in what becomes a
political struggle to establish the independence of judges? If there are
such, this should embolden today's young lawyers. At least the verdict
is still out on the legacy they may leave. Is the drift out of human

rights organizations perhaps an indication of the way society is changing, talking to itself, and sometimes acting in an organized and concerted fashion, as we saw in Chapter 12? Tanya Lokshina had suggested: 'This diverse, differentiated, multicoloured social talking-shop, not a human rights but a much broader social get-together, that'll be the engine of progress.' And she went on to argue: 'Perhaps we can simply say that, in time, traditional human rights activity will transform itself into human rights organizations of a Western type, very professionalized.'

That will depend upon whether other types of organizations take on what we might call social responsibilities, and new political parties find a following. If there was a sudden crisis, a major incident, domestic or international, or a substantial fall in living standards caused by a recession, there could be serious protests on the streets. A marked fall in Putin's popularity could persuade others in the leadership to replace him, possibly by a more conciliatory figure with a new economic team, but equally possible would be the choice of a more aggressive, nationalistic team. In either case the outcome would be an elite choice. There is no organized, concerted, political opposition, either liberal, or nationalist, or left wing that has a following and could take advantage of popular discontent to dislodge the present regime.

However, Russia, a huge multi-ethnic country, with its partly state-owned, partly private economic and financial interests, its oligarchs, new middle class, and pockets of dire poverty, its authoritarian rulers and corrupt state administration, and its now emerging civil society, countless lawyers, and openness to the world is moving on from its present post-Soviet stage.

What is lacking? In many respects, Russia today is still a country, with 'a civil society that lacks citizens', a society whose members will act (sometimes) to defend their own personal interests, and then retreat again. Sustained collective action is rare. The intellectual and academic community, with odd exceptions, does not come out publicly in support of the civic or human rights' activists. Their message that we, as citizens, are responsible for our state and society, still speaks to few. Solzhenitsyn, in the Soviet period, wrote of 'when breathing and consciousness returns'. Russia, we could say, is now very much awake but its citizens still have to accept that they are responsible for their society and its government's actions.

Perhaps the best way to look at the Russian human rights community during this period is to see it as playing a role in the creation of a thinking, acting, conflict-ridden society, whose citizens will come to accept their responsibilities, and where organizations, with new ideologies, will one day provide a basis for political change. Some like to describe the human rights community as the vanguard or the nucleus of this new active society. I would claim for it a rather different role – one that has upheld the right of organizations to exist, independent of the state, their right to criticize the authorities, to challenge them in court, and to defend the rights of the vulnerable. These, I would argue, are critical elements to be included in any political programme aiming at a democratic order and accountable government. Once that is achieved, then it will be possible to argue (and disagree) openly over what is justice, which rights are the more important, and how to realize them.

NOTES

Introduction

1. See Further Reading for selected sources.
2. There is an extensive literature on the dissident movement, which lies outside the scope of this book. However, two works which directly relate to the theme of 'legacies' of the past and human rights are: Robert Norvath, *The Legacy of Soviet Dissent* (London and New York, 2005), and Benjamin Nathans, 'The dictatorship of reason: Aleksandr Vol'pin and the idea of human rights under developed socialism', *Slavic Review* 66/4 (2007), pp. 630–63.
3. Both Yury Orlov, the founder, and Liudmila Alekseeva, were in the USA.
4. Anatoly Adamishin, and Richard Schifler, *Human Rights, Perestroika, and the end of the Cold War* (Washington, 2009), p. 93.
5. In Chapter 5 we see the 2001 Congress in action. Data on participants vary in different sources.
6. This, and Orlov's comments are taken from copies of their presentations.
7. I use the word 'branches' but these are all autonomous organizations which have chosen to 'join' the International Memorial Society. See Chapter 10 for discussion of this issue.

Chapter 1   Perestroika to 1993: Seedbed for Human Rights

1. See Further Reading for more on Kovalev.
2. In the newly constituted Moscow Helsinki Group, Larisa Bogoraz, Sergei Kovalev, Vyacheslav Bakhmin, Lev Timofeev and Gleb Yakunin were from the dissident community, and Liudmila Alekseeva and Yury Orlov, both now in the USA; Genry Reznik, Lev Ponomarev, and Aleksei Simonov were newcomers.
3. The Society's early years are well chronicled: see Further Reading.
4. The Congress of People's Deputies elected a smaller Supreme Soviet whose members sat in permanent session.

5. Mary McAuley, *Soviet Politics 1917–1991* (Oxford, 1992), pp. 100–1 includes this account.

Chapter 2   Human Rights Organizations: First Shoots

1. Богораз, Л. И. ред., *История, философия, принципы и методы правозащитной деятельности: Сб. материалов семинара Московской Хельсинкской группы "Права человека"*, Series 1, edition 2, (Moscow 1995) p. 6. Kovalev, writing at the same time (*XX век и мир*, 6/91, p. 9) suggested that within the human rights dissident community there had always been the 'legalists' (*zakonnye*) who wanted the laws observed and the 'politiki' who wanted radical changes to the political system – but that in the present situation all had thrown themselves into politics.
2. The *Chronicle of Current Events* was a key underground publication distributed between 1968–83 to which a number of dissidents (including Kovalev) contributed.
3. http://www.prison.org. I am quoting from an early publication, no longer available.
4. Abramkin, suffering from ill health, died in January 2013.
5. Threatened with eviction by a steep back dated rise in rent in 2013. http://mright.hro.org.

Chapter 3   Early Debates Over Rights and Strategies

1. *О соблюдении прав человека и гражданина в Российской Федерации в 1994–1995 годах: Доклад Комиссии по правам человека при Президенте Российской Федерации* (Moscow, Iurid. lit., 1996). (The observance of the rights of man and citizen in the Russian Federation in 1994–1995. The report of the President of the Russian Federation's commission for human rights.) Trs. Catherine Fitzpatrick.
2. *Правозащитники о себя, Бюллетень по правам человека*, 1997, №. 9
3. *XX век и мир*, 1991, p. 6.
4. *Между прошлым и будущим* (Moscow, independent publ. Pik, 1999), pp. 136, 140–1.
5. And Sachs repeated this, elaborating on the issue, at a London meeting in 2013.
6. A key Western donor, more detail in Chapter 5.
7. The announcement was available on an earlier version of the MHG website.
8. Vyacheslav Bakhmin, a former dissident, imprisoned for his views, worked as programme officer for more than one Western foundation during our period.

Chapter 4   Local Differences, Tackling Isolationism

1. Krai is the Russian term used for some (faraway) regions.
2. 'Правозащитное движение и механизмы защиты прав человека. Санкт-Петербург, 13–14 июня 1998г'. Stenographic report. Citizens Watch, St Petersburg.

3. See Chapters 10 and 12.
4. I write about this in an article in *Разномыслие в СССР и России (1945–2008)*, ed. B. M. Firsov (St Petersburg, EUSPb, 2010).
5. Since 2011 items have been regularly translated and appear in *Rights in Russia*: http://hro.rightsinrussia.info/hro-org/parole.
6. See Further Reading for a translation of one of the volumes.
7. To defend Article 31 – the right to demonstrate – see further details in the Introduction.

Chapter 5   Western Assistance, An Extraordinary Congress

1. See Further Reading for some key contributions to the discussion.
2. Western governments' aid programmes: the American government's USAID, National Endowment for Democracy, Eurasia Foundation, and IREX; the British Know How Fund, and Westminster Foundation; the Swedish (SIDA), Swiss (Liberty Road), Dutch (Matra) and Canadian governments' aid agencies. The European Commission had a human rights programme, as did the United Nations' High Commissioner for Human Rights. The Americans dominated among the private foundations: George Soros' Open Society Institute, the Ford Foundation, and the MacArthur Foundation all had Moscow offices, as did the German foundations, funded by political parties (the Konrad Adenauer, Friedrich Ebert, Heinrich Boll, and Friedrich Neumann Foundations). Representatives of the Mott Foundation, and the Jackson Foundation paid visits to make grants in the field of human rights and visit grantees. The Sigrid Rausing Trust, based in London, supported human rights, and in 2002 the Oak Foundation appeared. Perhaps somewhere in the order of $10–15 million was awarded annually from 1995–2005, with some of the funding going to the 'Western partners', and in grants ranging from $10,000 to several hundred thousand.
3. A further challenge, facing any grant maker, it how to refuse requests. The best advice I was given before starting to work in this field was 'Just remember that it's unpleasant to have to ask for money, and it's unpleasant to have to refuse it.' The ability to grant or refuse a request for money puts the grant maker in a position of power, not a pleasant one. This is especially so when you listen, with a sinking heart, to a proposal that you know has not a chance of succeeding ('I want to transform the legal culture of Buryatiya with a series of brochures that I and my son will write') but which is of passionate concern to its author who, probably, is living close to the breadline. Of course there are those who are in it for the money, and judgement about people is crucial. But there remain those bearers of unlikely ideas whom you must turn down, gently, and who will never understand why you refused them.
4. *Перспективы гражданского общества в России*, p. 39, in http://www.levada.ru/books/perspektivy-grazhdanskogo-obshchestva-v-rossii-2011. In later chapters further material is taken from this survey, referred to as Volkov 2011.
5. Marek Nowicki: see http://hro.org/node/181 for photograph and lecture that captures him as teacher. Also http://www.hfhr.pl/wp-content/uploads/2011/06/

marek_nowicki_what_are_human-rights.pdf. And for in memoriam: http://www.hro.org/node/2924.

6. Wiktor Osiaty…nski, *Human Rights and Their Limits* (Cambridge, 2009).

7. The details and quotations are taken from the materials distributed to those attending the Congress. Some were published by www.hro.org. Lev Ponomarev subsequently edited and published materials from the congress as *Всероссийский чрезвычайный съезд в защиту прав человека. Москва Январь 2001* (Moscow, 2001).

8. 'The need to invent, rather than reclaim, public space explains in part why the path toward a civil society was so rocky.' Kathleen E. Smith, *Remembering Stalin's Victims* (Ithaca, 1996), p. 199.

Chapter 6   The Civic Forum of 2001: To Tango or to Sit It Out?

1. *Izvestiya*, 10 June 2001.
2. http://kremlin.ru/events/231.html 15 June 2001.
3. http://www.strana.ru/stories/2001.07.11.
4. http://RIAN.ru, 23 June 2001.
5. *Nezavisimaya gazeta*, 16 November 2001.
6. *Obshaya gazeta*, no. 43, October 2001.
7. *Center for Pluralism newsletter*, Winter 2002, pp. 15–16.
8. Elena Koval at a conference in December 2000 organized by Vyacheslav Igrunov, which brought academics and a few activists together; the following quotation by Kiril Kholodkovsky, is taken from a similar conference hosted by the Ebert Foundation in March 2001.
9. Z. Svetova, *Novye izvestiya*, 20 September 2001.
10. Exceptions were Leonid Gordon (IMEMO) and Alexander Gorelik (Krasnoyarsk).
11. A curious informal activity, spawned by a shortage economy.
12. Sergei Markov in interview with Elena Topeleva, Agency for Social Information, 3 September 2001.
13. Yury Dzhibladze, a young doctor at the time of perestroika, whose interest in non-violent campaign tactics and good English had taken him first to the Eurasia Foundation as a grant-maker, then to Columbia University, to study human rights, was now running his own organization Democracy and Human Rights. For more detail, see Chapter 8.
14. *Izvestiya*, 2 November 2001.
15. *Izvestiya*, 13 November 2001; *Nezavisimaya gazeta*, 16 November 2001.
16. *Novye izvestiya*, 20 November 2001.
17. *Nezavisimaya gazeta*, 16 November 2001.
18. *Правозащитное движение сегодня: проблемы и перспективы* (Moscow, Demos, 2005), p. 127. We come back to this, with more detail, in Chapter 7.

19. *Nezavisimaya gazeta*, 18 November 2001
20. *30 Oktyabr*, no. 20, 2001
21. *Moskovsky komsomolets*, 22 November 2001
22. *Novye izvestiya*, 20 November 2011
23. *Nezavisimaya gazeta*, 24 November 2001; *Novye izvestiya*, 27 November 2001 (referring to a well-known line from Galich, a song-writer: 'write to us, write to us, and we'll read what you write, and we'll read what you write').
24. Some were invited but refused (for example, Pustintsev).
25. *The Telegraph*, 19 January 2012.

Chapter 7   Activists and Popular Attitudes

1. The organizing committee, apart from themselves, included members of the original dissident community (Alekseeva, Daniel, Roginsky), perestroika activists (Averkiev, Dzhibladze, Gefter, Yurov), those of a post-Soviet generation (Taubina, Shvedov), and Elena Topoleva (Agency for Social Information). The conference proceedings were published as *Правозащитное движение сегодня: проблемы и персепктивы* (Moscow, Demos, 2005). All quotations, including that by Korotaev, above, are taken from pp. 83–143 (which include the survey materials presented to the participants) and recommendations.
2. Levada Centre surveys: see www.levada.ru/arkhiv. Interestingly enough, law students in the late nineties, attending summer schools, when asked to draw up a bill of rights for a community, usually failed to include 'right to a fair trial'. Some of the Levada material is included, or referred to in the 2005 volume, and also by Rusakova (see below).
3. T. P. Gerber, S. E. Mendelson, *How Russians think about Human Rights*, Ponars Policy memo no. 221, 2002.
4. Е. Русакова, 'Внешний имидж и общественная поддержка' (2006), www.hro.org/files/Rusakova.pdf.
5. Conference materials (2005), p. 143: Rusakova (2006, p. 4) quoting Levada survey 2005.
6. I am here summarizing points made in his article in *Civitas*, 1 (2003), pp. 22–3.
7. Conference materials (2005), pp. 86–7; 127.
8. A popular view, as summarized by Rusakova (2006).
9. 2004 conference materials; Ella Paneakh, 'EU Human Rights Policy towards Russia', *The EU-Russia Centre Review* 16 (2010), pp. 36–40.
10. Quoted by Rusakova.
11. Small grants programme referred in Chapter 5.
12. http://www.cgo.perm.ru.
13. Volkov, 2011, p. 37.
14. http://www.msps.su/. Originally the Moscow School of Political Studies, set up in 1992, the School renamed itself in 2013, following an investigation by the procuracy under the foreign agents law. See the website for its many activities.

Chapter 8   Army and Police Reform

1. See Further Reading both for the social movements' literature and for the topics covered in these chapters.
2. My apologies if I have wrongly remembered her name.
3. In his report for 2012 (see Chapter 12), he takes up certain issues involving the use of conscripts.
4. Brian D. Taylor 'From Police State to Police State. Legacies and Law Enforcement in Russia', in Mark Beissinger, Stephen Kotkin (eds), *Historical Legacies of Communism in Russia and Eastern Europe* (Cambridge, 2014), quotations from pp. 135, 145–6.
5. Taylor's 2006 article (see Further Reading) provides more detail on both this, and INDEM's projects, and on the crisis centre in Ekaterinburg.
6. Federal Law No. 18-FZ, 10/01/2006, followed by Decree No. 212 of 15/04/2006. NGOs were required to register both with the tax authorities and with a new agency, the Federal Registry Service, and to submit in much more detail their sources of funding, expenditure, planned activities, and current activities; failure to submit an annual report, on time, could being disbandment; requests for further documents could be issued at any time. The FRS could also refuse to register, and hence close an organization. Elena Klitsunova, *Promoting Human Rights in Russia by supporting NGOs*. Centre for European Policy Studies, Working document, no. 278, 2008 (http://www.ceps.eu).
7. Volkov 2011, pp. 44–5.
8. Полный текст 'Анализ нарушений прав человека сотрудниками российских правоохранительных органов', http://publicverdict.ru/topics/research/analiz.html.
9. See http://eng.publicverdict.ru/topics/library/7388.html for the memorandum on the Concept of Police Reform, and http://publicverdict.ru/topics/reform/8690html.
10. http://publicverdict.ru/topics/news/8530html.
11. http://publicverdict.ru/topics/reform/8690html.
12. The report on this meeting, 10 April 2012, no longer appears on the Council's Kremlin website. For a condensed version, http://publicverdict.ru/topics/seminars/10167.html.
13. Volkov, 2011, p. 32.

Chapter 9   Prison Inspectors, Juvenile Courts, Domestic Violence and Refugees

1. Четверикова И. В, 'Институционализация общественного контроля соблюдения прав человека в местах принудительного содержания (в рамках наблюдательных комиссий)' (EUSPb, diploma thesis, M.A., 2011) has a good chapter on the background to the legislation, and an analysis of commission reports.

2. Z. Svetova, *Novye Izvestiya*, 20 November 2001.

3. These included remand centres, and colonies, the detention centres (under the police), the places of detention and punishment under the security services and armed forces, and the special schools under the ministry of education.

4. A commission should have a minimum of five and a maximum of 20 unpaid members recommended by affiliated organizations (e.g. ex-prison officers, veterans), by social or human rights NGOs which had existed for five years or more; a list (with no more than two from any one organization) should be submitted to the (federal) Civic Chamber, which would determine the final choice for each regional commission. Members must be 25 years or older. NGOs should support their members financially. Their term of office was to be two years (reset in 2011 at three years). The commissions should report, in detail, to the Civic Chamber each year. One sighs to see that an institution was created, with very complex rules – a pocket book for the commission member, produced by Babushkin, makes daunting reading – one whose reporting procedures can only encourage the hapless commission secretary to tick boxes and claim all kinds of imaginary visits and outputs.

5. *Novaya gazeta*, 1 January 2013; see also http://ovdinfo.org/news/2013/11/01/obnarodovany-novye-sostavy-onk-pravozashchitniki-ne-v-bolshinstve.

6. A recent case, where the prison governor is only now on trial for the abuse prisoners were subject to, demonstrates the limits to monitoring, and the testimony of the Pussy Riot duo witnesses to practices that continue.

7. However, as we see in Chapter 11, the Voronezh activists have developed some innovative approaches.

8. Дети в тюрьме, issue 1, Moscow Centre for Prison Reform, 2001.

9. I have written at length on juvenile justice in Russia and England and Wales (see Further Reading) and here draw from these publications. For an up-to-date account on Russia, see L. M. Karnozova, Responses to infringements of the law by young offenders in the Russian Federation, in the third International Crime and Punishment Film Festival. Juvenal Justice. Academic papers, ed. Prof Adem Sozuer (Istanbul, 2013).

10. http://rusk.ru/ 17 December 2007; http://r-v-s.su/.

11. Справка по результатам обобщения информации судов субъектов РФ об использовании ювенальных технологий судами общей юрисдикции, подготовленная Рабочей группой при Совете судей РФ по вопросам создания и развития ювенальной юстиции в системе правосудия РФ: unpubl.memo.

12. http://refugee.memo.ru/.

13. Human Rights Watch has focused on these issues in a letter of 16 January 2014 to the UN Special Rapporteur on Human Rights of Migrants: http://www.hrw.org/news/2014/01/16/russia-letter-un-special-rapportuer-human-rights-migrants-and-un-independent-expert.

14. For an interview with Gannushkina on Radio Svoboda, translated into English, see: http://hro.rightsinrussia.info/hro-org/migrants-1.

Chapter 10   Past And Present:
The International Memorial Society

1. Beissinger and Kotkin, ch.1, pp. 1–27.
2. Между прошлым и будущим, p. 191.
3. An interview with Roginsky from http://www.colta.ru (31 January 2014), titled 'What is Memorial?', translated in Rights in Russia (10 February 2014). It is even more complex than this. The International Society has individual members as well as organizations (registered as legal entities); the Russian Memorial Society, which exists on paper but does not undertake any funded activities, includes both the registered and some non-registered organizations. Long and wearisome negotiations with the Ministry of Justice over the status of the Russian Society (which is a separate legal entity from the International Memorial Society) and changes to the Civil Code persuaded the Society to redraft both charters in 2014. Not surprisingly Western commentators confuse 'the Russian Memorial Society' with 'the International Memorial Society', which, as of the end of 2014, was not under threat. See http://www.hro.org/node/20981 for statement by Elena Zhemkova, 17 November 2014, hro.org/node/20619 for the detailed legal explanation, and hro.org/node/21243 for the January court case.
4. See Chapter 11.
5. This, a successful and popular project, based on the well-established EUStory, which started in Germany funded by the Korber Foundation, and which produces fascinating essays (within a few years over 1,500 were coming in each year), has its local winners as well as those who make it to Moscow to collect their prizes as national finalists. It is too early to say whether its young participants or their teachers will go on to influence the teaching or understanding of history in their localities, and more widely, attitudes to historical memory. The project did bring many local organizations together but brought them no closer to the human rights activists working on Chechnya.
6. Sarah E. Mendelson and Theodore P. Gerber, 'Activist Culture and Transnational Diffusion: Social Marketing and Human Rights Groups in Russia', Post-Soviet Affairs (2007) 23, 1, pp. 50–75.
7. http://Colta.ru interview.
8. See Chapter 6 for Podrabinek on the Civic Forum.
9. See Chapter 4 on leaders leaving office feet first.
10. Is it the same in Germany or Italy I wonder? It would be interesting to compare the impressions of observers from, say, Italy, Sweden, Argentina and the USA to see what that might tell us of different political cultures.

Chapter 11   Young Lawyers Step Forward

1. Protocol 14, ratified by the Duma in 2010, has brought some relief, and a reduction in numbers coming from all the countries, including Russia. ECHR website www.echr.coe.int.

2. See Further Reading, Bowring in particular.

3. See Further Reading.

4. See Chapter 4 for Nikitin, Chapter 6 for Pasko.

5. Although, see Chapter 12, Pustintsev thought the process was now well underway.

6. In the summer of 2014 Pavlov's wife's resident status in Russia was unexpectedly annulled; she left at short notice, with their child, for Prague.

7. Volkov, 2011, pp. 21, 49.

8. Maria Sereda has since moved to work for Amnesty in Moscow.

9. *Правозащитное движение сегодня* (Moscow, Demos, 2005), p. 101.

Chapter 12   Twenty Years On: Human Rights, Society and Politics

1. January 2012, Interview for Rights in Russia: http://www.rightsinrussia.info/archive/interviews-1/simonov.

2. 'Российский неполитичный активизм: наброски к портрету героя'. The research, funded by the Mott Foundation, was carried out between March and November 2012, and covered a range of issues, as well as localities, and urban/rural differences. Http://www.grany-center.org/catalog/analiz/details_849.html Quotation, p. 55.

3. Volkov, 2011, p. 19; further quotations from pp. 23–4, 39, 42.

4. Future quotations from GRANI are taken from pp. 14, 22–3.

5. We draw on the annual reports presented by the Federal Ombudsman's Office for 2008–2012, available on http://ombudsmanrf.org/doklady.

6. Carine Cleman, Olga Miryasova, Andrei Demidov, *От обывателей к активистам. Зарождающиеся социальные движения современной России*. Trikvadrata, Moscow, 2010. All quotations are drawn from pp. 234–9, 250, 315, 348–50, 610–12.

7. 57,000 in 2010, 24,000 in 2012. The number of appeals is not large for a country the size of Russia, and there is no way of knowing when turning to the ombudsman is seen as worthwhile. The introduction of ombudsmen by the majority of the subjects (regional authorities) of the Federation – 71 in all by 2012 – surely also affects the federal figures.

8. The SOVA Center for Information and Analysis (www.sova-center.ru) monitors and reports on the use of anti-extremist legislation, and on incidents involving racism and xenophobia.

9. I am drawing on GRANI, pp. 53–8.

10. The events were extensively covered in the Western press. For the NGO 'foreign agents' law, the most important piece of legislation for the human rights organizations: Federal law No 121-FZ 20 July 2012. 'О внесении изменений в отдельные законодательные акты Российской Федерации в части регулирования деятельности некоммерческих организаций, выполняющих функции иностранного агента' // «Российская газета», 23 July 2012.

11. Volkov, p. 39; Collective Action, p. 612.
12. Statement by 4 Perm NGOs 20 May 2013. Translation from Rights in Russia, Weekly update 21, 27 May 2013.
13. The law required the NGO to make the request to register; its refusal could result in heavy fines, and closure. The procurator could require changes to a charter, impose administrative penalties, issue a warning. For a detailed account, and of individual organizations, see the Human Rights Watch website: http://www.rightsinrussia.info/international-comment/hrw-13 and further updates.
14. http://closedsociety.org/.
15. http://kremlin.ru/news/19146.
16. http://spb-egida.ru/story/rima-sharifullina-prokurature-esli-im-poruchili-ubrat-sornyaki – to-zachem – je-korchevat-rozyi Bold in the original.
17. http://www.hro.org/node/18258.
18. http://www.civildignity.ru/ru/application-results.

Conclusion

1. *Между прошлым и булущем.* independent publ. Pik, 1999, p. 119.
2. See Further Reading, Donnelly, pp. 204–6.
3. For the Russian reader, Vladimir Pastukhov 'Конституция несуществующей России', http://www.polit.ru/article/2014/03/29/constitution/ may be of interest.
4. Without in any way depreciating the courage of LGBT activists, it is the actions of their vociferous political opponents that have recently made their cause widely known and publicized.

DRAMATIS PERSONAE

To aid the reader, I have included further details for those individuals who appear frequently, speaking or acting, in different chapters. Where one exists, I include a website address. By inserting an individual's name, or 'human rights activists in Russia', in www. yandex.ru, and clicking on pictures or images, a variety of photographs and more information on an individual becomes available.

Abramkin, Valery, founder and chair of Prison and Freedom, subsequently Moscow Centre for Prison Reform (1989–2013, dec), http://www.prison.org/

Alekseeva, Liudmila, chair of the re-established Moscow Helsinki Group (1996–), http://www.mhg.ru

Altshuler, Boris, founder and chair of Rights of the Child, Moscow (1991–), http://right-child.ru/

Auzan, Alexander, professor Moscow State University, founder and chair of the Consumers Confederation (1989–)

Averkiev, Igor, founder and chair of the Perm Human Rights Centre (1993–2003), then of the Perm Civic Chamber (2003–), http://www. pgpalata.ru

Babushkin, Andrei, founder and chair of Committee for Civil Rights, Moscow (1997–), http://www.zagr.org

Bakhmin, Vyacheslav, board member Moscow Helsinki Group, and of the Sakharov Centre, http://www.sakharov-center.ru, consultant to western foundations

Belyaev, Sergei, founder and chair of Litigator, Ekaterinburg (1993–)

Bituitsky, Vyacheslav, chair of Voronezh Memorial Society (1991–), board member of International Memorial Society, member of Migration Rights

Blinushov, Andrei, chair of Ryazan Memorial Society (1991–), board member of the International Memorial Society, co-founder and editor of http://www.hro.org/

Bogoraz, Larisa, chair of the re-established Moscow Helsinki Group (1991–1996, dec)

Chikov, Pavel, founder and chair of Agora, Kazan (2006–), http://openinform.ru/

Daniel, Alexander, board member International Memorial Society, http://www.memo.ru

Drozhzhakov, Vitaly, trade union organizer Krasnoyarsk, member of St Petersburg Human Rights Resource Centre, http://www.hrrcenter.ru/

Dzhibladze, Yury, founder and president of the Centre for the Development of Democracy and Human Rights, Moscow (1998–), http://www.demokratia.ru

Fedotov, Mikhail, chair of the President's Council for the Advancement of Civil Society and Human Rights (2010–), http://www.president-sovet.ru

Gannushkina, Svetlana, founder and chair of Civic Assistance Committee (1990–), and of Migration Rights (1996–), Moscow, http://refugee.ru and http://refugee.memo.ru, board member of the International Memorial Society, and the Sakharov Centre

Gefter, Valentin, director Human Rights Institute (1996–), http://www.hrights.ru and board member of Sakharov Centre

Gorelik, Alexander, professor of criminal law, Krasnoyarsk State University, founder and chair of Committee to Defend the Rights of Citizens (1992–2007, dec)

Kalikh, Alexander, chair of Perm Memorial Society (1990–2010), board member International Memorial Society

Kalyapin, Igor, entrepreneur and activist, founder and chair, Committee against Torture (2000–), Nizhny Novgorod, http://www.pytkam.net/contacts.regional-representative-offices/163

Kanevskaya, Maria, founder and director of the Human Rights Resource Center (St Petersburg) (2008–) http://www.hrrcenter.ru/

Kovalev, Sergei, chair of the Committee on Human Rights of the Russian Supreme Soviet (1990–1993), of the President's Commission on Human Rights (1994–1996), president of the Institute of Human Rights (1996–), president of the International Memorial Society (1994–), board member of the Moscow Helsinki Group, and of the Sakharov Centre.

Krivenko, Sergei, leader of Coalition Army and Reform, board member International Memorial Society.

Lokshina, Tatyana, Moscow Helsinki Group (1998–2004), Demos (2004–2008), Human Rights Watch (2008–) http://www.hrw.org

Lukashevsky, Sergei, Moscow Helsinki Group (1998–2004), Demos (2004–2008), director of the Sakharov Centre (2008–) http://www.sakharov-center.ru

Lukin, Vladimir, founding member of Yabloko, ombudsman, Russian Federation (2004–2014) http://ombudsmanrf.org

Marchenko, Veronika, founder and chair of Mother's Right, Moscow (1989–), http://www.mright.hro.org

Melnikova, Valentina, Executive Secretary of Union of Soldiers' Mothers Committees of Russia (1998–) http://ucsmr.ru

Orlov, Oleg, chair Human Rights Centre, International Memorial Society (1993–2012), board member of International Memorial Society, http://www.memo.ru

Pamfilova, Ella, chair of the President's Council for the Advancement of Civil Society and Human Rights (2004–2010), ombudsman Russian Federation (2014–)

Pisklakova, Marina, chair of ANNA, Crisis Centre (1995–), http://www.owl.ru/anna

Ponomarev, Lev, early member of the Memorial Society, elected to Russian Congress of Deputies 1990-1993, founder and executive director of For Human Rights (1997–), http://www.zaprava.ru

Pustintsev, Boris, founder and chair of Citizens Watch, St Petersburg (1992–2013, dec), http://www.citwatch.org

Roginsky, Arseny, board member, chair of International Memorial Society (1992–) http://www.memo.ru

Samodurov, Yury, founding member of Memorial Society, director of the Sakharov Centre (1996–2008)

Sereda, Maria, member of the Ryazan Memorial Society; Amnesty International, Moscow (2012–), http://amnesty.org.ru/

Shvedov, Grigory, board member of International Memorial Society, editor of *30 October*, founder and editor of *Caucasian Knot* (2001–) http://www.kavkaz-uzel.ru

Simonov, Aleksei, founder and chair of Glasnost Defence Foundation, Moscow (1993–)

Sokiryanskaya, Katya, Memorial Society, Nazran (2003–2008), Memorial Human Rights Centre (2009–2012), International Crisis Centre, Moscow (2012–)

Taubina, Natalya, director of For Civil Society (1997–2004), director of Public Verdict (2004–) http://publicverdict.ru

Yurov, Andrei, founder and honorary president of the Youth Human Rights Movement – MPD, Voronezh (1998–), http://yhrm.org/

FURTHER READING

Here I offer the reader, who does not know Russian, a selection of English-language publications which address the issues, or discuss organizations that feature in the book, and from which I have benefited. I have tried to cater for those who, for example, may know the human rights or social movements literature but for whom Russia is largely unknown territory, and vice versa. It probably does not need saying that several of the Russian organizations have an English translation on their websites (see Dramatis Personae), easy to find, and that the UN Committees' websites include the Country Alternative Reports. The Human Rights Watch country reports are on its website.

Human Rights

Donnelly, Jack, *International Human Rights* (3rd edn, Westview, 2007).
Douzinas, Costas, *The End of Human Rights* (Oxford, 2000).
Moyn, Samuel, *The Last Utopia: Human Rights in History* (London and Cambridge, 2010).
O'Neill, Onora, 'The dark side of human rights', *International Affairs* 81, 2 (2005), pp. 1–14.
Osiatynski, Wiktor, *Human Rights and Their Limits* (Cambridge, 2009).
Stammers, Neil, *Human Rights and Social Movements* (London, 2009).

Social Movements/Civil Society

Cook, Karen S., Russell Hardin, Margaret Levi, *Cooperation without Trust?* (New York, 2005).

Goldstone, Jack (ed.), *States, Parties, and Social Movements* (New York, 2003).

Snow, David A., Robert D. Benford, 'Master frames and cycles of protest', in Aldon D. Morris, Carol McClurg Mueller (eds), *Frontiers in Social Movement Theory* (New Haven, 1992), pp. 133–55.

Tarrow, Sidney G., *Power in Movement: Social Movements and Contentious Politics* (2nd edn, Cambridge, 1998).

Russia: State and Society

Politics

Gelman, Vladimir, *Authoritarian Russia: Regime Change after the Soviet Union* (Pittsburg, 2015).

Lipman, Maria, Nikolay Petrov (eds), *Russia 2025. Scenarios for the Russian Future* (Basingstoke and New York, 2013).

Politkovskaya, Anna, *Putin's Russia* (London, 2004).

Robertson, Graeme, *The Politics of Protest in Hybrid Regimes: Managing Dissent in Post-Communist Russia* (Cambridge, 2010).

Shevtsova, Lilya, *Russia Lost in Transition, The Yeltsin and Putin Legacies* (Washington, 2009).

Civil Society

Evans, Alfred B., Laura A. Henry, Lisa McIntosh Sundstrom (eds), *Russian Civil Society: a Critical Assessment* (New York, 2006) has articles on Soldiers' Mothers, Crisis Centres, and Migrants, among others.

Greene, Samuel A., *Moscow in Movement: Power and Opposition in Putin's Russia* (Stanford, 2014).

Henry, Laura A., 'Shaping Social Activism in Post-Soviet Russia: Leadership, Organizational Diversity, and Innovation', *Post-Soviet Affairs*, 22/2 (2006), pp. 99–124. On environmental NGOs but relevant to the wider issues.

Howard, Marc Morje, *The Weakness of Civil Society in Post-Communist Europe* (Cambridge, 2003).

Johnson, Janet Elise, Aino Saarinen, 'Assessing civil society in Putin's Russia: The plight of women's crisis centers', *Communist and Post-Communist Studies*, 44 (2011), pp. 41–52.

Mendelson, Sarah, John Glenn, (eds), *The Power and Limits of NGOs* (New York, 2002).

Mendelson Sarah, and Theodore P. Gerber, 'Activist Culture and Transnational Diffusion: Social Marketing and Human Rights Groups in Russia', *Post-Soviet Affairs*, 23/1 (2007), pp. 50–75.

Human rights

Adamishin, Anatoly, Richard Schifler, *Human Rights, Perestroika, and the End of the Cold War* (Washington, 2009).

Bowring, Bill, *The Degradation of the International Legal Order?* (London, 2008).

Dauce, Francoise, 'Activists in the Trap of Anti-Politics: An Exploration of the Powerlessness of Human Rights NGOs in Russia', *Laboratorium* 2 (2010) pp. 86–102.

Gerber, Theodore P., Sarah E. Mendelson, *How Russians think about Human Rights*, Ponars Policy memo, 221 (2002).

Gilligan, Emma, *Defending Human Rights in Russia: Sergei Kovalyov, Dissident and Human Rights Commissioner 1969–2003* (London, 2004).

May, Rachel A., Andrew K. Milton (eds), *(Un)civil Societies. Human rights and democratic transitions in Eastern Europe and Latin America* (Lexington, 2005).

Moscow Helsinki Group, *Human Rights in the Russian Regions* (trs. Tanya Lokshina, Moscow 2001).

Sajo, Andras (ed.), *Western Rights? Post-Communist Applications* (The Hague, 1996).

Sinikukka, Saari, *Promoting Democracy and Human Rights in Russia* (Abingdon, 2010).

Western assistance

Henderson, Sarah, *Building Democracy in Russia. Western Support for Grassroots Organizations* (Ithaca, 2003).

Keck, Margaret E., Kathryn Sikkink, *Activists Beyond Borders* (Ithaca, 1998).

Sundstrom, Lisa M., *Funding Civil Society. NGO Development in Russia* (Palo Alto, 2006).

Weiler, Jonathon, *Human Rights in Russia. A darker side of reform* (Boulder, 2004).

Individual organizations or topics

Adler, Nanci, *Victims of Soviet Terror: the story of the Memorial movement* (Westport, 1993).

Ashwin, Sarah, Simon Clarke, *Russian Trade Unions and Industrial Relations in Transition* (Warwick, 2003).

Beissinger, Mark R., Stephen Kotkin (eds). *Historical Legacies of Communism in Russia and Eastern Europe* (Cambridge, 2014).

Gilligan, Emma, *Terror in Chechnya: Russia and the Tragedy of Civilians in War* (Princeton, 2010).

McAuley, Mary, *Children in Custody: Anglo-Russian Perspectives* (London, 2009).

Norvath, Robert, *The Legacy of Soviet Dissent* (London and New York, 2005).

Smith, Kathleen E., *Remembering Stalin's Victims* (Ithaca, 1996).

Taylor, Brian D., 'Law Enforcement and Civil Society in Russia', *Europe-Asia Studies* 58/2 (2006), pp. 193–213.

———, *State Building in Putin's Russia: Policing and Coercion after Communism* (Cambridge, 2011).

INDEX

internet, use of, 3, 11-13, 15, 22, 90,
    95, 101, 105, 196, 248, 259,
    266–9, 283–7, 303 hro.org,
    101–2
Isayev, Sergei, 84, 221

journalists, *see* media
justice system,77, 124, 160, 166–7,
    212, 226–8, 261–2, 292, 310,
    314–15, 322
  codes, 8, 60, 124, 140, 225, 232,
    261, 287
  independence of judges, 14, 64, 69,
    168, 183, 209, 261, 291, 301,
    317, 322
  Investigative Committee, 213
  jury system, 261
  law-enforcement agencies, 61, 71,
    208, 214, 292
  see also ministry of justice,
    penal system, police, prosecutor's
    office
juvenile justice system, 224–33
  Centre for Judicial Reform (Moscow),
    226
  Chance (Ekaterinburg), 226
  colonies, 216, 221, 223, 229–30,
    232–3
  Council of Judges, 232
  juvenile courts, reform attempts,
    183, 186, 215, 227–8, 230–2
  NAN (Moscow), 226, 231

Kalikh, Alexander, 247–50, 254
Kalinin, Yury, 216, 232
Kaliningrad, 18, 174, 188
Kalyapin, Igor, 59–61, 113, 182, 186,
    196, 198, 203–4, 206–9, 242,
    260, 273–4, 303
  Committee Against Torture, 113,
    203–4, 210, 260, 268, 307
Kandyba, Nikolai, 53, 69, 71, 73, 77
Kanevskaya, Maria, 17–9, 117, 262,
    270–2, 276

Karaganov, Sergei, 194
Kartashkin, Vladimir, 78, 81, 91–5,
    132, 152, 186
Kasyanov, Mikhail, 14, 16, 144–8
Khasbulatov, Ruslan, 44–5
Khodorkovsky, Mikhail, 11, 17,
    42, 154, 156, 204–5, 268,
    305
  Open Russia foundation, 11, 156,
    205
  YUKOS 17, 207, 305
Kholodkovsky, Kiril, 135–6
Komi republic, 103, 104, 187, 220
  see Sazhin
Kon, Igor, 45
Korotaev, Aleksei, 30, 115–6, 155,
    164, 171, 282, 321
Kotlyar, Tatyana, 74
Kovalev, Sergei, 15, 64, 253–4
  before 1993, 25-6, 28–9, 30, 32,
    41, 47
  Kovalev commission, 67–71
  1996–2014, 15, 19, 63, 78, 96, 122,
    133, 148
  public positions, 15–6, 72–5, 81,
    82, 122, 139, 140, 144, 148, 165,
    281, 287, 315–16
  see also ombudsman, President's
    Human Rights Commission
Kozlov, Aleksei, 286
Krasnodar, 84–5, 86, 211
Krasnov, Mikhail, 79–80
Krasnoyarsk, 18, 73–4, 84, 86, 88,
    90, 93, 112, 210, 222, 226,
    228–30, 233, 247, 260, 217,
    275, 288
Kremlin children, 35
Krivenko, Sergei, 188, 189–92, 195,
    248, 303
Kuklina, Ida, 193

Lakhova, Ekaterina, 230–1
Latypov, Robert, 177, 178, 249–51,
    254, 275

Nikitin, Alexander, 90–1, 93, 95, 265
Nizhny Novgorod, 25, 59, 86, 89, 90,
113, 192, 275
International Society for Human
Rights, 102, 113
see also Kalyapin
Nowicki, Marek, 104, 106, 116–9,
270, 276

ombudsman
children's ombudsman, 227, 271
legislation on, 41, 69, 71, 83, 168,
185, 317
regional, 95, 174, 222, 233, 278
terms of office and reports, 96, 220,
261, 264, 284, 287, 290–5, 298–9
Kovalev, 67, 68
Lukin, 19, 87, 98, 107, 174, 190,
194, 304, 311
Mironov, 83, 90, 92, 146, 217
Open Society Foundation (OSI, Soros),
79, 100, 112, 120, 172, 206
Orenburg, 95, 204
Orlov, Oleg, 13, 16, 19–20, 25, 27–8,
29, 50, 67, 75–6, 147, 186, 309,
314, 320
see also Memorial Human Rights
Centre
Orlov, Yury, 79–80
Ours (pro-Putin Youth Organization),
186

PACE, 68
Pamfilova, Ella, 19, 131, 138, 142, 152,
186, 190, 192, 201, 304
Pashin, Sergei, 90, 95, 96, 209, 217,
260
Pasko case, 151–2, 265, 275
Pavlov, Ivan, 265–8, 270, 271, 275,
300, 307
Pavlovsky, Gleb, 130, 131, 136–7,
140, 141–4
penal system, 7, 41, 243, 308
ministerial oversight, 83, 216

Penal Reform International, 219
prison (public) inspectorate, oversight commissions, 20, 21, 70,
152, 183, 215–21, 221–4
prison service, 83, 145, 204, 224,
228, 233
reform of, 29, 39, 49, 147, 195
see also Abramkin, Gorelik, juvenile
colonies
People's Assembly, 140
perestroika, 4, 8, 9, 15, 16, 22, 25–30,
32–40
Perm, 42, 43–4, 61, 63, 84, 86–7, 89,
90, 112, 223
Centre for Civic Education, 172,
174–5, 210
GRANI, 285–6, 296–7, 300–3
Human Rights Centre, 74, 84, 158,
221, 277, 300–3
prison colonies and oversight,
221–4
Perm-36, 250
see also Averkiev, Latypov, Memorial
Pisklakova, Marina, 52, 56, 233–7
Podrabinek, Alexander, 48, 133, 134,
142, 253
Pokras, Alla, 219–20, 229
police
brutality, corruption, 1, 58, 85, 101,
158, 196–9, 202–5, 211
reform of, including working group,
20, 63, 93, 104, 183, 199–201,
207–8, 210–4
structure, 183, 196–8, 209
see also Kalyapin, Taubina
political parties
Communist party (post-1991), 75,
83, 90, 153
Democratic Russia, 9, 26, 30, 44, 62,
75, 78, 217
Demsoiuz, 60
Liberal Democratic party, 153
Russian Social-Democratic party, 62
SPS, 189

1 and 2 Living chain around KGB headquarters, Lubyanka Square, on the first 'Political Prisoners' Day', 30 October 1989.

3 Protester from Demsoiuz is led away from the 30 October 1989 demonstration.

4 Requiem for dead soldiers organized by Mother's Right, 1994.

5 Svetlana Gannushkina of Migration Rights meeting with Yezidis, refused citizenship, in Krasnodar in 2005.

6 Domestic violence poster of the early 2000s, used by ANNA.

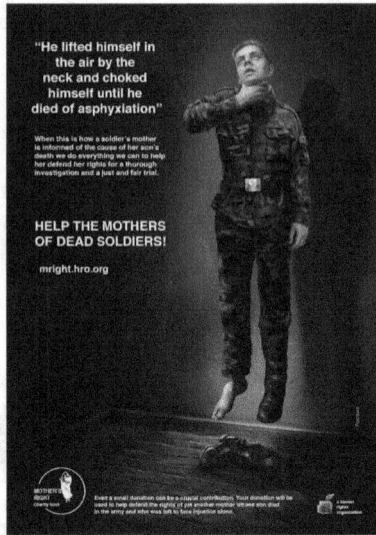

7   Poster used by Mother's Right, 2010.

8   Liudmila Alekseeva and Nina Tagankina (Moscow Helsinki Group) debate their right to hold a public meeting in Pushkin Square with law enforcement officers in 2007.

9 Court hearing of Bolotnoe demonstrators, Black Friday, Moscow, February 2014.

10 Demonstrators outside the court are removed by OMON (Special Services).

11 March in St Petersburg protesting against the new law prohibiting discussion of LGBT issues with minors, 2013.

12 Putin meeting with activists, January 2014, to discuss appointment of a new ombudsman. On the right is Alekseeva, on the left, Babushkin and Gannushkina. Vladimir Lukin, the outgoing ombudsman, is far right, opposite Elena Topoleva of the Civic Chamber.

13   Sergei Kovalev, International Memorial Society.

14   Liudmila Alekseeva, Moscow Helsinki Group.

15   Arseny Roginsky, International Memorial Society.

16   Lev Ponomarev, For Human Rights and Liudmila Alekseeva.

17   Oleg Orlov, Memorial Human Rights Centre (with poster of Natalya Estemirova, murdered in Grozny in 2009).

18   Valery Abramkin, Moscow Centre for Prison Reform.

19   Svetlana Gannushkina, Civic Assistance Committee, Migration Rights.

20   Boris Pustintsev, Citizens Watch.

21 Andrei Blinu-shov, Memorial Society, Ryazan.

22 Igor Kalyapin, Committee Against Torture.

23 Igor Averkiev, Perm Civic Chamber.

24 Grigory Shvedov, *Caucasian Knot*.

25 Marina Pisklakova, ANNA.

26 Pavel Chikov, Agora.

27 Tanya Lokshina, Human Rights Watch.

28 Maria Kanevskaya, Human Rights Resource Centre.